Policy Conflicts in Post-Mao China

An East Gate Book

East Gate Books

Policy Conflicts in Post-Mao China

A Documentary Survey, with Analysis

JOHN P. BURNS
STANLEY ROSEN
editors

M. E. SHARPE, INC.
Armonk, N.Y.
London, England

To our parents,
Al and Frances Rosen and
Harold and Helen Burns

East Gate Books are edited by Douglas Merwin,
120 Buena Vista Drive, White Plains, New York 10603

Available in the United Kingdom and Europe from M. E. Sharpe
Publishers, 3 Henrietta Street, London WC2E 8LU.

Library of Congress Cataloging in Publication Data

Main entry under title:

Policy conflicts in post-Mao China.

    Contains material translated from the Chinese press.
    ''East gate books.''
    Includes Bibliographies.
    1. China—Politics and government—1976-   —Sources.
2. China—History—1976-   —Sources.
3. Chinese newspapers. I. Burns, John (John P.) II. Rosen, Stanley,
1942–
JQ1502.P65 1986   951.05′7   86-907
ISBN 0-87332-337-8
ISBN 0-87332-338-6 (pbk.)

Printed in the United States of America

CONTENTS

ACKNOWLEDGMENTS

THIS BOOK WOULD not have been possible without the advice and encouragement of like-minded colleagues who felt, as we did, that primary source materials are an indispensable aid in the study and teaching of Chinese politics. Among the many, several individuals are deserving of special mention. Perry Link provided the majority of the cartoons and the two comedians' dialogues (which were translated by Tom Gold and Robert Tharp). Professor Link collected the cartoons from exhibitions in Guangzhou and Beijing in 1979 and 1980. Jonathan Unger provided the valuable interview on agricultural decollectivization. Dorothy Solinger suggested articles on commerce and industry and aided with their interpretation; in addition, she offered helpful suggestions on the introduction. Lowell Dittmer graciously shared with us his collection of post-Mao documents. Irving Epstein, Nina Halpern, and Carol Hamrin commented on a draft of the general introduction. Mark Selden and Brantly Womack contributed their counsel at several stages of the project. For their varying responses at the earliest stages of this effort, we thank David Bachman, Richard Baum, Gordon Bennett, Tom Bernstein, Marc Blecher, David Chu, Deborah Davis-Friedmann, Howard Goldblatt, David Goodman, Karl Herbst, Harlan Jencks, Joyce Kallgren, Richard Kraus, Peter N. S. Lee, Steven Levine, Kenneth Lieberthal, Andrew Nathan, Michel Oksenberg, Elizabeth Perry, Barbara Pillsbury, Lester Ross, Peter Seybolt, Susan Shirk, Lynn T. White, Allen Whiting, Christine Wong, Wong Siu-lun, and David Zweig. Finally, the encouragement and patience of Doug Merwin of M. E. Sharpe has been essential from the very beginning.

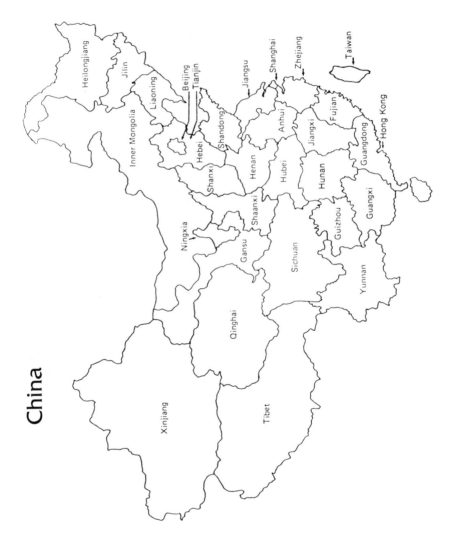

China

GENERAL
INTRODUCTION

AMONG THE SENIOR leadership of post-Mao China a consensus has emerged that rapid economic development should be given high priority. This policy orientation, the leadership generally concedes, necessitates certain other policies. First, it requires the active cooperation of China's intellectuals, scientists, and technicians. Political authorities are as a result attempting to woo this group by liberalizing Party controls over their professional activities, by abandoning the practice of using class labels to curb their behavior, and by "licensing" certain forms of limited participation. Second, leaders also agree that fostering rapid economic development requires the institutionalization of the political system, the regularization of the bureaucracy, and the abandonment of the ad hoc mass mobilizations that characterized the Maoist era. Third, in the leadership's view rapid economic development also requires the rule of law to reduce the arbitrariness of administration and to protect both specialists and politicians from the abuses that many of them experienced during the Cultural Revolution. Finally, the new policy orientation requires the rapid expansion of both human and capital resource bases. On these requirements, there is little dispute.

If China's political leaders have agreed on the broad outlines of the policy orientation, and on the general requirements for beginning to realize rapid economic development, they have failed to agree on a host of other political, economic, and social issues. Within the Party and within society public debate has centered on (1) the methods that are appropriate for achieving these goals; (2) the likely consequences of rapid economic development for the Party, and the new relationship of the Party with the state and society; (3) the nature of the state in the changed circumstances brought on by rapid economic development; and (4) the lessons to be drawn from the thirty-five years of post-Liberation China. More generally, having discredited the radical version of Chinese socialism as "sham Marxism," the leadership must decide which components of the post-1949 central belief system should be retained or refashioned for the formation of the new "socialism with Chinese characteristics."

Elite groups and individuals in post-Mao China have publicly advocated competing policy options and have sought support for their programs from among specialized constituencies. To a limited extent advocates have turned to national state and Party forums, such as the Standing Committee of the National People's Congress and the plenums of the Party's Central Committee. Although these institutions for the most part have continued to reflect the results of policy-making, they have on occasion acted as a channel for articulating different policy options. The policy process in contemporary China has thus become more of a process of negotiation, coalition building, and compromise as leaders have backed competing policy options and sought largely short-term victories.

This situation has resulted from several factors. First, post-Mao China has lacked a charismatic leader who can personally dominate the policy process. Although Deng Xiaoping has been undoubtedly the most powerful of China's current leaders, he has shared power with others and decisions have been made collectively. Second, an increasingly complex economy has contributed to the emergence of competing policy options. Whereas "Maoist radicals" often tended to view policy differences in terms of a struggle between "two roads"—the socialist road and the capitalist road—those in policy-making positions today see policy conflict in less apocalyptic terms. As a result, it has become less necessary—as well as more difficult—to link tightly policy decisions made in diverse policy arenas. When one notes, as well, that leaders now rely more heavily on technical and specialist advice in each policy arena, it is not surprising that policy options have multiplied.

Third, local and regional interests have fostered complexity in the policy process. Given China's large geographic area and huge population, this is of course not a new phenomenon. However, such centrifugal tendencies have been furthered by national policies that promote decentralization as a means to accelerate local and regional growth. A good example of this is Selection 46, in which Shen Yue, the secretary of the Liaoning Provincial CCP Committee, attempts to justify his province's (and, in effect, all of Northeast China's) concern with the development of heavy industry at a time when many in the Center were pushing for more investment in light industry. The potential clash between national priorities and local interests—and the increased opportunities for local officials to pursue such interests under the decentralized "open policy" initiated by Deng Xiaoping—was demonstrated most dramatically in the notorious "Hainan Island Scandal," which broke in August 1985. Granted a range of tax and duty exemptions previously limited to the country's four "special economic zones," Hainan Island was encouraged to attract foreign investment to develop its backward and impoverished resources. Instead of a development strategy based on investment, which would require years to succeed, the island's top officials opted for a shortcut. Using their duty free status, they imported luxury items that could be resold at high profits to China's inland provinces. Despite warnings from higher levels, local authorities brought in 89,000 motor vehicles, 2.9 million color television sets, 250,000 video tape recorders, 122,000 motorcycles, and so forth, all for resale. The motor vehicles brought in at the island's two main ports over a 14-month period exceeded the total imported by the rest of the country in a year. In the end, the $1.5 billion scandal cut deeply into China's foreign exchange reserves and increased criticisms of the dangers of the open policy.[1]

The eighty-seven selections included in this reader are intended in part to document the emergence and range of competing policy options. Our introduction will provide a context for the selections and consists of three main sections. First, an overview of Chinese politics from 1976 to 1985 will examine the major trends and conflicts that have marked the last decade. This will be followed by a discussion of the sources available for research on contemporary Chinese politics. A brief final section presents the Chinese political system as it emerges from the selections in this reader. In each section our comments will be illustrated by reference to our selections. Before turning to the main body of the introduction, however, it is necessary, to avoid misunderstanding, to distinguish the purpose of this book.

The preparation of this reader began as a response to the teaching needs of the two editors and after informal discussions with a number of like-minded colleagues. Over the years, we have found the use of primary source materials in our courses to be an essential aid in the understanding of Chinese politics. Students can better appreciate and evaluate the secondary sources that commonly serve as their textbooks if they are also familiar with the building blocks of research—the primary sources. The student who realizes why it matters whether an article on philosophy is published in *Renmin ribao* (People's Daily) or in *Zhexue yanjiu* (Philosophical Research) (see the introduction to the Literature and Art section for the answer); who can recognize the different purposes and the relative importance of published contributions that have bylines, that are signed "Commentator," or that appear as "letters to the editor"; and who can suggest reasoned explanations for the publication of some articles in the open press and others—on the same subject—only in the internal press has already learned a good deal about the Chinese Communist Party's (CCP) communications with its membership and with the public at large. By extension, the student has enhanced his/her understanding of the Chinese political system.

If one aim of our book is to sensitize students to the wide variety of primary sources available, and the proper use and interpretation of these sources, the creation of a guide to the informed reading of the Chinese media is not our sole purpose. Equally important, we seek to use primary sources to illuminate some of the more contentious issues in China today. We are concerned with the *conflicts* over *policy* in a wide variety of areas. In general, our section introductions discuss the forms such policy conflict may take. To preempt our critics, however, we must indicate what has *not* been intended. Our reader does not include the "major documents" of post-Mao China. You will find very few Central Committee documents or speeches by the nation's top leaders. We are not presenting "a broad survey of significant statements that the Chinese Communists have made about themselves and their objectives," as John Lewis did so effectively over twenty years ago.[2] Despite our stress on conflict, this is not primarily a volume on elite-level Chinese politics. We offer none of the writings of Deng Xiaoping, Hua Guofeng, Chen Yun, et al., to examine "factionalism" at the top of the political system. Nor is our basic purpose to offer a political history of post-Mao China, although a knowledge of the sequence of events since 1976 will greatly enhance the use of this book; thus, we offer a brief account of key developments in this introduction and append an extensive chronology at the end.[3]

Our reader differs from previous compilations of primary source materials both in the breadth of material selected and the treatment of the policy process. Relatively few of our documents directly represent the views of individuals involved in the *formulation* of policy. Rather, we have focused at least as heavily on the *implementation* of policy. This distinction between formulation and implementation is of course not always clear, since policy-making tends to be a continuous process. Policy feedback during the implementation stage may thus reappear as an input in a new policy formulation. Therefore, in addition to our three selections from Central Party offices (Selections 34, 40, and 86), the two attributed contributions from prominent Party officials (Selections 46 and 65), and editorials and commentaries that reflect authoritative voices within the Party leadership (Selections 1, 26, 33, 41, 42, 43, 45, 55, 56, 57, 62, 63, and 82), we have included inputs into the policy process from various levels of the political system. For example, there are demands from organized occupational and social groups (Selections 27 and 32), investigative reports by intrepid journalists on corruption (Selections 36, 37, 51, and 52), and many "letters to the editor" of newspapers and magazines requesting clarification of a controversial policy or objecting to implementation at the basic level (e.g., Selections 7, 8, 9, 10, 11, 19, and 20).

With the liberalization of Party controls over professional activities, the role of intellectuals has changed markedly from the difficult years of late Maoism. In addition to choosing selections that address the changing status of intellectuals directly (Nos. 29–31), we have sought to document this new tolerance by including examples of intellectual contention on issues of public policy (e.g., Selections 74 and 75) and the results of surveys collected by Chinese social scientists on a variety of social problems (Selections 16, 66, and 87). This in fact represents one of the most fascinating and intellectually exciting developments in post-Mao China; *viz.*, the commentaries on state policy by Chinese social scientists. It is becoming necessary to treat at least some of the writings of China's intellectuals as *secondary*, rather than *primary* sources.

Chinese Politics Since 1976

The urge to periodize post-Mao developments is overwhelming, but daunting. On the positive side, one can be guided by the Chinese authorities, who find such periodization essential, not least as a means of communication within the Party and to the masses. Thus, historic benchmarks are established. Before the Cultural Revolution (1966–1976), Chinese commentaries chronicling the regime's achievements often began with the standard phrase "since Liberation (1949). . . ." During the greater part of the 1970s, when many of the achievements of the 1949–1966 period were being questioned and the Cultural Revolution was still being highly praised, it was common to preface the recitation of successes with the words "since the Cultural Revolution. . . ." Post-Mao China has continued this practice. The key event, interestingly enough, is neither the death of Mao (September 1976) nor the purge of his radical supporters, dubbed the "Gang of Four" (October 1976), but rather the decisions enacted by the Third Plenum of the Eleventh CCP Central Committee (December 1978). Indeed, this plenum endorsed major changes in the political, economic, and social spheres. Most prominently, it shifted the country's policy orientation away from class struggle and toward economic development. Among its important initiatives were sweeping personnel changes, including the promotion to the Politburo of four supporters of Deng Xiaoping; the abandonment of the ambitious ten-year economic development program associated with Mao's successor and then-Party chairman and premier, Hua Guofeng; the first steps in an ongoing rural reform that has contributed to a large increase in agricultural output and peasant incomes; and the abolition of the previous practice of discriminating against people of "bad" class background, such as former landlords, rich peasants, capitalists, and their offspring. Most observers, including the editors, would agree that the December 1978 plenum was the key turning point in post-Mao China. The careful reader will therefore note that the earliest documents in this collection date from January 11 and 17, 1979 (Selections 17 and 61). Following the decisions of the Third Plenum, they reflect the narrowing of the focus of class struggle and the promotion of the new rural policy, which allows peasants to "become rich through labor." Equally revealing is Selection 11, from September 1979, in which political instructors, so important during the Cultural Revolution years with their emphasis on "politics in command," suddenly find themselves facing an openly hostile audience of students. Because of the Third Plenum's importance as a turning point in post-Mao politics, our chronology provides a rather detailed account of Deng's rise at the expense of his political opponents prior to December 1978.

If a general consensus on the significance of the Third Plenum is easily reached, the periodization of post-1978 developments is somewhat more problematic. Much depends on what one chooses to investigate and one's framework of analysis. For Lowell Dittmer, who is tracking ideological change, the "Deng Xiaoping reform regime" can be divided into periods of the "thaw" (fang), lasting from December 1978 until the Sixth Plenum of the Eleventh Central Committee (June 1981), and "ideological retrenchment" (shou), lasting approximately from the Sixth Plenum until the end of 1983 (Dittmer also distinguishes two earlier periods—"late Maoist" and the "Hua Guofeng interregnum"—in his periodization).[4]

For Dorothy Solinger, who is investigating economic development strategy, and Carol Hamrin, who is looking more broadly at alternative "visions" for China's future held by senior political leaders, developments in post-Mao China are best understood in terms of competition and coalition building among three broad bodies of opinion. Hamrin distinguishes three distinctive "policy packages" or sets of solutions to the problems associated with China's modernization. All have coexisted since 1979, and each has roots in the Maoist era. In 1976–77, under the leadership of Hua Guofeng, Ye Jianying, and Li Xiannian, a conservative package of economic, social, personnel, and foreign policies predominated. Its advocates favored only limited modification of the mid-1970s approach associated with Mao Zedong. By 1978–1980, an alternative pragmatic reform had been revealed. As articulated by Deng Xiaoping and protégés like Hu

Yaobang and Zhao Ziyang, the program called for bold experiments that required fundamental departures from many of the accepted practices of post-1949 China, and that in turn carried major implications for the economic and social structure and for China's international orientation. Starting in 1979, but achieving greater success in 1980–81, a more *orthodox reform* prescription, linked to rehabilitated veterans like Chen Yun and Peng Zhen, emerged in reaction to Deng's bolder initiatives. If the "conservatives" were sympathetic to many of Mao's ideas and the "pragmatic reformers" were willing to embark upon uncharted waters, the "orthodox reformers" were satisfied that the policies of the Eighth Party Congress (1956) and the post-Great Leap Forward (early 1960s) had worked well before and were still relevant. Expressing concern over the consequences of Deng's initiatives for China's Marxist-Leninist heritage, they have been unwilling to grant the pragmatic reformers a free hand.[5]

Periodizations such as those above, centered on elite-level policy packages or broad ideological trends, can be extremely helpful in organizing data and analyzing political developments at the Center. These same periodizations, however, may be misleading when one focuses on policy implementation across a wide variety of policy arenas. For example, as noted in the Literature and Art section below, one can chronicle at least a dozen shifts in the political climate for writers and artists since the death of Mao. Similarly, many of the debates and problems discussed in the Education section—the value of key schools, the indiscriminate transfer of teachers to other lines of work, the discrimination against women, and so forth—have been consistent issues of contention dating back to Maoist China. Therefore, we have chosen to organize our chronological overview of post-Mao China in a more conventional manner, conveniently using key Party congresses, conferences, and plenums as historical benchmarks.

Our account will be "reform-oriented," since the emphasis is on the rising influence of Deng Xiaoping and the formulation and implementation of policies associated with his political line. Moreover, greatest stress will be placed on introducing the major political events in these years, rather than on any detailed account of factional policy or bureaucratic divisions among the leadership. Nor is this the place to cover, even superficially, developments in each policy arena. The appended chronology and, to a lesser extent, the section introductions are intended to fill this gap.

January 1976 (Death of Zhou Enlai)– August 1977 (Eleventh Party Congress)

The death of Premier Zhou is an appropriate place to begin, given his role as the delicate balancer of Chinese politics. Zhou's death, at a time when the debilitating illness of Chairman Mao was readily apparent to China's elite, intensified the ongoing succession struggle. Leftists in the Party, led by Mao's wife, Jiang Qing, had accepted only grudgingly Deng Xiaoping's return to office in 1973. There followed several years of jockeying for power, as Deng and his moderate supporters gradually attempted to undo some of the policies initiated by the radicals during the Cultural Revolution. Zhou Enlai had mediated between these groups, and with his death, the fragile accommodation that characterized these years seemed on the verge of coming apart. Since neither side was strong enough to appoint its own candidate as Zhou's replacement, a compromise candidate—Hua Guofeng—was chosen as acting premier.

In April, during the Qing Ming festival, a time for honoring the dead, tens of thousands of Beijing residents filled the city's huge Tiananmen Square, just south of the Imperial Palace, and close by Zhongnanhai, the headquarters of the Party. Some among them placed wreaths in honor of Zhou Enlai on the Martyrs' Monument and wrote poems that made veiled criticisms of the country's leftist leaders. A riot ensued, which authorities only brought under control after the Square was cleared and hundreds were arrested. Immediately after the incident, the leftist-dominated Politburo announced that Deng Xiaoping was to blame for this "counterrevolutionary" affair, and he was dismissed from his posts as a vice-chairman of the Party and as a vice-premier. At the same time, the Politburo appointed Hua Guofeng as Party first vice-chairman and as premier. Deng retreated to Guangzhou in South China under the protection of senior military leaders.

Then in September, Mao Zedong died. After several weeks of indecision, the leftist leaders put pressure on the other, more conservative Politburo members to fill the vacant Party chairmanship with one from among their number. In early October, the leftists published articles critical of Hua's leadership, thus forcing a showdown.[6] On the evening of October 6, Hua, with Ye Jianying's support, engineered the arrest of Jiang Qing, Wang Hongwen, Zhang Chunqiao, and Yao Wenyuan, later dubbed the "Gang of Four." Subsequently, Hua Guofeng became chairman of the Party and head of the Party's Military Affairs Commission. Despite the continuation of familiar Maoist policies in agriculture (e.g., further developing collectivization, high rates of capital accumulation, and so forth), Hua had signaled his intention, by December 1976, to follow a more balanced approach to economic development.

With the removal of the "Gang of Four" from top leadership positions, the rehabilitation of Deng Xiaoping became a controversial issue.[7] Some senior leaders, who in 1976 had approved of his removal, were reluctant to reconsider their decision. To do so would be to admit that Mao Zedong, who had personally ordered Deng's dismissal, had been wrong. In the course of this debate a group emerged that professed its loyalty to the memory of Mao, led by Wang Dongxing, Mao's former chief bodyguard. In February he published the later infamous statement known as the "two whatevers," ("whatever policy Chairman Mao has decided upon, we shall resolutely defend; whatever instructions the Chairman has issued, and propagated in the media, we shall steadfastly obey"), a ploy designed to make Deng's rehabilitation more difficult. Later, Hua Guofeng aligned himself with the "two whatevers" group (including Politburo members Wang Dongxing, Wu De, Ji Dengkui, and Chen Xilian). By March, however, after the intervention of Ye Jianying, a Party Work Conference agreed that Deng should be restored to office, paving the way in July for the Third Plenum of the Tenth Central Committee to reinstate him as a Party vice-chairman, vice-premier, and chief of staff of the People's Liberation Army (PLA). From the summer of 1977, then, Deng officially returned to office. He did not, however, assume overall control and was confined to supervising developments in science, technology, and education policy.[8]

Meeting a month later, the Eleventh Party Congress was the product of compromise. The Congress returned to power representatives of the "two whatevers" group (it reelected Hua Guofeng as Party chairman and Wang Dongxing as a vice-chairman). But it also reelected Ye Jianying, Li Xiannian, and Deng Xiaoping as vice-chairman. The Congress adopted a new Party constitution and heard reports from Hua and Ye defending the Cultural Revolution. Deng was able to have his protégé Hu Yaobang appointed to head the Central Committee's Organization Department, however. This appointment was significant, for Hu Yaobang then dramatically speeded up the rehabilitation of veteran cadres who, like Deng and Hu, had been victims of the Cultural Revolution.[9] Ultimately, some 2.9 million rehabilitations followed.[10] The stories of their suffering dominated the "wounded literature," which began to be published in late 1977.

August 1977–December 1978 (The Third Plenum of the Eleventh Central Committee)

This period is marked most prominently by the increasing influence of Deng Xiaoping and the declining power of Hua Guofeng. Deng's initiatives against his opponents in a sense began at the Fifth National's People's Congress (NPC) in February 1978. Although the NPC elected Hua as premier and endorsed his ambitious Ten-Year National Development Plan, with its emphasis on the further rapid development of heavy industry, Deng was able to place his allies in important posts in the State Council.[11] Deng's momentum began to build, and his disagreement with Hua on a variety of issues became increasingly visible. For example, at the National Science Conference in March, Deng called for the selection of the best talents in science and technology, who would have "conditions created for them to engage in research work with single-minded devotion." Hua, on the other hand, insisted that "the most powerful base and inexhaustible source of strength for the modernization of science and technology in our country are the masses of the people in their hundreds of millions. . . ."[12] Deng also began to discuss the need for large-scale foreign investment in China's development process.[13]

The pressure on Hua came from several fronts simultaneously. Provincial leaders associated with Deng were pushing for agricultural and industrial reform. Wan Li, in Anhui Province, promoted experiments to reform the rural incentive system; Zhao Ziyang, in Sichuan Province, began decentralizing controls over industry, granting more autonomy to industrial enterprises.

A media campaign to demystify Mao served Deng's interests well. In May, *Guangming ribao* (Guangming Daily) published an article arguing that "practice is the sole criterion of truth." Truth could not be found, in this view, from slavish adherence to dogma, but could only be discovered in the real world. The implication that political authority should rest on results, not on the cult of personality, suggested that a possible reevaluation of Mao was necessary. Deng's endorsement of this slogan in June was followed in July by the first publication of a 1962 speech in which Mao admitted responsibility for the disasters of the Great Leap Forward. By implication, if Mao was fallible then, he could have made further mistakes, such as dismissing Deng Xiaoping from office and promoting Hua Guofeng.

In November, Deng's veiled attacks on Hua Guofeng culminated in open criticism of Hua at a Central Work Conference, during which Hua was obliged to make a self-criticism. Hua lost much of his influence during this meeting, and his supporters were replaced during the subsequent Third Plenum. Deng scored another victory at this time when Beijing authorities reversed their assessment of the Tiananmen riots. The demonstration was officially declared to be a "revolutionary" act, and those arrested were released and honored.

For the first time since the Hundred Flowers Campaign in 1957, unofficial magazines, journals, and posters began to appear in Beijing (and a number of other cities), voicing popular dissatisfaction with the authorities. In its early stages the "Democracy Movement," as it later came to be known, focused on critical evaluations of Mao and of Hua Guofeng. Although it was composed of disparate elements, its members agreed on a number of issues, as they demanded the institutionalization of democracy through elections, the rule of law, and the provision of human rights for China's citizenry.[14] For a brief period, then, Deng's campaign to demystify Mao and to criticize the "Whateverists" moved to the streets of China's large cities. At the Third Plenum in December, Deng decisively defeated the "Whateverists." Sweeping personnel and policy changes, eighteen months after being restored to power, established Deng as China's de facto leader (see appended Chronology).

December 1978–September 1980 (Third Session of the Fifth National People's Congress)

If the previous period represented the steady rise of Deng and his allies, the twenty-odd months from the Third Plenum of the Eleventh Central Committee of December 1978 to the Third Session of the NPC of September 1980 saw the consolidation of Deng's power in both the Party and the state. At the Fifth Plenum of the Eleventh Central Committee in February 1980, Deng's "practice faction" (shijian pai) followed up its earlier successes at the Third Plenum with equally impressive personnel adjustments. The so-called "Small Gang of Four"—aka "Whateverists"—were compelled to resign their posts while Deng protégés Hu Yaobang (appointed as general secretary of the Party) and Zhao Ziyang entered the Politburo's standing committee.[15] The September 1980 NPC sessions brought in Zhao Ziyang as premier in place of Hua Guofeng and witnessed the public reprimand of leading members of the so-called "petroleum group," whose emphasis on heavy industry contrasted with the light industry/agriculture emphasis of Deng's "new economic group" (Selection 44). It was a period in which the reformers pushed ahead on virtually all fronts. Our best cartoons and the two comedians' dialogues (Selections 35 and 53) were either exhibited or published in this relatively open atmosphere.

Representative of the initiatives at this time was Deng Xiaoping's address to an enlarged session of the Politburo from August 18 to 23, 1980. He pointed out that reform of the state structure was necessary to reduce bureaucratism; to terminate life tenure for cadres; and to eliminate overlapping responsibilities, the patriarchal style of leadership, and the over concentration of power. He argued that steps should be taken to promote democracy and collective leadership and to strengthen the socialist legal system. Finally, Deng maintained that a major effort was necessary to recruit and promote cadres who were revolutionary, young, better educated, and who possessed appropriate specialized knowledge.[16]

At least two of our documents reflect the optimism of autumn 1980. Selection 81, the deathbed appeal of Chinese actor Zhao Dan, calls for a reduction in Party control of the arts. And, although delivered only in October 1980, the speech by Liao Gailong, a policy researcher in the Party Secretariat (Selection 18), discusses the possibilities for democratic reform. However, neither Zhao's appeal nor Liao's broad-ranging proposals were adopted; on the contrary, by the end of the year the reform movement generally had been placed on the defensive.

September 1980–September 1982
(Twelfth Party Congress)

In many areas, the momentum of the reformers slowed down in this period. In cultural matters, there were warnings about the dangers of "bourgeois liberalization"; in economic affairs, a variety of problems caused, in part, by policies associated with decentralization, led to recentralization measures by the central government. More specifically, by the end of 1980 inflation had become a serious problem. The greater reliance on market mechanisms, the rise in agricultural purchase prices, the granting of autonomy to local authorities and enterprises to retain profits, the rise in wages and bonuses, all contributed to higher prices. Decentralization increased substantially the amount of "extra-budgetary" funds, which were not controlled by the state plan, and which were used for capital construction and other budgetary expenditures at the local level. Under these conditions, the reform of the urban industrial economy, associated closely with Premier Zhao Ziyang, was postponed, with concessions made to the advocates of heavy industry and central planning (see selection 46 for their viewpoint). The one major breakthrough for the reformers was their success in the restructuring of the Party, state, and military bureaucracies.

Bureaucratic reorganization—carried out primarily in 1982—led to the retirement of thousands of elderly officials and their replacement by those younger and better educated. The number of ministries, commissions, and agencies under the State Council fell from 98 to 54, coupled with a staff reduction from 49,000 to 32,000. In addition, the number of vice-premiers fell from 13 to 2. Ironically, the bloated bureaucracy had been owing, in part, to reformist attempts to circumvent conservative control over the planning process by creating, from 1979 to 1981, a number of additional state commissions to compete with the State Planning Commission and the State Economic Commission. In similar fashion to the state organs, the Party Central Committee trimmed its bureaucracy by 17.3 percent at this time.

At the Sixth Plenum of the Eleventh Central Committee (June 1981), Hua Guofeng was replaced as Party chairman by Hu Yaobang, and Deng Xiaoping became chairman of the Party's Military Affairs Commission. Nevertheless, the Plenum can be considered a compromise, particularly when one examines the "Resolution on Some Questions in the History of Our Party," a lengthy document issued at this meeting. Although Mao was condemned for his role in initiating the Great Leap Forward and the Cultural Revolution, great pains were taken to separate the persona of Mao from Mao Zedong Thought, which was said to remain relevant to present-day China. On other subjects, such as class struggle (see Selection 3), the final resolution seems to reflect a measured compromise among various Party factions.

The Twelfth Party Congress, meeting in September 1982, further established a framework for organizational change. A new Party constitution abolished the post of Party chairman, making the Secretariat—under Hu Yaobang and staffed by "reformers"—the operational center of the Party. A new Central Advisory Committee was created to serve as a "halfway house" for elderly Central Committee members on their way to full retirement. Hua Guofeng moved one more step down, from the Politburo to the Central Committee. Nevertheless, while Deng had established the mechanisms for substantial personnel changes, such changes were far from being realized. In fact, the Politburo that emerged at this time was an even more elderly body than its predecessor. As one perceptive observer pointed out, Deng had once again settled for establishing a framework for the future success of his policies while refraining from using that framework immediately to compel his opponents to submit.[17]

September 1982–September 1985
(Special National Party Conference)

A number of the initiatives for which Deng and the reformers had been laying the groundwork in prior periods now began to bear fruit. In this regard, the major events were the Special Party Conference of September 1985 and the earlier Third Plenum of the Twelfth Central Committee in October 1984. At the same time, however, there were indications, particularly in 1985, that the reform program's momentum had slowed down and future stern tests awaited.

The Third Plenum in October 1984 produced the long-delayed Central Committee plan for the reform of the urban industrial economy. Although it is far too early to predict long-term success or failure, the plan juxtaposes a rosy vision of a future efficient Chinese industry guided in part by market forces, with statements indicating an acute recognition of the difficulties of instituting the reforms necessary to realize this vision. The creation of an urban industrial economy in which prices better reflected relative scarcities; in which enterprises had become "relatively independent entities" with substantial discretionary power to plan and market their output, fire workers, and set wages and prices; and in which inefficient enterprises were subject to closure would likely face substantial opposition from a variety of urban constituencies. Urban residents have long benefited from a variety of subsidies that have kept prices low and prevented inflation, but the cost to the state has been huge. Price reform would upset this system. For example, the 20 billion yuan subsidy paid by the state to keep agricultural prices low has been a major cause of government deficits. The implementation of the 1984 plan, particularly the five-year program of price reform, represents a bellwether for the success of the entire reform strategy.

In the realm of ideology and culture, Deng moved deftly to his left and right over this period, generally keeping the initiative in his hands. The most publicized attack on the right was the campaign against "spiritual pollution" initiated at the Second Plenum of the Twelfth Central Committee in October 1983. Defined by Deng at this plenum as "disseminating all varieties of corrupt and decadent ideologies of the bourgeoisie and other exploiting classes and disseminating sentiments of distrust toward the socialist and communist cause and to the Communist Party leadership," the campaign was extended by "leftist" and conservative Party members well beyond the parameters set by Deng. By early 1984, when it became clear that social stability was being threatened, that entrepreneurial peasants and urbanized intellectuals were being intimidated, and that eager foreign investors were being scared off—in other words, that the Four Modernizations program on which the legitimacy of Deng and the Party rests was being jeopardized—the drive against spiritual pollution was in effect called off.[18]

From the other direction, in 1984 there unfolded an "antileftist" emphasis on the need to "totally negate" the Cultural Revolution. Aimed particularly at the military, which had been slow to admit that it erred in "supporting the (Red Guard) left" during that upheaval, one purpose of the exercise was to convince skeptics, yet again, that all Red Guard factions, regardless of orientation or conduct, had been wrong and should be condemned.[19] Both initiatives—the elimination of spiritual pollution and the total negation of the Cultural Revolution—were inseparable from the three-year Party rectification campaign that was launched in 1984 (see Selection 36). In the context of the rectification, most observers viewed Deng's initial move against spiritual pollution primarily as a means to prepare the groundwork for his later, more difficult thrust against "leftist" and conservative opponents, the goal being to replace them with reliable, pragmatic successors.

The September 1985 Special Party Conference sent somewhat mixed signals regarding the strength of the reformers. Because it is the most recent major Party gathering, it is appropriate to close our chronology with a brief discussion of its decisions. For the reformers, the meeting held many positive aspects. Using the framework established at the Twelfth Party Congress in 1982, there were important changes in personnel. For example, sixty-four members or alternative members of the Central Committee resigned and were replaced; ten of the twenty-four Politburo members resigned and were replaced by five newcomers (see Appendix). The proposal for the Seventh Five-Year Plan (1986–1990) was adopted, reaffirming the nation's commitment to attracting foreign investment, limited private enterprise, and decentralization of economic decision-making.

In juxtaposition to these positive developments, the conference clearly revealed the conflicts among the leadership over economic reform. At its most fundamental, the conflict centered on how to operationalize the ubiquitous slogan "(building) socialism with Chinese characteristics," a "buzzphrase" for the entire Dengist reform program. As one report in the *Far Eastern Economic Review*, citing an official of the State Economic Commission who asked not to be named, summarized the main conflicts: First, how can China revitalize its enterprises but still remain socialist? On the one hand, there is the reformers' demand that enterprises, particularly industries, should be given power of "self-determination" with regard to pricing, wages, production levels, product line, and development. At the same time, keeping to the "socialist road" implies that these same enterprises must adhere to the overall economic plans drawn up at the center. Second, what is the role of market forces in a planned economy? Third, how is the government bureaucracy to be restructured so that cadres will administer, and not manage (i.e., interfere with) economic institutions? For the cadres themselves, there is equal uncertainty. How is the shift from direct to indirect control and from direct mandatory planning to indirect and guidance planning to be done? Where do "economic levers" like taxation and supply and demand start operating?[20]

Dislocations in various aspects of the economy following the implementation of the October 1984 reforms strengthened those, like Chen Yun, who have long been advocating the principles of classical socialist economic planning. Chen's speech at the September 1985 conference—in which he criticized over-reliance on market forces at the expense of planning, assailed corruption and the relaxation of ideological and political work, and warned about the rapid development of rural industry and its implications for future grain production—was widely reported, both in China and the West. By the end of the Seventh Five-Year Plan (1990), we *may* know the outcome of this debate.[21]

Primary Sources and the Study of Contemporary China

The compilation of primary source documents in text form as an aid to understanding Chinese politics did not originate with this volume; rather, it has a long history. In a rough sense, one can almost chart the state of the study of Chinese politics through the appearance of primary source collections over time. Using this perspective, the editors believe that this collection is different from previous compilations and fills a gap in the existing literature. Most previous volumes have concentrated heavily on official Party documents, such as laws and directives of the regime, and on official policy statements, such as speeches and writings of the central leadership. The primary intent of these earlier readers was the explication of basic institutions and policies, "to understand how the Chinese Communist government and Party are organized, how they exercise their control, and what the major policies of economic and social development are."[22] The related emphasis on Marxist ideology and doctrine as stated by Party leaders made some of these studies valuable as "guidebook(s) to Communist *aspirations*," to quote one author.[23] Those writing before the Cultural Revolution generally tended to see a unified leadership, with relatively little conflict at the top of the political system.[24] Where inner Party conflict was stressed, it was usually addressed in terms of a united higher leadership facing resistance from cadres at lower levels and disaffected masses, particularly in the aftermath of the Great Leap Forward (1958–1960). The translation and publication of captured internal Party documents from the early 1960s, when economic conditions were perhaps at their harshest, contributed to a picture of China in which the gap between central leaders and basic level cadres had become extremely wide, and in which the demoralization of the latter had reached alarming proportions, highlighting the failures of "political indoctrination." [25]

The revelations made public during the Cultural Revolution, spearheaded by the enormous documentation on inner Party developments published in the Red Guard newspapers and pamphlets, provided researchers with a very different picture of Chinese politics. Many scholars, following in the wake of the analysis being done in China itself, stressed the conflict at the very top of the political system, the "two line struggle" which permeated all policy arenas.[26] With the apparent victory of the "revolutionary" line in the Cultural Revolution, a host of primary source collections appeared, documenting the "fruits of revolution" in each policy arena.[27]

Documentary collections from the late 1970s, during the transition from Maoist China to Dengist China, stressed the fundamental conflict faced by all revolutionary societies: the "great debate" over the proper relationship between revolution (class struggle) and modernization (industrialization and economic growth). It was a time when the Cultural Revolution was still being praised, when Mao was still being extensively cited, and when the ascension of the "pragmatic reformers" was not yet clear.[28] With the favorable re-reevaluation of the 1949–1966 period and the across-the-board denunciation of the Cultural Revolution initiatives, however, scholars became persuaded that a more permanent conflict perspective, particularly at the elite level, was necessary in analyzing Chinese politics.

This collection makes its appearance at a time in which foreign scholars have unprecedented access to information from the People's Republic. In terms of documentary material, authorities in China at all levels have begun what can only be described as a publishing explosion. China has made available thousands of new books, journals, magazines and statistical compendia. Thus, more documentary material now exists on Chinese politics, economics, and society than at any time since 1949 (see below). Far more unexpected and exhilarating to longtime China scholars has been the direct access to the country and its citizens.

In 1978, China International Travel Service received 124,000 foreign tourists, greater than the total number of tourists received from the mid-1950s through 1976. Following dramatic increases each year since, by 1984 China was attracting 1.13 million foreign tourists (this does not include those from Hong Kong and Macao, or overseas Chinese; the total number of visitors in 1984 was 12.85 million). Visitors to China increasingly include professional delegations—such as economists, political scientists, and sociologists—and individual travelers, relatively free to travel to the steadily growing number of cities open to foreigners. The traffic in the other direction has likewise been surprising, as students, visiting scholars, and professional delegations have made their way to the West. From 1978 until mid-1985, the Chinese government had sent 29,000 students to study abroad. In addition, 7,800 students had found nongovernmental funds and were supporting themselves overseas. Over 15,000 students had already returned to China.[29] Western social scientists have begun to spend extended periods in Chinese universities and research institutes lecturing; to a lesser extent, they have also been able to do research in China's libraries, government offices, and urban and rural fieldwork settings. For their part, Chinese social scientists have arrived in the West to engage in research under a variety of national programs. Limited collaborative research projects are currently at a nascent stage, but there is cause for optimism.

Inevitably, such access has influenced our assessment of the Chinese policy process, particularly as it relates to policy implementation. When combined with a more open official press, in which senior leaders may, at selected times and in carefully circumscribed ways, express dissatisfaction with various consequences of the current policy line, in which local officials are similarly given an opportunity to present their views, and in which intellectuals may contend to a limited extent over nonthreatening policy issues in specialized academic journals, it is not surprising that scholars have discovered that policy conflict at both the elite and mass levels is more complicated than previously thought. One recognition of this is the recent popularity of models of the political process in which contention among elites involves three, rather than two, political lines.[30] Another manifestation is the visible activity of opinion groups—including both categoric and professional groups—in defending their "interests." Our reader is a product of this more open period. We have sought to benefit from the greater variety of primary sources now available for the study of China. It is to these sources that we now turn.[31]

Documentary Material

Changes in the methods used to study China and in the number and variety of sources have not diminished the importance of documentary material; on the contrary, the publishing explosion has made such material much more important than ever. Documentary material originating in China can be divided into official and unofficial material, and public or private (or "internal") material. Official material refers to those items published by government or Party sources and not to the status or the content of the material. These data include, for example, the national press, such as *Renmin ribao* (the Party newspaper); *Guangming ribao* (aimed at the country's intellectuals); and *Gongren ribao* (Workers' Daily), all of which are available outside of China, and *Jiefang junbao* (Liberation Army Daily), circulation of which is restricted. Starting from 1978, authorities have permitted the circulation outside of China of many South China provincial newspapers, a rich source of material on local affairs. Since 1983, more North China provincial newspapers have been made available as well. In addition to these publications, speciality newspapers focusing on the economy, finance and trade, agriculture, youth, the arts, and so forth have also been published in increasing number. The Catalog of Newspapers and Magazines available for subscription from the Shanghai Post Office as of late 1984 included 156 national, provincial, and municipal newspapers (although some are difficult to order directly from outside China). An equal number of newspapers, generally from smaller cities or from less open geographical areas, were still designated "for circulation only within China" (see below).

It is important that these newspapers, despite their "official" status, be kept distinct from documents issued directly by the Party or government. *Renmin ribao*, for example, contains a wide range of materials, including Party and government directives (such as Selections 34 and 86), unsigned editorials (Selections 42, 45, and 56), authoritative commentaries (Selections 1, 26, 33, 41, 45, 57, 62, and 63), signed articles that allow for more open discussion of controversial subjects (Selections 29, 30, 59, 64, 72, 74, 75, 76, and 81) or which provide exposés of improper behavior by Party and state officials (Selections 21, 36, 37, 51 and 52), and letters to the editor critical of local policy implementation (Selection 80).

The Party publishes its own theoretical journal, *Hongqi* (Red Flag), and other more specialized journals, including *Dangde shenghuo* (Party Life), which specialize in Marxist analysis and discussions of how Party members ought to behave. These journals have been a principal channel for communicating to Party members the purpose and methods of the Party rectification.

In addition to these journals, academic and professional bodies in China have published their own magazines and journals. These have included the *xuebao* issued by many universities and journals on sociology, social science, economics, law, political science, international relations, geography, population, and history, to name but a few. These journals contain articles written by academics and professionals on a wide range of topics. Editors have published in these places more theoretical articles and mingled them with prescriptive pieces, investigation reports, and short communications. The Shanghai list cited above contains thousands of these general and specialty magazines, conveniently dividing them into the same "open" and "restricted" categories as the newspapers.

The government also publishes its own reports, papers, and documents. The State Council, for example, three times a month circulates a summary of directives issued by the body, together with notices, agreements signed with foreign countries, and approvals given to action taken by local governments, in the *Guowuyuan gongbao* (State Council Bulletin). The government also has begun once again to issue statistical yearbooks and other compendia of economic data on a vast scale. These contain a wide range of material measuring the economic and social health of the country. Examples include the *Zhongguo jingji nianjian* (Chinese Economic Yearbook) and the *Zhongguo tongji nianjian* (Statistical Yearbook of China).

Translations of some of the more common periodicals, especially of articles appearing in the national press, can be found in translation serials published by the United States Department of Commerce (Foreign Broadcast Information

Service—FBIS—Daily Report and the various series published by the Joint Publications Research Service [JPRS], including Political, Sociological and Military Affairs; Economic Affairs; Science and Technology; Agriculture; and Translations from Red Flag) and by the British Broadcasting Corporation (Summary of World Broadcasts). Taiwan also publishes useful translations of internal documents in the monthly journal *Issues & Studies* as well as heavily edited and therefore less reliable translations of material originating in China and Hong Kong in *Inside the China Mainland* (monthly). M. E. Sharpe, Inc. publishes a series of translation journals of material from China. These quarterly journals include *Chinese Economic Studies*, *Chinese Education*, *Chinese Law and Government*, *Chinese Sociology and Anthropology*, *Chinese Studies in History*, and *Chinese Studies in Philosophy*. We have drawn on translations from *Chinese Education* and *Chinese Sociology and Anthropology* in this reader. An important source offering analysis of a wide range of primary source materials is the 10-page *China News Analysis*, based in Hong Kong (published 48 times a year).

Authorities in China have for several years published indices to numerous national and provincial newspapers. While these indices are generally available in Chinese libraries, Western libraries commonly have holdings only for the *Renmin ribao* and *Guangming ribao* indices, which are most easily obtainable through foreign subscription. In addition, beginning in 1981, the Chinese People's University in Beijing has allowed a multi-volume compendium of selected articles from journals published in China to circulate abroad. Although much of the material in this valuable source duplicates items available elsewhere (e.g., *Renmin ribao* articles, reprints from university journals, and so forth), a fair amount of the material stems from less generally available sources. These volumes are offered on subscription under the title *Zhongguo renmin daxue shubao ziliao she: fuyin baokan ziliao*. For 1983 and 1984 the series was restricted "for circulation only within China" (*xian guonei faxing*); fortuitously, it became available to subscribers abroad once again in 1985, with the number of titles increased from around seventy-five to ninety-nine (not including indices). As an example of the breadth of this material, there are seventeen separate titles for different aspects of education. Earlier volumes in the series, back to 1979, can often be found in Chinese libraries. Some U.S. libraries have been able to obtain the missing 1983 and 1984 volumes, and the Universities Service Centre in Hong Kong has obtained a set of all issues from 1980 to the present.

A particularly valuable source, although difficult to find, is the *Quanguo baokan suoyin* (Index to Newspapers and Periodicals from the Whole Country), issued in natural science and social science/humanities editions by the Shanghai library each month. Organized according to very detailed subcategories, this journal lists restricted as well as open publications and not surprisingly is for circulation only within China. Nevertheless, a few fortunate U.S. libraries have managed to secure subscriptions through bulk materials exchanges.

Many official documents have been circulated internally and not published in the public press. Authorities in Taiwan have at times been able to obtain and publish copies of these materials, often in *Zhonggong yanjiu* (Studies in Chinese Communism) and, in English, in the "documents section" of *Issues & Studies*.

The reliability of such sources has often been demonstrated either by reference or subsequent publication in the mainland press of the document in question. Because of their scope and authoritativeness, we have taken the large majority of our selections from open official sources. Of the eighty-seven readings, fully seventy-nine can be said to come from such sources, although some—like the comedians' dialogues in *Tianjin yanchang*—are from relatively unfamiliar publications. Broken down further, we find that fifty-five selections are from "national" newspapers, magazines, and services such as *Guangming ribao*, *Renkou yanjiu* (Population Research), and *Xinhua* (New China News Agency) releases. The remaining twenty-four are from provincial newspapers, magazines, and radio broadcasts. This can be a bit misleading since newspapers like *Yangcheng wanbao* (Yangcheng Evening News) and magazines like *Huangjin shidai* (Golden Age)—both from Guangzhou—are distributed throughout the country. Given its importance as the Party's mouthpiece, we have taken twenty-five selections from *Renmin ribao*. Eight selections were published originally in English.

A brief comment on these English-language sources may be helpful. Generally, material in English addresses issues considered of interest to foreigners (Selection 6 on lotteries, Selection 25 on workers, and Selection 32 on women), refutes "erroneous" conceptions of developments in China (Selection 2, which takes issue with a *New York Times* editorial on the political implications of China's new economic reforms), and provides rather sanitized information on developments in China and China's foreign policy positions. For example, although not fully comparable, it is interesting nonetheless to compare Selection 25 on Chinese workers, which overemphasizes the right of workers to strike and use their trade union for political participation, with Selection 28, originally published in Chinese, which is a detailed account of the problems of Party committees and Party secretaries in factories, after the new system in which the plant manager assumes all responsibility of operations has been set up. The latter selection, unlike the English article, makes no mention of the role of workers' councils and trade unions in either personnel decisions or in the supervision of management.

The importance of the United States Department of Commerce Translation Services can be seen in the fact that forty-two of the selections were either translated (thirty-nine) or reprinted (three English selections) in the aforementioned FBIS Daily Report. Ten reports were translated (nine) or reprinted (one) in JPRS.

The official sources listed above are clearly the scholar's most important resource. A word, however, should be added regarding the "unofficial" or "people's" publications, distributed by China's Democracy Movement activists from 1978 to 1981. Most prevalent during 1978–79, primarily in large cities, they included journals specializing in political criticism (e.g., *Tansuo* [Exploration], *Beijing zhichun* [Spring], and *Renwu* [Duty]) and those that focused more on short stories, poetry, and literary criticism (e.g., *Jintian* [Today]). The best of the politically oriented journals at times offered a fascinating commentary on material in the official press and published the valuable writings of political thinkers such as Wang Xizhe, whose unedited views were unacceptable in official circles. These unofficial publications have been reprinted in a wide variety of places; some are available in English.[32]

In addition to the official and unofficial documentary materials, both of which are public (*gongkai*), there exists an even larger category of private, internal (*neibu*) materials, useful for doing research on China. These materials are published by many Party, government, academic, and professional organizations in China and include the results of investigation reports (such as the periodical *Nongcun fazhan yanjiu* [Rural Development Research], published by the Chinese Academy of Social Sciences); authoritative interpretations of past events (such as *Zhonggong dangshi nianbiao* [Outline of Major Events in Chinese Communist Party History], published by the Party History Research Office); articles critical of authorities for failing to implement local policy (Selection 40); and material on a host of other issues. We have already referred to important publications that carry the designation "for circulation only within China." This, however, merely represents the most accessible of the *neibu* materials. There are also newspapers, magazines, reports, and books that carry designations such as "internal circulation only" (*neibu faxing*)—referring to "internal" within China or within the unit issuing the publication—those that add the phrase "pay attention in protecting this source" (*zhuyi baocun*) to the above designation, and so on. In short, the internal press consists of a hierarcy of restricted material. The tip of the hierarchy is said to be a twice daily publication entitled "internal reference" (*neibu cankao*), with access reportedly limited to around 1,000 high officials. It should be noted that internal circulation material at the base of the hierarchy, such as translations of selected articles from the Western press, is generally available to most Chinese citizens.

As a rule, internally circulated materials tend to be more reliable and more detailed than those published in the open press. They also tend to be much more critical of developments in China. When Party General Secretary Hu Yaobang, in a recent speech published in *Renmin ribao*, told newspapers that 80 percent of their reports should be devoted to the country's achievements, and only 20 percent left to shortcomings, he was, in effect, making a distinction between the open press, to which such standards refer, and the internal press, which is much less subject to these constraints.[33]

Some examples of the open/internal distinction may be helpful. Selection 24, from the official media, relates an open attack on Party and government offices by villagers on Hainan Island. The report concentrates on the severe punishment meted out to the villagers while ignoring the motive for the attack. The same report, in the internal press, would presumably include details on the motivations of the attackers and perhaps be less concerned with emphasizing the punishment. In this case, the report in the open press serves as a warning to potential evildoers, while the internal press serves more to impart information. Selections 38, 40, and 85, on the other hand, are examples of reports in publications generally available to Chinese, but kept from foreigners. Selections 38 and 40 are notable because they reveal the depth of problems in the area of Party personnel policy. Unlike the discussion of this issue in the open press, which tends to be very general, these internal reports are replete with statistical data. Selection 85 points to a controversial aspect of a highly successful policy—the behavior of new rich peasants who have prospered under the production responsibility system—raising questions which, if published in the open press, might imply official dissatisfaction with the policy.

Less easily categorizable are the Hong Kong magazines. Hong Kong Chinawatchers have benefited even more from the new open policy than Western Sinologists. As Chinese, many of whom are former residents of post-1949 China, they combine extensive contacts with an unparalleled knowledge of the politics, society, and culture of the country. Hong Kong magazines have therefore become a major source for the study of China, with information on policy conflict among senior leaders and on intellectual issues—particularly in such fields as literature, art and journalism—perhaps given greatest attention. Editorially, these publications have strongly supported the liberalizing reforms of Deng Xiaoping and his colleagues, while offering frequent criticism of senior leaders opposed to the liberalization. In addition to their own analyses, these magazines have occasionally published otherwise unavailable documents (such as Liao Gailong's "1980 Reform" speech included in this collection) or reprinted banned or heavily criticized literary works from Chinese magazines. Among the more important Hong Kong journals are *Zhengming* (Contention), *Jiushi niandai* (The Nineties, formerly *The Seventies*) *Dongxiang* (Trend, no longer published), *Jingbao* (The Mirror), and *Guangjiaojing* (Wide Angle). Except for our two interviews with Chinese émigrés (Selections 70 and 71), only Selection 44—on the struggle between advocates of different approaches to developing the Chinese economy—originates from Hong Kong. This report is typical of the "inside" analysis available only through Hong Kong sources. Both the FBIS Daily Report and JPRS provide translations from Hong Kong media reports on China.

Literary and Artistic Sources

A second source of material on China includes the works of fiction, short stories, poetry, plays, films, comedians' dialogues, cartoons, reportage, biography, and autobiography that have been published in China. China has a long tradition of using the cultural arena to wage political struggle indirectly. Forbidden areas of discussion may be broached for the first time in a short story, a film, a play, or even a cartoon. A critical airing of social or political problems can be more palatable and seem less threatening to the leadership if presented in the form of fiction, perhaps using a traditional art form and offered as comedy.[34] From these sources we gain a better understanding of the pervasiveness of bureaucracy in China, the arrogance of some officials, the suffering of China's intellectuals during the Cultural Revolution, the corruption of local leaders, and the confusion of ordinary people as they try to comply with authority or participate in politics. Because of space considerations, it has been difficult to make full use of these valuable sources. Nevertheless, we have selected two comedians' dialogues (*xiangsheng*), one on the pervasiveness of and necessity for "connections" and "networks" to accomplish virtually anything in a society still marked by an acute scarcity of commodities (Selection 35), and the other about a very, very cautious factory manager (Selection 53). Sprinkled throughout the book, in appropriate locations, are twenty cartoons, offering a pictorial counterpoint to the textual material. Neither the comedians' dialogues nor the vast majority of the cartoons have appeared in English previously. Moreover, since contention over literature and art policy tends to be more open and direct than in more overtly political arenas, we have devoted an entire section to this sector (Selections 81–85).

Research in China

A third source for doing research on contemporary China involves traveling to China and working either in a library or archive, or doing interviewing fieldwork. Since 1979, Americans in limited numbers have been able to do both. Scholars have had access to important libraries in Nanjing, Beijing, and Shanghai. In addition, they have been permitted to do research in urban industrial enterprises, commercial establishments, and government offices. Our understanding of the contemporary political process in China has been much enhanced by interviews with officials at all levels in these organizations. The interview data has been fruitfully combined with documentary material available in the specialized libraries of these units.

After a brief period of virtually unrestricted access to some of China's villages, American scholars have had only limited opportunities for fieldwork in the countryside. Since January 1981, authorities in China have severely restricted rural fieldwork, and American researchers have been generally limited to two week trips to selected rural sites. However, important studies based on these limited fieldwork opportunities are beginning to appear.

Interviewing in Hong Kong

A fourth source of material on contemporary China includes interviews with legal and illegal immigrants from China (the aforementioned Selections 70 and 71), conducted at the Universities Service Centre in Hong Kong. Particularly during the years when American scholars were prevented from doing research in China, this source proved invaluable. Throughout the 1960s and 1970s large numbers of mostly illegal immigrants arrived in Hong Kong, mainly from rural Guangdong. They provided useful factual information on the implementation of policy in China. Their own rather negative experiences in China, however, often biased their judgment about political affairs. In 1980, when Hong Kong abolished its practice of tacitly accepting illegal immigrants, the character of immigration from China changed. From 1980, tens of thousands of legal immigrants continued to arrive in Hong Kong each year, but unlike their predecessors, they were mainly from Fujian and other parts of China. They were often urbanites, and many of them had more years of education than did previous groups of immigrants. Both these groups have enhanced our understanding of Chinese society; indeed, since 1965 countless studies of contemporary China have been written based wholly or in part on their testimony.[35] Our two examples of émigré interviews concern the effects of the new agricultural policies on different aspects of rural life.

A Concluding Note

The picture of Chinese politics that emerges from this reader is very much a function of our focus and methodology. Putting relatively less emphasis on elite-level politics and greater stress on the implementation phase of the policy process; choosing a wide variety of sources, including the writings of local officials and ordinary citizens (there are fifteen "letters to the editor" of newspapers and magazines in this collection); and including policy arenas such as literature and art and population, where individual values openly conflict with state policy, it is not surprising that we discover a rather decentralized political system in which intermediate and lower-level cadres have considerable scope for resisting the policy directives of senior leaders.

Our approach highlights a number of elements of the Chinese political system that elite-level analyses frequently obscure.[36] For example, these readings reveal the crucial role of mid-level and basic-level cadres in policy success—and the advantages and disadvantages of holding a cadre position. As Selection 76 on rural education and Selection 86 on family planning show, there is great pressure on local cadres to take the lead in implementing unpopular policies, to set an example for their less politically conscious neighbors. At the same time, as Selections 77 and 79 show, these same cadres are best placed to provide desirable jobs and educational opportunities for their offspring. Selection 68 reveals the great power basic-level cadres can exercise over local residents. In this case, it took the most powerful person in the province—the first secretary of the provincial CCP committee—to rectify the case of a broken contract. Even the county CCP committee had been unable (or unwilling) to alter the decision local village cadres had made against a specialized household.

Moreover, by employing a wide range of source material, we can look at the same phenomenon from different angles. In the case of China's extensive *guanxi* (relationship) networks, we can see how the authoritative "Commentator" states the problem in general terms in *Renmin ribao*, the Party newspaper (Selection 33); how the problem is treated in an official Circular from the Party's Central Discipline Inspection Commission (Selection 34); how China's comedians present the issue of "unhealthy tendencies" in slapstick form, portraying "backdoor relationships" carried to absurd extremes (Selection 35); how investigative reporters use detailed case studies to expose particularly serious instances of the practice (Selections 36 and 37); how it is discussed in a letter from a personnel cadre to an internally circulated publication (Selection 38); and how it appears in "natural" form as young Party members being surveyed reveal their unwillingness to speak out for justice: "one more foe is another wall, but one more friend is one more road" (Selection 66). While each source highlights different aspects of the problem, the different accounts provide reinforcing documentation as to the pervasiveness of the phenomenon.

The intricate, complex relationship between higher and lower level units that emerges from our documents is intriguing. Clearly, higher-level organs (such as industrial companies, bureaus, and municipal and provincial Party committees) have a stake in the success of units under their supervision (such as factories). This has certain implications for policy. It has meant, for example, that collectives or individuals associated with the larger organ must be defended or protected when problems arise, as was the case with the nationally renowned wealthy peasant who went bankrupt (Selection 67). In that case, blandly accepting the bankruptcy of a peasant previously praised by *Renmin ribao* for becoming rich under the new agricultural reforms might lead other potentially bold peasants to question the Center's long-term commitment to the reforms. He could not be allowed to go under. More often, protective networks do not run from the Center to the individual, but rather occur at the middle levels of the Party and state bureaucracy, as Selections 36, 37, 51, and 52 reveal. To break through this local network of interests, central Party leaders have endorsed selected investigative reporters in their efforts to root out corruption or opposition to central policies. The most prominent of this new breed of investigative reporter is the well-known writer Liu Binyan, whose exposés of bureaucracy and corruption have made him the bane of mid-level—and, at times, high-level—officials since 1957. Some China-watchers, particularly in Hong Kong, in part chart the level of openness in the mainland by the amount of freedom accorded Liu Binyan in gathering and publishing his reports.[37] Liu's reports are indeed exceptional (Selections 36 and 37); not only do they name names, but at times even provide the street addresses of the persecuted victims!

The Party still officially subscribes to a modified "mass line" philosophy, which harkens back to Yanan-style democracy of the 1930s and 1940s. In their writings and speeches, central leaders like Hu Yaobang and Xi Zhongxun place great emphasis on the importance of letters and visits from the masses.[38] However, as Selection 22 shows, newspapers attempting to investigate complaints are accorded little cooperation. More often, there is great resistance, even harassment, of reporters pursuing a story. One source of protection, albeit rare, is the direct intervention of a Chinese leader in support of a journalist. For example, after the first installment of Ding Jizhi's hard-hitting two-part exposé of the Xian City Cement Plant (Selections 51 and 52), Hu Yaobang was cited in *Renmin ribao* urging Party, government, and army leaders in Hubei Province (where he was visiting) to read Ding's report. Hu pointed to leftover factional problems from the Cultural Revolution, continuing bureaucratic practices, and discrimination against intellectuals as typical problems awaiting solution. When Ding's second installment appeared in *Renmin ribao* four days later, it carried the weight of Hu's prior endorsement.[39]

Finally, our documents reveal how opposition to an established state policy can be manifested by focusing on the policy's negative side effects. For example, in our commerce section, several of the selections (Nos. 55–57) strongly support the continued development of the individual economy. However, several others (Selections 58–59), by investigating actual conditions in some of China's largest cities, point to the serious problems that have arisen as a consequence of the policy. Since the promotion of the individual economy has been positively endorsed officially since 1979, critics cannot attack the policy itself, but must couch their criticisms in acceptable form.

Notes

1. *New York Times*, December 13, 1985, p. 4; FBIS Daily Report, September 10, 1985, pp. W10–W20 (*Zhengming*, September 1985).

2. John Wilson Lewis, *Major Doctrines of Communist China* (New York: W. W. Norton, 1964).

3. For the use of primary source documents to trace the political history of post-1949 China, see Harold C. Hinton, *The People's Republic of China, 1949–1979: A Documentary Survey* (Wilmington, Delaware: Scholarly Resources, 1980), 5 volumes; Mark Selden, *The People's Republic of China: A Documentary History of Revolutionary Change* (New York: Monthly Review Press, 1979); and Robert R. Bowie and John K. Fairbank, eds., *Communist China 1955–1959: Policy Documents with Analysis* (Cambridge, Mass.: Harvard University Press, 1962).

4. Lowell Dittmer, "Chinese Marxism Since Mao" (paper prepared for the conference "To Reform the Chinese Political Order," June 18–23, 1984, Harwichport, Massachusetts).

5. Dorothy Solinger, "The Fifth National People's Congress and the Process of Policy Making: Reform, Readjustment, and the Opposition," *Asian Survey* 22:12 (December 1982), pp. 1238–1275; Carol Lee Hamrin, "Competing 'Policy Packages' in Post-Mao China," *Asian Survey* 24:5 (May 1984), pp. 487–518.

6. Roger Garside, *Coming Alive: China After Mao* (New York: New American Library, 1981).

7. Parris H. Chang, *Elite Conflict in the Post-Mao China*, rev. ed. (Baltimore: Occasional Papers/Reprints Series in Contemporary Asian Studies, University of Maryland, School of Law, 1983), No. 2 (55), p. 3.

8. Hamrin, "Policy Packages," p. 495.

9. Chang, *Elite Conflict*, p. 6.

10. Kenneth Lieberthal, "Bureaucratic Reforms Since Mao" (paper prepared for the conference "To Reform the Chinese Political Order," June 18–23, 1984, Harwichport, Massachusetts, p. 43).

11. Chang, *Elite Conflict*, p. 7.

12. See the widely different speeches at the National Science Conference by Deng (*Peking Review* 12 [March 24, 1978], pp. 9–18) and Hua (*Peking Review* 13 [March 31, 1978], pp. 6–14).

13. Hamrin, "Policy Packages," p. 496.

14. Kjeld Erik Brodsgaard, "The Democracy Movement in China, 1978–1979: Opposition Movements, Wall Poster Campaigns, and Underground Journals," *Asian Survey* 21:7 (July 1981), pp. 747–774.

15. Lowell Dittmer, "China in 1981: Reform, Readjustment, Rectification," *Asian Survey* 22:1 (January 1982), p. 33.

16. *Selected Works of Deng Xiaoping, 1975–1982* (Beijing: Foreign Languages Press, 1984), pp. 302–325.

17. Kenneth Lieberthal, "China in 1982: A Middling Course for the Middle Kingdom," *Asian Survey* 23:1 (January 1983), p. 33.

18. Thomas B. Gold, " 'Just in Time!' China Battles Spiritual Pollution on the Eve of 1984," *Asian Survey* 24:9 (September 1984), pp. 947–974.

19. Thomas P. Bernstein, "China in 1984: The Year of Hong Kong," *Asian Survey* 25:1 (January 1985), pp. 43–44.

20. Mary Lee and David Bonavia, "Socialist Balancing Act," *Far Eastern Economic Review*, October 10, 1985, pp. 36–38.

21. See *China News Analysis* No. 1301 (January 1, 1986) for an analysis of the plan and *China News Analysis* Nos. 1291 (August 15, 1985), 1292 (September 1, 1985), 1293 (September 15, 1985), and 1295 (October 15, 1985) for details on the September 1985 Conference. Chen Yun's speech is translated in FBIS Daily Report, September 23, 1985, pp. K13–K16 (NCNA, English, September 23, 1985).

22. Theodore H. E. Chen, ed., *The Chinese Communist Regime: Documents and Commentary* (New York: Frederick A. Praeger, 1967).

23. Lewis, *Major Doctrines*, p. 7 (emphasis added).

24. Even the best documentary studies were unable to set out clear divisions within the Chinese leadership, but discussed the "balance of forces" within the Party in the general terms of a dominant "radical wing" and a much weaker "rightist opposition." See, for example, *Communist China 1955–1959: Policy Documents with Analysis* (Cambridge, Mass.: Harvard University Press, 1962).

25. J. Chester Cheng, ed. *The Politics of the Chinese Red Army* (Stanford: Hoover Institution Press, 1966); C. S. Chen and C. P. Ridley, eds., *Rural People's Communes in Lien-chang* (Stanford: Hoover Institution Press, 1969).

26. A pioneering work in setting out elite divisions over policy—although not necessarily in terms of a two-line struggle—through the study of documents is Richard Baum and Frederick C. Teiwes, *Ssu-Ch'ing: The Socialist Education Movement of 1962–1966* (Berkeley: Center for Chinese Studies, University of California, Berkeley, 1968).

27. See, as examples, David Milton, Nancy Milton, and Franz Schurmann, eds., *The China Reader, Vol. 4: People's China* (New York: Vintage, 1974); Peter J. Seybolt, ed., *Revolutionary Education in China: Documents and Commentary* (White Plains, N.Y.: International Arts and Sciences Press, 1973); Steven Andors, ed., *Workers and Workplaces in Revolutionary China* (White Plains, N.Y.: M. E. Sharpe, 1977). The importance of the Red Guard newspapers in providing information about elite-level politics can be seen in Kenneth Lieberthal, *A Research Guide to Central Party and Government Meetings in China 1949–1975* (White Plains, N.Y.: International Arts and Sciences Press, 1976). Of the 233 meetings this *Guide* includes for the 1956–1966 period, information on over 25 percent was derived from just one Red Guard source per meeting.

28. The most substantial work, Mark Selden's *The People's Republic of China: A Documentary History of Revolutionary Change* (New York: Monthly Review Press, 1979), goes back to 1946 and seeks "to capture the views of major protagonists in successive debates that shaped the formation of an independent road to socialism." While Selden sees the debate as a struggle within the revolutionary camp, a more radical perspective is offered in Raymond Lotta, ed., *And Mao Makes 5: Mao Tsetung's Last Great Battle* (Chicago: Banner Press, 1978). In Lotta's account, the "coup" of October 1976 was a victory of the "Rightists" over the revolutionaries. This book remains the most complete collection in English of the writings associated with the "Gang of Four."

29. JPRS-CPS-85-112, November 4, 1985, p. 37 (*Banyuetan*, August 25, 1985). The Seventh Five-Year Plan called for still more students to be sent abroad.

30. See Dorothy J. Solinger, ed., *Three Visions of Chinese Socialism* (Boulder, Colorado: Westview Press, 1984), and Hamrin, "Policy Packages."

31. The classic account of the proper use of the diverse sources available for the study of contemporary China remains Michel Oksenberg, "Sources and Methodological Problems in the Study of Contemporary China," in A. Doak Barnett, ed., *Chinese Communist Politics in Action* (Seattle: University of Washington Press, 1969), pp. 577–606.

32. For English translations see, *inter alia*, Gregor Benton, ed., *Wild Lillies, Poisonous Weeds: Dissident Voices from People's China* (London: Pluto Press, 1982); Anita Chan, Stanley Rosen, and Jonathan Unger, eds., *On Socialist Democracy and the Chinese Legal System: The Li Yizhe Debates* (Armonk, N.Y.: M. E. Sharpe, 1985); David S. G. Goodman, ed., *Beijing Street Voices: The Poetry and Politics of China's Democracy Movement* (London: Marion Boyars, 1981); and James D. Seymour, ed., *The Fifth Modernization: China's Human Rights Movement, 1978–1979* (Stanfordville, N.Y.: Human Rights Publishing Group, 1980).

33. Hu Yaobang, "On the Party's Journalism Work," FBIS Daily Report, April 15, 1985, pp. K1–K15 (*Renmin ribao*, April 14, 1985). On China's internally circulated media, see Michael Schoenhals, "Elite Information in China," *Problems of Communism* 34:5 (September–October 1985), pp. 65–71; Jorg-Meinhard Rudolph, "China's Media:

Fitting News to Print," *Problems of Communism* 33:4 (July–August 1984), pp. 58–67; and idem, *Cankao Xiaoxi: Foreign News in the Propaganda System of the People's Republic of China* (Occasional Papers/Reprints Series in Contemporary Asian Studies, School of Law, University of Maryland), 1984, No. 6.

34. There is a great deal of self-censorship among cultural workers, however, and some works have been singled out for official criticism. Such criticized works include "If I Were for Real," by Sha Yexin, Li Shoucheng, and Yao Mingde; "In the Archives of Society," by Wang Jing, both translated in Lee Yee, ed., *The New Realism: Writings from China After the Cultural Revolution* (New York: Hippocrene Books, 1983), pp. 102–141 and 261–322. The most publicized work that was officially criticized is of course the filmscript "Unrequited Love" (*Kulian*), by Bai Hua.

35. Most recently, see Anita Chan, Richard Madsen, and Jonathan Unger, *Chen Village* (Berkeley: University of California Press, 1984), and Martin K. Whyte and William L. Parish, *Urban Life in Contemporary China* (Chicago: University of Chicago Press, 1984).

36. For a discussion of models based on elite-level analysis, see Harry Harding, "Competing Models of the Chinese Communist Policy Process: Toward a Sorting and Evaluation," *Issues & Studies* 20:2 (February 1984), pp. 13–36, and Chalmers Johnson, "What's Wrong with Chinese Political Studies?" *Asian Survey* 22:10 (October 1982), pp. 919–933.

37. See, for example, *Jiushi niandai* (The Nineties) 189 (October 1985), pp. 92–109; *Zhengming* (Contention) 86 (December 1984), p. 9; 78 (April 1984), pp. 25–26; and *Far Eastern Economic Review*, December 26, 1985, pp. 39–40.

38. FBIS Daily Report, October 15, 1985, pp. K2–K4 (*Renmin ribao*, October 8, 1985); FBIS Daily Report, November 27, 1985, pp. K29–K31 (*Renmin ribao Overseas Edition*, November 17, 1985).

39. FBIS Daily Report, April 20, 1984, p. K6 (*Renmin ribao*, April 19, 1984).

FURTHER READINGS

Bowie, Robert R., and John K. Fairbank, eds. *Communist China 1955–1959: Policy Documents with Analysis*. Cambridge, Mass.: Harvard University Press, 1962.

Brodsgaard, Kjeld Erik. "Paradigmatic Change: Readjustment and Reform in the Chinese Economy, 1953–1981, Part II." *Modern China* (April 1983), pp. 253–272.

Butterfield, Fox. *China: Alive in the Bitter Sea*. New York: Bantam Books, 1982.

Chang, King-yuh, ed. *Perspectives on Development in Mainland China*. Boulder, Colorado: Westview Press, 1985 (twenty-two articles covering politics, the military, economics, and foreign policy).

Chang, Parris H. *Elite Conflict in the Post-Mao China*. Rev. ed. Baltimore: Occasional Papers/ Reprints Series in Contemporary Asian Studies, University of Maryland, School of Law. 1983, No. 2 (55).

Chen, C. S., and C. P. Ridley, eds. *Rural People's Communes in Lien-chiang*. Stanford: Hoover Institution Press, 1969.

Cheng, J. Chester, ed. *The Politics of the Chinese Red Army*. Stanford: Hoover Institution Press, 1966.

China Under the Four Modernizations, Parts I and II. Selected papers submitted to the Joint Economic Committee, Congress of the United States. Washington, D.C.: U.S. Government Printing Office, August 13 and December 30, 1982.

Dittmer, Lowell. "Structural Change in the PRC, 1976–1982." Paper prepared for the California Regional Seminar in Chinese Studies, Center for Chinese Studies, University of California, Berkeley, November 4–5, 1983.

Garside, Roger. *Coming Alive: China After Mao*. New York: New American Library, 1981.

Ginsburg, Norton, and Bernard A. Lalor, eds. *China: The 80s Era*. Boulder, Colorado: Westview Press, 1984.

Goldstein, Steven M. *China Briefing, 1984*. Boulder, Colorado: Westview Press, 1985 (articles cover politics, culture, society, foreign policy, and economics).

Goodman, David S.G. *Groups and Politics in the People's Republic of China*. Armonk, N.Y.: M. E. Sharpe, 1984.

Hamrin, Carol Lee. "Competing 'Policy Packages' in Post-Mao China." *Asian Survey* 24:5 (May 1984), pp. 487-518.

Harding, Harry. "Competing Models of the Chinese Communist Policy Process: Toward a Sorting and Evaluation." *Issues & Studies* 20:2 (February 1984), pp. 13-36.

Hinton, Harold C. *The People's Republic of China, 1949-1979: A Documentary Survey*. Wilmington, Delaware: Scholarly Resources, 1980, 5 volumes.

Huntington, Samuel, and Clement H. Moore, eds. *Authoritarian Politics in Modern Society: The Dynamics of Established One-party Systems*. New York: Basic Books, 1970.

Huntington, Samuel, and Joan Nelson. *No Easy Choice*. Cambridge, Mass.: Harvard University Press, 1976.

Johnson, Chalmers. "What's Wrong with Chinese Political Studies?" *Asian Survey* 22:10 (October 1982), pp. 919-933.

Lampton, David M. *Policy Implementation in Post-Mao China*. Berkeley: University of California Press, forthcoming.

Lewis, John Wilson, ed. *Major Doctrines of Communist China*. New York: W. W. Norton, 1964.

Lieberthal, Kenneth. "Bureaucratic Reforms Since Mao." Paper prepared for the Conference on "To Reform the Chinese Political Order," Harwichport, Massachusetts, June 1984.

Lieberthal, Kenneth. *A Research Guide to Central Party and Government Meetings in China 1949-1975*. White Plains, N.Y.: International Arts and Sciences Press, 1976.

Lotta, Raymond, ed. *And Mao Makes 5: Mao Tsetung's Last Great Battle*. Chicago: Banner Press, 1978.

Maxwell, Neville, and Bruce McFarland, eds. *China's Changed Road to Development*. Oxford: Pergamon Press, 1984.

Moody, Peter R., Jr. *Chinese Politics After Mao: Development and Liberalization, 1976 to 1983*. New York: Praeger, 1983.

Nathan, Andrew J. "A Factional Model for Chinese Politics." *The China Quarterly* No. 53 (January-March 1973), pp. 34-66.

Oksenberg, Michel. "Sources and Methodological Problems in the Study of Contemporary China." In A. Doak Barnett, ed. *Chinese Communist Politics in Action*. Seattle: University of Washington Press, 1969, pp. 577-606.

Pye, Lucian. *The Dynamics of Chinese Politics*. Cambridge, Mass.: Oelgeschlager, Gunn and Hain, 1981.

Resolution on CPC History 1949-81. Beijing: Foreign Languages Press, 1981.

Selden, Mark, ed. *The People's Republic of China: A Documentary History of Revolutionary Change*. New York: Monthly Review Press, 1979.

Selected Works of Deng Xiaoping 1975-1982. Beijing: Foreign Languages Press, 1984.

Shaw Yu-ming, ed. *Power and Policy in the PRC*. Boulder, Colorado: Westview Press, 1985.

Shirk, Susan L. "The Political Economy of Chinese Industrial Reform." Paper prepared for the Conference on "To Reform the Chinese Political Order," Harwichport, Massachusetts, June 1984.

Solinger, Dorothy J. "The Fifth National People's Congress and the Process of Policy Making: Reform, Readjustment, and the Opposition." *Asian Survey* 22:12 (December 1982), pp. 1238-1275.

Tien, Hung-mao. *The Communist Party of China: Party Powers and Group Politics from the Third Plenum to the 12th Party Congress*. Baltimore: Occasional Papers/Reprints Series in Contemporary Asian Studies, University of Maryland, 1984, No. 61.

Tsou Tang. "Prolegomenon to the Study of Informal Groups in CCP Politics." *The China Quarterly* No. 65 (March 1976), pp. 98-114.

Whitson, William W. "Organizational Perspectives and Decision-Making in the Chinese Communist High Command." In Robert A. Scalapino, ed. *Elites in the People's Republic of China*. Seattle: University of Washington Press, 1972.

Wolfgang, Marvin E., ed. *China in Transition*. Special Issue of *The Annals of the American Academy of Political and Social Sciences*, November 1984 (articles cover politics and bureaucratic reform, law, industry, agriculture, population, and foreign policy).

Yu Guangyuan, ed. *China's Socialist Modernization*. Beijing: Foreign Languages Press, 1984 (776 pages, primarily on economic developments between 1977-1980, with long chapters on such topics as agriculture, industry and transport, commerce, banking, finance, population, urban employment and wages, science and technology, and economic relations with foreign countries).

I
STRUCTURE
and PROCESS

A. Theory and Ideology

WHEN MANY OF THE fundamental verities of post-1949 Chinese political theory and ideology were decried as "sham Marxism" by Party reformers, several nagging questions floated to the surface. First, and most obviously, what theory and ideology was to replace the discredited radical version of Marxism-Leninism-Mao Zedong Thought? What could be salvaged from the "socialism" practiced under late Maoism, and what needed to be jettisoned? Second, what role should ideology play in guiding the extensive reforms considered necessary in developing "true socialism"? Third, what were the theoretical and ideological lessons to be drawn from the Cultural Revolution "catastrophe"? What new relationship between leaders and led—between the Party and society— was necessary in the era of the Four Modernizations? The readings in this section address these questions.

It is useful to start with an overview of the ideological platform on which the reform movement is based. Although ideological zigs and zags have appeared from 1979 to the present and analysts often subdivide this period into phases of "liberalization" and "retrenchment," the overall thrust has been in a "liberal" direction; thus, our summary will stress this more liberal ideological conception. As Lowell Dittmer has described it, the basic premise is that the revolution has been completed. With the socialization of the means of production, the bourgeois classes lost their economic base and are doomed to eventual extinction (as a class); class struggle has essentially come to an end. The main contradiction in socialist society is a nonantagonistic one between advanced and backward economic sectors; the solution lies not in redistribution, but in the completion of the modernization process. The key to modernization is economic development; with the growth of the productive forces, the relations of production may be assumed to adapt to this growth without undue political attention. Socialism is not seen as a short transition phase from capitalism to communism, but a relatively stable mode of production that fuses selected aspects of both capitalist and communist modes of production. The socialist system is marked by: (1) predominantly public ownership of the means of production (although collective and even individual ownership are allowed to coexist with state ownership); (2) distribution on the basis of labor; (3) the regulation of social production primarily by the law of value (i.e., profit as the main criterion for economic efficiency). Socialism is distinguished from capitalism primarily in terms of ownership of the means of production. After the transfer of ownership, the socialist mode is so firmly established that selected elements from capitalist systems may be introduced (management systems, material incentives, markets) without endangering the socialist nature of society. Because there is no danger of regenerating capitalist elements within the social formation, the concerns that troubled Mao, such as the rise of a new bourgeoisie within the Party, are unnecessary. Class struggle under these conditions is subordinated to the central task of economic construction.[1]

It follows from this that ideology and politics must play subordinate roles, primarily to "serve" and to "guarantee" the success of the economic reforms. Such "absurdities" as "putting politics in command," "giving priority to politics," and considering ideological work to be in the "supreme position of 'commander in chief'" have been extensively criticized in the Chinese press; as a result, political work cadres have become demoralized and feel that "political work will become something unnecessary and useless."[2]

Selection 1 is included not only for its importance as a policy statement, but also because of its impact on Western analysis of China. One of a series of commentaries in *Renmin ribao* (People's Daily), *Hongqi* (Red Flag), and other media following the October 1984 "Decision on Reform of the Economic Structure," it was a message to Party and state cadres that successful implementation of economic reform and, therefore, of the entire Four Modernizations program, required a new understanding of basic Marxist theory. As one recent report acknowledged, "When some people discovered that certain phrases and policies in the [October 1984] 'Decision' were different from their past understanding of socialism, they considered these to be a deviation from Marxism. In fact, the concept of Marxism they have in mind is actually not Marxism, but the outcome of the 'leftist' ideological influence."[3]

One sentence in Selection 1—"We cannot expect the writings of Marx and Lenin of that time to provide solutions to our current problems"—attracted immediate foreign attention. The Associated Press sent a story marked "Urgent" over the wires, with the headline "China Abandons Marx." Confronted by this scoop, the home offices of many American newspapers sent their own urgent queries to correspondents stationed in Beijing, saying: The Associated Press has come up with this bombshell, where's *your* report? In short order, America's leading correspondents, including many with little knowledge or experience of China, offered their assessments. William Safire of *The New York Times* enthused, "When it comes to world history . . . the big event of 1984 was surely the rejection of Marxism and embrace of capitalism by the Government of a billion Chinese." Flora Lewis, in the same paper, called the announcement "breathtaking," and a "historic watershed." Joseph C. Harsch, in *The Christian Science Monitor*, spoke of China, "once among the most fanatically communist [countries], [having] repudiated the doctrines of Marx and Lenin."[4] Taken aback by the reaction in the West—as *Time* magazine reported the complaints of one

Chinese intellectual, "Such a fuss is the last thing we wanted. We need a quiet revolution"—Chinese newspapers and magazines intended for foreigners sought to set the record straight, as Selection 2 indicates.

There are, however, important developments occurring in the Chinese economy, and they do involve revisions of what has heretofore been taken as basic Marxism in China. As subsequent articles in the Chinese press have made clear, it is not the Chinese "updating" of Marx that is particularly controversial—after all, Mao had been doing this since the 1920s and 1930s—rather, it is the attempts to build socialism through the development of a commodity economy.[5]

While Marx had analyzed in great detail the structure of capitalist society and had outlined the nature of a future communist society, he had not considered the process by which a socialist system established in a pre-capitalist society would make the transition to communism. Having absorbed the lessons of unsuccessful Maoist experiments like the Great Leap Forward, which attempted a "shortcut" transition to communism by the premature imposition of advanced methods of production on a backward economic base, Deng and his strategists have stressed the necessity of a long-term, sustained economic development to create the preconditions for communism. But the reformers have sailed into relatively uncharted Marxist waters by arguing that, given China's backwardness, the necessary economic growth must be accomplished through the development of a commodity economy, an economic system Marx had associated with capitalism. As one *Renmin ribao* commentary put it, "Marx predicted that commodities and money would be unnecessary under socialist conditions. However . . . commodities and money are necessary for socialist society . . . and commodity production . . . must be vigorously developed."[6]

Robert Delfs has indicated the profound implications of such a policy—and the reasons why many Chinese cadres are skeptical of this approach. If China is a developing commodity economy, then structurally the Chinese economy should resemble a capitalist economy in many respects, and many of the laws that govern capitalist economic development should also apply to China. Commodity exchange would be similar in both economies. While the Chinese are at pains to point out the basic differences between capitalist commodity economy and China's socialist commodity economy—first, land and other important means of production are owned by the whole people, though they may be used and operated by collective groups and individuals; second, planning plays an important role in the socialist commodity economy—the growing similarities to a capitalist system (as China introduces "socialist" financial markets and "socialist" stock exchanges) are rather unnerving to the orthodox who have not sufficiently "emancipated their thought."[7]

Selections 3, 4, and 5 concern the relationship between the Party (state) and society in the transition to communism. The limits imposed on the position, scope, and methods of class struggle under socialism (Selection 3) have already had a major impact on Chinese social and political life. There has been a demonstrable decline in the level of political coercion in the system, one that has benefited the masses as well as the elites. Recent protests over socio-economic issues by a variety of groups have not only shown that freedom of action has expanded, but also that official reaction is likely to be milder. What might once have been labeled as serious crimes against the state, as "counterrevolutionary acts," are now more often treated as social grievances, perhaps not legitimate, but at least understandable. They are seen as social phenomena likely to occur in a period of rapid economic and social development, not as a challenge of a political nature to authority. Ironically, this enlightened attitude is likely to increase the number of such protests.[8]

Selection 4 is in part a legacy of the Cultural Revolution. The concept of a selfless, incorruptible, prescient Party of stalwart revolutionaries serving as a vanguard for the masses had been battered badly, first by the revelations of the Cultural Revolution, and then by the counter post-Cultural Revolution revelations. Virtually no Party member of any influence had emerged unscathed. The Party's loss of prestige was part of a more general "crisis of confidence"; this phrase became so prevalent in society that the Chinese press felt compelled to acknowledge and discuss it openly. Written at the beginning of a period of retrenchment, after the high tide of reform in the summer-autumn of 1980, and just prior to the final crackdown of "Democracy Movement activists," the selection is one of many articles at this time that sought to refute the notion that leading Party members had become a "new class" and that the basic contradiction in Chinese society was between this new class and the people as a whole. Such ideas had been expressed by the most radical of the rebel Red Guard groups in the late 1960s and were echoed in the writings of some of the Democracy Movement activists, most of whom had been Red Guards. The article affirms that "unhealthy tendencies" such as privilege-seeking still exist within the Party, but argues that this is owing to a "bureaucratism" that is inevitable because of China's historical legacy and economic backwardness, and not owing to a "bureaucratic class," which is impossible under socialism. Bureaucratism is expected to disappear as socialism matures.[9]

Selection 5, offering a critique of "some comrades" who suggest that the Marxist concept of alienation may be applicable to socialist states, is of most interest if viewed in the political context of 1983-84, although the issue it raises is likely to remain a source of controversy. Some background is necessary. While alienation had been a topic in academic circles going back at least to the 1960s, its revival in the 1980s must be understood in part as a reaction to the Cultural Revolution. Seeking an explanation for some of the negative phenomena under socialism, those who warned of the dangers of alienation spoke of the potential conflict between Party/state bureaucrats and the population at large, albeit, unlike some of the democracy activists, they did not see the conflict in class terms, or even as unmanageable. From 1978 to November 1983, over 600 articles on the subject of alienation had appeared in newspapers and magazines, although it was during a series of symposiums on Marxism from March-May 1983 that the debate took on prominent political overtones. The March 1983 publication in *Renmin ribao* of a speech by Zhou Yang, a deputy director of the Party's Propaganda Department and the president of the All-China Federation of Literary and Art Circles, played an important role in escalating the academic debate into a political-ideological problem. Zhou's speech referred to *economic* alienation, resulting from ill-conceived policies in economics; to *political* alienation, owing to the abuse of power by Chinese officials (the specific subject of Selection 5); and to *ideological* alienation, represented most obviously by Mao's cult of personality.[10] For our purposes, the storm that centered around Zhou's speech is worth discussing because it reveals how academic debates can become political issues and why conclusions reached on theoretical questions may be seen as politically explosive by China's leaders. Zhou's views were considered important for three reasons. First, he has been an important figure as an academic bureaucrat going back to the 1930s, presenting the Party line to intellectuals in the humanities. As of 1983, he held at least 15 separate offices at the central level.[11] Second, Zhou had delivered a major speech in 1963 highly critical of academics in China who had used Marx's early writings on alienation to justify a positive evaluation of the concept of humanism; Zhou's intervention had effectively stifled further open discussion. When he reversed his position in the early 1980s, it therefore had an important impact. Third, according to Hong Kong sources, Zhou had delivered a speech reflecting his new views to literary and art workers in 1982, immediately arousing opposition at senior levels of the Party; major Party newspapers would not publish his views. By March 1983, the climate had improved, and Zhou offered to present his ideas at a symposium commemorating the 100th anniversary of the death of Marx. Despite opposition, and a delay of the symposium, Zhou went ahead. Hu Qiaomu, a member of the Party Politburo, with views on alienation much more orthodox than Zhou's, reportedly suggested Zhou's speech be published in the journal *Zhexue yanjiu* (Philosophical Research), thus guaranteeing a small audience and a restriction of the discussion to academic circles. However, Wang Ruoshui, the deputy editor-in-chief of *Renmin ribao*, and also an authority on Marx's views on alienation, managed to publish the speech in his newspaper, the Party's most important mouthpiece, thus guaranteeing wide circulation and raising the ''academic'' controversy to a much higher level. The removal of Wang and another senior editor from their posts on the newspaper quickly followed.[12]

   With the onset of the campaign against ''spiritual pollution'' in October, the writings of Zhou and Wang on alienation (and humanism) came under strong attack. Zhou was compelled to make a self-criticism in November. The conclusion to (this phase of) the debate appeared in a long, authoritative article by Hu Qiaomu in January 1984, in which the applicability of the concept of alienation to socialist society was rejected.[13] Why was alienation such a threatening concept to Party leaders? Selection 5, published just three days after Hu Qiaomu's article, provides some answers. An argument that alienation, however modified, was present under socialism as well as capitalism would inevitably lead to calls for a reduction in the power of the state and the Party. In an interview given to a Western professor, the director of the CCP's Propaganda Department, Deng Liqun, went further. Specifically criticizing Wang Ruoshui for ''writing as though alienation were in fact inevitable under socialism,'' he argued that Wang was providing ''a theoretical basis for the activities of the dissidents, by suggesting that a new cultural revolution was necessary to overturn the privileged caste of Party bureaucrats."[14]

Finally, Selection 6 was chosen as an example of the social experimentation that has accompanied the reform program. In the same way that political and economic reforms have been marked by trial and error, as the leadership casts about for an appropriate "socialism with Chinese characteristics," a similar probing is taking place within society. Distinctions among what is encouraged, permitted, tolerated, or prohibited remain uncertain. Put another way, the line between the "healthy" and the "unhealthy"—even between socialist and capitalist practices—at times appears indeterminate. Judging from Selection 6, economic reform and the "open policy" will no longer include lotteries•

Notes

1. Lowell Dittmer, "Chinese Marxism Since Mao" (paper prepared for the conference "To Reform the Chinese Political Order," Harwichport, Massachusetts, June 1984, pp. 42–44). Although Dittmer divides the Deng Xiaoping reform era into "liberalizing" (December 1978–June 1981) and "retrenching" (June 1981–end of 1983) periods, we have drawn primarily from his delineation of the "liberal" period. An important component of the retrenchment period is the introduction of the concept of "socialist spiritual civilization," along with the admission that advanced material civilization may not lead to a similar level of spiritual development. Thus, socialist modernization is generally now taken to include both material and spiritual civilization. It is useful, also, to spell out more fully the official policy on class struggle. Although the 1982 Constitution of the Communist Party states that "most of the contradictions in Chinese society do not have the nature of class struggle, and class struggle is no longer the principal contradiction," an ideological justification for future campaigns against "spiritual pollution" is introduced in the same paragraph: "However, owing to domestic circumstances and foreign influences, class struggle will continue to exist within certain limits for a long time, and may even sharpen under certain conditions." Thus, the second part of the paragraph unties the Party's hands for intervention, but the first part binds it to milder and less frequent intervention. The Constitution can be found in *Beijing Review* No. 38 (September 20, 1982), pp. 8–21. The quote is from p. 9.

2. FBIS Daily Report, June, 11, 1985, pp. K7–K11 (*Liaowang*, May 20, 1985); FBIS Daily Report, April 17, 1985, pp. K14–K18 (*Renmin ribao* [People's Daily], April 12, 1985). Chen Yun, an octogenarian member of the standing committee of the Politburo and the chairman of the Party's Central Discipline Inspection Commission, warned in a speech at the September 1985 special Party Conference that the neglect of politics had gone too far. Addressing a host of problems—both economic and ideological—that have appeared under the new economic reforms and the "open policy," Chen charged that the problems "can be directly attributed to the relaxation of ideological and political work and the decline in the function and authority of the departments in charge of ideological and political work. We should take this as a lesson." His speech and its dissonance with the remarks of other top officials were widely noted in the Hong Kong and Western press. See, for example, *Far Eastern Economic Review*, October 3, 1985, pp. 10–12.

3. FBIS Daily Report, February 27, 1985, p. K18 (*Guangming ribao* [Guangming Daily], February 4, 1985).

4. *The New York Times*, December 10 and 11, 1984; *The Christian Science Monitor*, December 14, 1984. Correspondents with expertise on China, such as Jim Mann of the *Los Angeles Times*, offered more balanced assessments. *Renmin ribao* amended the offending

sentence the following day, inserting the word *all* before "our current problems."

5. Robert Delfs, "Reports of a Death Greatly Exaggerated," *Far Eastern Economic Review*, March 21, 1985, pp. 88 and 91.

6. FBIS Daily Report, December 21, 1984, pp. K1–K2 (*Renmin ribao*, December 21, 1984).

7. Delfs, "Reports of a Death." On the differences between the three types of commodity economy—simple commodity economy, capitalist commodity economy, and socialist commodity economy—see FBIS Daily Report, August 28, 1985, pp. K7–K10 (*Guangming ribao*, August 10, 1985).

8. FBIS Daily Report, June 25, 1985, pp. W1–W3 (*South China Morning Post*, June 24, 1985).

9. For a presentation and critique of theories of class formation under state-socialism, see David Lane, *The End of Social Inequality?: Class, Status and Power Under State Socialism* (London: George Allen & Unwin, 1982), pp. 126–151. For a provocative analysis of China's "bureaucratic system," see the essays by Li Yizhe and Wang Xizhe in Anita Chan, Stanley Rosen, and Jonathan Unger, eds., *On Socialist Democracy and the Chinese Legal System: The Li Yizhe Debates* (Armonk, N.Y.: M. E. Sharpe, 1985).

10. JPRS 83667, April 15, 1983, pp. 46–62 (*Renmin ribao*, March 16, 1983). The alienation debate is discussed in Bill Brugger, "Alienation Revisited," *The Austrialian Journal of Chinese Affairs* No. 12 (June 1984), pp. 143–151, and Wang Chang-ling, "The Debate About 'Alienation' Among Mainland Scholars," *Issues & Studies* 21:3 (March 1985), pp. 90–103.

11. Malcolm Lamb, *Directory of Officials and Organizations in China, 1968–1983* (Armonk, N.Y.: M. E. Sharpe, 1983).

12. FBIS Daily Report, December 9, 1983, pp. W1–W9 (*Zhengming*, December 1983).

13. FBIS Daily Report, February 7, 1984, pp. K1–K33 (*Renmin ribao*, January 27, 1984).

14. Stuart Schram, " 'Economics in Command?' Ideology and Policy Since the Third Plenum, 1978–1984," *The China Quarterly* No. 99 (September 1984), p. 448. The zigs and zags continue. As Schram points out, Hu Qiaomu's authoritative article had become somewhat irrelevant to the main trend within a few months. Moreover, by mid-1985, Wang Ruoshui was again publishing articles on humanism in the national press. See FBIS Daily Report, June 24, 1985, pp. K1–K3 (Zhongguo xinwen she [China News Agency], June 22, 1985).

1

Commentator

THEORY AND PRACTICE

How CAN WE do departmental work better? On December 5, 1984, in our commentator's article "The Part and the Whole," we specifically talked about the problem of correctly handling the relationship between the part and the whole. Here we wish to talk about the problem of the relationship between theory and practice.

Any item of important work is guided by theory. It is guided either by a correct theory, or by an incorrect theory. At the same time, any item of important work has its own characteristics and specific conditions. In addition, these characteristics and conditions are always changing. Exactly identical things are rarely seen, and there is nothing that does not change. If we are to do departmental work well, the first thing is to know theory and the second thing is to know practice; and these two must be closely integrated.

One of the great contributions of Comrade Mao Zedong is that over the last few decades he advocated the integration of theory with practice. The victory of the Chinese revolution was gained under the guidance of this brilliant thinking of Comrade Mao Zedong. Later, mistakes occurred in our work, which were owing to the violation of the principle of integrating theory with practice. The history of our Party tells us that integrating theory with practice is the magic weapon needed for us to win victory. Whoever looks down on theory will lose his bearings; whoever looks down on practice will become an empty talker. Therefore, our slogan is: Integrate theory with practice closely.

To master theory, it is necessary to study earnestly. There are many classical works of Marxism, and it is necessary to select the major works to study, and to study consistently. At present it is necessary to emphasize learning some economic theory, and it is also necessary to learn some modern knowledge of science and technology. In studying Marxism, it is important to pay attention to learning the universal laws expounded by the classical writers, as well as the stand, viewpoint, and method in observing and solving problems. We should not cling to some individual phrases or some concrete theses. One hundred and one years have passed since the death of Marx. His works were written more than 100 years ago. Some were his tentative ideas at that time, and things have changed greatly since then. Some of his tentative ideas were not necessarily very appropriate. With regard to many things, Marx and Engels did not experience the process, and Lenin did not experience that either. They did not have the opportunity to deal

Renmin ribao [People's Daily], December 7, 1984. Translation from FBIS Daily Report, December 7, 1984, pp. K1–K2.

with them. We cannot expect the writings of Marx and Lenin of that time to provide solutions to our current problems. All this should have our consideration in our studies.

Comrade Mao Zedong once sharply criticized some people by saying: "Up until the present, some people still regard individual phrases in Marxist-Leninist works as a ready-made panacea, with which they seem to be able to cure all diseases without an effort." "This is childishly ignorant, and we should enlighten them." We should not adopt a dogmatic attitude toward Marxism. The era is developing, and new situations and new problems keep arising. Using some theses in the articles of Marx and Lenin to frame real life will only hamper the progress of history. As descendants of Marx, we have the duty to enrich and develop Marxism in practice.

To understand practice, it is necessary to go deep into practice. At present, the biggest practice in China is the Four Modernizations drive and quadrupling total industrial and agricultural output value. In studying the Four Modernizations, the best combination of theory with practice for theoretical workers and propagandists is to plunge themselves into the Four Modernizations. Departure from this practice means lagging far behind the situation. The economy is a large ocean where many problems are not explained in books; therefore we are required to carry out investigation in practice in order to work out methods for solving the problems. It is necessary to read books and listen to reports, but it is impossible to read too many books, and only listening to reports will not do us any good. To study and solve economic problems, it is necessary to immerse oneself in the economy and reforms. It will take several years of arduous effort to make oneself familiar with the economy. Comrades engaged in theoretical and propaganda work who did not pay attention to the study of economics should now make up their minds and concentrate their efforts on studying the economy for three to five years.

2

Tong Gang

CHINESE-STYLE SOCIALISM MISJUDGED

A RECENT *New York Times* editorial commenting on China's economic reforms concluded that "if this economic revolution is allowed to run its

China Daily, January 11, 1985. Reprinted in FBIS Daily Report, January 14, 1985, pp. K11–K12.

course, it is bound to produce a comparable upheaval of the political system." Few Chinese would agree.

The New York Times has implied that China's economic flexibility can lead only to a fundamental political change. The article stated that the Chinese were reevaluating parts of traditional socialist theory because "nothing in Marx, Lenin, Stalin, or Mao could teach them how to make 800 million peasants grow enough to feed themselves." The Chinese have become flexible—but they are not "ditching" their ideology, as the *Times* said. In fact, what's happening is the formation of a unique brand of socialism with Chinese characteristics.

There are Westerners who are fond of saying China is going capitalist. But they are the only ones saying it; the Chinese certainly aren't. Westerners have noted the existence of billboards and other types of advertising; they read that China is encouraging consumerism; they see that private enterprises have returned.

A socialist economy is a planned economy, and today China recognizes that the best results come from a planned market-oriented economy. To invigorate the economy, China must first put life into the market. But Westerners tend to think of the market as something peculiar to a capitalist economy. This is hardly the case. A market economy must exist both in capitalist and socialist societies. As Alvin Toffler said in his book *The Third Wave*, the market is just a mechanism through which an exchange takes place.

Encouraging real growth is the key, and the place where real growth originates is in the market. The Chinese, unlike Westerners, see no contradictions between socialism and consumerism. China believes that socialism should boost production in order to meet the increasing demand of consumers. The changes in Chinese society are so profound that no conclusion can be drawn without seeing the whole picture. It is irresponsible to say China is going capitalist, and such comments merely reflect a poor understanding of the nation.

Some Westerners, it seems to me, are blinded by their preconceptions. They are too familiar with stereotypical socialism in China, which includes the communes and the "iron rice bowl." These Westerners sometimes mistake socialism with Chinese characteristics for capitalism and unbridled free enterprise.

It is true that China allows pockets of capitalism in such places as the special economic zones. Private enterprises have also sprung up. But all these measures are implemented only as a supplement to the socialist economy. In a word, China knows its goal: to perfect socialism in such a way as to provide a rich and abundant life for the people.

3

—

Hu Lu

A FEW QUESTIONS ON CLASS STRUGGLE UNDER PRESENT CONDITIONS

WHY DO WE say that the current struggle "to deal blows at serious criminal activities in the economic field is a major manifestation of class struggle in the economic sphere under the new historical conditions of China's socialist society"?

This thesis in the "decision on dealing blows at serious criminal activities in the economic field" of the CCP Central Committee and the State Council is based on actual conditions in the economic field in our country. If the serious criminal activities in the economic field are allowed to spread unchecked, it will be impossible for our modernization program to be carried on smoothly. Obviously the struggle against serious criminal activities in the economic field is vital to the success or failure of the socialist modernization drive and the prosperity or decline of our Party and state. It is a serious struggle of Communists and the masses of the people who uphold socialism against elements hostile to and undermining socialism, a conflict of fundamentally opposed interests, and there-fore a major manifestation of class struggle in the economic sphere under the new historical conditions of China's socialist society.

As the exploiting classes have been eliminated as classes, why is there still a class struggle? What are the different characteristics of the class struggle under present conditions from the class struggle of the past?

The "Resolution on Certain Questions in the History of Our Party since the Founding of the PRC" unanimously adopted by the Sixth Plenum of the Eleventh Party Central Committee clearly points out: "Class struggle no longer constitutes the principal contradiction after the exploiters have been eliminated as classes. However, owing to certain domestic factors and influences from abroad, class struggle will continue to exist within certain limits for a long time to come and may even grow acute under certain conditions. It is necessary to oppose both the view that the scope of class struggle must be enlarged and the view that it has died out."

This is a scientific conclusion reached by applying the fundamental principles of Marxism on the class situation and class struggle under the new historical conditions of China's socialist society. It is also an important guiding principle for us to correctly understand the current class struggle in our country.

Judging by a host of facts, class struggle will continue to exist within certain

Wenhui bao [Wenhui News], June 9, 1982. Translation from FBIS Daily Report, June 18, 1982, pp. O3–O5 (excerpts).

limits for a long time to come mainly because: (1) Although the exploiting classes have been eliminated as classes, their remnants and other hostile elements are still around and will make trouble when they find an opportunity. (2) The ideology of the exploiting classes will continue to exist for a long time to come and still can corrupt some people. (3) The exploiting classes have been eliminated as classes only on the mainland. In Taiwan, Penghu, Quemoy and Matsu as well as in Hong Kong and Macao, the exploiting system still exists and the exploiting classes are intact. The reactionaries among them and those blinded by greed inevitably will try in every conceivable way to corrupt the mainland. (4) Internationally, imperialism and hegemonism are always trying in every possible way to infiltrate, undermine, and subvert our country politically, economically, ideologically, and culturally. (5) With the development of economic relations with foreign countries, decadent capitalist ideas and the bourgeois lifestyle will invade us through various channels.

Under present conditions, class struggle is mainly against counterrevolutionaries and enemy special agents; various kinds of criminal offenders and other bad elements; new exploiters engaged in graft, embezzlement, and speculation; some remnants of the "Gang of Four"; a small number of unreformed landlords and rich peasants and some remnants of other old exploiting classes. This struggle is different from the class struggle of the past mainly because the above-mentioned elements hostile to and undermining socialism can no longer form an open and whole class after the exploiting classes have been eliminated as classes.

Now that class struggle is stressed in dealing resolute blows at serious criminal activities in the economic field, are we going to repeat the past mistakes of "taking class struggle as the key link" and enlarging the scope of class struggle?

The answer is definitely no. "Taking class struggle as the key link" was a slogan raised shortly before the "Cultural Revolution." Practice has proven that this slogan is totally erroneous and has caused very serious consequences. The Third Plenum of the Eleventh Party Central Committee resolutely ended the use of the erroneous slogan "taking class struggle as the key link," which does not apply to socialist society, and made the important decision to shift the whole Party's work emphasis to socialist modernization, thus, fundamentally correcting the erroneous "left" guiding ideology. At the same time, the Party Central Committee summed up the Party's experiences and lessons in class struggle, both positive and negative, and made a correct appraisal of class struggle under present conditions in our country. The class struggle we have talked about since the Third Plenum of the Eleventh Party Central Committee is basically different from "taking class struggle as the key link." The difference is manifest in the following:

1. Class struggle now occupies a different position in our society. The Party Central Committee clearly pointed out that after the completion in the main of socialist transformation and the elimination of the exploiting classes as classes, the principal contradiction in the country is no longer class struggle, but the contradiction between the people's growing material and cultural needs and the backward social production. Class struggle, including dealing blows at serious

criminal activities in the economic field, must be subordinated, of service, and of help to the central task of economic construction.

2. The appraisal of the situation of class struggle is different. In the past, under the influence of erroneous "left" ideas, it was held that class struggle existed all the time in all places, and a large number of social contradictions which did not fall within the scope of class struggle were all regarded as class struggle. Now the Party Central Committee has clearly pointed out that class struggle exists only within certain limits. The "resolution" of the Sixth Plenum of the Eleventh Party Central Committee also points out: "We must correctly understand that there are diverse social contradictions in Chinese society which do not fall within the scope of class struggle and that methods other than class struggle must be used for their appropriate resolution."

3. The method of class struggle is different. Because class struggle is no longer the principal contradiction in today's society, we need not and should not launch turbulent mass movements like we did in the past, but should solve problems of class struggle which exist within certain limits in the same legal way cases are handled, using socialist law as the weapon and following judicial procedures. The current struggle against serious criminal activities in the economic field is being waged in this way. Therefore, in practice we are not "taking class struggle as the key link" and will not again make the mistake of enlarging the scope of class struggle.

4

Wang Hongchang and Liu Mengyi

DOES A "BUREAUCRATIC CLASS" EXIST WITHIN THE PARTY?

Bureaucratism Represents a Force Alien to the Socialist System

Preventing and overcoming bureaucratism is a fixed and unchanging guideline for our Party. Since the founding of the new China, the Party Central Committee has repeatedly stressed that we must treat the prevention and elimination of bureaucratism as an important task in strengthening and improving Party leadership. Especially since the Third Plenum of the Eleventh Party Central Committee, the Party Central Committee has adopted a series of relevant

Zhongguo qingnian bao [China Youth News], February 7, 1981. Translation from FBIS Daily Report, February 23, 1981, pp. L27–L30.

measures. It has effected readjustments and reforms organizationally and in regard to the system has achieved conspicuous results. However, if the phenomenon of bureaucratism that has inevitably existed under the socialist system and under the dictatorship of the people's democracy is lumped together with the version of bureaucratism in the old society, which served private ownership under the dictatorship of landlord and bourgeois classes, or if we even claim that there exists ''a bureaucratic class'' within the Party, this is entirely wrong. The phenomenon of bureaucratism that exists today is inherent in the socialist social system based on public ownership and opposed to the people's democractic dictatorship. We must not fail to take note of this. We must also distinguish between two different versions of bureaucratism under two different social systems. We must refrain from taking superficial phenomena as essential points and freely exaggerating the seriousness of bureaucratism under the socialist system. Our doing so is wrong and harmful in regard to both theory and practice.

Marxism holds that as an idea, bureaucratism is determined by a given economic foundation and is the superstructure serving a given economic foundation. There was no bureaucratism before the existence of private ownership. With the appearance of the system of private ownership, bureaucratism arose to defend it. In a slave society, slave owners needed a set of appropriate bureaucratic political systems to protect the economic interests of their own class and maintain the rule of a minority over the majority. Bureaucratism in feudal society originated from the feudal despotic system. It not only had its roots in the feudal economy but was inseparable from the feudal state system. In order to maintain their economic interests and their feudal despotic rule, the landlord class and its chief representative—the feudal emperor—had to subject the people to oppression, exploitation, and rule through bureaucratic organs at all levels and professional bureaucrats of various ranks. Though resolute in its opposition to the feudal landlord class, the bourgeoisie does not oppose private ownership. It also never opposes the rule of a minority over the majority. Therefore, with the establishment of the bourgeois economic system and political system, bureaucratic politics geared to capitalist features have arisen. Of course, bureaucratism in capitalist society is sharply different from its counterpart in feudal society in form and in pattern. This is because the bourgeoisie still wants to continue raising the democratic banner in deceiving the masses of people and thus needs a relatively unobtrusive version of bureaucratism. But bureaucratism, whether represented by feudal society or capitalist society, will never change in its nature when it comes to maintaining private ownership, exploitation and the rule of a minority over the majority. From this it can be seen that the old version of bureaucratism is basically opposed to the masses of laboring people and represents an antagonistic contradiction. To solve such a contradiction, we cannot possibly do so through the exploitation system itself and can only do so through antagonistic and violent armed revolution—smashing the old state machinery and overthrowing the whole exploitation system.

Under the socialist system and under the dictatorship of the people's democracy, for both historical and realistic reasons, we cannot immediately get rid of bureaucratism. First, socialist society has not been offered on a silver platter. It has managed to emerge from the old society and inevitably embodies the remnants of the old society. The new China has been established and developed on a semifeudal and semicolonial basis. Despite our success in democratic revolution and socialist revolution and in eliminating private ownership, the bureaucratism rooted in Chinese officialdom for several thousand years could not possibly have disappeared with the establishment of the socialist system. Like a ghost, it still haunts our political life. Second, a backward economy is what bureaucratism relies upon for its existence and is its breeding ground. Despite a collective agriculture introduced in our country long ago, given no basic change in manual work, productivity is still very low. A large number of urban factories are still backward in their technology. Certain traces of small production have not been completely eliminated. Just as Lenin pointed out, bureaucratism is "the superstructure of scattered and apathetic small producers" and its economy is rooted in "the disorganized and apathetic state of small producers" (*Collected Works of Lenin*, vol. 32, p. 343). This is to say that without a great increase in productivity and with no basic change in the backward state of the economy, we cannot talk about the thorough elimination of bureaucratism. Third, owing to certain defects existing in the leadership of the Party and the state and in the economic management system and the cadre system, coupled with the backwardness of our education, science, and technology, we have found it difficult to improve upon and perfect the democratic system and the legal system, thus providing a chance for the existence and development of bureaucratism.

The Idea of a "Bureaucratic Class" Is Absurd

Summing up the phenomenon of bureaucratism existing under the socialist system to infer the existence of a "bureaucratic class" is not only incompatible with the actual objective conditions of our country but also theoretically goes against the fundamental principles of Marxism. The Marxist concept of classes is put in terms of different economic positions, which are taken as the yardstick with which to differentiate classes. This is to say that under given social conditions, who is in possession of the means of production and how these means of production are used are expressed as the economic and political positions of different classes. Our country long ago did away with private ownership, exploitation, and the exploiting classes and established a socialist society following the system of public ownership. The means of production are owned by the working class and the masses of laboring people. Despite different kinds of work taken up by the people in the process of social production, there is no longer the relationship between the exploiter and the exploited. Instead there exists the relationship of mutual help and cooperation between comrades. Our state organs and their management workers do not possess the means of production. Nor do they practice exploitation. Though some people assume "bureaucratic airs" and develop certain unhealthy practices, such as seeking privileges and so forth, how can they be described as a "bureaucratic class" serving private ownership?

Based on the Marxist method of class analysis, Lenin further pointed out the relations among the masses, the class, and the political party. Lenin held that in class society, the masses were divided into classes that were generally led by political parties. Especially in modern society, any political party belongs to a given class, serving its fundamental interests. Never has there been a case in which a class belongs to a political party. The proletarian political party is the representative of the fundamental interests of the working class and the masses of laboring people. Its birth and growth are inseparable from the working class and the masses of laboring people. The Chinese Communist Party is the outstanding representative of the Chinese working class and laboring people. This has been repeatedly proved by sixty years of history. Just as the masses of people have realized from practice, without the Chinese Communist Party, there would be no new China. Without the Chinese Communist Party, there would be no socialism. Without the Chinese Communist Party, the realization of the Four Modernizations could not be achieved. If the relationship between class and the political party is reversed and if a "class" within the Chinese Communist Party is arbitrarily created and is used as an excuse to attain the aim of opposing and removing the Chinese Communist Party, this would clash with what the working class and the masses of laboring people know and their wishes.

In fact, even under the old social system, "bureaucrats" were also only part of the ruling class. These bureaucrats could not act against the interests and wishes of the whole ruling class. There basically existed no independent economic interests. For example, in feudal society, the landlord class was the ruling class. But the "bureaucrats" who emerged to exercise power only represented a very small number of the members of the landlord class. What these people said and did could not run counter to the fundamental interests of the landlord class. If such was the case, they would be removed from office. Bureaucratism under the dictatorship of the people's democracy (or proletarian dictatorship) is a reflection of nonproletarian ideas among the revolutionary ranks and is condemned by the great majority of people in society. Speaking honestly, there really exist unhealthy practices within the Party. There are really an extremely small number of leading cadres who seek privileges. Opposing bureaucratism is right and proper. But it must be noted that we cannot equate individual phenomena with universal phenomena. Nor can we magnify something limited to a part into something that affects the whole. By no means are all the Party members or the majority of Party members affected by unhealthy practices. Also by no means are all the leading cadres or the majority of them seeking privileges and practicing bureaucratism. Still less is there a so-called "bureaucratic class."

Firmly Bear Historical Lessons in Mind

The lessons we have learned are painful. During the ten years of turmoil, to subvert the people's democratic dictatorship and usurp Party and state power, the

Lin Biao and Jiang Qing counterrevolutionary cliques applied the methods used against class enemies toward those variously guilty of bureaucratism. They ruthlessly persecuted many good cadres who maintained close ties with the masses and with reality—treating the latter as a "bureaucratic class." Prompted by ulterior motives, they put forward such reactionary slogans as: "The Great Cultural Revolution" provides a solution to "the contradiction between the new Cultural Revolution and the old government," "thoroughly smash public security, procuratorial, and law enforcement organs," and so forth. All "leaders" prior to "the Great Cultural Revolution," at every level from the state chairman down to the workshop and production team leaders, regardless of how high or low their "official" rank, were labeled "advocates of the black line," "members of the bureaucratic class," and "capitalist-roaders" and were all "toppled and discredited" or subjected to even greater humiliation. As a result, good people suffered while bad people held power. Feudal despotism reigned supreme. This almost led to the ruin of our Party and state. What serious consequences resulted, just because a problem of bureaucratism or a contradiction among the people that could have been solved through the socialist system itself was arbitrarily made into a contradiction between ourselves and the enemy and tackled by resorting to "ruthless struggle and relentless blows."

Our approach to opposition against bureaucratism must not be carried beyond given limits. This is to say that it must be down-to-earth. Stalin pointed out: "If the struggle against bureaucratism within our state machinery is carried so far as to ruin the state machinery and leave its reputation in tatters and so far as to bring about the collapse of the state machinery, then this is acting against Leninism and is to forget that our machinery is Soviet machinery and is the highest exponent of all existing state machinery in the world" (*Collected Works of Stalin*, vol. 10, p. 273). The Lin Biao and Jiang Qing counterrevolutionary cliques did carry things so far. At present, an extremely small number of people are bent on making trouble in the world. They are harping on the old tune that "there exists a bureaucratic class within the Party." Their ultimate aim is also to bring about the collapse of our Party and state machinery.

Every upright man can see that since the Third Plenum of the Eleventh CCP Central Committee, the Party Central Committee has done a large amount of work to prevent and overcome bureaucratism and has achieved conspicuous results. However, given a short period of time, we cannot possibly have thoroughly solved all the problems that have accumulated over the years. Thorough solution of these problems takes time and calls for a process of work. Every Communist Party member and revolutionary comrade should advance in a steady and orderly manner under the unified guidance of the Party Central Committee. We must persist in Party leadership, doggedly follow the socialist road, uphold the people's democratic dictatorship, adhere to Marxism-Leninism-Mao Zedong Thought, continuously improve on and perfect the socialist democratic system and the legal system, energetically develop productivity, and share the same will in properly readjusting the national economy. So long as we do so, bureaucratism among our ranks can surely be gradually overcome. With the advance of the socialist cause, bureaucratism will eventually be thoroughly eliminated.

5

Li Yanshi

COMMENTING ON THE SO-CALLED "ALIENATION OF POWER"

WHEN COMMENTING ON so-called socialist alienation, some comrades are very fond of talking about "alienation of power." They think that the "existence of organs of state power implies alienation in the political field." To bring into play the role of organs of state power, socialist states "must place themselves above society and issue orders to their citizens, and the external strength of state power will gradually become larger." As a result, organs in power will become the "bureaucratic" organs, and the "servants of the people" will become the "masters of the people." It is necessary to analyze and clarify these erroneous views.

The fundamental starting point of the thoery of "alienation of power" is to regard all power and all organs that issue orders as an alienated force that is placed above society. This will inevitably negate the fundamental difference between socialist and capitalist countries and make people fall into the mire of anarchism.

When studying the origin of states, Engels, starting from a host of historical facts, explained how organs of official business and the democratic system in primitive society were gradually abandoned and replaced by organs of violence, which were divorced from social production and the masses, and carried out class oppression. He pointed out that "this force, which emerged from society but was above society and was divorced daily from society, was a state." Obviously, what Engels referred to here is an exploitative class state, either slave-owner states, feudal lords' states, or bourgeois states, states by which a few exploiters rule the laboring masses. Therefore, they are above and opposed to society. The organs of power in these states are special organs of violence that are used to exercise dictatorship over the laboring masses.

Can we say that a socialist state is an alienated force that is above society and is daily being divorced from society? Can we apply the concept of "alienation of power" when studying a socialist state? Let us see how Engels and Lenin expounded on the Paris Commune—the first state of proletarian dictatorship in human history. In *State and Revolution* Lenin said: " 'The commune was not a state in its original sense'—This is Engels' important thesis. . . . The commune was no longer a state, for it supressed the minority of citizens (exploiters) instead of the majority of citizens and smashed the bourgeois state machine. Citizens came up to the stage to replace the special strength that had been used to carry out

Nanfang ribao [Southern Daily], January 30, 1984. Translation from FBIS Daily Report, February 8, 1984, pp. P1–P3.

suppression. All this shows that the commune was not a state in its original sense.'' This means that the commune was not an alienated force that was above society. As far as the nature of a state, which is a total of class oppression, is concerned, a state of proletarian dictatorship is still an organ of violence of one class against another and is still a state in its original sense. But being an organ that is organized by the majority of citizens and by which the majority of laborers rule a few exploiters, it is not an alienated force that is above society.

A socialist state exercises the functions of resisting foreign aggression, suppressing the resistance of domestic exploiters, and organizing social production. The people regard their state as a concentrated representative and force safeguarding their fundamental interests. In the course of exercising their functions, organs of state power naturally will issue orders, formulate plans and measures, and guide and organize the masses in realizing their fundamental interests. How can we regard a socialist state and its orders as ''an alienated'' and ''external'' force?

Of course, in a certain period of time, the masses' direct participation in state administration is limited to a certain extent. When exercising their powers and issuing orders on behalf of the people, organs of state power must avoid issuing ''confused orders'' and ''compulsory orders.'' But in any case, all this is to perfect the system of democratic centralism. It in no way means turning state power into an ''alienated strength'' that is opposed to the people.

To expound the so-called ''alienation of power,'' some comrades have even gone so far as to say that in socialist society, ''following the constant development of the social productive forces, the state will gradually become the large owner of more and more production materials, technological and management personnel, and products. As a result, laborers will obey its orders and deployment. Therefore, in a sense, socialist society 'still retains a bourgeois state without the bourgeoisie.' '' This is ridiculous! Everyone knows that Lenin, in a given sense, explained that the functions of a proletarian state still retained the traces of the old society in protecting the bourgeois rights of equal labor and the exchange of equal labor in the course of safeguarding workers' labor results. This does not mean in the least that laborers are in class antagonism against the state.

Many of the comrades who have put forward the theory of ''alienation of power'' subjectively want to stress the importance of opposing bureaucratism and preventing ''servants'' from changing into ''masters.'' However, because they have inappropriately used the concept of ''alienation,'' they have consciously or unconsciously cast doubts on the socialist system and created confusion.

First, the concept regards the phenomenon that will possibly occur and can be overcome as one that is inevitable and cannot be overcome. That organs of state power can become ''bureaucratic'' organs and that servants of society can become masters of society are only a kind of possibility. As long as we constantly carry out the struggle against bureaucratism, we can absolutely overcome such phenomena. If we regard such phenomena as the manifestation of ''alienation of power,'' this will be the same as asserting that as long as there are organs of state power, they will inevitably become bureaucratic organs through ''alienation,'' and "servants" will inevitably become "masters" who place themselves above society. Because "alienation" contains the seed of an inevitable self-emergence, it will make us think that the root cause of bureaucratism is the socialist system itself instead of the vestiges and influence of the old society.

Second, the concept regards local phenomena as universal ones and secondary aspects as principal ones. In socialist state organs, bureaucratism is only a local phenomenon, while serving the people and being willing to be servants of society are the principal aspects of the people's political power. If we regard bureaucratism as a manifestation of "alienation of power," this will be the same as saying that wherever there are organs of state power, there will surely be "bureaucratism." In the minds of some philosophers, the concept of "alienation" contains the meaning of the "external" development of things, so being "bureaucratic" is regarded as the principal aspect of socialist states.

Third, the concept regards many necessary things in the political life of our present state as very unfortunate things, because many philosophers interpret "alienation" as the "distortion of human nature" and "overcoming alienation" as the "restoration of human nature." If we use this concept to explain the political life in socialist society and put forward the theory of the "alienation of power," we will inevitably interpret proletarian state power and orders issued by organs of power as something that is "not suited to human nature." Interpreting everything as an abnormal, "alienated" phenomenon can only make people take a very passive attitude toward their country.

This attitude will obviously make people cast doubt on the socialist system. The crucial point of the theory of the "alienation of power" is to fundamentally negate socialist and communist society, which is the most perfect and the most rational society.

Some comrades who have put forward the theory of "alienation of power" think that they are summing up the lesson of the "Cultural Revolution," eradicating "leftist" influence, and preventing the reoccurrence of such a "centralized rule" as exercised by the "Gang of Four." Their motives are understandable, but they have departed from the four basic principles and have mistakenly summed up past lessons. We must analyze, according to the four basic principles, why the "Gang of Four" was able to exercise centralized power in the "Cultural Revolution" and how arbitrary attitudes emerged within the Party. The "Resolution on Certain Questions in the History of the Party Since the Founding of the PRC" points out: "Gradually building a high degree of democracy under the socialist political system is one of the fundamental tasks in socialist revolution. We have not attached great importance to this task since the founding of the PRC, and this has become an important condition for initiating the 'Cultural Revolution.' This is a bitter lesson." Only by strengthening the people's democratic dictatorship and perfecting the democratic life of the Party and state can we prevent people like Lin Biao and the "Gang of Four" from usurping Party and state leadership again. All practices weakening state power and the Party leadership over the state's political life will only provide opportunities for evildoers to carry out usurpation activities. Advocates of the theory of the "alienation of power'' have departed from the four basic principles and mistakenly used the concept of ''alienation.'' As a result, they are unable to make a clear break with ''leftist'' elements and have embarked on the evil road of negating the socialist system.

6

Li Xiaojia

LOTTERY CLAMPDOWN PROVES LUCKY FOR CONSUMERS

China Daily Applauds Clampdown on Lotteries

IF YOU COULD believe the advertisements, the easiest way to get a color TV set in China over the past few months would have been to buy a lottery ticket.

Millions of consumers believed it. Crowds waited in long queues in department stores, small shops, even railway and bus stations to buy a chance on winning a television, imported refrigerator, or even a car—an item rarely available to private owners in China.

The lottery craze got out of control.

Last week, a State Council circular put an immediate ban on lotteries run by commercial and industrial enterprises. It also prohibited individuals or organizations from using lotteries to raise money for public use. Stiff penalties—including fines, disciplinary action, and confiscation of goods—were announced.

The ban was necessary.

Lotteries are harmful because they make people think that they can get rich quickly through chance alone, which runs against the traditional idea that the way to wealth is through hard work.

Young people in particular were easily seduced by these corrupt ideas, and this could have serious consequences.

''You spend so little and could get so much,'' some young people say. But they fail to realize how minute their chances really are, especially in a country of one billion consumers. Lotteries led millions of people to spend their money for no purpose whatsoever.

The craze climaxed when the lunar new year's eve program televised a lottery in front of a studio audience of 20,000 and 200 million television viewers throughout the country. This cast an unpleasant shadow over China's most

China Daily, March 15, 1985. Reprinted in FBIS Daily Report, March 19, 1985, pp. K21–K23.

important traditional festival. China Central Television (CCTV), after being criticized by newspapers throughout the country, issued an open self-criticism.

But it wasn't until the State Council directive that most lotteries actually ceased. A few still are allowed. Local governments, for instance, will be permitted to allow raffles to collect money for social welfare causes, but these experiments must not be allowed to continue, the circular said. Similarly, banks which have sponsored savings deposits with lotteries will be allowed to continue, but they were directed not to expand.

The problem is that some people seem to get addicted to lotteries, despite the fact that they never win. A friend of mine had bought more than 20 tickets for different lotteries. And he would have just kept on buying, figuring one day he was bound to get lucky.

Lotteries obviously are just a disguised form of gambling, which has serious implications since it involves a great number of people. Gambling is banned in China—it is only right that lotteries should be banned too.

I find it hard to believe that any kind of lottery could be in the best interests of the country.

The consumers were duped. Department stores and shops attached lottery tickets to goods that they had a hard time selling. People were pushed into buying things they neither needed nor wanted because they held out the remote promise of winning something of value. Stores should instead focus on providing higher quality goods. The lotteries were actually distorting supply and demand and could have led to blind production.

Several years ago, the People's Bank of China ran a lottery to encourage people to open savings accounts. Only the winners got interest paid on their accounts.

Lotteries are nothing but tricks to get money out of people's pockets. There are other ways to encourage people to save, and appeals for voluntary donations for such urgent causes as rescuing starving pandas or restoring the Great Wall have been successful.

If lotteries were allowed to continue, the scale of this kind of "extortion" would only rise.

One good thing has come out of the lottery craze. It has made people think about just how far the economic reforms should go.

It is true that China needs urgent reforms to invigorate its economy, which has been stagnant several times over the past thirty years. But does it mean that the reform should cast away all the traditional values together with the defects? Or does it mean that all the high ideals that have supported the Chinese people for so many decades should no longer be treasured?

The answer obviously is "no." The present reforms promote new ways for individuals to enrich themselves, but the main emphasis is still on the hard work that is needed to further the country's development, and not on wealth for its own sake.

Also, learning from abroad means bringing in the good things, advanced technology and management techniques, for instance, but not negative things such as lotteries.

By encouraging some people to get rich first, the government does not intend to encourage a polarized society of two classes. The purpose is clear here: Let some become wealthy first and then help others to become better-off along with them. Lotteries certainly do not serve this purpose.

Recently, Party and government officials in many places have abused their power to run enterprises, engage in various trades, resell state materials that are in short supply, trade in foreign currencies at huge profits, and spend public funds freely entertaining friends or sending gifts.

Many work units recklessly distribute bonuses and other material goods among their personnel, thus causing the state serious losses. Some shops have seized the opportunity to drive up prices.

Many of these activities have been conducted under the guise of reform and the "open policy."

This is harmful and deceptive. Such "reform" will lead China nowhere.

I am glad that these activities have aroused sufficient public attention.

After all, the reforms must be in the best interest of all Chinese people. They should not just offer a chance for a few profiteers to get wealthy through illegal means.

FURTHER READINGS

Brugger, Bill, ed. *Chinese Marxism in Flux, 1978–1984*. Armonk, N.Y: M. E. Sharpe, 1985.

Chan, Anita, Stanley Rosen and Jonathan Unger, eds. *On Socialist Democracy and the Chinese Legal System: The Li Yizhe Debates*. Armonk, N.Y: M. E. Sharpe, 1985.

Deng Xiaoping. *Selected Works, 1975–1982*. Beijing: Foreign Languages Press, 1984.

Dittmer, Lowell. "Ideology and Organization in Post-Mao China." *Asian Survey* 24:3 (March 1984), pp. 349–369.

Issues & Studies 21:3 (March 1985). Special Issue on Mainland China's Ideology: Continuity and Changes (pp. 14–134).

Joseph, William A. *The Critique of Ultra-Leftism in China, 1958–1981*. Stanford: Stanford University Press, 1984.

Kraus, Richard Curt. *Class Conflict in Chinese Socialism*. New York: Columbia University Press, 1981.

Lotta, Raymond, ed. *And Mao Makes Five: Mao Tsetung's Last Great Battle*. Chicago: Banner Press, 1978.

Martin, Helmut. *Cult and Canon: The Origins and Development of State Maoism*. Armonk, N.Y.: M. E. Sharpe, 1982.

Nee, Victor, and David Mozingo, eds. *State and Society in Contemporary China*. Ithaca: Cornell University Press, 1983.

Schram, Stuart R. *Ideology and Policy in China Since the Third Plenum, 1978–84*. London: Contemporary China Institute, 1984.

Schram, Stuart, ed. *The Scope of State Power in China*. London: School of Oriental and African Studies, forthcoming.

Selden, Mark, and Victor Lippit, eds. *The Transition to Socialism in China*. Armonk, N.Y.: M. E. Sharpe, 1982.

Teiwes, Frederick C. *Leadership, Legitimacy, and Conflict in China: From a Charismatic Mao to the Politics of Succession*. Armonk, N.Y.: M. E. Sharpe, 1984.

Womack, Brantly. "Modernization and Democratic Reform in China." *The Journal of Asian Studies* 43:3 (May 1984), pp. 417–439.

B. Political Socialization

WHEN CHINA'S POST-MAO leadership denounced the Cultural Revolution stress on politics and class struggle as "sham Marxism," arguing instead that the primary task of a nation that has already undergone socialist transformation should be the rapid development of its economy, they presented the country's political workers with a major challenge. This challenge was nothing less than the development of a new standard of morality and a convincing central belief system to displace the discredited radical version of Marxism-Leninism-Mao Zedong Thought. For many youths, the most enduring lesson of the Cultural Revolution years—marked as they were by the gyrations at the top of the political system, culminating in the purge of the "Gang of Four" in October 1976—was that all ideological-political commitments must be viewed with a heavy dose of skepticism.

The readings in this section reflect the uncertainties of political workers and young people as they respond to post-Mao policies. Can Chinese youth be instilled with a new ethic of competition and entrepreneurship while maintaining "socialist" values? What does "politics" mean in the context of the pursuit of socialist modernization? Officially, socialist modernization is defined as the realization of a high level of both spiritual and material civilization, but the two values, much as the "Red and Expert" formula so prominent in the Maoist years, seldom fit comfortably into one package.

The uncertainties of political cadres and youth reflect, in part, divisions among China's leaders over the proper solution to the "youth problem." Although in virtual agreement that a serious problem exists, suggested solutions have varied, with the most crucial distinction pitting those advocating a strategy of "accommodation" to youth interests against those more concerned with the "control" of youth behavior. In a sense, these divergent strategies can be labeled "economic" and "political." The major testing ground for these approaches has been the Communist Youth League (CYL), a political organization that enrolls the country's most progressive youth between the ages of fourteen to twenty-eight. The CYL's primary tasks include the socialization of China's young people and the training and tempering of those who will be recruited into the Communist Party.

Those in the leadership urging accommodation trace the youth malaise to the stultifying control exercised over the CYL by Party organs and to the lack of concern for the real interests of youth. For them, the negative feelings associated with politics and ideology stem not from an insufficient stress on those subjects, but from too much political control. With a definition of politics more closely linked to modernization and material development, these reformers seek to reinvigorate youth work and allow the CYL greater autonomy in conducting its affairs. Their goal has been to increase the prestige of the League so outstanding youth will once again clamor to join. If the CYL could again appear to youth as a vital organization and an important route to social mobility, both recruitment and socialization could be greatly facilitated.

Other leaders, particularly those specializing in political and ideological work, have not been convinced that the solution lies in less control; on the contrary, it has been the very laxity in ideological-political work that has led to the current dilemma. More fearful about opening the League to independent-minded youth who find traditional political appeals irrelevant, they seek to tighten the political standards for CYL membership, to reintroduce ideological-political work into schools at all levels, and to place the League even more tightly under Party control.

In short, is it more important to make the CYL "relevant" or to promote "communist ideology" within the organization? The accommodators would turn the League into an organization whose functions would be integrated with—and subordinated to—economic requirements. They seem content to downplay the stress on ideological-political values until a higher level of material civilization has been reached. The youth press is replete with accounts of local CYL branches that have reached out to youth—by setting up marriage introduction bureaus, by purchasing soccer balls to inspire workers who prefer sports to productive labor, and so forth. For political work cadres, such arguments are unconvincing and dangerous. To defer ideological-political education is to guarantee the spread of the "bourgeois ideology" and "spiritual pollution" that will accompany an unalloyed stress on economic development.

The views of both camps are reflected in youth work. Thus, the CYL has been ordered to encourage youth "to become rich" while leading them to develop a communist world outlook. To appeal to youth interests, the League needs to exercise independent political, economic, and social initiatives; but it must also accept the "absolute" leadership of the Party. Nevertheless, the gap between the economic and the political in youth work has become extremely wide, with most youth opting for economic success and generally ignoring political appeals. This, in turn, has contributed to the paralysis of the League. It may be unrealistic to expect youth striving to become "10,000-yuan households" to reach out and revive a moribund ideological-political organization; they are too busy being productive.

The first three selections are concerned with recruitment into the CYL under current conditons. Selection 7 reflects the dilemma of League cadres in the countryside as they try to determine a youth's political consciousness after the decollectivization of agriculture. As the editor's response indicates, the old formula that emphasized a direct concern for the collective no longer applies. A recent report from the Central CYL Secretariat was unambiguous in noting that the primary task of rural League branches is to help youth get rich. CYL cadres from new wealthy peasant households make up only 10 percent of all League cadres in the countryside; the goal is to bring this figure up to 50 percent.[1] Selections 8 and 9 show the decline in importance of the League in secondary schools and universities. Before the Cultural Revolution the competition to enter the League was keen, since membership imparted high social status and political activism was a factor in university selection. Moreover, League members engaged in a wide variety of extracurricular activities. In the current era, with academic achievement determining university entrance and upward mobility, CYL membership is often bestowed rather than sought, and League functions have greatly declined.

The post-Cultural Revolution reaction against many of the nation's most well-known model personages and units—they were said to have been fabricated by the radicals for ulterior motives—has had a devastating effect on individuals who appear more "progressive" than their peers. At a time when official policy urges individuals and families to get rich through hard work, those who work for the "common good," for nonmaterial rewards, are often looked upon suspiciously by co-workers. The problems and pressures model workers face has been a common theme in the press, with Selection 10 offering a typical example of the "activist dilemma." As Richard Solomon pointed out a decade and a half ago, for the Party to operate successfully in society, it must attract many more people than it can recruit. Policy implementation is most successful when many aspirants compete for coveted slots within the Party. The relationship between Party members, activists, and ordinary masses has always included a certain amount of tension, but mass ostracism of activists seems to have reached its zenith in the post-Mao period.[2]

Selection 11, from 1979, and Selection 12, from 1984, are two sides of the same coin. When the Party shifted the work of the whole country to socialist modernization (read economic development) after the Third Plenum of the Eleventh Central Committee in December 1978, political work cadres began to feel irrelevant, as revealed in Selection 11. After more than five years of attempting to adjust political lessons to the new situation, middle school students, as the survey cited in Selection 12 shows, still find such lessons of little use.

The search for proper social relationships in a society that encourages competition and rewards the victors with material benefits is highlighted in Selections 13, 14, and 15. Selection 13 is the provocative opening essay in a forum encouraging readers to discuss the development and maintenance of friendships under highly competitive conditions. As the writer reveals, the stakes are high, and those who fail are seldom accorded any sympathy. Selections 14 and 15 are contributions from the widely publicized forum to learn from Zhang Hua. Because they demonstrated the extent to which pragmatic materialism had affected student attitudes, and governed the relationship between individuals of "unequal value,'' the results of this forum were presented in such Western media as *The New York Times*. Some of the participants, such as Duo Yan, whose letter is included here, showed a rationality that even human capital theorists might have found embarrassing. Briefly, Zhang was a twenty-four-year-old medical student in Shaanxi Province who leaped into a nightsoil pit to rescue a sixty-nine-year-old peasant from drowning. Along with the peasant, however, Zhang was overcome by methane fumes and died in the hospital after he was rescued in turn by a passing dairy worker. Zhang was posthumously hailed as a national hero for his selfless act, and an extensive media campaign—including the obligatory diary excerpts—was launched in China's major newspapers. Shanghai's *Wenhui bao* departed from most newspapers that followed the usual practice of merely enumerating in glowing terms what other university students could learn from Zhang Hua's lofty ideals. In publishing Duo Yan's dissenting letter, which called the attempted rescue of the old peasant an emotional act that in fact damaged the long-term interests of the state, and in soliciting responses to refute Duo Yan's views, the paper was overwhelmed by 1,600 letters within a few days, with the dissenter garnering a good deal of support.

In the last several years, our knowledge of Chinese society has been greatly enhanced by the work of Chinese social scientists. In particular, academic journals have been publishing the results of survey data in a wide variety of fields, including the attitudes of students and workers. The survey of senior high graduates included here (Selection 16) is but one example of this rich new source of data. Not surprisingly, this and similar surveys reveal that the large majority of Chinese students aspire to a university education and look down on manual labor; this is particularly the case for those who have gained entrance to the elite "keypoint" schools. The detailed examination of student interests and job preferences shows how far we have come from the days when Chinese students, asked what they would like to do, would often give the then socially acceptable answer: "Whatever the Party (state) asks me to do." Unfortunately, because attitude surveys are not available from earlier periods, it is difficult to assess whether we are merely seeing a change in *norms*, or whether youth *values* have in fact undergone a fundamental alteration in post-Mao China. Presumably the answer lies somewhere in between•

Notes

1. Li Yuanchao, "Nongcun tuan zuzhi yao dailing qingnian zhifu" (Rural CYL Organizations Must Lead Youth to Become Rich), *Nongcun qingnian* (Rural Youth), No. 3 (November 1984), p. 5.

2. Richard Solomon, "On Activism and Activists," *The China Quarterly* No. 39 (July–September 1969), pp. 76–114.

7

Letter to the Editor

HOW SHOULD THE CRITERIA FOR ADMISSION TO THE COMMUNIST YOUTH LEAGUE BE ADMINISTERED AFTER INSTALLATION OF THE PRODUCTION RESPONSIBILITY SYSTEM?

Comrade Editor:

Since the production responsibility system was installed in the countryside, we have been at a loss how to administer the criterion for recruiting new members of the Communist Youth League. To determine whether or not a youth meets the standard of a League member, our previous practice was to find out whether or not he devoted himself to the interests of the public, loved the collective, and did his share for the construction of a socialist new countryside. Now production is contracted out to individual households. With the overall contracting system being implemented, the young people are confined to the small world of a family or a household, calculating how to increase the family income and earn a greater bonus for overfulfillment of production quotas. In this way, how can we examine and determine whether a youth has a high degree of political awareness and possesses the collectivist spirit of devoting himself to the interests of the public?

Please give us an answer.

Yours,

Wang Baochang et al., Sichuan

Comrades Wang Baochang and Others:

We must examine young people who apply for League membership strictly according to the League membership requirements set forth in the League constitution. The constitution of the Communist Youth League states in explicit terms that a League member must "implement the Party's general and specific policies, enthusiastically fulfill the tasks assigned by League organizations, and play an exemplary role in studies, labor, and work."

"Shixing zerenzhihou, zenyang zhangwo rutuan biaozhun?" *Zhongguo qingnian* [China Youth], No. 16 (August 26, 1981), p. 21. Translation from *Chinese Education* 18:1 (Spring 1985), pp. 10–12.

Right now, different forms of the production responsibility system are being implemented across the countryside; it is precisely the major policy the Party has adopted to regulate production relations. Quite a few young people who apply for League membership are in full support of the policy. They take the initiative in contracting production projects that call for more intensive labor and higher skill in an effort to wrest continuous high yields in the land they have contracted for. This embodies precisely the exemplary role they play in carrying out conscientiously the Party's general and specific policies. Whether a rural youth can wrest high yields, make more contributions, and provide the state and the collective with more agricultural and sideline products has now become a basic criterion for assessing his genuine love of the state, his concern for the collective, and whether or not he is doing his part for the socialist cause. To define without analysis the endeavor of doing a good job with the land one has contracted for as a move to "further one's own interest" is incorrect.

Implementing the different policies the Party adopts toward rural areas adds new content to the criterion a League organization should administer when recruiting new members. For example, whether or not a youth supports the line, the general and specific policies of the Party, and abides by the decrees, rules, and regulations issued by the state serves as a specific criterion for assessing his political awareness. Since implementation of the overall contracting system, for another example, investigation must be made to determine who works the hardest, who studies science and makes use of science, and who provides the state and the collective with more agricultural and sideline products. All this will serve as ironclad evidence. Compared with the previous practice of "everyone eating from the same big pot," don't things at present provide us more accuracy in administering the criterion of recruiting new League members?

Obviously, the situation has changed, but the requirements for a League member set forth in the League constitution remain the same. The problem is some comrades still judge candidates by old standards when recruiting them. In their eyes, going to work like a swarm of bees and allowing "everyone to eat from the same big pot" are precisely a wholehearted devotion to the interests of the public and a love for the collective, while spending more energy on the land one has contracted for is "calculated" to further one's own interests. In this way, they feel everything is out of step with their standard and most young people, it seems, do not measure up to League member requirements. Under the new circumstances, therefore, the basic condition for one to administer correctly the criterion of admitting new League members is to catch up rapidly with the changed situation in terms of one's way of thinking. Of course, this does not mean that we can willfully tamper with the League member requirements set forth in the League constitution and lower our demands on progressive youth. That, too, would also be incorrect.

Organization Department,
League Central Committee

8
—
Letter to the Editor

WE CANNOT LOWER OUR STANDARDS IN RECRUITING LEAGUE MEMBERS

Comrade Editor:

We are Communist Youth League cadres at the grass-roots level in a university. On the eve of the college entrance examination every year, as we understand it, League organizations in some middle schools, in cooperation with their schools' efforts to raise the promotion rate, do a rush job of recruiting into the League students who have yet to attain the standard of a League member, so as to create conditions for meeting the requirement of enrolling the better qualified. In this way, they not only damage the prestige of the League organization but also impede the healthy growth of the young students.

Take, for example, the League branch of a 1980 class in our institute. Out of the twenty-nine League members of the whole class, twenty were admitted on the eve of their graduation from high school. Twelve of them were urged by their teachers to join the League. Some of them had not even filled out the application form. There was also a strange case in which some student who had already entered the college suddenly received League membership credentials, which were transferred from his former middle school, although he did not know how and why he had been admitted.

We find that League members recruited in a crash program are lacking in a sense of discipline and basic knowledge of the League organization. We held a small quiz in a League branch and asked five simple questions such as "Why should a League member pay his membership dues regularly?" To our surprise, as many as eleven members of the branch failed to pass. Some members never took part in League activities and regular League sessions. All this exerts a negative influence on the young students who want to make progress. One student remarked: "What's the difference whether you join the League or not? Some League members in my class acquit themselves worse than I do!"

It is our belief that we should not blame the League members for the above problem; it is the League organizations that recruited them that should bear the responsibility. To crash recruit new League members on the eve of the college entrance examination is an indiscreet move violating the principle of

"Fazhan tuanyuan buke jiangdi biaozhun." *Hubei qingnian* [Hubei Youth], No. 6 (June 1981), p. 10. Translation from *Chinese Education* 18:1 (Spring 1985), pp. 13–14.

organization. The once-a-year college entrance examination is now approaching. It is hoped that middle school League organizations in all places will adopt a positive and cautious attitude in recruiting new members. We also request the leading bodies of League organizations at all levels to pay full attention to this problem and put a stop to the unhealthy practice of rush recruiting new League members on the eve of the college entrance examination.

Liu Xianfan

Li Hongbo

9

Letter to the Editor

IS THE ACTIVITY OF "CREATING AN ENTIRE CLASSROOM OF LEAGUE MEMBERS" CORRECT OR NOT?

Comrade Editor:

Last semester our school mounted an activity called "creating an entire class-room of League members," calling upon young people of every classroom to exert themselves for admission into the League within the semester. The school leadership used this as a criterion to assess the performance of every class in terms of its political work and the progress of students' studies. Thus the League branches of each class blindly emphasized quantity and vied with each other in recruiting new members under the pretext of "allowing not a single comrade-in-arms to fall behind." If things go on like this, I am afraid, the Chinese Communist Youth League will lose its role as a mass organization of the progressive young people. Comrade editor, please tell me whether the activity of "creating an entire classroom of League members" is correct or not.

Yours,

Hongliu of Linxiang County, Hunan Province

"Gao 'chuang tuanyuanban' huodong duibudui?" *Zhongguo qingnian* [China Youth], No. 16 (August 26, 1981), p. 21. Translation from *Chinese Education* 18:1 (Spring 1985), pp. 15–16.

Comrade Hongliu:

Your school mounted the drive of "creating an entire classroom of League members," calling upon all young people to join the League before the end of the semester. On the surface, it was a move emphasizing recruitment of new League members. In fact, it was a wrong action.

The Communist Youth League is a mass organization of the progressive young people. Its progressiveness and mass participation complement each other. An absence of either of the two will make the League essentially incomplete. The progressiveness and mass character of the Youth League constantly finds its expression in the League membership. In this sense, doing a good job of recruiting new members holds the key to combining the two aspects. The practice of closed-doorism is, of course, incorrect. That will alienate the League organizations from the broad masses of young people. Nor is it practical, however, to require that every youth should measure up to the requirements of a League member within a short period of time. It is an objective fact that among the students of a class are those who are advanced, those who are intermediate, and those who fall behind. The activity of "creating an entire classroom of League members" is prone to a one-sided emphasis on the quantity of League members. It may lead to rush recruiting and take in some young people who still fall short of the requirements of a League member, thus undermining the progressiveness of the Youth League.

A correct approach calls for an "active and planned recruitment." This means that ideologically we should attach importance to cultivating activists and do solid work to promote them energetically. When they attain the standard of a League member, we should admit them in a timely and planned way. Thus we can continuously expand the League organization and improve the quality of League members.

Yours,

Ju Yunfeng

10

Letter to the Editor

BEING ADVANCED RESULTED IN VEXATION

Comrade Editor:

My good friend little Chen has always been energetic and conscientious about her

"Xianjin fan'er dailaile kunao." *Huangjin shidai* [Golden Age] (Guangdong), No. 8 (August 1981), p. 15. Translation from *Chinese Education* 18:1 (Spring 1985), pp. 27–28.

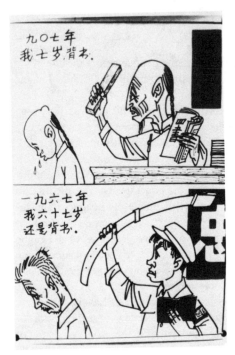

In 1907, when I was seven years old, I had to recite my lessons from memory.

In 1967, when I was sixty-seven years old, I still had to recite my lessons from memory.

THE MORE THINGS CHANGE, THE MORE THEY REMAIN THE SAME

Fanlao huantong, by Liao Bingxiong

This cartoon uses irony to show the persistence of Chinese cultural forms. Despite the very different subject matter, there is a great affinity between the young student memorizing the Confucian classics in the Qing (Manchu) dynasty and the old intellectual memorizing Mao's quotations under the supervision of a Red Guard. Moreover, the "radical" style of the Cultural Revolution is equated with the "feudal" style of traditional China.

work. She is assiduous and not upset by criticism. The masses praise her and the leadership has a good impression of her. She has been repeatedly elected an advanced producer of the factory.

Since she became well-known, however, she has been subject to increasing censure. Some people say she knows how to ingratiate herself with the leadership and gets credit for all the good things done by others. Some people believe one will be under pressure working together with her, will be asked to perform hard work, will have bad luck, and will be taken advantage of. There are still others who think her pursuit of the advanced status is for the purpose of becoming an "official." As a matter of fact, little Chen has no intention to become an "official" at all. The leadership truly had the idea to promote her to some official position. But she thought herself unqualified, unable to shoulder the responsibility, and she turned down the offer in all sincerity. Since others keep heaping reproach on her and the leadership always adds to her "work load," little Chen is extremely annoyed and constantly laden with anxiety. Unfortunately, she made a mistake in her work recently. The leadership cautioned her to guard against conceit and impetuosity, while others made more insinuations against her. I sympathize with little Chen and shudder at her experience of becoming an advanced worker.

Yours,

Li Xiaoling

11

Letter to the Editor

POLITICAL INSTRUCTORS SHOULD GET RID OF THEIR DEPRESSION

Comrade Editor:

We both are political instructors in a middle school. One has been engaged in educational work for many years, and one has recently taken up his educational post. In the course of teaching, we have come to understand some common problems involving students in their study of politics. These problems affect directly the teaching of political classes and the work of ideological education in the school; they need to be addressed immediately.

After the smashing of the "Gang of Four," especially since the reform of the college entrance examination system, the students' mental outlook experienced a dramatic change. From the attitude of regarding "study as useless," they have reversed themselves and now study assiduously. But politics classes are an exception. The students no longer treat politics courses as lessons on current events, but merely as a formality. The theories are divorced from reality and inapplicable to practical problems. Quite a few students are of the opinion that political theory is not a science but something that can be changed at will. They raise doubts about certain basic principles, saying, for example, "the superiority of the socialist system is not evident in China"; "despite the system of exploitation in capitalist society, the broad masses of people there have a high standard of material life

"Zhengzhi jiaoshi yao cong kunao zhong baitou chulai." *Xin shiqi* [New Times], No. 1 (September 1979), p. 42. Translation from *Chinese Education* 18:1 (Spring 1985), pp. 75–76.

ENOUGH TO BLOW YOUR HAT OFF
Nufa chongguan, by Liao Bingxiong

Confronted by a liberalized cultural policy that allows a relatively more open depiction of emotions in films, literary works, and in social life generally, some senior cadres have reacted very negatively to what they consider "spiritual pollution." As this cadre "blows his top," a queue, worn by all Chinese males during the Qing/Manchu dynasty, is revealed. This shows the "feudal" mentality of such conservative critics.

which we cannot match"; " the theory that imperialism is decadent and moribund does not tally with reality"; etc. Some even assert that "education in solely a Marxist point of view is the road that leads young people to ignorance." Consequently, they take a completely different attitude toward mathematics, physics, and chemistry than toward politics. Achieving good scholastic attainments in the former, they believe, will have a bearing not only on the Four Modernizations of the country but also on their own future. On the contrary, the study of politics will avail one nothing. Because of this, even though politics classes meet only two or three periods a week, classrooms are not always available. If we say there still is some "enthusiasm" for the course, it is manifested solely in the crash review of lessons before examination.

Marxism-Leninism-Mao Zedong Thought is the guiding thought for our Party and the state, the guide to our actions. Owing to the rampant distortion and damage of Lin Biao and the "Gang of Four," however, some young folks misunderstand and are skeptical about Marxism-Leninism. Furthermore, they have no personal experience in the difference between the old and the new societies, and they are simpleminded and naive. Thus they only see what is on the surface and not the essence, only one side and not the whole situation. Consequently, they have a variety of ideological problems, which are precisely the expression of problems in society. It goes without saying that we cannot expect to solve the problems with a few politics classes.

Right now, we are at an historical turning point as the whole Party shifts the focus of its efforts onto the great undertaking of socialist modernization. To enhance the nation's consciousness of Marxism-Leninism-Mao Zedong Thought, especially that of the younger generation, has become a major task that brooks no delay. It is the unshirkable duty of political instructors to take on this glorious and formidable mission. Nevertheless, problems we encounter in our work have become obstacles to our advance. We hope you can help us in this regard.

Sincerely,

Liu Hua and Shi Lanying

August 1979

12

WHY DON'T MIDDLE SCHOOL STUDENTS LIKE TO TAKE POLITICS CLASSES?

Beijing Youth News published on May 22 a report of an investigation conducted by its reporter Wu Peihua of some middle school students. The report shows that almost 95 percent of the students investigated say they dislike the politics course most. Their reasons:

First, the teaching material is empty and abstract.

The politics textbook for the junior middle school is *Ideological Cultivation of Young People*. Logically speaking, this should be the spiritual nutrition that

"Weishenme zhongxuesheng bu xihuan shang zhengzhike?" *Beijing qingnian bao* [Beijing Youth News], May 22, 1984, reprinted in *Baokan wenzhai* [Digest of Newspapers and Periodicals], May 29, 1984, p. 3. Translation from *Chinese Education* 17:4 (Winter 1984–85), pp. 72–73.

middle school students are in need of. But the textbook gives very few vivid examples and is filled with slogan-like big talk so that the students are scared when reading it. It seldom touches upon the worries and difficulties students encounter in their lives. As time passes, an idea has taken root in the students' minds, that is, there is no use studying politics. In senior middle schools the students study the textbooks of political economy and philosophy. These textbooks involve many concepts and are difficult to understand. The syllabus provides that the two courses be taught within a period of one year. Thus the enormous and complex teaching materials are compressed into "ship biscuits" and students find them abstract and remote from their lives.

Second, the teacher monopolizes the class and monologizes from beginning to end.

In giving lectures the teachers act as if they were reciting from memory, and some teachers just simply read from the textbooks. They only give the students dull and dry conclusions rather than teaching them how to analyze and solve problems. Sometimes they try to dodge contradictions in real life and forbid the students to raise questions. If the students offer opinions contrary to the teacher or textbook, they are likely to be reprimanded for "imagining things" or even "having problems with their thinking." The students make a strong appeal: "We hope we can be given the time to think and the opportunity to express ourselves."

Third, the method of examination is mechanical and rigid.

Because of the rather important proportion politics holds in the total score for the college entrance examination, nobody can afford to treat the subject lightly. Right now the practice of reviewing the politics lessons is for the teachers to concoct scores of questions and provide standard answers. The students start to commit the answers to memory one week beforehand. During the examination, they just put down the mechanically memorized answers to the right questions. Some students tried to answer the questions the way they understood, but always lost in terms of test scores. To make things secure, nobody dares to "take reckless action" again.

13

Chen Ze

I

I AM SO happy and relaxed this summer vacation. I can go wherever I

"Zai jingzheng zhong neng fazhan youyi ma?" [Can Friendship Be Fostered Amid Competition?]. This section, "Wo," appeared in the "High School Days" Column, *Zhongguo qingnian* [China Youth], No. 6 (June 1982). Translation from *Chinese Education* 18:1 (Spring 1985), pp. 43–48.

want without trying to hide myself. There is no longer any anxiety bearing down on me all day. Even watching TV is more interesting than in the past, for my parents do not repeatedly urge me to study with that worried look of theirs. Perhaps you may say: What's the big deal? Is there anybody who is not happy and relaxed during a summer vacation? But as far as I'm concerned, I would not have dared to play and feel happy three days ago, not to say in the three previous years, had I not known my test scores for promotion to senior high school.

Three years ago I graduated from primary school. Because I was naughty and ignorant in my childhood, I failed to pass the high school entrance examination. I had no choice but to stay on in the primary school along with another eighty or so unfortunate children who had the same bad luck as me. As a primary school with high school classes attached, it did not even offer a complete high school curriculum. Thus we stayed on for six months, and then even this primary school refused to keep us any longer.

Fortunately, there are still many good people in this world. We were finally allowed to continue our education many days after other students had already started the term. The school that we entered was called the "second division" of a key high school. It was said to be a school but was not recognized by the Bureau of Education, which even refused to provide our teachers with teaching material. Two dark and dirty rooms outside of the school were found and designated to be our classrooms. We didn't have a bell to call us to classes; we didn't have sitting-up exercises during the break; we had no eye exercises, no singing, and no sports. All that should be had in [school] life we didn't have.

Life completely changed for me, and I felt unhappy every day. This was not because of the poor conditions of study, but because all of a sudden I seemed to become much lower than others. I never went out to play, not because I didn't want to play but because I was too ashamed to face anyone else or to look for former playmates. Nor would their parents allow them to play with me, as I was a student of the "second division." It is also because of this that my relatives tended to give me a cold shoulder. Later we were allowed to move into the school proper but retained the name of "second division." In the physical culture class, when our classmates got into mischief, the teacher would rebuke us: "You are of the 'second division.' What do you run wild for? If you want to run wild, you better think whether this is the place for it!" At this all the classmates lowered their heads. I really hated the name "second division." Whenever people mentioned the "second division" or asked me which school I attended, I felt as if a needle had been stuck into my heart, and I was extremely unhappy.

We were human the same as others, but why were we denied the fine feelings and warmth between man and man? More than once when I heard the ridicule of people, saw the sneers of relatives, or the silent tears of my mother, I secretly burst into tears. I hated myself for being no good, but I was not a person to live on the sympathy and pity of others. I could never bring myself to believe that I was inferior to others. I simply had to work hard, to make a desperate effort.

Thus I embarked on a struggle, a lonely and difficult road I had never experienced before. But I had to make a good show. From that time onward, I never went out except to go to school. On the road, I always dipped my head and

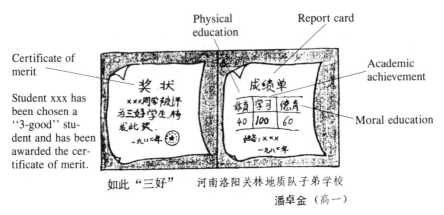

"THREE GOOD" IS DETERMINED IN THIS MANNER?
Ruci sanhao by Pan Zhuojin (first year senior high student from Henan Province)
Source: Zhongxue sheng [Middle School Student], No. 3 (March 1983), p. 81.

Chinese students are urged to be good in athletics, study, and morality ("three-good"). Those that achieve three-good status are commended and sometimes rewarded. Because achievement in study is so important currently in China, students are often granted three-good status on high grades alone.

hurriedly walked forward; I had no intention to run into an acquaintance, still less the talented students of the key schools and key classes. On returning home, I would bury myself in books, studying and studying without a break.

Sometimes, I wished I could have the help of my classmates. But once I saw that some of them, fearful that others might outstrip them, "kept their knowledge secret" and resented each other, I did not want to turn to them. For my part, I too wanted to guard against others.

Thus, I stayed at my desk all by myself numerous cold, wintry nights, as well as hot summer days. My brains were strained by work but my heart was so hollow and cold. Before me was a dim light and behind me a lonely shadow. A series of scenes from my childhood reappeared in my mind's eye:

In summer when flowers were in full bloom, I went with my little playmates to catch frogs at the pond. After we caught the frogs, we piled the earth high and built low terraces along the bank of the pond and then dug a big waterhole. Laughing heartily, we watched the frogs jump from the diving platforms and race in swimming.

After a rainfall, we would dig caves in the side of a hill, with one cave linked to another. Behind them there were also hidden holes and tunnels just like a labyrinth.

In the freezing cold winter, we would go skating and play games on nearby ponds and fight with each other on the "war chariots" that we made ourselves with boards and angle iron. . . .

This golden childhood was happy. Our little playmates were so close to each other that if anyone was bullied all others would feel bad. Whenever one got something good, the others would share his joy. And if anyone found a pretty cigarette case, he would show it around and nobody would feel jealous of him. But what about now? Why should people distrust and even guard against and oppose each other?

After all, our carefree childhood is gone forever. I must face reality. After three years of hard work, I have passed the examination and been admitted to a key class that I don't like. Despite this, new anxieties begin to grip my heart.

I am still a student, and there will be plenty of examinations down the road. Can I win in every examination? It seems to me life is filled with competitions. The people around me are each a classmate, a friend, and at the same time a competitor. The winners of the competitions earn the admiration of others, and the losers suffer discrimination. I have great sympathy for those who lose and often pray that I may never become a loser in my life. I yearn for the day when there is no more competition among people so that everyone can get along with others in friendly affection and lead a life of dignity.

14

Letter to the Editor

Is It Worthwhile for a College Student to Risk His Life to Rescue an Old Peasant?

[*Wenhui bao* Editor's Note] In a movement to learn from some advanced figure, we occasionally come across some objection from a number of young people. A case in point is the view presented here by a college student on the merit of Zhang Hua's sacrifice. To push the movement to learn from martyr Zhang Hua's spirit further ahead, we publish in our newspaper the full text of the letter and solicit from our readers answers to the question or articles in response. (Please address all letters and manuscripts to the editorial group for the column "The University in Society.") In this way, we can arrive at a correct view on the problem through ideological exchange and mutual help.

Comrade Editor:

Your newspaper published on page 1 of the October 18 issue the story of Zhang Hua, a third-year student of the No. 4 Army Medical College. True, the spirit

"Daxuesheng maosi jiu lao nong zhidema?" *Wenhui bao* (Shanghai), November 9, 1982, p. 4. Translation from *Chinese Education* 18:1 (Spring 1985), pp. 39–40.

displayed by Zhang Hua in rescuing the old peasant in disregard of his own safety deserves to be praised and encouraged. But whether it is necessary for him to risk his life is a question we all need to think over.

Zhang Hua was twenty-four years old, the most promising period of one's life. In addition, he was a third-year student of an army medical college, a prospective professional that the nation needs for its socialist construction. In contrast, the old peasant was already at the advanced age of sixty-nine. I admit that the old peasant can do his share for society. But it cannot conceivably be compared with what Zhang Hua might have done in the days ahead had he survived.

Furthermore, it is no easy matter for the state to train a college student, whose own value far exceeds that of an old peasant. As a college student, therefore, one should be aware of the preciousness of one's life. One should make use of one's limited life to create for the state a value larger than his own rather than exchanging it for the life of a sixty-nine-year-old peasant. Anyway, it is not worthwhile to exchange gold for a like amount of stone.

It is therefore my opinion that every one of us must take into account the interests of the entire country and the entire nation as well as what the state expects of us when deciding to take an action. Under no circumstances should we be swayed by our emotions.

Yours,

Duoyan, student of Hangzhou Normal College

15

Letter to the Editor

A Letter from Duoyan's Schoolmate

SUPPOSING "DUOYAN" WERE to fall into a manure pit; let us do some calculation according to his theory.

"Duoyan's" schoolmates should not rescue him. They have all about the same value. To rescue him would be like gaining six of one at the expense of half a dozen of the other. If things went wrong, both of them might be lost. In sum, it is not worthwhile.

The teachers of "Duoyan" should not jump into the manure pit to rescue him, either, for that would be like trading big "gold" for small "gold." Of course,

" 'Duoyan' de tongchuang laixin." *Wenhui bao* (Shanghai), November 16, 1982, p. 4. Translation from *Chinese Education* 18:1 (Spring 1985, pp. 41–42.

that would not be worthwhile.

Then get a middle school student to rescue "Duoyan." Well, some calculations have to be made to determine whether the student's future value will outweigh that of "Duoyan." Perhaps he may even become an outstanding figure like Lang Ping or Chen Jingrun some day.

Still less should any worker or peasant come to the rescue of "Duoyan." How can a creator of socialist material wealth risk his life in order to rescue a consumer?

According to "Duoyan's" theory, all those who understand the value of life and are resolved to dedicate themselves to some meaningful pursuit should not rescue "Duoyan," a person who is not clear about the value of life. This is because all of them are "gold" when compared with "Duoyan," while "Duoyan" is nothing but "stone."

"Duoyan," oh, "Duoyan"! Around you are any number of people who have moral integrity and understand the value of life. Please conscientiously learn from them! Last summer students of the class of 1979 of the biology department in our college made a trip to Putuo for fieldwork. Two girl students were swept away by ocean waves. Many students jumped into the raging billows one after another to rescue them in defiance of the danger. How should a matter like this be explained?

It is hoped "Duoyan" can understand the value of life so that he can truly "use his limited life to create for the state a value larger than his own."

Yours,

Wen Zi, Hangzhou Normal College

16

Lan Chengdong and Zhang Zhongru

ASPIRATIONS AND INCLINATIONS OF THIS YEAR'S SENIOR HIGH SCHOOL GRADUATES

A Survey of Three High Schools in Shanghai

IN 1982 THERE will be 36,000 new senior high school graduates in Shanghai, mostly seventeen and eighteen years of age. Psychologically, youth

"Yingjie gaozhong biyesheng de zhiyuan qingxiang." *Shehui* [Society], No. 2 (May 1982), pp. 22–25. Translation from *Sociology and Society in Contemporary China, 1979–1983* (a special issue of *Chinese Sociology and Anthropology*), edited and translated by David S. K. Chu (Armonk, N.Y.: M. E. Sharpe, 1984), pp. 159–169.

WHEN A MAN ATTAINS THE TAO
[ENLIGHTENMENT AND
IMMORTALITY], EVEN HIS
PETS ASCEND TO HEAVEN
Yiren dedao, by Fang Cheng

A man's success benefits his subordinates, relatives, and anyone else associated with him. Although not expressed directly in the cartoon, a leader's fall from grace will also bring negative consequences to those associated with him.

of these ages already possess a basic self-concept and happen to be at a crucial stage in their process of individual socialization. Just before graduation, they are at the crossroads of life, their idealized futures filled with rose-colored longings. But simultaneously they face a grim reality: besides only a minority of them who can enroll in colleges to pursue advanced studies and some who are able to enter specialized secondary and polytechnic schools, the vast majority must face directly the problem of finding employment. The graduates have to make difficult choices about their individual futures. An understanding of their aspirations and preferences has definite reference value for concerned departments.

Recently, using mainly the questionnaire method, we conducted a survey of aspirations and inclinations of 150 senior high graduates in 4 classes (including one liberal arts class) of 2 ordinary and one key-point high school in Hongkou District.[1]

The students were asked to fill in items [on questionnaire forms] on their own academic achievement, parents' occupations and cultural levels, the rank order of their aspirations, etc. In addition, the students were asked to evaluate a list of 38 occupations and types of work according to the degree of their preferences and to give scores to 138 questions.

The results obtained are summarized and analyzed as follows:

I. Students' Aspirations (See Table I:1):

Table I:1

Student Aspirations

Sex	School type	Enter university	Apply to secondary technical	Apply to polytechnical	Get job
M	Key HS	92.9%	0	0	7.1%
M	Ordinary HS	50.0%	32.4%	11.7%	5.9%
F	Key HS	100%	0	0	0
F	Ordinary HS	40.5%	42.9%	11.9%	4.7%

The data from Table I.1 indicate the following:

First, among the majority of students, the "theory of schooling is useless" already has no market. Regardless of whether from key-point or ordinary high schools, the percentages of students wishing to study in colleges, secondary specialized schools, or technical schools all exceed 90 percent. In our survey, we discovered that students from ordinary high schools with mediocre school records, even below-average students, all indicate applying to colleges as their first choice; only an extreme minority indicate a willingness to work right away, and these consist of students with opportunities for "substitution" [dingti].[2] The present situation is vastly different from the era of the "Gang of Four" when to be uncivilized and ignorant was considered glorious.

Second, there is little interest in general manual labor. Fewer than 12 percent of boys and girls from ordinary high schools applied to technical schools, and not a single one from the key-point high school was willing to apply to a secondary specialized (not to mention polytechnical) school. True, China's Four Modernizations need large numbers of high-level technicians, but at present there is greater shortage of middle-level technical personnel and skilled workers. According to responses of some key-point high school students, because their teachers expect them all to enter colleges, secondary technical schools are beneath consideration. We believe, however, that it is still necessary to emphasize a pre-Cultural Revolution slogan: "one red heart; two kinds of preparation"—it is better to accept the choice of the country.

II. Analysis of Various Factors Influencing Student Aspirations and Preferences

1) Relationship Between Parental Occupations and Graduates' Aspirations (See Table II:1)

Correlational statistical analysis obtained Ty ≅ 0.048, indicating that parental occupations and graduates' aspirations do not have any correlation. On the basis of the data, parents nowadays generally all hope for their offspring to have higher education.

Table II:1.

Parental Occupations and Graduates' Aspirations

Parental occupation	Cadre	Intelligentsia	Worker	Other
[Aspiration]				
College	29	29	47	0
Secondary specialized school	6	3	20	0
Polytechnic school	4	1	3	1
Get a job	1	2	4	0

Ty ≅ 0.048

2) Relationship Between Parental Cultural Level and Graduates' Aspirations (See Table II:2)

A G ≅ 0.42 is obtained from correlational statistical analysis, i.e., using parental cultural levels to predict graduates' aspirations can reduce the error by 42 percent, indicating that parental cultural levels have a relatively large correlation with graduates' aspirations and preferences. Parents with higher cultural levels have a stronger desire for their children to have a higher education than do parents with lower cultural levels.

Table II:2

Parental Cultural Levels and Graduates' Aspirations

Parental cultural level	High	Medium	Low
[Aspiration]			
Attend college	39	56	10
Apply to secondary specialized school	4	18	7
Apply to polytechnic school	3	3	3

G ≅ 0.42

3) Correlation Between Student Achievement and Graduates' Aspirations (See Table II:3)

Table II:3

Achievement and Graduates' Aspirations

Achievement	Good	Medium	Low
[Aspiration]			
Attend college	45	53	7
Apply to secondary specialized school	5	23	1
Apply to polytechnic school	0	8	1

$G \cong 0.52$

A $G = 0.52$ is obtained from statistical analysis, indicating a relatively large correlation between achievement and aspirations; the better the student's achievement, the higher the aspiration. Knowing the student's achievement to predict his/her aspiration can reduce the error by 52 percent.

4) Correlation Between Student Valuation of Occupations and Graduates' Aspirations (See Table II:4)

Table II:4

Occupational Valuation and Graduates' Aspirations*

Occupational valuation	A	B	C
[Aspiration]			
Attend college	96	9	0
Apply to secondary specialized school	6	23	0
Apply to polytechnic school	1	8	0

$G \cong 0.95$

*Category A indicates occupations that require higher education. B indicates jobs that require secondary education. C indicates manual labor in general.

A $G \cong 0.95$ is obtained from correlational statistical analysis, i.e., using [student's] valuation of occupations to predict graduates' aspirations can reduce the error by 95 percent, indicating a very strong correlation between them. It is worth noting that an obvious bias exists in these students' valuation of occupations, i.e., higher esteem for mental work and low esteem for manual labor. Below let us consider students' evaluations of specific social occupations and their interests and hobbies that may further explain this question.

III. Student Evaluation of Occupations and [Their] Interests and Hobbies (See Table III:1)

Table III:1

Students' Evaluations of 38 Types of Occupations and Jobs

Rank order	Occupation	Score
1	Engineer	112
2	Doctor	107
3	Technician	107
4	Journalist	69
5	Judge	61
6	Author	57
7	Lawyer	54
8	Cadre	48
9	Natural scientist	40
10	Office worker	34
11	Athlete	30
12	Electronics worker	28
13	Soldier	27
14	College teacher	20
15	Light industry worker	20
16	Musician	11
17	Artist	5
18	Social scientist	−11
19	Actor	−21
20	Machinist	−25
21	Sailor	−54
22	Secondary school teacher	−60
23	Shop employee	−71
24	Driver	−78
25	Nurse	−82
26	Primary school teacher	−114
27	Railroad worker	−122
28	Service worker/attendant	−126
29	Kindergarten teacher	−127
30	Construction worker	−134
31	Barber	−142
32	Textile worker	−148
33	Iron and steel worker	−148
34	Cook/kitchen staff	−154
35	Farmer/peasant	−171
36	Dock worker	−172
37	Sanitary worker	−189
38	Self-employed worker	−208

The 138 items in the student "Interest Questionnaire" are summed up into twenty-three specialties and occupations, some of which are not included in Table III:1, but most are. We tabulated the students' five most liked [preferred] and three most disliked occupations, categorized by sex for comparison. (See Table III:2)

From these two tables, we can see some interesting questions worthy of further study.

Table III:2

Graduates' Interests and Preferences

Rank male		Score	Rank female		Score
		Most Liked			
1	Astronomy	21	1	Literature	27
2	History	19	2	Art	23
3	Literature	13	3	Astronomy	22
4	Law	12	4	Law	16
5	Service trades	12	5	Chemistry	13
		Most Disliked			
1	Agriculture	−31	1	Agriculture	−34
2	Forestry	−16	2	Electronic technician	−30
3	Geology	−14	3	Industrial worker	−22

A. The reason that engineers head the list and natural scientists are ranked only ninth is possibly because students have a relatively clear and definite concept of engineers and are more familiar with their work. The broader concept of natural scientist includes not only physicists but also agricultural scientists. Social scientists ranked eighteenth; it appears that students understand their work even less. And also very possibly they confuse social scientists with those who "lived off politics" [literally, "eat political rice" [*chi zhengzhi fan*] during the "Gang of Four" period.

B. Secondary school students often merely admire certain occupations by name without really knowing what they involve, as illustrated by the profession of physician which ranked in second place. In the "Interest Questionnaire," medical studies scored very low, ranking not even among the top five. This is because the "Interest Questionnaire" determines the psychological manifestations of respondents through the use of several indicators that express in detail the necessary requirements of being a physician, such as desiring to learn to dress wounds and to make emergency rescues of the injured, desiring to do experiments on animals, to be very interested in dissection of human anatomy, in the physiological characteristics and various bodily organs, etc. The questionnaire survey shows that many high schoolers have no interest in these things.

C. Considerations of material benefits in society have a great influence on high school students. Electronics and light industry workers are ranked in the forefront. In particular, electronics, ranked twelfth, is even ahead of college teachers [fourteenth]. Possibly this is because the [former] occupations are closely related to people's living standards. A more likely possibility is that in recent years these occupations have relatively greater incomes from bonuses, and that there is preferential purchase of goods internally [in departments where one works]. A few years ago, machinists and other heavy industry workers were much sought after; there was a saying: "those who could do lathe work, benchwork, and planing" need not worry and could go anywhere in the world. Nowadays, during the period of [economic] readjustment, there are reduced production assignments for machinery occupations and relatively fewer bonus awards. And in comparison with electronics and other newly developing industries, working conditions in machinery occupations are inferior and labor more strenuous. Textile workers must work all three shifts [in rotation] and the work is hard. Although sailors and railroad workers have relatively high salaries and welfare benefits, they must be away from home for years so that they also rank low on the list. These facts indicate that there is great need to strengthen labor education among young students, through which to foster in them aesthetic feelings toward all productive labor and to direct students to more rational occupational directions.[3]

D. There is need to raise the social status of teachers, especially that of secondary, elementary, and kindergarten teachers. Science and technology are important for the Four Modernizations, and education is the foundation of science and technology. The level of education directly determines the development of science and technology; education is a kind of intellectual investment. A society in which a teacher's status is not high is surely a society of slow development.

E. High school students' preferences for certain occupations are initially promoted by curiosity and do not necessarily create any true sense of duty or mission. E.g., the "Interest Questionnaire" shows that male students like astronomy best, and females also like it very much. But when we questioned several students in detail, they indicated that they do not like it so much. Analysis reveals that there were some problems with several measures related to astronomy in the "Interest Questionnaire." Initially, strong interests are expressed [by respondents] when they are asked about radio and television programs that introduce conditions of other stars and planets, about scientific research data and conditions of outer heavenly bodies brought back by artificial satellites launched by China and foreign countries, and about reports related to flying saucers and whether there is life in outer space. But if further questioned about being very interested in observing the stars for a long time without getting tired, it is certain that a great majority of students will give a score of minus two, indicating strong dislike.

F. Certain traditional concepts are deeply rooted so that cook/kitchen staff, dock worker, and sanitation worker ranked the lowest. Table III:1 indicates that farmer/peasant ranked thirty-fifth; according to our observations at the time, many did not want to reveal their inclination disliking agriculture so that they all expressed "not sure." A minority of students obviously deliberately filled out the opposite of their real aspirations, but the truth is evident when one compares their responses in the "Interest Questionnaire." In general, both male and female students indicate that they are most uninterested in agriculture. The actual reason for this may be that now since there is no longer [the policy of] going to settle in the countryside, there is no need to worry about it, so that there is also no need to reveal one's inclination of looking down on agriculture.

G. Self-employed occupations constitute one of the realistic ways out for graduates; consequently, that a majority of students make no secret of their strong dislike for them is worthy of attention and research. From teachers in charge of classes, we understand that students believe that individuals in self-employed enterprises lack security and have an uncertain future; work units owned by the whole people are "iron rice bowls." Since in Shanghai enterprises and units of the whole people and of large collectives are already overcrowded to a worrisome degree, a large part of the labor force flow should be toward those in self-employed businesses and in repair and service trades which are precisely the ones needed by society. Today, how to change the phenomenon of people without jobs and jobs without people is a matter that needs to be studied and resolved as a whole by concerned departments. A pressing matter at hand is how to further mobilize the enthusiasm of youth for individual self-employment. According to statistics, to date in Shanghai there are only a little more than 10,000 persons in self-employed businesses, an obviously negligible figure in a large city with a population of ten million. This city's labor force resources are rich, with great potential to be tapped.

IV. The Most Worrisome Matter for Current Graduates

On the item on what is your greatest worry currently, 68 percent of the students are worried that they may not be able to get more schooling, 17.3 percent are anxious that they may not be able to find jobs, and only 5.3 percent indicate that they have no anxieties or concerns, no worrisome matters on their minds. Most of the latter are students of science classes [majors] from the key-point high school, who also have relatively good grades and relatively strong self-confidence.

Additionally, this item also revealed a tiny few students with somewhat eccentric thinking, e.g., a liberal arts student in the key-point high school indicated that his greatest worries were "policy changes, more [political] campaigns and movements, outbreak of war, [and] destruction of the universe."

Some other students seem to think that besides attending college, there can be no contribution to society. One student wrote: "Failing to gain admission to college, one becomes a consumer of wealth and not a creator of wealth." On the item of his occupational valuation, besides expressing his strong liking for engineers, and a liking for authors, journalists, natural scientists and technicians, he indicated a strong dislike for all manual labor occupations.

Notes

1. In interpreting the data from this survey, it should be noted that being the home of Fudan University and its Branch Campus, Hongkou District may not be typical of Shanghai as a whole.

2. As a means of easing the unemployment problem in large urban areas, at this time a policy allowed for job "substitution," i.e., a high school graduate may preferentially take

over a job vacated by a parent upon the latter's scheduled or early retirement.
3. Implicitly but clearly, the authors of this article do not accept the notion that high school graduates on the job market and workers have their own *rational* considerations in job preferences if choices are available. The rationality of the former may be at odds with socialist goals and ideals which attempt to downplay inequalities in the division of labor.

FURTHER READINGS

Chan, Anita. *Children of Mao: Personality Development and Political Activism in the Red Guard Generation*. Seattle: University of Washington Press, 1985.
Chinese Sociology and Anthropology. Quarterly translation journal, published by M. E. Sharpe, Armonk, N.Y.
Chu, David S. K., ed. *Sociology and Society in Contemporary China 1979–1983*. Armonk, N.Y.: M. E. Sharpe, 1984.
Hooper, Beverley. *Youth in China*. New York: Penguin, 1985.
Liang Heng and Judith Shapiro. *Son of the Revolution*. New York: Alfred A. Knopf, 1983.
Liu, Alan P. L. "Opinions and Attitudes of Youth in the People's Republic of China." *Asian Survey* 24:9 (September 1984), pp. 975–996.
Martin, Roberta. "The Socialization of Children in China and on Taiwan: An Analysis of Elementary School Textbooks." *The China Quarterly* No. 62 (June 1975), pp. 242–262.
Ridley, Charles P., Dennis Doolin and Paul Godwin. *The Making of a Model Citizen in Communist China*. Stanford: Stanford University Press, 1970.
Rosen, Stanley. "Education and the Political Socialization of Chinese Youth," in John N. Hawkins, ed. *Education and Social Change in the People's Republic of China*. New York: Praeger, 1983, pp. 97–133.
Rosen, Stanley. "Prosperity, Privatization and China's Youth." *Problems of Communism*, March-April 1985, pp. 1–28.
Shirk, Susan. *Competitive Comrades: Career Incentives and Students Strategies in the People's Republic of China*. Berkeley: University of California Press, 1982.
Solomon, Richard. *Mao's Revolution and the Chinese Political Culture*. Berkeley: University of California Press, 1971.
Watson, James L., ed. *Class and Social Stratification in Post-Revolution China*. Cambridge: Cambridge University Press, 1984.
Whyte, Martin K. *Small Groups and Political Rituals in the People's Republic of China*. Berkeley: University of California Press, 1974.
Whyte, Martin King, and William L. Parish. *Urban Life in Contemporary China*. Chicago: University of Chicago Press, 1984.

c. Political Participation

CONFLICT IN THE arena of political participation has centered around the degree to which China's political institutions should be autonomous from Party control, and the role that groups should play in the political process. Although post-Mao China has witnessed a general retreat by the Chinese Communist Party in the affairs of the government and the economy, the Party's new role has remained both ambiguous and controversial. Senior Party leaders have for the most part ended the practice of cadres simultaneously holding both government and Party posts, and have proscribed Party secretaries from interfering in the day-to-day running of government institutions and economic enterprises. The duties of Party secretaries in the new regime, however, have remained unclear. In addition, conflict has continued to surround elite-level attempts to institutionalize channels of participation. Should the Party be able to predetermine the results of elections? To what extent should the press be permitted to criticize Party officials?

When they took the decision to give top priority to economic development, China's leaders of necessity began to expand the scope of political participation to include the specialists, technicians, and other intellectuals whose services the political elite had done without for more than a decade. Brought in from political limbo, latent groups of managers and intellectuals began to assert their interests both vis-à-vis other groups in Chinese society and vis-à-vis the Party. In this sense, China has not escaped the dilemma of other one-party states whose leaderships have set out on ambitious economic development programs. Rational decision-making under conditions of technological complexity has required that Party leaders share power with groups of specialists and experts and that Party officials rely more heavily on institutionalized processes.[1] The selections in this section, then, reflect the conflict over the Party's role in the modernization process that has characterized post-Mao China.

Some local officials have resisted the attempts of China's national leaders to reinvigorate institutional channels of participation and to share power with some groups in Chinese society. In part this reflects the fear of local cadres that their power was being reduced. Others simply did not understand the need to replace mass campaigns with stable, bureaucratic processes. Local officials signaled their displeasure by interfering in local elections, by obstructing investigative reporters, and by continuing to discriminate against "mental" workers.

Before participation could be put on a more institutional footing, however, authorities had to dismantle the mass campaign apparatus, which radicals in the Party had relied on during the Cultural Revolution. The device of class labels, used to control "enemies" and to mobilize "the people," was closely associated with the campaigns. By abolishing the general use of these labels, authorities signaled the end of campaigning as a channel of mobilized participation (Selection 17).

In a speech delivered at a National Party school forum in October 1980, Liao Gailong, a research fellow of the Policy Research Office of the Party Secretariat, made a strong plea for democratic institutional reform (Selection 18). Coming just months after Deng Xiaoping's Politburo speech on the same theme, Liao contributed to the debate among senior Party leaders over their evaluation of the Cultural Revolution and of Mao Zedong's role in it, the results of which they later published in the "Resolution on Certain Questions in the History of Our Party." While going much further in his recommendations for institutional change than did either the "Resolution" or subsequent official policy, Liao was clearly in the reformists' camp. The speech, dubbed the "Gengshen Reforms," was significant because, when compared to the policies actually adopted, it indicated that the Party's senior leadership canvassed a relatively wide range of opinions on the issue. The Cultural Revolution scars were still deep and fresh enough for the Party to seriously consider implementing proposals that had appeared to be radical when suggested by the "Democracy Movement" from 1979 to 1980, or that previously had been condemned as "bourgeois."

Liao advocated substantial changes in China's national and local political institutions to implement procedural democracy. He suggested that the National People's Congress (which he described as a "rubber stamp") be reduced in size, that it be divided into two houses, and that it set up a system of powerful standing committees. He endorsed the end of the "fusion" of the Party and state (this had only led to "autocratic rule") and sounded a general retreat for the Party from its traditional role as controller of mass organizations, such as trade unions, and the media. Indeed, Liao suggested, national Party organs should be decentralized, with three weakened committees checking and balancing one another, in the fashion of "bourgeois" institutions, to prevent leadership abuses.

Although Party leaders were willing to preside over a retreat from the day-to-day running of the government and the economy, they were unwilling (or unable) to decentralize the Party itself, perhaps fearing regionalism or, worse, anarchy. Most of Liao's suggestions have not been implemented. Still, authorities have strengthened the NPC standing committee system, and they have attempted to carve out separate areas of responsibility for Party and state cadres.

Conflict over the role of Party leaders in the reform of China's election system is illustrated in Selections 19–21. In a letter to the editor, a writer complains that officials improperly intervened in a local election in Guangdong (Selection 19). It is wrong to assume that only leaders understand the real interests of the masses, the letter asserts. Selection 20, however, rebuts this argument and points out that the masses, left to their own devices, would choose popular fellows who only have the short-term welfare of the people in mind. Although *Nanfang ribao* (Southern Daily) offers no solution in this matter, we can assume that, in general, official China prefers more guidance than less. Certainly that has been the experience of local elections since 1980.[2]

The significance of having been elected to office is addressed in Selection 21, in which Party members are admonished to respect the mandate of popularly elected non-Party officials. In this view, then, representativeness (*daibiaoxing*) is acquired not only by the more orthodox means of serving the people's interests, but also by winning elections.

In addition to voting in elections, citizens in post-Mao China have used written forms of participation, such as representations to the media and big-character posters, and less institutionalized means such as politically motivated violence (Selections 22–24). Although the media in China have functioned primarily either to smooth the process of policy implementation or to communicate elite goals to the people, they have also acted as a channel for ordinary people to bring to light instances of cadre abuse. In Selection 22, journalists indicate the problems they face when investigating these cases. Like bureaucrats everywhere, local cadres in China sometimes obstruct the gathering of material that shows them in a bad light, refuse to give their permission for damaging material to be published, and drag their feet at making changes that would disrupt cozy, often mutually beneficial relationships with other leaders.

During the heyday of the Democracy Movement in Beijing, officials debated the merits of big-character posters as a channel of participation (Selection 23). Many cadres undoubtedly preferred to discourage citizens from writing posters. Cadres associated the posters, anonymously authored and difficult to control, with the chaos of the Cultural Revolution. Nevertheless, during sessions of the NPC, some delegates argued that posters were an appropriate vehicle for criticizing local leaders: "The masses could judge for themselves whether the poster was positive or negative." These views did not, however, win the day, and in the 1982 State Constitution authorities omitted any reference to the citizens' right to use posters.

Paradoxically, as China's leaders attempted to institutionalize participation, violence as a means of political expression became increasingly common.[3] Although Selection 24 leaves many questions unanswered, it highlights the delicate nature of the middleman role played by local officials. Faced with what they obviously felt was an intolerable situation, villagers on Hainan Island openly attacked government and Party organizations. The villagers' motive in this case, while assuredly political, went unreported in the official press. Publication of the incident served to teach by negative example the value of respect for authority.

While authorities regularized the channels of participation, they relaxed controls over the activities of groups in Chinese society. The result has been an increasingly obvious clash of interests both among groups and between social groups and the Party. Although authorities used trade unions to mobilize workers to implement Party policy and to discipline the labor force, in Selection 25 they acknowledge the right of workers to strike in protest over entrenched "bureaucratic" management. Still, the piece undoubtedly exaggerates the ability of workers to participate in politics through trade unions. In Selection 26, officials remind workers that they have not been left behind in the economic reforms that were implemented first in the countryside. The article acknowledges that workers have their own demands and urges them not to become impatient as they see their incomes fall gradually behind those of the peasants. These selections, then, illustrate conflicts between workers, on the one hand, and managers and peasants, on the other.

In the post-Mao reforms of the economy, enterprise managers as a group began to make demands for more autonomy vis-à-vis the Party (Selections 27–28). In Selection 27 Guangdong managers argue that their newly acquired powers should be codified, and in particular that their control over personnel matters, heretofore the prerogative of Party committees, should be explicitly acknowledged. The Party in retreat was required to reexamine its role in these circumstances. Selection 28, while acknowledging that the power of Party secretaries has been "reduced," underlines the continuing interest of Party secretaries in personnel matters. The secretary's role, however, has remained ambiguous. Interestingly, Selection 28, in contrast to Selection 25, fails to mention the role of workers' councils and trade unions in either personnel decisions or in the supervision of management.

Nowhere have the changes been greater than in the Party's reappraisal of the role of intellectuals (Selections 29–31). In Selection 29, authorities urge cadres to "serve" and to "show concern for" intellectuals, who are needed to implement the Party's economic development program. After years of discrimination against them, the Party has brought back intellectuals from the political wilderness. Politics no longer means zealous attendance at meetings, but has been redefined to include the pursuit of learning, professionalism, and developing expert knowledge (Selection 30). The new status of intellectuals is reflected in Selection 31. Cadre resistance to justly rewarding mental workers or "ninth category" elements, who they discriminated against during the Cultural Revolution, must be stopped. Interestingly, the piece also reflects the problems that leaders in administered, nonmarket economies face when attempting to reform the wage system. How should the value of the contribution of intellectuals (or any other group) be determined?

Finally, in Selection 32, a writer examines the role of women in the labor force. Although some officials have argued that "the woman's place is in the home," Women's Federation officials, reflecting the interests of women (as articulated in opinion polls) have fought back to defend group interests.

In the process of developing the economy, Chinese authorities have relaxed restrictions on groups in society, with the result that some groups have begun to make demands of Party and state officials. At the same time, authorities have embarked on a major reinvigoration of China's political institutions designed to channel and to contain the new demand-making•

Notes

1. Samuel Huntington and Joan M. Nelson, *No Easy Choice: Political Participation in Developing Countries* (Cambridge, Mass.: Harvard University Press, 1976), p. 166.

2. See Andrew J. Nathan, *Chinese Democracy* (New York: Alfred A. Knopf, 1985), Chapter 8; and Barrett L. McCormick, "Reforming the People's Congress System: A Case Study of the Implementation of 'Strengthening Socialist Law and Socialist Democracy' in Post-Mao China," in David M. Lampton, ed., *Policy Implementation in Post-Mao China* (Berkeley: University of California Press, forthcoming).

3. Elizabeth J. Perry, "Rural Collective Violence: The Fruits of Recent Reforms," in Elizabeth J. Perry and Christine Wong, *The Political Economy of Reform in Post-Mao China* (Cambridge, Mass.: Harvard University Press, 1985), pp. 175–192.

17

STRESS POLITICAL STAND, NOT CLASS ORIGIN

THE COMMUNIST PARTY'S policy on descendants of former exploiters was reaffirmed by the *People's Daily* today in an editor's reply to a letter from three Heilongjiang peasants whose parents were former landlords or rich peasants.

Party policy is that while a persons's class origin is noted, the theory that class origin decides everything is rejected and the stress is placed on a person's political stand.

"Because of our family backgrounds," wrote Li Xianai, Wang Zhongyao, and Liu Shuhua of Nahe County, "we used to be discriminated against. We had no right to speak at meetings or to take part in political activities. Leaders of our production team did not dare to have close contact with us for fear that they might be accused of confusing class alignment. Nor did we dare to mix with them because people would say that we were trying to corrupt the leadership." "We felt that there was no place for us in the new society in which we have grown up," they added.

Fortunately, they had the sympathy of a member of the work team sent by the county Party Committee to their village in March last year. "He told us that so long as we love the Party and socialism, we could be united with the people. At first, we took his words with a grain of salt. But later on, we were convinced of the truth of what he had said," they continued. The man got them to attend meetings and take part in political activities. Whenever their families had difficulties, he was always on hand to help. "We were so happy, like orphans who found the embrace of a mother. We did our best at work and last year we were elected model workers."

Commenting on the letter, the editor's note pointed out that the policy of putting the stress on political stand rather than on class origin is a Marxist policy that is in the interests of the people. "Nevertheless," it went on, "there are obstacles to the implementation of the policy. In many places, there is still discrimination against descendants of former landlords and rich peasants. This is abnormal and harmful to socialism."

The children of former landlords and rich peasants are not exploiters, the editor stressed. "We must unite with them so long as they are not reactionary. It is nearly thirty years since New China was founded, and most of these people are grandchildren or even great grandchildren of former exploiters. If their parents were not landlords or rich peasants, these people should not be classified as coming from families of exploiting classes."

Xinhua [New China News Agency], English. From FBIS Daily Report, January 12, 1979, pp. E5–E6.

Only by carrying out resolutely the policy of stressing one's policy stand rather than one's class origin can it be possible to unite the maximum number of people in the modernization effort, the editor's reply concludes.

18

Liao Gailong

THE "1980 REFORM" PROGRAM IN CHINA (PART IV)

The Essence of the "1980 Reform" Is to Achieve the Democratization of the Party and the State

The Party Central Committee, the Standing Committee of the National People's Congress, and the State Council are currently engaged in revising the Party constitution and state constitution on a comprehensive scale and formulating overall plans for economic construction, so as to work out detailed programs for socialist construction, socialist political and cultural construction, military construction, foreign policies, as well as Party-building. All these tasks can be accomplished only by fully relying on the masses and the mass line of the Party, and by pooling the experiences of the whole Party and whole nation. The Party Central Committee has decided to convene the Sixth Plenum at the end of this year [1980] to discuss and adopt resolutions on certain historical issues that have arisen since the founding of the People's Republic. The Twelfth National Congress of the Party, which will be convened next year, will discuss and adopt a new Party constitution, formulate a draft plan for national economic development, adopt the draft new constitution of the People's Republic of China, and elect the leading bodies of the Party according to the new Party constitution. The Fourth Plenum of the Fifth National People's Congress, to be convened in the latter part of next year, will discuss and adopt the new constitution and plans for long-term economic construction. According to the resolutions of the enlarged meeting of the Party Central Committee Politburo that was convened in August this year, and the resolutions of the subsequent Third Plenum of the Fifth National People's Congress, we have started to carry out reforms of the Party and state systems and so on, which are reforms conducive to our country's socialist conditions. This

Qishiniandai [The Seventies] (Hong Kong), No. 134 (March 1, 1981) (excerpt). Translation from FBIS Daily Report, March 16, 1981, pp. U1–U19.

year is 1980, and in China's lunar calendar it is called Gengshen [*geng* stands for the seventh of ten heavenly stems and *shen* for the ninth of the twelve earthly branches] year (the year of the monkey). I think these reforms may be collectively termed the "1980 Reform" or "Gengshen Reform." I think in the future annals of the People's Republic of China, this reform of the socialist system—the Gengshen Reform—implementation of which has begun in 1980, will probably be highly appraised. The program of this reform was laid down in Comrade Deng Xiaoping's speech at the enlarged meeting of the Politburo convened on August 18. The Party Central Committee has ordered that this speech be communicated to the non-Party workers throughout the whole country. Comrade Hua Guofeng's speech at the Third Plenum of the National People's Congress convened on September 7 carries important explanations of and further elaboration on this program. Now the 1980 Reform is a reform of the system of Party and state leadership, that is, a socialist democratic reform. What are its contents? I will now give a few words of explanation. The essence of this reform can be completely expressed in one phrase: to achieve the democratization of the Party and the state. Comrade Deng Xiaoping's speech on August 18 already points out the correct direction of this reform. I will divide the discussion of the democratization of our country's political life into two parts: first, the democratization of the state; and second, that of the Party.

A Thousand Deputies of the People; the National People's Congress to Be Divided into a House of Regional Representatives and a House of Social Representatives, Each of Which Will Impose a Constraint on the Other

Comrade Deng Xiaoping's speech mentioned the points explained below about democratizing our country's political life.

First, the constitution must be revised to help firmly establish our country's socialist democratic system. What kind of democratic system do we intend to establish? The answer to this question must be reflected in the new constitution. At the conference of the Party committee secretaries of various provinces and municipalities, which was convened in September, Comrade Hu Yaobang said: "The constitution needs major revisions." Only the first version of our constitution, which was adopted in 1954, was fairly good. The constitution was later revised after the Ninth, Tenth, and Eleventh National Congresses of our Party, and in the words of Comrade Hu Yaobang, it became worse with each revision. I think Comrade Hu Yaobang's appraisal has important implications. The Third Plenum of the Fifth National People's Congress has adopted the proposal of the CCP Central Committee on revising the constitution and has given rise to the formation of a constitution revising committee, which has started working. Comrade Deng Xiaoping's speech on August 18 points out the principle for revising the constitution: our constitution must be perfected, must be clear and accurate, and must genuinely ensure that the masses of people can enjoy adequate democratic rights and the right to manage the state and various enterprises and businesses, that various nationalities can really practice regional autonomy, that the people's congresses at various levels will be improved, and so on. The principle of disallowing the overcentralization of power will also be reflected in the constitution. These were Comrade Deng Xiaoping's words.

Here I want to discuss the problem of improving the system of the people's congresses. We must try our utmost to enable the people's congresses at various levels as well as their standing bodies quickly to become perfect and to become authoritative organs of power that represent the people. This is our aim. In addition to ensuring the necessary centralization of power, we must appropriately decentralize the power to the localities, so that the local people's congresses will have greater power to handle local problems. In particular, we must take effective measures to conscientiously strengthen the national autonomous power of the autonomous regions of various nationalities and strengthen national unity. Because of the prolonged sabotage by Lin Biao and the "Gang of Four," the contradictions among nationalities are rather intense at present. In particular, we must correctly implement our policy of national autonomy in Xizang [Tibet] and Xinjiang to resolve the national contradictions in these regions. We have a tentative idea about the National People's Congress. At present, the National People's Congress is made up of 3,400 to 3,500 deputies. Only in Beijing is there a sufficiently large conference hall to hold so many people. There are many difficulties in the conducting of meetings. Aside from the reading of declarations, it is impossible to speak at the assembly or to hold discussions. Therefore, only group discussions are possible. Thus, it is very inconvenient to convene such a congress that is attended by so many people, or to convene it frequently, or to let it last a longer period of time. Therefore, we are considering reducing the number of deputies from 3,400 or 3,500, to say, 1,000. Of course, there must not be too few deputies. Such a reduction will be conducive to expanding democracy. Although the number of deputies decreases, democracy will be enhanced. In fact, 1,000 will still be a large number. Therefore, we also consider dividing the people's congress into two houses, just as the division of the congresses of many countries into an upper house and a lower house. The Supreme Soviet of the Soviet Union is also divided into the Soviet of Nationalities and the Soviet of the Union. We should prepare to adopt the plan of dividing the National People's Congress into two houses. One will be called the House of Regional Representatives, whose members will represent various localities. The other will be called the House of Social Representatives, whose members will represent the interests of various strata and various enterprises. The House of Regional Representatives will have fewer members, say 300, and will also be called the first house. The House of Social Representatives, or the second house, will have a larger number of members, say 700. These two houses will jointly exercise legislative power and the power of creating various systems, jointly supervise the government's work, and jointly exercise the highest state power. The two houses of such a people's congress will impose a constraint on each other. Neither one of them will have the final say. If one house makes an incorrect decision, the other will be able to rectify it. Such a congress system will facilitate the consideration of the interests of various localities and various nationalities as well as facilitate the handling of contradictions among various parts of the people, that is, the contradictions among people of various occupations and various strata. The common responsibility of the two houses will be the correct handling of contradictions among the people. Moreover, in order that the state budget and the state's economic construction plans may be worked out expeditiously and that the conditions and experiences in implementing the plans and budgets may be studied and summed up opportunely, the meetings will probably have to be convened more frequently, say twice a year. The duration of each meeting should also be longer. At present, each session lasts for something more than a week to around ten days. Actually such a meeting is to adopt certain laws that have been formulated by our Party and organs beforehand. It is probably correct for people to call our National People's Congress a "rubber stamp." The same is true for the Soviet of the USSR, at which people just raise their hands to adopt those documents that have been fully prepared by the Party organs. Therefore, merely convening two meetings a year will not be adequate for our purpose; we should also increase the number of standing bodies of the congress. Both houses must have their standing bodies, which should be simple in structure as well as capable and vigorous. Therefore, their members must be fewer. At present, the conducting of meetings is not convenient for those standing committees with around 300 members. However, it will be easy for a standing committee with 60 to 70 members to convene a meeting. At present, the members of our standing committees are old people. Some of those seventy- or eighty-year-old people have difficulty in walking and must be supported by other people, and may even be unable to attend meetings. Are they not committee members in name only? In the future, our standing committee members will all be young, healthy, and capable of working 8 hours a day. They should be experienced, and their abilities should be up to a certain standard. They will work full time as committee members and will not perform other duties. The head of a department cannot be concurrently a standing committee member of the National People's Congress. A standing committee should be at the same level as a department. Each 50- to 70-member standing committee should be capable and organizationally simple. Its members should work all year long in the committee. Aside from going to the localities for investigation work, they will discuss problems at meetings, perform legislative duties and various planning tasks, make comparisons between our country and foreign countries as well as between the present and the past, and thus help ensure the interests of the people of socialism. Just as bourgeois parliaments safeguard the interests of the bourgeoisie, we must ensure the interests of the proletariat and the people. In addition, various kinds of special committees, such as economic, financial, and labor committees, should be formed in both houses. The special committees should employ the right scholars, experts, and consultants and organize various brain trusts. Thus, the organs of power will become authoritative and effective organs of power that can represent the people. The People's Congress will thus carry out the regular work of law making and supervising the government.

Three Principles of the Legal System

To strengthen socialist democracy and the legal system, we must work in conjunction with the whole nation to gradually perfect our constitution and laws and turn them into an indestructible force through indomitable struggles. We must build a perfect socialist legal system and must not allow anyone to damage this system. We must establish the principles of this socialist legal system. We should have these three principles.

The first principle is that all are equal before the law. All are equal with respect to the obligations and rights specified by the law. No one will be allowed to enjoy any special privileges above the law or any protection that enables him to evade legal obligations or punishment by law.

The second principle is that the law safeguards the personal freedom and other civil rights of all citizens. Illegal infringement or encroachment must be penalized by law. During the "Great Cultural Revolution," people could arrest you, search your house, and confiscate your property at will, and could extort a confession from you by torture. In the future, these will be impossible. Anyone who commits illegal infringement will be punished by law. Our public security organs will arrest anyone who arbitrarily searches other people's houses, confiscates their property, or arrests them, and will conduct investigations and require him to bear legal responsibilities.

The third legal principle is that when judicial officials conduct a trial, they will only respect the facts and the law. No one will be allowed to interfere in the independent activities of the judicial officials in their work. In short, the judiciary must be independent. Even Party committees will not be able to interfere in this independence. When a court of law passes a verdict, it will not have to send it to any Party committee for examination. A Party committee will not have such power. It will be responsible for political leadership only, and not for passing verdicts. It must not interfere in judicial work. Only thus can judicial independence be achieved.

All these basic principles of the legal system must become common knowledge understood by every household and norms observed by everyone in the political life of the whole Party and whole nation. These principles must be generally applicable.

The Work of the Party and the Work of the Administrative Organs Must Be Divided

The second area of democratization of our country's political life is to eliminate the phenomenon of fusion of the Party and the administrative organs, with the Party undertaking administrative work, and to separate the work of the Party from the work of the administrative organs. The Party's work must be separated from the work of various economic and cultural organizations, mass organizations, the media, and so on. The so-called unified leadership, the fusion of Party and administrative organs, and the undertaking of administrative work by the Party provided an asylum for a dictator to exercise autocratic rule and resulted in the violation of the principle of socialist democracy that should have been the source of vigor in our country's political life. How should these defects be remedied? Comrade Deng Xiaoping's speech on August 18 pointed out the need to really build the governments at various levels, from the State Council to the localities, and to build a powerful and effective working system that extends from top to bottom. In the future, the State Council and various local governments will discuss, make decisions on, and issue documents concerning all the work that lies within the jurisdiction of the government, and the Party Central Committee or the local Party committees at various levels will not give instructions or make decisions about such work. Of course, governmental work will be carried out under the Party's political leadership. Therefore the work of the government will increase and Party leadership will also be strengthened. That is, the government will assume the sole responsibility of doing governmental work, and Party committees or Party committee secretaries will not exceed their function and meddle in the government's affairs. The Party committees should perform their own duties, formulate as well as supervise the implementation of the Party's line, principles, and policies, and carry out the Party's organizational propaganda and disciplinary work. The Party should also exercise political leadership over the government's work, propagate and implement the Party's line, principles, and policies through the Party members who work in the government, and must not use the method of coercive decrees. In particular, the Party should not interfere in the government's routine work. Only thus can the government's work and the Party's political leadership be simultaneously strengthened. Otherwise, if the Party is not separated from the government and if the Party undertakes the government's work, then the government will be weakened, because it will not be able to assume sole responsibility for its work, and Party leadership will also be weakened, because it will be engaged in governmental work and will inevitably commit the errors of bureaucracy and routinism. Then, the political leadership of the Party as well as the propaganda work and organization of the Party committees will be weakened. Don't people talk about the Party neglecting self-supervision? It is because the Party meddles in government affairs and cannot manage itself satisfactorily. That is, it does not do its own proper work.

If We Do Not Change Our Course, We Will Also Experience a Crisis Like the "Polish Crisis"

Similarly, the Party should ensure that various financial, economic, educational, scientific, and cultural organizations as well as various mass organizations and the media will be under the correct leadership of the Party's line, principles, and policies. If the Party's line, principles, and policies are not correct, the Party will be unable to exercise leadership. The Party must ensure that such organizations will work independently, efficiently (which is a particularly important point), and in coordination, and that they do their utmost in the interests of the masses whom they represent. In social life and state life, differences of opinion are normal, and the Party and the state should prevent their degeneration into antagonism and should guide the organizations concerned in resolving these differences rationally and in a democratic way. Only thus can a socialist society be lively and vigorous. Only thus can splits and disturbances in a socialist society be avoided as far as possible. At present our mass organizations include trade unions, youth leagues, women's federations, science associations, and writers' unions. In the past the Party ran the business of these mass organizations, so that these so-called mass organizations became bodies similar to Party organs. They have been unable to represent the interests of the masses, to provide a link between the Party and the masses, or to serve as a means by which the Party can correctly handle the contradictions among the people. Thus we have been deceiving ourselves. The workers are not permitted to elect the officials of the so-called trade unions. The Party just arbitrarily appoints the officials. Thus the unions do not represent the workers' interests. Lenin said that even under the socialist system trade unions must still safeguard the interests of the laborers, that is, workers. He said that when part of the workers have a conflict of interests with the economic management personnel of the state enterprises or with the state organs, the trade unions concerned must quickly and satisfactorily resolve the conflict through negotiations or consultations with the administrative authorities of the enterprises or with the state organs, or resolve the conflict by persuading the workers. He said, for one thing, that the trade unions must help the workers whom they represent gain the maximum amount of benefit, but without simultaneously harming the interests of the state, of economic construction, and of other members of the population; and for another thing, the trade unions must provide political education for the workers. In particular, the trade unions must teach the workers that the working class is the leading force in the country and society, and that the interests of the whole are identical to those of the individual. However, when Comrades Li Lisan and Lai Ruoyu, who were responsible for leadership over the trade unions at that time, wanted to act in this way and to safeguard the workers' interests, they were imperiously and unjustly branded with the labels of syndicalism, economism, and opposing the Party and socialism. Comrade Li Lisan was thus unjustly denounced in 1951. Comrade Lai Ruoyu was similarly denounced in 1958, and the four labels were hurled at him. (Li Lisan was charged with syndicalism and economism and was not considered as an anti-Party and antisocialist element. The anti-Party and antisocialist labels were hurled at Lai Ruoyu.) They were blamed quite imperiously and unjustly. This could only ruin the link between the masses of workers and the Party and trade unions, so that the Party and trade unions were divorced from the masses of workers. Such an erroneous "left" deviationist practice is breeding a crisis of the Polish type. We all know what has happened in Poland. If we do not change our course, the same things will happen to us. Will the working class not rise in rebellion? Therefore, our trade unions and mass organizations must be thoroughly reformed and the masses of workers must be allowed to enjoy freedom and democracy in electing their own trade union leaders and officials of their leading bodies, so that the masses of workers will be able to form their own trade unions. These leaders and leading bodies must faithfully represent the masses of workers and independently work for the socialist trade unions. Mass organizations of workers, young people, women, scientists, and writers are socialist organizations, and the Party should also exercise political leadership over their work through the efforts of Party members who work in these mass organizations, who will propagate and implement the Party's line, principles, and policies. However, the Party must not interfere in the routine business of these organizations or arbitrarily dismiss the leaders of these organizations from their posts.

Establish Independent Peasant Associations

The peasants, who account for over 80 percent of the total population of our country, have not yet formed organizations that represent their interests, namely, national and local peasant associations at various levels. Some foreign friends have raised this question: Why don't you establish peasant associations? I think this is a very reasonable idea. The absence of peasant associations is unfavorable to safeguarding the peasants' interests and to strengthening the worker-peasant alliance. The National People's Congress will be divided into a House of Regional Representatives and a House of Social Representatives, and the latter will consist of the deputies elected by the people in various strata and various occupations. Therefore, I think the establishment of an independent peasant association—an all-China peasants' union or association— is inevitable. We should not fear that this peasant association will rise in rebellion. It will not do so. In the past some people said that peasant associations were unnecessary, because the National People's Congress and the people's congresses at various levels did represent the peasants. Actually, these congresses are not devoted to representing the peasants; they represent the whole people, the people of various strata. The peasants should have their own independent organizations. Only thus can the contradictions among the people be correctly handled. The prices of our agricultural products have remained low for many years. The price scissors [price differential between agricultural and industrial products] have not narrowed. On the contrary, they have sometimes widened. The peasants' interests cannot be safeguarded. Even now, rice is grown at a loss. All these undesirable phenomena may be eliminated if the peasants have their own independent organizations.

Will the contradictions among the people increase and intensify if various units and organizations assume sole responsibility for their work under the leadership of the Party's line, principles, and policies, and if national and local peasant associations at various levels are established? I do not think so. On the contrary, this will be a practical measure of great significance that will genuinely help correctly handle the contradictions among the people and help mobilize all positive factors.

Journalists Should Report
News Independently

Moreover, the relationship between the Party and the media should also undergo a similar change. The Party has resolved to adopt the policy of informing the people of everything in principle. As Comrade Wan Li said at the National People's Congress, we have resolved to tell the people everything, including financial deficits. It has been made public that the financial deficit amounted to over 18 billion yuan last year; it was no longer kept secret from the people. In order that the media can play the role of quickly and effectively propagating the policies and decrees of the Party and the government, can opportunely inform the people of all important events aside from a minority of secrets concerning national defense and diplomacy, and can opportunely reflect the people's criticisms of and suggestions to the Party and state organs, we should permit, require, and encourage the media, the journalists, and the commentators to independently assume the responsibility of reporting or publishing news, letters from the masses, and comments. I think that such broad freedom of the press, freedom of speech, and freedom of publication, which exist under the leadership of the Party's line, principles, and policies, is of prime importance to democratizing the Party and the state. It will be a key step in promoting the democratization of the Party and the state. Of course, the mass media, journalists, and commentators must be responsible to the Party and the people. If they violate Party discipline or state decrees, they should be investigated for legal responsibility by the Party organs for inspecting discipline and by the judicial organs of the state. Although the specific elaboration in the latter part of the foregoing discussion represents my personal opinions, the aforesaid principle that the media should independently assume their responsibility under the political leadership of the Party has already been decided.

Democratizing the Management of
Enterprises and Other Businesses

The third aspect of the democratization of our country's political life is to reform the system of leadership adopted by various enterprises and business units. Comrade Xiaoping said in his August 18 speech that we must make the necessary preparations and then gradually alter the present system whereby the factory directors and managers assume responsibility under the leadership of the Party committees. We must conduct experiments and then implement on a gradually increasing scale a new system whereby the factory directors and managers assume responsibility under the leadership and supervision of factory management committees, company directorates, or economic committees of integrated economic organizations. Moreover, we must also consider reforming the system whereby the heads of schools, universities, and various institutes assume responsibility under the leadership of the Party committee, step by step and with due preparations. Why must we effect such reforms? It is because that kind of system of leadership being practiced in enterprises and businesses, called the leadership of the Party committees, is actually a system of dictatorial rule by the Party committee secretaries, who have the final say on any matter. Moreover these Party committee secretaries are mostly laymen in the enterprises and businesses over which they exercise leadership. Thus, the Party committees and their secretaries inevitably act against the principle that Party leadership should be confined to political leadership. At the enterprises and businesses, they interfere in work with which they are absolutely unfamiliar. Thus, the responsibility of the Party to exercise political leadership is weakened or even abandoned, and the administrative leadership over and management of the enterprises and businesses are also weakened and hampered. Moreover, this so-called system of the leadership of Party committees, which actually allows the Party committee secretaries to wield absolute power, is completely contradictory to the democratization of enterprise or business management. The enterprises and businesses should be managed by the masses, not by the Party. The people are the masters of the enterprises. If the Party manages them, then the masses will not consider the factories as theirs, but will consider them as belonging to other people, and [this] impairs the right of the masses to be the masters. Such an undemocratic system, marked by overconcentration of power, is quite unfavorable to modernizing and democratizing enterprise management and making it scientific. On the contrary, we must implement the principle of separating the work of the Party from the work of administrative organs in the enterprises and businesses and enable the administrative and management personnel of the enterprises and businesses to independently assume the responsibility of managing the enterprises and businesses. Moreover, we must enable the Party committees of the enterprises and businesses to free themselves from the routine affairs that should not be managed by them, so that they will be able to concentrate their efforts on ideological, political, organizational, and supervisory work. Doing a good job of such work is actually their principal obligation and their proper duty. Of course, this is a major reform, and before the regulations concerning the new system are worked out, the existing system must still be practiced to avoid confusion. Nevertheless, in practicing the existing system, the defect of the Party committee secretaries enjoying absolute power must be overcome. We should not allow one person alone to have the say and should practice the mass line.

Direct Democracy Should Be Practiced at the Grass-roots Levels

The fourth aspect of the democratization of our country's political life is to democratize the enterprises and business units and to practice democracy in the government in the social life of the grass-roots levels. To achieve this, in our economic reform we must integrate the expansion of enterprise decision-making power with the democratization of enterprise management. What we call enterprises here include rural communes and production teams. Such an expansion of decision-making power does not mean the expansion of individual persons' power to have the say; it means the expansion of the democratic power of the masses. In his August 18 speech, Comrade Xiaoping said that the general institution of workers' councils and workers representatives' meetings in the enterprises and business units had already been decided upon long ago, and the question now is to popularize and perfect such a system. Workers' councils existed before the Great Cultural Revolution, but were later abolished. The workers' councils and workers' representatives' meetings will have the power to discuss and make decisions on important matters of the workers' own units, will have the power to recommend to higher levels the dismissal of incompetent leading personnel of their own units, and may gradually come to practice the election of an appropriate range of leaders. Obviously the workers' councils or workers' representatives' meetings will elect and give rise to leading bodies that will manage the enterprises or businesses, will include the administrative leaders of the enterprises or businesses as their members, and will help enable the working masses to become the real masters of various enterprises or businesses. As for the practicing of direct democracy at the grass-roots levels, the new constitution will specify the principle that in the government and the social life of the grass-roots levels, direct democracy must be fully implemented in every residential district, so that every citizen will really be able to participate in discussing and making decisions on various public affairs which are directly related to their livelihood and interests. The democratization of enterprise and business management and the implementation of direct democracy at the grass-roots levels will constitute a firm and reliable basis for a highly democratic socialist political system. The adoption of these important measures will provide ample evidence that our Party completely trusts and relies on the people and faithfully serves the people. None of the states in the West nor any of the social capitalist and social imperialist states under the cover of pragmatism or pragmatic socialism dare practice such democracy. The Soviet Union knows that it is not practicing scientific or Marxist socialism. It calls its own system pragmatic socialism. However, it is actually practicing social capitalism and social imperialism. It is very afraid of and never talks about letting the masses manage the enterprises or practicing direct democracy. However, we dare to do it and will certainly do it. The discussion above concerns democratizing our country's political life and provides an outline of the highly democratic political system we mentioned earlier.

The Party Center Will Set Up Three Committees to Mutually Supervise and Constrain One Another

In his speech of August 18 on democratizing the political life of the Party, Comrade Xiaoping not only put forward the general principle of reforming the present system of Party and state leadership marked by concentration of power, but also put forward the two specific reforms described below. The first will be the reform of the highest leading bodies of the Party. The new national congress of the Party will not elect and give rise to a single Central Committee that enjoys absolute power, but will elect three parallel central committees that will mutually supervise and impose constraints on one another. In his speech of August 18, Comrade Deng Xiaoping said that the Party Central Committee has already set up a discipline inspection committee, and the establishment of a consultative committee, whose name is to be finalized, is under consideration. These two committees, together with the Party Central Committee, will be elected at the national congress of the Party. Each of them will have clearly defined tasks and jurisdictions of its own. We should also consider establishing similar corresponding bodies to work in parallel with the State Council. Then, a large number of old comrades, who originally worked in the Party Central Committee and the State Council, will be able to put their experience to use and will be able to play a guiding, supervisory, and advisory role. Moreover, this will help enable the groups in the Central Committee and State Council that perform day-to-day duties to become simpler in organization, become more capable, and gradually become younger.

I think that the most important implication of this measure is that it will be conducive to overcoming the defect of overconcentration of power in the Party. This measure amounts to an appropriate division of power within the central leading body, with the three central bodies mutually supervising and imposing constraints on each other, so that they will be able to jointly and correctly exercise the highest leadership power of the Party when the national congress of the Party is not in session. We see that the National People's Congress will be divided into two houses, and the State Council is going to have its supervisory and advisory agencies, which may be called the executive committee or consultative committee or something else. The judicial organs of the state have already been divided into the Supreme People's Procuratorate, the Supreme People's Court, and the Ministry of Public Security, which mutually impose constraints on one another. These are all examples of the appropriate division of power and mutual restriction. These are correct measures that prevent the abuse of power in general or by any single body. Democracy is a unity of many coordinated varieties of things. Under socialist democracy, these varied, coordinated, and unified bodies will form an automatic regulatory system that will correctly handle the contradictions among the people as well as the contradictions between the enemy and ourselves, and which will prevent the degeneration of socialism or the outbreak of rebellions or other unexpected incidents. We want to build such a system, which will help prevent and rectify errors. If, on the contrary, Party and state power is overly concentrated, then actually we can only have unity in form, which is mechanical, as well as bureaucratism and autocracy, which suppress the people's creativity and enthusiasm in many varieties of things. Although we have unity in form and a very high degree of centralization, actually our system will be bureaucratic, autocratic, and powerless. Such a system, marked by overcentralization of power, is against, contradictory to, and incompatible with the principle of socialist public ownership and socialist democracy, as well as against basic Marxist principles.

Abolish the Politburo and Establish Executive, Supervisory, and Discipline Inspection Bodies

Some comrades propose that the three central bodies should be named according to their particular duties, for example, the existing Central Committee may be renamed the Central Executive Committee. This name was adopted by our Chinese Communist Party during the initial period after its founding. Its duty will be to implement the resolutions of the national Party congress, and therefore we use the term executive. It will be an executive body and will be the counterpart of the State Council. As for the second committee, Comrade Deng Xiaoping initially inquired whether it might be called the consultative committee. Of course it may be given some other name. The name of Central Supervisory Committee has been proposed because its main duty will be to make recommendations, to exercise supervision and inspection, and to urge other bodies in their work. It will supervise the work of the Central Executive Committee. Its members will be the revolutionaries of the older generation, who have rich experience, are still be able to work, but are rather weak physically. Each of these old comrades will seem to have a scepter. If the Central Committee commits an error, they will knock their scepters and warn that there is an error that must be rectified. We must let them give such warnings and rectify the errors of the Central Executive Committee. There must be a standing committee under the Central Executive Committee, and the Politburo must be abolished. When Lenin set up the Politburo, it was parallel to the Organizational Bureau. Later the Organizational Bureau was abolished. Why do we still call ours a politburo? This is unreasonable. We should call it a standing committee. The plenum of the Central Executive Committee will elect the standing committee. There will also be a Secretariat of the Central Executive Committee to perform routine duties. Correspondingly, the Central Supervisory Committee will elect its own standing committee, whose power will correspond to that of the standing committee under the Central Executive Committee, and will have its own secretariat, whose staff will be the sturdier old comrades, who will perform routine work. The third body will be the Central Discipline Inspection Committee, whose duty will be to maintain good discipline in the Party, to rectify the Party's style of work, as well as to exercise supervision and inspection and carry out rectification when violations of Party discipline occur. Its tasks will be clear-cut. These three bodies will be jointly responsible to the National Party Congress. What should be done if some controversy arises among them? If their views differ, they may convene a joint conference. If any controversies are not successfully resolved at a joint conference, a national congress of the Party should be convened. Such a congress may be convened at any time because it is a permanent organization. This authoritative organization will then make the final decision. Thus, there will be a safeguard against our Party committing major errors in political leadership. Major issues will be discussed by the whole Party.

Another important implication or purpose for establishing three Central Committees is that this will enable some very experienced old comrades to play a guiding, supervisory, and advisory role more satisfactorily, that is, to do what they are most capable of. Thus, they will not be overtired. Their weakness is that they are easily overtired. We will kill them if we ask these old and feeble comrades to work eight hours a day in the office. Thus our purpose is to bring their good points into play and get around their weaknesses. Moreover, our new system will help enable the groups working in the Central Committees and State Council to be simpler in organization, to be more capable and efficient, and to gradually become younger, so that the leading groups of the Party and the state will not get older and less efficient. At present, our leaders are getting so old that they cannot even walk, but they are still working in leading positions. To change this situation will be the first step to be taken in democratizing the political life of the Party.

The Draft Party Constitution Adopted at the Fifth Plenum of the Central Committee Must Be Largely Revised

The second step to be taken is that the Party committees at various levels and various leading bodies must gradually implement the principle of democracy and genuinely practice the system whereby leadership is integrated with the assumption of responsibility for different tasks by different individuals. The key measure in genuinely implementing the principles of democracy and collective leadership will be the implementation of the democratic voting system that allows each person to cast one vote. Comrade Deng Xiaoping said that if the Party committees at various levels really want to implement the system that integrates collective leadership with the assumption of responsibility for different tasks by different individuals, they must be able to clearly distinguish those matters that should be discussed collectively from those that should be the responsibility of certain individuals. Important matters must be discussed by the collective, and relevant decisions must be made by the collective. In voting on a resolution, we must strictly observe the rules that the minority must be subordinate to the majority and that each person can cast only one vote. A secretary will only have the right to cast one vote and will not have the [final] say. Any task that has been collectively decided on must be done, with each individual responsible for one part of the work. No one will be allowed to shift his duties onto other people. Anyone who neglects his duties must be investigated and held responsible.

To achieve the democratization of the political life of the Party, the Party Central Committee has resolved to make further and drastic amendments to the draft Party constitution adopted at the Fifth Plenum of the Central Committee. The new constitution, in addition to giving expression to the two major reforms mentioned above, must establish the following important principles, which have been written down in the "Resolution on Certain Questions in Our Party's History." First among these principles is that we must correctly fix the position of the Party in state activities. Our country's people's democratic dictatorship must be led by the Communist Party. Leadership requires a certain degree of authority, and therefore leadership must be correct. Errors are unavoidable in exercising leadership. However, to prevent the aggravation of errors, we should impose a certain limit on authority of any kind and must not have absolute authority. The practice of Party leadership over the people's democratic dictatorship does not imply that the Party's activities may be free from any restriction. Any restriction that is appropriate will not hamper the correct and effective leadership of the Party and will also restrain the Party when it commits errors. In the first place, the Party organizations at all levels, ranging from the central committees to the grass-roots organizations, must rigorously observe the constitution and laws, which are created by the Party and the people, in all their activities. All Party activities must be carried out within the limits of the constitution and the laws. Otherwise, all state organs and the people will have the power to boycott the activities. They will have the power to resist and oppose any Party organizations or leaders that break the law. This is a matter of principle. No Party organization or leader should have unlimited powers. They should set an example in observing the constitution and the laws.

Second, the relationship of unity and mutual supervision between our Party and other parties and groups or the masses who follow our Party must be strengthened. We must persist in and continue to implement the principle of permanent coexistence and mutual supervision with regard to the relationship between the CCP and other parties and groups. Non-Party personages who take up leading duties should be assigned the relevant posts and should have the relevant power and responsibility, as Party members do. The Party should help them overcome their difficulties and provide them with favorable conditions for their work. Our Party must continue to invite, on our own initiative, other parties and groups and personalities without any Party affiliation to discuss major issues and to attend certain Party meetings. Thus, our Party organizations may discuss with them ways of solving the problems in the life of our state as well as jointly carry out criticism and self-criticism with them.

Third, our Party must adhere to and perfect the system of democratic centralism. We must resolutely implement the principles that the Party Central Committee has resolved of guarding against the overconcentration of power in any individual leaders, abolishing the system of lifelong tenure, and reducing publicity of individuals. Moreover, the correct relationship among Party members at various levels must be specified. Only in their work must those at the lower levels be subordinate to those at the higher levels. In other respects, all Party members must be equal. There is no such thing as a higher-class Party and a lower-class Party. No one must be allowed to place himself above the Party organization, or to enjoy special privileges that are not specified in the Party regulations, the laws of the state, or other rules and regulations. Any rules or regulations that provide for unreasonable privileges must be amended. Moreover, every level of the Party, whether it be high or low, must supervise the other levels. At various Party meetings, the vast numbers of Party members and the organizations at the lower levels will have the right to voice criticism of the organizations at the higher levels or the leaders at any level. We must continue to devote our efforts to perfecting our Party system and its organization, bodies, and so on, and must strengthen supervisory measures to prevent Party organizations at various levels from violating the Party codes or Party constitution. If such violations occur, then we will be able to discover and rectify them more opportunely.

Will the Reform Be Abortive?

We have discussed the main contents of the 1980 Reform or socialist reform. Some people worry about whether this reform will be aborted or are skeptical about its success. Some people even compare our 1980 reform with the reform movement of 1898. They say that the forces of the traditionalists and the resistance are too strong, and that if the pace of the reform is too fast, it may end up like the reform movement of 1898, which failed utterly and ended with the murder of Tan Sitong and his co-workers—the group of reformers known as the six gentlemen. People who hold such views are pessimistic about the prospects of this reform. I think that this comparison is incorrect. At that time, Kang Yuwei and Liang Qichao, who initiated the reform movement of 1898, relied on the poor young Guangxu emperor, who had no real power and was controlled by the Empress Dowager, the leader of the diehards. Therefore, it was easy for the diehards, who mastered the whole forces of the Qing dynasty, to crush the reform movement with bloodshed. Is the situation in 1980 identical or similar to the situation in 1898? The resistance to reform does exist and will continue to exist in the future. When Marx wrote the draft of the book *The Civil War in France* in 1871, he foresaw that the cause of rejuvenation, namely, socialist reform and construction, would be hampered and delayed because of the resistance arising from vested interests and class selfishness, and would consequently have to undergo a long process of development. We should be able to envisage this.

19

Letter to the Editor

HIGHER LEVELS FIXING THE TEAM LEADER IS NOT DEMOCRATIC

LAST YEAR WE WENT to a production brigade in the countryside and came across the following case: A production team held an election to decide on the choice of its team leader. Most members of the team were in favor of Yahuo, who was impartial and had the lofty aspiration to change the backward

"Shangmian quanding duizhang jiushi bu minzhu." *Nanfang ribao* [Southern Daily], February 14, 1979, p. 3. Translated by Ai Ping.

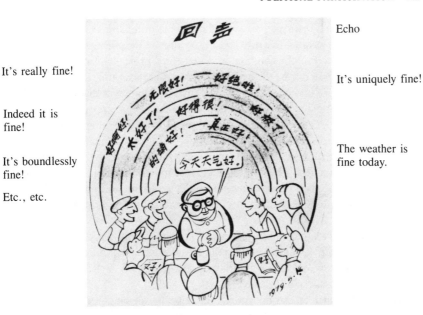

It's really fine!

Indeed it is fine!

It's boundlessly fine!

Etc., etc.

Echo

It's uniquely fine!

The weather is fine today.

ECHO

Huisheng, by Huang Weiqiang

When the leader declares his position, no matter how trivial the issue, his subordinates try to outdo each other in voicing agreement.

appearance of the production team. He was concerned about both production and income and willing to guide the members in following the path of getting rich together. Nevertheless, the commune leadership was against the choice; they thought Yahuo followed the tail of the masses, yielding to the masses' desire for making money and was indifferent to the commune-sponsored water conservation project. As the masses' desire was out of line with the leadership's intention, the commune sent people to persuade the team members not to elect Yahuo but another villager by the name of Yaming as the team leader. The team members were not convinced. Finally, the commune, disregarding the masses' opposition, issued a notice to the production brigade approving of Yaming as the team leader. The production brigade had no choice but took the notice to the production team and made the announcement. When the team members heard about the choice of Yaming as their leader, they said discontentedly: "Since the higher authorities have decided to designate Yaming as the production leader, why did they ask us to hold the election? All they had to do was to issue a notice. Why should they take all the trouble to do this?"

Things like this are a common occurrence in the countryside. Similar cases also happen in elections held in factories and government offices. In electing model workers, and respresentatives and members of leading bodies, the general practice is for the leadership to present a slate and the voters either approve it by a show of hands or circle the candidates' names on a preset ballot. The leadership will send people to persuade the workers if any differences arise and will force the masses to vote for candidates whom they dislike. Once you raise an objection, you will be criticized as advocating "absolute democracy," "bourgeois democracy," etc. Does such a practice conform to the principle of people's democracy? As far as we know, some leading cadres still maintain a wait-and-see attitude toward the democratic election of team and group leaders, section chiefs, and workshop directors. They are afraid that democratic elections may generate confusion and that good people may not be elected to the leading posts. They are fearful that the Party leadership might be weakened because of the democratic process.

The above shows that leading comrades, under the influence of Lin Biao and the "Gang of Four," still entertain quite a few misconceptions about "What is socialist democracy? What is bourgeois democracy?" or "Does democracy generate or eliminate confusion?"

In order to clarify these questions, we hope the news media can conduct a discussion on the issue of democracy so as to enhance the understanding of all of us.

20

Letter to the Editor

THIS SORT OF FIXING IS NECESSARY

HAVING READ THE articles on "How to Foster Socialist Democracy" published in your newspaper, I disagree with the views contained in the article "Higher Levels Fixing the Team Leader Is Not Democratic." [Selection 19]

In regard to the issue of elections, it is necessary to foster democracy and to solicit the opinions of the masses. However, we cannot follow behind the masses and appoint as cadres whoever is chosen by them. The reason is twofold: First, the position of the masses often prevents them from making an overall appraisal of a cadre, and their view tends to be one-sided. Second, right now in some units, especially the grass-roots units in the countryside, the masses are still affected by a strong feudal patriarchal mentality. In conducting an election, some people, instead of furthering the interests of the Party and the collective, often proceed

"Zhezhong 'quanding' shi biyaode." *Nanfang ribao* [Southern Daily], February 21, 1979. Translated by Ai Ping.

from the benefit of an individual, a small group, or even a feudal patriarchal faction. Consequently, the cadres they elect do not meet the requirements of cadres of the Party. There is such a case in our area.

We had a person who was not politically adept, but he really knew something about production and had a rich knowledge of the ways of the world. Some people remarked: ''To get rich we must rely on him.'' Therefore, quite a few members of the production team voted for him during the election of team cadres. There was another who came from a poor family, was politically adept, and was also quite good at production. But the masses thought he was incapable of developing connections to earn extra income for the production team. During the election very few people voted for him. Having conducted an overall evaluation of the two candidates, the Party committee at the higher level vetoed the person elected by the majority of the team members and upheld the person disliked by quite a few of them. Was such a decision on the choice of cadre correct? I think so. This is because ours is not a democracy in absolute terms but a democracy under centralized guidance. We cannot emphasize either democracy or centralism at the expense of the other.

21

Shui Fang

WHOM DOES HE REPRESENT?

WHILE CHEN SUIHENG, a deputy mayor of Nanjing and not a Communist Party member, was investigating the city's sanitation, he criticized the work of the Jiangsu provincial bureau of environmental protection. The bureau chief was displeased and said: ''I represent the Communist Party. Whom does he (meaning Chen) represent?''

In the opinion of the bureau chief, he himself represents the Communist Party because he is a Party member. But, is an individual Party member the same as the Party? The answer, of course, is no. To determine whether a Party member represents the interests of the Party, it is insufficient just to see whether he is a Party member in name. It depends on whether he acts according to the Party's line and policies and whether he really measures up to the standards of being a Party member. Everyone can see that in his attitude toward criticism the bureau chief did not in the least have the appearance of a Communist Party member, for a Party member cannot reject well-intentioned criticism (whether from the leader-

---

'' 'Daibiao shei' ban.'' *Renmin ribao* [People's Daily], April 11, 1983. Translated by Ai Ping.

ship or from the masses), even if the criticism is not completely correct.

When Chen Suiheng was challenged, he didn't argue. Later, when Hui Yuyu, governor of Jiangsu Province, learned about the affair, he said to Chen: "You could have told the bureau chief that you represent the people of Nanjing, because you have been elected by the city's 3.6 million people." In his investigation of Nanjing's sanitation, Chen was using the people's power, representing their interest. How could the bureau chief criticize this?

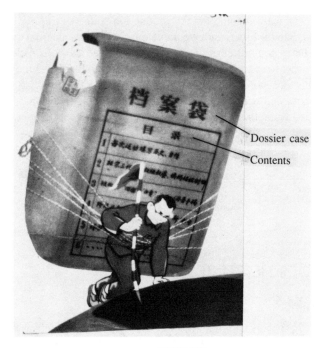

BURDEN
Baofu, by Jiang Peiyang

This shows the burden intellectuals in post-1949 China have not been able to escape: their class origin and political record follow them wherever they go.

Communist Party history demands that Party members cooperate with and respect the office of those comrades who are not Party members. Comrade Mao Zedong several decades ago criticized Party members and cadres who abuse comrades outside of the Party. This bureau chief and any other comrades who share his views should ask themselves: Do the people's representatives have the power to supervise their work? Do their words and behavior conform to the state constitution and Party regulations? Only after they have considered these questions can they meet the demands of our times in their own words and behavior.

22

DISCUSSING THE THREE DIFFICULTIES OF NEWSPAPERS BECOMING CRITICAL

A Monthly Review of Incoming Letters and Visits

IN OCTOBER THIS newspaper received 13,333 letters and 1,204 visits from its readership, a total of 14,537. As work for wage adjustments and school entrance examinations had been basically completed, there were 3,799 fewer incoming letters and visits than in the preceding month. One hundred and forty-three letters (visits) were published or reported in the newspaper and other internal publications, and a few of them were also handled by the newspaper itself. All the rest were turned over to the departments concerned for settlement.

The letters and visits focused on the following problems: (1) Easing up of economic policies led to an increase of traffickers who bought things in other places to be resold in Shanghai. Consequently, it became increasingly more difficult to buy train, bus, and steamer tickets and the hotels were all overcrowded. (2) Public vehicles were jam packed and the quality of service needed further improvement. Many readers suggested changes in the new regulations set forth by the Public Transportation Company on renewing monthly tickets. (3) The service of shop assistants in a few stores worsened after the conclusion of the "double good" movement. They refused to answer any questions from customers and even went to the extreme of beating or abusing them. (4) After newspapers reported the story of how Chen Aiwu criticized the minister of commerce for using his privileged position to get free meals, quite a few readers wrote to us to report similar incidents in Shanghai. They suggested that leading organs of the municipality put a brake on such irregularities. (5) Hard hit by frequent natural disasters this year, agricultural income is on the decline. Quite a few commune and production brigade leaders in the suburbs are pessimistic about the year end distribution, and a lot of commune members have gone outside to take up odd jobs or engage in business, thus adversely affecting agricultural production.

A newspaper speaks for the Party and the people. In order to give expression to the people's voice and demand and forge close ties between the Party and the people, we often select a portion of the readers' letters to be published as newspaper criticism. This work has enjoyed the strong support and close cooperation of leaders of most units, who regard criticism by the masses as a driving force to help them overcome bureaucracy and improve work. Nevertheless, we also feel deeply the obstruction and difficulties for newspapers to launch criti-

"Tantan baozhi kaizhan pipingde san nan." *Jiefang ribao* [Liberation Daily], November 18, 1980, p. 2. Translated by Ai Ping.

cism. Recently the *People's Daily* published a commentary entitled "Bring to the People the Message That 'Much Distress Regenerates a Nation,' " which explained, from the viewpoint of combining theory with practice, the necessity for newpapers to launch criticism. The article was well written, and we were greatly educated and encouraged after reading it. Availing ourselves of the opportunity to review incoming letters and visits this month, we would like to talk to the broad masses of readers about the problems we encounter in launching criticisms.

Difficulty Gathering Material

In publishing a reader's letter criticizing a certain unit or a certain cadre, the first difficulty we encounter is obstruction in the process of gathering material and checking the facts. Once we received a letter from a few rank-and-file cadres from Wanxiang Commune in Nanhui County reporting that one principal leader of the commune Party committee, taking advantage of his position and power, used public funds to build his own house and involved himself in entertaining guests and taking gifts. We dispatched a reporter to check the facts. On arriving at the commune office, our reporter found a comrade on duty bending over a newspaper while eating fruit. The reporter identified himself and asked the comrade on duty to find for him the person responsible for discipline inspection in the commune. The comrade on duty replied in a cheerless tone : "Now is the busy farming season. No one is available." Having no other alternative, the reporter was compelled to go elsewhere to inquire about the matter. Later he learned that the person he had to interview was now at a certain production brigade. The reporter then came back to the commune office and asked the comrade on duty to help him make a phone call to get in touch with that person. Pointing to the telephone set, the comrade on duty said: "To make a phone call doesn't cost you a penny. Can't you dial it youself?" With this, he lowered his head again to continue reading the newspaper. The reporter asked for his name and observed that a person on duty had the obligation to help make contacts. Suddenly [the comrade on duty] flew into a rage and shouted: "The secretary of Wanwu Production Brigade Party Branch was criticized in your newspaper. (*Note:* This referred to an incident a few days before when our newspaper published a reader's letter to criticize the branch secretary's ostentation and extravagance at his son's marriage.) Do you also want to criticize me in the newspaper for not having helped you make a phone call? You should not wilfully make trouble and keep finding fault with us."

In gathering material for critical articles, at times we also encounter obstruction from the leadership above. A few workers of Aizhen Electrical Appliance Factory in Chuansha County paid a visit to our newspaper to report that a dispute between the factory and two adjacent production teams had caused a shutdown of production in the factory, and they asked us to send people over to investigate. The next day one of our reporters went to the factory to talk to the Party branch leader. The branch leader reluctantly said: "This morning the deputy secretary of the county agricultural machinery industry bureau Party committee called us to say:

'If reporters from the *Liberation Daily* come to your factory for fact-finding, you should not talk with them.' Since the leadership gave the 'instruction' beforehand, this really puts us in a spot.'' Nevertheless, to solve the problem the branch leader agreed to brief the reporter on the situation. Why did the bureau leader issue the "prohibitive" instruction? It was because when the workers returned from their visit to the newspaper, they immediately spread the word throughout the factory. It happened that the bureau leader was also in the factory at that time. Fearful that the factory leader might "divulge" to the reporter something harmful, he called early next morning to warn the factory.

The above two incidents are typical of the ones our reporters encountered in their trips to gather material and check facts. There are often cases in which they get a perfunctory response, are given a cold shoulder, or have a warm reception first and a "cold" reception later. (If the reporter comes to cover some advanced deeds, the unit he visits welcomes him with a smiling face and serves him a cold drink in summer and hot tea in winter; later when they find out that the reporter has come to check facts about a criticism, they will find a pretext to stay away and allow the reporter to sit waiting or turn him over to some other organization.)

Difficulty Getting Manuscripts Approved

Newspapers that launch criticism run into the additional difficulty of getting the manuscripts approved. Some critical letters scheduled to be published are choked off for various "reasons" when submitted to concerned departments at a higher level for examination and approval. Submission for approval often turns out to be submission for "execution."

A few months back a reader wrote to us to report that a certain commune, disregarding the commune members' financial condition and the condition of their houses, ordered all of the commune members to pull down their houses and move so that they could launch a new peasants' housing estate project. The houses of some commune members had been newly built. The loans on the old houses had not been paid off before they were forced to raise money again in order to build the new estate. They poured out endless grievances. To build the new housing estate, vast stretches of fertile land were turned into housing foundations. Because the former foundations were built on inferior soil that had a lot of gravel, this land could not immediately be used for cultivation, which hurt agricultural production to a certain extent. Disregarding the realities of the commune, the leadership also embarked on huge projects to build roads and construct canals, arousing strong objection from the commune members. Our reporter submitted the galley proof of the letter to the county Party committee for examination and approval. One leader of the Party committee remonstrated: "Their projects have been discussed by the county Party committee. It was the advanced experience of a fraternal province. If you were to put it in the newspaper, wouldn't the whole thing be messed up?" He stubbornly refused to approve its publication, and the letter was thus nipped in the bud.

What we encounter even more often in getting manuscripts approved is stalling. Qingong Garment Factory expanded its workshop in violation of a construction ordinance, affecting the daily life of its neighbors. Because of this, residents of Lane 641 of Huangpi South Road paid a call on us. Our newspaper printed a galley proof of their letter of criticism and submitted it to the Municipal Garment and Accesories Industrial Company for examination and approval. A comrade from the company's office immediately responded: "We will certainly study this problem and have it resolved properly. But please do not publish it in the newspaper." At that time, we thought that since they were ready to take remedial action, there would be no necessity to publish the letter. However, a few months elapsed, and by the end of October the problem remained unresolved. There were also other cases in which the leaders, having read the galley proof of letters of criticism, refused to allow them to be published under the pretext that they were aimed at "an advanced collective" or "an advanced individual." Or in some cases these leaders might seek the good offices of others to come to our newspaper to intercede. And they might also try to drag their feet by using the pretext: "We are not clear about the situation and need to do some investigation."

Difficulty Getting Things Settled

We often hear people say that once a criticism is published in a newspaper, the problem will be readily solved. As a matter of fact, this is not necessarily true.

On September 1 we published a reader's letter that criticized a Wang X of the Plastics Section of the Municipal General Merchandise Purchase and Supply Center. He had availed himself of the opportunity of transferring downward the cooperative production of certain products to extort money from two enterprises run by production brigades. The next day our reporter contacted responsible comrades of the Plastics Section Party branch, asking them to look into the matter and report back to us how they resolved the problem. By October 25, the reporter had contacted them four more times, asking them to expedite the matter. Nevertheless, they only tried to explain things away for Wang instead of taking action to correct his mistakes.

On April 10 our newpaper published a reader's letter entitled "It Is No Good to 'Shield People on Their Own Side,' " which criticized individual comrades of the construction company under the Light Industry Bureau for shielding Gao X, a technical cadre of the company, who defaulted in paying his rent. A responsible person of the department concerned in the Light Industry Bureau attached great importance to the matter. He personally attended the meeting held by the real estate management station that had jurisdiction over Gao's house to show support for the reader's criticism. However, certain people of the construction company now still believe that Gao had his reasons for defaulting in paying the rent. With their sympathetic backing, Gao was more than 700 yuan in arrears as of October 31.

There are also leaders of some units who, instead of being glad to have their errors pointed out and corrected, fly into a rage when others point out their errors. Some give a "cold shoulder" to criticisms launched by the newspaper; they take

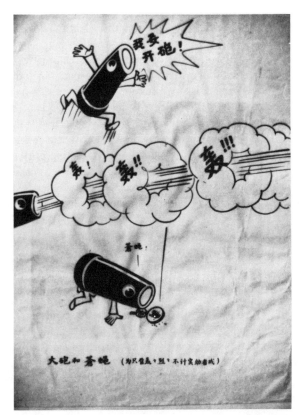

I want to fire
the cannon!

(Sound of cannon)

A fly

THE CANNON AND THE FLY
Dapao he cangying, by Tan Yuzhao

This cartoon ridicules the mass campaign method of policy implementation, so prominent a feature of the Maoist period. At the beginning of a campaign, a (symbolic) cannon is fired and the masses are mobilized to participate actively, with great results promised. In the end, however, as the discovery of the fly in the cartoon indicates, the results are minimal.

no action or give no response despite repeated inquiries from the newspaper. Some try to track down the authors of the critical letters in an attempt to retaliate. And some even come to our newspaper to make a scene. Many readers feel strongly about this and suggest that the newspaper choose some typical cases and expose them instantly. We think this is a good idea.

The "three difficulties" confronting our newspaper in publishing criticisms mirror the unhealthy work-style among certain Party organizations and individual leading cadres. They lack the spirit of conducting criticism and self-criticism and do not have a democratic way of doing things. They have no intention of accepting the masses' supervision. Therefore they are afraid of criticism rather than welcoming it.

Launching criticism and self-criticism is one of the Party's three great work-styles. That we are capable of conducting criticism and self-criticism, including making public criticism in the newspaper, is an expression of the Party's firmness and strength. The history of our Party shows that whenever criticism and self-criticism are well conducted in the Party, democracy is adequately practiced in both the Party and the state. Conversely, whenever intra-Party criticism and self-criticism are poorly handled, democracy is at a low ebb. Conducting criticism and self-criticism is also a principal measure in the acceptance of the masses' supervision. Therefore the resolution to improve newspaper work adopted by the Party Central Committee in 1954 requires that cadres at all levels "warmly welcome and resolutely protect criticisms by the laboring people from below." It is our hope that cadres in vast numbers, according to the requirements of the Central Committee's resolution, will treat criticisms from the people correctly, including criticisms made by the masses through the newspaper. With the help of everyone and with an attitude of being friendly with others and curing the disease to save the patient, we are prepared in the future to continue doing well the work of conducting criticism and self-criticism in the newspaper. Conscientious and responsible, we must dig deep into the problems so that all the facts can be verified and made clear as much as possible, or at least involve minimum discrepancies. If criticisms made by the newspaper are incorrect, we welcome explanation or even rebuttal from the person under criticism. We are also willing to make self-criticism openly. At the same time, it is our hope that Party organizations at different levels will lend us active support in our endeavor to conduct even better criticism and self-criticism, especially criticism from below.

23

LIAONING NPC DEPUTIES DEBATE ABOLISHING BIG-CHARACTER POSTERS

WHETHER BIG-CHARACTER posters [*dazibao*] should be abolished or not was the subject of a hot debate among deputies from Liaoning Province to the current session of the National People's Congress yesterday. The

Xinhua [New China News Agency],English, June 29, 1979. From FBIS Daily Report, June 29, 1979, pp. L3–L4.

deputies were gathering in a panel discussion on how to protect the people's democratic rights.

Forty-six-year-old peasant deputy Gan Yuanli proposed abolishing the use of big-character posters. He listed the following reasons:

—During the Great Cultural Revolution, many people put up big-character posters to practice bourgeois factionalism in an attempt to crush other factions.

—The form of the big-character poster is liable to be used by people to slander others, creating a very bad influence and bringing about confusion.

—Big-character posters cost a lot in ink and paper and result in great waste.

"Ours is a socialist country, and the people are the masters of the country. We have a rich democratic life. For instance, the people take part in and manage state affairs. The workers participate in management of enterprises, and rural commune members take part in discussions on farm production," he said.

This secretary of the general Party branch in Dingjiakou Production Brigade in Liaoning Province, who has worked in the countryside for more than twenty years, cited his own experience to show that it was better not to write big-character posters any more.

Following the toppling of the Gang of Four, he went on, democracy had been developed and production carried on in spite of the lack of big-character posters. The masses were applauding the fact that those people who used to use big-character posters to make trouble now had to do their own farmwork themselves. There were seven teams in his brigade, and each team called a general meeting once a month to hear the views of the peasants. Leaders at various levels often went among the masses to solicit their opinions. The Party members made criticisms and self-criticisms at meetings once every ten days. Moreover, brigade and team leaders convened meetings once a month to report on their work to the commune members in the brigade. Furthermore, all production brigades and teams had suggestion boxes to collect the opinions of the peasants, and special persons were designated to reply to criticisms by the masses at regular intervals. "This is the democratic life of our commune members, and we do not want to put up big-character posters," he said.

Deputy Yang Yuwei, a twenty-seven-year-old worker at the Dalian Chemical Plant in northwest China, said, "I don't quite agree with Deputy Gan Yuanli. The big-character poster is still a form to promote democracy. But it should be used properly." He said that workers in his plant were still putting up big-character posters to criticize their leaders or to suggest measures to control pollution and improve the work-style of the leadership. The plant leadership attached great importance to the views of the workers.

Yang Yuwei said, "We must not negate without exception the role of the big-character posters in promoting democracy." But he proposed that posters like those put up at Xidan in Beijing be abolished for the reason that if anyone had some views to raise, he could put up posters at his own unit or in his own locality.

Shen Hongtao, professor of physics at the Northeast Engineering Institute, said he objects to abolishing the posters at Xidan. If anyone wanted to put up a poster there, he said, let him do so. The masses can judge for themselves whether the poster is positive or negative. It was not right to ban posters by administrative decree. Professor Shen pointed out that the Chinese people are leading a rich democratic life. Democracy in China is enjoyed by the majority of the people and is different in nature to that in capitalist society. The big-character poster is only a supplementary form of democracy. "However," he stressed, "if anyone tries to slander others with posters, as stipulated in the draft criminal law, he will have to be charged and punished for libel." His views were endorsed by other deputies at the discussion.

24

GUANGDONG REPORTS UNREST ON HAINAN ISLAND

THE TUNCHANG COUNTY People's Court on Hainan Island held a rally to pass verdicts on July 31. In accordance with the state law, chief criminal Wang Mingguang and core member Wang Dingji, who had participated in Tunchang County's recent serious criminal incident of beating, smashing and looting, were respectively sentenced to ten years and two years of imprisonment by the court, thus enforcing and vindicating the state law and resolutely safeguarding the Four Modernizations.

On July 8 this year, under the pretext of "applying for an audience with the higher authorities to appeal for help," some individual evildoers in Hainan Island's Tunchang County instigated and gathered together over 300 people in the county town who were unaware of the truth. They took no heed of dissuasion, forcibly occupied the county broadcasting station, and forcibly carried out agitating propaganda broadcasts. At the same time, they charged the county's Party and government organs and smashed the county CCP committee's general office, security office, and conference room. They rushed into seven rooms of the county guesthouse and carried out activities of beating, smashing, and looting there. At their instigation, some people forced their way into Renmin restaurant and Sanba restaurant, stole the restaurants' food, and damaged items. They also illegally searched the house of a principal responsible person of the county CCP committee and illegally confiscated his property. During the incident of beating, smashing, and looting, they snatched away large quantities of state and private property

Radio Guangzhou, August 17, 1979. Translation from FBIS Daily Report, August 22, 1979, p. Pl.

including official seals, documents, papers, and files, thus seriously disrupting the normal order in society, production, and work and adversely affecting the general situation of stability and unity.

The masses and cadres on Hainan Island and in Tunchang County were very indignant about the incident. They strongly demanded that public security and judicial departments severely punish the criminal elements in accordance with the law so as to safeguard the smooth realization of the Four Modernizations. After the incident, the county public security bureau, procuracy, and other organs carried out timely investigation work to track down the culprits. With the approval of the county people's procuratorate, Wang Mingguang and Wang Dingji, the ringleaders in beating, smashing, and looting, were arrested and charged in accordance with the law. The county people's procuratorate brought charges against them, and the county people's court tried them.

The cadres and masses of Tunchang County resolutely supported the action of the judicial organs in punishing the beaters, smashers, and looters according to law. They said: Beating, smashing, and looting are crimes. Since they have committed crimes, they must be punished according to law. The court has severely punished the criminals who sabotaged order in society, thus promoting uprightness and upholding the legal system. This finds great favor with the people.

25

WORKERS' MOVEMENT ENTERS A NEW PERIOD

Interview with Ni Zhifu, President of the All-China Federation of Trade Unions and Member of the Politburo of the CCP Central Committee

---

[*Beijing Review* Editor's Note] The interview begins with a review of the All-China Federation of Trade Unions' international activities and a discussion of the role of the trade union in the general mobilization of China's work force to modernize the country.

Defending the Workers' Interests

Q: The Constitution says that the working class is the leading class of the state. How does the trade union, a mass organization of this class, represent and

Beijing Review No. 7 (February 13, 1984), pp. 17–21 (excerpt).

defend the workers' rights and interests?

A: The Chinese workers have become masters of New China. They take part in the administration of state affairs, and, in particular, institute democratic management in enterprises. This is the basic and most important right of Chinese workers and staff.

First, workers make up a considerable proportion in organs of state power— the national and local people's congresses at various levels. On behalf of the workers and staff, they examine, discuss, and decide upon major state affairs and make proposals to defend the workers' interests.

Second, trade unions above the county level, together with other relevant departments, work out rules and regulations for labor protection, wages and bonuses, welfare and education, and other affairs concerning the interests of workers and staff. They also supervise their implementation.

Third, as a people's organization, the trade union occupies an important place in various local committees of the Chinese People's Political Consultative Conference (united front organization) where trade union council members discuss state affairs with members of various democratic parties and people's organizations.

Fourth, the trade unions mobilize workers and staff to take part in democratic management of their own enterprises. This is an important duty, as well as a manifestation of the workers' and staff's rights as masters.

It is also routine for the trade unions at all levels to urge administrative departments to solve urgent problems in the workers' and staff's daily lives, such as housing, child care, and welfare subsidies. The trade unions should do their best to help the workers and staff members, keeping their well being in mind and fighting against bureaucracy, which hurts the workers' democratic rights.

Democratic Management

Q: Can you tell me how the Chinese workers and staff members take part in enterprise management?

A: The Chinese workers and staff members take part in managing their enterprises mainly through workers' congresses. This is laid down in the Constitution. In 1981, the state published "Provisional Regulations for the Workers' and Staff Members' Congress," which says the congress is the power organ where the masses participate in enterprise management and decision-making, and supervise the work of cadres. The grass-roots trade unions are working bodies of these congresses. The State Council has called on all enterprises to establish this system.

Q: What have been the results so far?

A: We've made some progress during the past two years. About 200,000 enterprises and other units across the country have set up this kind of congress. Among the big and medium-sized enterprises, where the system is rather popular, a quarter have done well with democratic management.

Q: What are the criteria of efficient democratic management?
A: The criteria are as defined in the regulations. Major items such as production planning, management, and budgets and final accounts are all discussed and decided by the workers' congress. Problems closely linked with interests, such as housing distribution, regulations for rewards and punishment, use of welfare funds, etc., are decided by the congress through discussion. Wage increases, workers' training plans, and major rules and regulations for the factory are discussed at the congress before they are put into practice. The congress should also supervise the enterprise leaders' work, praising the good and criticizing the bad.

Q: Are there any problems?
A: Of course there are also many problems. First, some enterprises have not yet established the workers' congress system. Second, quite a number of congresses are not playing their role efficiently, and, even worse, in a few enterprises, the congress does not function at all.

To improve this situation, the Tenth Congress of the All-China Federation of Trade Unions adopted the following measures to promote the popularization of democratic management in enterprises.

—We will urge those businesses without congresses of workers and staff members to establish the system as soon as possible, taking this as one of the major considerations in the assessment of enterprises.

—We will popularize the system of assessing leaders through workers' congresses, and urge more enterprises to choose their leaders at various levels through democratic elections.

—We will see to it that the enterprises will, in line with the regulations, give play to the role of the congress as an organ of power. Leaders of enterprises must seriously implement the decisions of the congresses of workers and staff.

—The All-China Federation of Trade Unions will cooperate with the competent departments and give specific guidance to enterprises, so as to gradually perfect the system of democratic management.

Training Workers

Q: You have stressed the importance of raising the scientific and technological level of the workers in the modernization drive. What will the trade unions do in this field?
A: The present scientific and technological level of China's workers and staff cannot meet the demand of the modernization drive. For instance, engineers and technicians make up only 3 percent of all employees in industrial departments. About a quarter of the workers never finished junior middle school, and they need supplementary classes in liberal arts and technology. This is an urgent problem we must deal with.

In describing a trade union in a socialist country, Lenin said, ''It is an organization designed to draw in and to train; it is, in fact, a school; a school of administration, a school of economic management, a school of communism." During the new period, trade unions at various levels will pay more attention to training workers and staff members, helping relevant departments and institutes in government and business run their spare-time schools effectively, solving problems, and defending the workers' right to an education.

There are now more than 50,000 workers' schools, with 11 million students. Adding those enrolled in radio and TV universities, correspondence colleges, and various short-term courses, the figure may reach 20 million, or about one-fifth of all workers and staff in China.

We'll also train the trade union cadres in rotation. The Cadres' School of the All-China Federation of Trade Unions will become a college of the workers' movement, where trade union leaders above the county level will be trained, while cadres' schools of provincial trade unions will train leaders for grass-roots trade unions.

Are Strikes Illegal?

Q: The new Constitution has eliminated the regulations on strikes. Does this mean all strikes are illegal?

A: No, it doesn't mean that. But we are not in favor of solving problems through strikes, because they end up hurting the workers' interests.

In socialist China, the working class is the leading class of the country, and the businesses belong to either the state or the collective. There is no conflict of basic interests between the state, the enterprise, and the individual. To defend their rights and interests, the workers can solve their problems through the democratic channels mentioned before. It is not necessary for them to go on strike.

I'll give you an example. Not long ago, several workers in a color printing house in the city of Siping, Jilin Province, lost their fingers on the job because the deputy director did not care about the workers' safety. Li Yan, a deputy president of the factory's trade union criticized him, asking him to take necessary safety measures. Instead of correcting his mistakes, the deputy director retaliated against Li Yan. Angered, the workers sent an accusation against this bureaucrat to the higher-level trade union and the Party paper. Soon after, the higher-level Party committee and trade union sent people to look into the matter. As a result, the deputy director was dismissed from his post and punishment was meted out according to law. The safety facilities were installed, and Li Yan was praised as "a just and brave trade union cadre." Last October, she attended the Tenth National Congress of the All-China Federation of Trade Unions and was elected an alternate member of its executive committee.

Another example was the capsizing of the oil rig Bohai No. 2 on November 25, 1979, in which 72 people died and the state lost a lot of property. It was *Gongren ribao* (Workers' Daily), the newspaper of the All-China Federation of Trade Unions, which first made the facts of this case public. Through judicial proce-

Be Prepared for "Danger" in Times of "Peace"

A Portrayal of Some Cadres Who Have Been "Restored to Health"

Down with capitalist-roaders

Liberate your thoughts

BE PREPARED FOR DANGER IN TIMES OF PEACE
Ju an si wei, by Huang Weiqiang

Some rehabilitated cadres who had suffered during the Cultural Revolution are reluctant to take a stand in support of the new reforms because it might get them in trouble if the political line shifts once again.

dures, those directly responsible were sent to prison and the minister of the Petroleum Industry was forced to resign.

Fighting bureaucracy is one of the tasks set by the Tenth Congress, and this is resolutely supported by the Party and government. When the workers or their trade union find something in the production process which endangers the workers' safety, they warn the administrative personnel. In cases where bureaucrats do not heed the warning, the trade union may stop production or organize the workers to abandon a dangerous area. This is our special way of fighting against bureaucracy.

Q: Since the working class is the most advanced class, why do you still stress educating the workers in communist ideology?
A: Although the working class is the most advanced and disciplined class, workers cannot grasp the ideology of scientific communism automatically. Only

through conscientious study can the workers get a better understanding of the scientific ideology which defines their historical mission, and become a conscious motive force of history.

Another reason why we emphasize education is that with the retirement of the veteran workers, a lot of young people have joined the army of the working class. Sixty percent of the workers and staff were employed after the "Cultural Revolution." Having grown up during those years, they were not oppressed and exploited in the old society, and they lack a systematic knowledge of communism. Furthermore, since the implementation of the policy of opening to the outside world, some of them have been influenced by decadent bourgeois ideas, and a few workers and staff members do not observe discipline, neglect their duties, and even seek private gains through work.

The trade unions must educate their members with communist ideas so as to help them see their historical mission, overcome negative influences, and devote themselves to socialist construction. Through education, the Chinese working class will become a well-educated and disciplined mass with lofty ideals and morality. They will be pioneers in developing China's material wealth and socialist culture and ethics and will consequently better fulfill their duties as the leading class of the nation.

26
―――
Commentator

ONE CANNOT GET FAT FROM EATING ONE MOUTHFUL

WHAT IS THE purpose of reforming the economic structure? It is to develop the productive forces and enable the state to become powerful and the people rich. This requires a process of arduous effort by everybody working in concert. It is not possible "to get fat from eating one mouthful" and for everybody to wake up one morning as "10,000-yuan households."

Recent propaganda on the great successes of the rural reforms is absolutely correct. However, the excessive propaganda on "10,000-yuan households" in the rural areas has apparently given urban residents the mistaken idea that as a result of the rural reforms all the peasants have become rich and most have become

Renmin ribao [People's Daily], February 22, 1985. Translation from FBIS Daily Report, February 25, 1985, pp. K1–K2.

"10,000-yuan households." They infer from this that with the urban reforms now underway, it should be the turn of the urban staff and workers to become "10,000-yuan households." Many people compare their salaries with the rural "10,000-yuan households" and with certain individual urban entrepreneurs with high incomes, and the more they compare, the more they feel that their own income is low, and the more they hope to immediately become people with a "high income" amid the reforms that have just started. The comrades affected by such an idea regard certain current reforms as "Wu Song feeling unsatisfied with drinking beer."

Such an idea is not realistic. China is a large country with a poor foundation. In order to catch up with the living standard and labor productivity of the economically developed countries, we must make arduous efforts for several decades or longer. The rural reforms carried out first have attracted worldwide attention. We solved the long-standing problems of feeding and clothing the 800 million peasants, and the peasants of many localities have gradually become well off. However, compared with several hundred million peasant households, the "10,000-yuan households" are only a few drops in the ocean, and we are still far from reaching our goal.

The living standard of the people in urban areas has also improved markedly in recent years. Could most of the urban inhabitants have dreamed of purchasing household electric appliances like a television and so on before the Third Plenum of the Eleventh CCP Central Committee? We are now rapidly increasing the production of these products, and they will be gradually popularized in the households of urban inhabitants. The Party and government have done their utmost to improve the people's lives. Such a move, which is rooted in long years of indebtedness, is absolutely necessary. We hold that the people's consumption level should correspond with labor productivity. At present the economic results of many enterprises are not good enough, and their labor productivity is not high enough. If high salaries and bonuses exceeding the level of production development are paid out, then people will appear to become "rich" for a time, but the consequences can be none other than loss of control over consumption funds, market shortages, and big price fluctuations. Those who have temporarily risen to the status of "people with high incomes" will be dragged down by "high prices." In addition, the difficulties in future reforms and economic development will be increased. We cannot follow this way of reaping calamity while in pursuit of a hollow title.

Hard work and rousing ourselves for vigorous efforts to make the country prosperous are the fine tradition of our nation. We must lay a solid foundation for making the country powerful and the people rich, which has been the long-cherished aspiration of generations of Chinese people. The historical cause of overthrowing the "three big mountains" was great and unprecedented. The current task of building the Four Modernizations is greater and more arduous.

We must work hard in a steady and sound way for several decades to create and contribute more for society and seek a big improvement in living standards on the basis of a great development in production.

27

GUANGDONG FACTORY DIRECTORS DEMAND GREATER POWER

SIXTY-FIVE MEMBERS of the Guangdong Provincial Society of Factory Directors and Managers met this afternoon to discuss and adopt a letter to the Guangdong Provincial CCP Committee and People's Government and the Guangzhou City CCP Committee and People's Government, making a ten-point proposal on releasing their grip on factory directors and managers, demanding firm and all-round implementation of the regulations on the work of directors of state-run industrial enterprises promulgated by the central authorities, and asking for adequate self-management power and the authority to make decisions and exercise command. The main contents of the ten-point proposal are:

1. The provincial and city CCP committees and people's governments are asked to issue a formal document clearly specifying the expanded scope of power for enterprises to appoint or dismiss cadres and establish organizations, assigning the factory directors power to handle personnel and financial matters, and defining the concrete policies.

2. Factory directors and managers are to be elected democratically and appointed by the immediately higher level. As for appointment of their assistants, the factory directors and managers are to draw plans and submit them to the higher level for approval. The intermediate-level cadres are to be appointed or dismissed by the enterprises themselves. Reports on such appointments or dismissals should be submitted to the higher level for recording.

3. Directors of factories run by collective enterprises have the power to appoint or dismiss their assistants and intermediate-level cadres. Should the Party organizations disagree, the persons named by the factory directors may be used on a trial basis for three to six months before their appointments or dismissals are approved.

4. The factory directors and managers should be given power to handle financial matters. Their exercise of financial power should not be overly interfered with if they have not gone beyond the limits of the state policies, decrees, and regulations concerned.

5. The enterprises should be given the power to carry out their administrative restructuring and to make decisions on the establishment of organizations and the placement of cadres and managerial personnel, so that there may be a fixed number of personnel and fixed positions and that their personnel have required qualifications.

Radio Guangzhou, April 13, 1984. Translation from FBIS Daily Report, April 16, 1984, pp. P1–P2.

6. The enterprises should be assigned power to recruit or dismiss their personnel according to the principle of appointing those best fit for the jobs.

7. Under the premise of ensuring that the state obtains greater revenue, the amount of cash awards for staff and workers should be permitted to fluctuate with the amount of increase in taxes and profits submitted to the state by their enterprises, and there should be a maximum and a minimum amount of the awards. The enterprises should be permitted to retain a certain proportion of money from their total sales and use the money as production development funds.

8. The provincial and city authorities are asked to define the policies on learning the experience of the Shenzhen Special Economic Zone in carrying out economic restructuring.

9. The enterprises have the right to refuse to pay an unreasonable share of fees for idle personnel and to accept the unnecessary personnel rigorously assigned to them.

10. Leading organs, supervisory units, discipline inspection committees, and other organizations at all levels are asked to make greater efforts to inspect, supervise, direct, and help the enterprises, so that the enterprises may correctly exercise their self-management power.

28

Li Xin

PROCEED FROM THE OVERALL SITUATION OF REFORM, ESTABLISH A NEW PARTY-GOVERNMENT RELATIONSHIP

[*Xinhua*] Editor's Note: Some comrades report that since the introduction of the system of the plant manager assuming all responsibility for operations, the work of the Party committe has become difficult and the Party secretary has had nothing to do. This speech has given us new insight convincingly showing us that in the new situation of reform of the enterprise leadership system, the Party secretary can do a great deal of political work as long as he is an enlightened person who keeps the overall situation in mind, keeps a clear head on major issues, and does not get entangled in small details. It is entirely possible for the Party secretary and the manager of an enterprise to cooperate with each other in effectively invigorating the enterprise and raising its economic effectiveness.

How SHOULD THE Party committee and the Party secretary of a

Xinhua [New China News Agency], Chinese, February 7, 1985. Translation from FBIS Daily Report, February 15, 1985, pp. K2–K6 (excerpts).

plant do the work after the system of the plant manager assuming all responsibility of operations is introduced? This is also a new subject to me, one I have been exploring. Therefore, I will offer only my preliminary understanding of this question and my experience.

Emancipate Onself by Proceeding From the Overall Situation of Reform

I majored in civil engineering in college and worked in the Army before 1978. After being transferred to a civilian job, I was first appointed as Party secretary of the Beijing vinylon plant and then Party secretary of the Beijing printing and dyeing plant in 1983. Based on my practical experience, which has enhanced my understanding, I wholeheartedly support the decision of the Party Central Committee and the State Council to reform the enterprise leadership system.

1. Practical experience enabled me to understand that to extricate the Beijing printing and dyeing plant from its difficult situation, it was necessary to embark on the road of reform, and that reform of the enterprise leadership system was an important link in the entire chain of reforms.

When I began my work at the Beijing printing and dyeing plant, Comrade Xu Xiaochun was deputy manager of the Municipal Cotton Printing and Dyeing Company and concurrently manager of the Beijing printing and dyeing plant. Although we worked hard together at that time, the plant's difficult economic situation did not improve. Later Comrade Xu Xiaochun returned to the company, leaving the plant's production and administrative work in the charge of a deputy plant manager. During that time, the plant's economic performance did not improve and went from bad to worse. What was the problem, and what should be done to save the plant? I realized that to extricate itself from its difficult situation in the face of strong market competition, the plant must raise its competitiveness. This required two prerequisites: The state must invigorate the enterprise by reforming the excessively centralized economic system, and the enterprise leadership system must be reformed to enable an expert to assume all responsibility of the enterprise's production, management, and administrative work.

2. Practical experience enabled me to understand that in transforming an enterprise from a production-type enterprise to a production and management-type, it is necessary to select a capable person to assume the post of manager.

To achieve a breakthrough in the situation at the plant, higher authorities in the spring of last year decided to readjust and replenish our plant's administrative leading body. I was in favor of having Comrade Xu Xiaochun return to the plant to assume the manager's post. Although I noticed at that time that some people in our plant were rather critical of him, saying "he did not do well in the past and will not do well if he comes back," I believed that in the work of accelerating reform of the urban economic structure, Comrade Xu Xiaochun met three indispensable requirements as a good plant manager, aside from being an expert in technology and management. First, being imbued with a strong enterprising spirit, he regarded the plant as his home and devoted himself wholeheartedly to his work in order to run the plant well. Second, having an emancipated mind and innovative spirit, he dared to think, take action, make reform, and was full of ideas. Third, he had the perseverance and persistence to accomplish what he wanted.

3. Practical experience over the years of revolution taught me the importance of cooperation with the plant manager and of "harmony between the general and the prime minister."

With the introduction of the plant manager responsibility system, the Party committee's role and position in the enterprise underwent a new change. First, the Party secretary had to abandon his post as "commander in chief" and concentrate his efforts on ensuring fulfillment of production and operational tasks and on supervising implementation of the Party's principles and policies. Thus, with his real power reduced, the Party secretary faced greater difficulties in his work, causing ideological wavering among some Party cadres. Some of them told me that they did not understand my support for Comrade Xu Xiaochun's return to the plant and my willingness to cooperate with him, and they said that from now on the Party committee would not have the power to do anything and would become ineffective because of its lesser position. At this crucial moment, I thought about the following: As a Communist Party member, I should keep a clear head politically and consider questions from the overall viewpoint of reform. Even people in ancient times knew the importance of "harmony between the general and the prime minister." Why could I not cooperate with the plant manager in invigorating the enterprise? Hence, I felt much at ease in my thinking and, not caring about what other people said, I persistently stood on the front line of reform, supporting and leading reform.

[*Xinhua*] Editor's Note: Fame, gain, and power probably still weigh on the mind of some cadres who profess love for what they really fear. Only by removing this weight from his mind can a cadre march with a light pack on his back and match his words with deeds in reform. This experience provides much food for thought for all enterprise Party secretaries.

Wholeheartedly Support the Plant Manager in Promoting Capable People

Comrade Xu Xiaochun always believed that even with fairly good equipment, the plant would still be unable to promote production, primarily because of the contradiction between modern production and backward management, and that to resolve the contradiction, it was necessary to promote capable people. In the past, he hastily tried to promote to leading posts at various levels intellectuals who were well versed in technology and management and dared to blaze new trails, but he failed because the conditions were not ripe for it. Now, with his expanded decision-making power and the introduction of the plant manager responsibility system, he proposed appointing and removing cadres at plant and middle administrative levels. I agreed with his views, trusting that he had more contact with and better understood the technical and management cadres in the plant.

Because nomination, appointment, and removal of administrative leading cadres is made by the plant manager, does it mean that the Party committee does not have anything to do? Our experience shows that the Party committee must do a conscientious job in the following fields:

[*Xinhua*] Editor's Note: The following points are quite enlightening. They explain that even with the plant manager exercising the right to appoint or remove administrative cadres, the enterprise Party committee and Party secretary still have plenty of work to do. The problem is whether or not they take the initiative to do so effectively.

1. The plant manager wanted to promote some capable persons, but a handful of people opposed him and even concocted slanders against them. Under such circumstances, we conducted an earnest investigation to understand the real situation and to straighten out rights and wrongs.

2. Among the administrative leading cadres appointed by the plant manager, some were not Party members. After their appointments were announced, they were extremely diffident, fearing that the Party committee and Party members would not support them. To dispel their fears and enable them to go all out to do their work, we separately held talks with them to clarify our stand.

3. After the introduction of the plant manager responsibility system, some cadres in charge of workshops, sections, or offices who failed to adapt themselves to the change were disrespectful toward the newly appointed administrative leading cadres and did not cooperate with them. In view of this erroneous tendency, we stepped up efforts to educate and persuade such cadres and removed from the organization those who refused to change their attitude.

4. We did an active job in quickly recruiting Party members from among capable persons who had requested to be admitted to the Party and met the requirements for Party membership. Among the twenty-five newly appointed intellectual cadres who were not Party members, eleven have been admitted to the Party.

Keep to Principles When Dealing with Major Issues, Display a Good Style in Handling Minor Ones, and Establish a New Type of Relationship Between the Party and the Administrative Authorities

Implementation of the plant manager responsibility system—a major reform of the enterprise leadership system—means the changing of many-years-old conventions and habits in dealing with a lot of questions and the need to do away with old traditional concepts and work procedures. Because of this, there will inevitably be some contradictions, including questions of people's thinking and understanding as well as questions on practical work. Handling these questions properly concerns the issue of whether or not we will be able to arouse the initiative of the Party, the administrative authorities, and the staffs and workers and whether or not we will be able to unite all cadres to make a success of the work in every field. It is a matter that requires us to rack our brains. To establish a new type of relationship between the Party and the administrative authorities, I think that it is necessary to "keep to principles when dealing with major issues and display a good style in handling minor ones." In practice, we have paid attention to the following:

1. Conscientiously break with old ideas and make a change in thinking and style.

Implementation of the plant manager responsibility system requires establishment of a new type of relationship between the Party and the administrative authorities. Whether this relationship can be maintained, I think, depends mainly on the secretary. First of all, the secretary should take the Party's cause into account, attach importance to the overall interest, and break with the following three ideas on their own initiative: One is that he has absolute control in major issues, and that the plant manager can only act according to his instructions. Another is that the secretary is the No. 1 leader, while the plant director is the No. 2 leader. And third, is that the secretary commands everything, and that his words are decisive in all matters, big and small.

[Xinhua] Editor's Note: Perhaps these three ideas are commonly held by all comrades who have worked as secretaries of enterprise Party committees for a long time. The fact that in the new situation Comrade Li Xin is able to take the initiative in breaking with these ideas and replacing them with a new concept to cope with the reform reflected by the implementation of the plant manager responsibility system indicates that he is worthy of being called an enlightened Party committee secretary.

Second, the secretary should take the initiative in paying attention to the situation in production and operations and undertake ideological and political responsibility for any problem that appears in production, operations, and administrative or management work. The secretary should share burdens with the plant manager, help him solve problems, and act as his supporter. Third, the secretary should take the initiative in harmonizing the plant manager's relations with such mass organizations as the trade union and the CYL organization and see to it that the Party, the administrative authorities, the trade union, and the CYL organization cooperate in fulfilling the production task and all other work of the enterprise.

2. Give positive support in every way to the plant manager in carrying out the functions and powers of his production and operational command system. The Party committee's support for the plant manager is of special importance after the system of the plant manager assuming full responsibility is introduced. The Party committee should ensure that the plant manager can exercise his command power without impediments, and that his orders and prohibitions are strictly enforced.

3. Divide the work scientifically so that each has his own function and responsibility and, at the same time, cooperate closely to make the work of the enterprise a real success.

In implementing the plant manager responsibility system and dividing the work between the Party and the administrative authorities so that each has its own functions, it is necessary to pay attention to the need for sincere unity and close coordination. Every effort should be made to guard against the problem of each going his own way, thus resulting in the separation between political and economic work. In the past year, we have carried out our work in such a way as to focus on reforms and have made ideological and political work subordinate to and serve the purpose of economic reform. This has ensured our smooth progress in making reforms and resulted in a remarkable improvement of our economic results.

4. Take the overall interests into consideration and make positive efforts in every way to remedy the occasional negligence or mistakes on the part of the plant's administrative leadership instead of blaming it.

5. Fully understand the roles of guarantee and supervision and properly exercise the functions and power of the Party committee. I think a correct understanding of this point is necessary before the Party organizations in the enterprise can bring the roles of guarantee and supervision into full play. Guarantee and supervision are aimed at enabling the enterprises to do a good job and enlivening the enterprises by following the Party Central Committee's principles and policies. Therefore, guarantee and supervision are distinct and yet interrelated. They constitute an integral entity. We should say that guarantee is a premise and a basis, and supervision is a means. The aim of supervision is to ensure effective realization of guarantee. Also, guarantee and supervision in no way mean going down to all details. Instead, they should focus on the orientation and the implementation of the line, principles, and policies.

Do a Successful Job in Building the Political Work Contingent to Meet the Needs of the Situation

The original backbone political workers in our plant were mostly old hands who had worked since the plant's founding. Generally speaking, they had a rather poor educational background and were relatively advanced in age and old-fashioned in mind. At the beginning, many of them had doubts, could not understand, and were vexed by the many current reforms such as appointment of non-Party cadres, admittance of outstanding intellectuals into the Party, and institution of the plant manager's responsibility system.

Practice shows that we should actively adopt measures to raise the quality of the political work contingent and consolidate it so as to meet the needs of the situation.

First of all, we have paid attention to organizing political work cadres to study the Party's principles and policies so as to eliminate "left" influence, set right the guiding thoughts for various work, and raise their consciousness of making reforms. At the same time, we have strengthened the study of political work to be done under the new situation and have called on the political work cadres to pay attention to the renewal of their thinking, knowledge, and work methods.

> [*Xinhua*] Editor's Note: All political work cadres in the enterprises are faced with the work of "the three renewals." No progress equals regression. Only by renewal can we do pioneering work, make advances, and open up a new situation of political work in the enterprises.

We must also actively train those who are relatively young and promising among the political work contingent by sending them out for advanced study. To reinforce the political work contingent, we have selected those comrades who have education at or above the high school level; who support the line, principles, and policies formulated at the Third Plenum of the Eleventh CCP Central Committee; and who warmly love political work with a pioneering spirit and have the ability to communicate. We have arranged for those comrades who are no longer suitable for political work to do other work as appropriate.

Now, the political work and political work contingent are undergoing changes. Work adjustments have been made for twenty-five political work cadres in the plant. Several new secretaries of general Party branches of workshops and administrative sections and offices have shown relatively strong abilities in leadership, organization, coordination, and innovation. They have opened a new situation in ideological and political work within a short time. They are therefore considered capable persons for this work by the masses. Those veteran comrades who are now in the second line after the readjustment of the political work system have been assigned work suitable to their abilities.

29

Zheng Lizhou

INTEGRATION WITH INTELLECTUALS SHOULD ALSO BE ADVOCATED

THE QUESTION CONCERNING intellectuals is a hot topic of dis-

Renmin ribao [People's Daily], January 3, 1983. Translation from FBIS Daily Report, January 6, 1983, pp. K1–K2.

cussion at present. Once, when chatting with a comrade in charge of the Party's leading work, I said: "We have advocated the slogan of integrating oneself with workers and peasants for a few decades, and now it is also necessary to advocate integration with intellectuals." Looking surprised, he shook his head again and again: "Your mind may be excessively emancipated!" I immediately explained: "This is not my invention. It is put forward by Comrade Lu Dingyi in an article." This comrade took the newspaper that I showed him and read carefully. No longer shaking his head he said: "I need to consider this question carefully. . . ." Of course, how to approach and treat intellectuals correctly in the new historical period is indeed a question that our cadres should seriously consider.

It is not to create something new and unorthodox by advocating the integration with intellectuals; instead, it is an objective requirement posed by the historical change in the intellectuals' status and role in our country. Since the Third Plenum of the Eleventh Central Committee, the Party central leadership has explicitly declared: Workers, peasants, and intellectuals are three basic forces in our country; like workers and peasants, intellectuals are also a major force to be relied on in the building of socialism; and since the key to the Four Modernizations lies in the modernization of science and technology, it is particularly necessary to bring the role of intellectuals into full play. Now the intellectuals' status as a reliable force has been stipulated in the constitution and has been affirmed in the form of law. This requires us to establish a new notion and new relationship in approaching and treating intellectuals and to correspondingly change our work-style and method. The advocation of integrating oneself with intellectuals conforms with this new requirement under the new conditions. Though this is a simple reason, it represents an important breakthrough and a major change in theory and policy. So it is not easy to put it into practice. This is because many of our comrades have not yet changed their old notions and have not yet eliminated various prejudices against intellectuals, and they are still influenced by "leftism." Nowadays, few people still treat intellectuals as the enemy, but then quite a few people still treat them as outsiders and guests rather than comrades in our ranks. If even the question of what kind of people intellectuals are has not been solved, how can we have the desire to integrate ourselves with intellectuals? Of course, man's cognition follows a process and always tends toward correctness and being perfectly in step through repeated experiences, comparisons, revisions, and complements in practice. It is no wonder that some cadres still harbor prejudice in approaching intellectuals. From recognizing that intellectuals are people on our own side and understanding that they constitute a reliable force with which one can consciously contact, approach, and even identify with, there are requirements one higher than another, and people's understanding needs to be enhanced to a higher and higher degree. We hope those comrades whose understanding fails to keep abreast with the development will better force themselves to interact with intellectuals so as to make this process of integration a course of changing one's notions, eliminating prejudices, and enhancing understanding.

The integration with intellectuals involves substantial content and various methods. In undertaking it, the most important matters can be summarized in a few words: study, approach, and service. The vast majority of China's intellectuals love socialism and the motherland and possess actual capability and professional knowledge, all of which are needed in the modernization drive. All this is worth our studying. In particular, the progressive intellectuals like Jiang Zhuying and Luo Jianfu have lofty sentiments, a strict scientific attitude, and a selfless spirit of dedication. We should earnestly learn from them.

To integrate oneself with intellectuals, one must modestly learn from them. This is the first point. Leading cadres and intellectuals should be both students and teachers to each other and should learn from and help each other. In order to learn from and help intellectuals in key points, we need to come into contact with them and have an intimate understanding of them. Owing to the influence of their educational conditions, social circumstances, living habits, working methods, and tortuous experiences over many years, intellectuals have their own characteristics. Leading cadres should take the initiative in often coming into contact with them so as to narrow the gap between them, promote mutual understanding, exchange and harmonize each other's sentiments, identify themselves with intellectuals, and realize a genuine integration. This is the second point. To integrate oneself with intellectuals should, in the final analysis, give effect to serving them. In order to enable intellectuals to contribute their wisdom and intelligence with ease of mind and high spirits, a basic condition is that we trust them politically, support them in their work, and show concern for their lives, creating all necessary conditions for them. Many revolutionaries of the older generation have repeatedly indicated that they are willing to work for intellectuals as assistants, servants, supporters, and heads of logistic work and make every effort to serve them. This serves as an example for our whole Party and leading cadres at all levels. Some people think that the work of serving intellectuals does not tally with their status. Now they should draw a deep lesson by comparing themselves with the farsighted actions of the old comrades. Being willing to serve intellectuals in fact is a question of whether one is concerned with the Party's cause and the people's interest. Showing concern for intellectuals is equal to showing concern for the socialist modernization cause; and serving intellectuals is to serve the socialist modernization cause. Our leading cadres should approach and realize this question in this way and be resolute in serving intellectuals heart and soul.

As far as intellectuals are concerned, they should of course not relax their study and the effort to improve themselves; still less should they merely wait for other people to integrate with them but not energetically integrate themselves with workers and peasants. It is still important and imperative for intellectuals to integrate themselves with workers and peasants, and get access to and learn from workers and peasants so as to draw nourishment to enrich themselves mentally. Especially at present, when some workers and peasants may still harbor some misunderstanding toward intellectuals and, being limited by its economic conditions, the state has not yet been able to solve many actual problems that intellectuals are faced with, intellectuals should not grumble and take a passive attitude.

Rather, they should take a correct attitude toward these problems. With the close combination of the three basic forces, namely, workers, peasants, and intellectuals, the objective of creating a new situation in socialist modernization will certainly be achieved, and our state and our nation will certainly become more prosperous and developed.

30

Fang Qingrong

AN ANALYSIS OF "SHUNNING POLITICS"

IN DEALING WITH knowledge and intellectuals, we have to eliminate many erroneous concepts. "Shunning politics" is one of them.

When the slogan "stressing politics" was in vogue, some comrades used to say this of the intellectual about whom they were talking: "Regarding this comrade, he devotes all his time to his studies and shuns politics." In those days, the comment "shunning politics" was almost the same as "taking the road of becoming bourgeois specialists," and it carried much weight. Even if the person who was thus labeled might by chance escape being criticized or struggled against, he "could not be assigned to important posts."

What is politics? How can one be considered as good in politics? According to past understanding, politics means class struggle. Therefore, during the period when "class struggle was taken as the key," the chief requirement for being good in politics was whether one "took an active part in class struggle" in addition to having a good class origin. To be specific, only if one took an active part in various criticism meetings, struggle meetings, and study meetings, reciting quotations, making pledges, and loudly shouting slogans, could one be regarded as one who "stressed politics." At present things have changed and the understanding of politics has also changed. Nevertheless, to date there are still some people who regard participation in political activities and various kinds of meetings as the chief criterion for judging whether a person is good in politics or not. How does this comrade fulfill his own job? What is his professional level? What achievements and attainments has he made in the field in which he has specialized? What contributions has he made to the people? All these seem to have nothing to do with politics. In fact, this is a harmful, one-sided view.

If, for the sake of the modernization of the motherland, a person studies hard, endeavors to gain proficiency, and makes achievements in his own job, he is concerned with politics and is good in politics. Let us take, for instance, Luo Jianfu and Jiang Zhuying who, for the sake of the motherland's undertaking of

Renmin ribao [People's Daily], January 24, 1983, p. 5. Translation from FBIS Daily Report, January 27, 1983, pp. K19–K20.

scientific research, studied assiduously day and night, took infinite pains in their work, and made outstanding contributions to their respective research fields. Did all this not prove that they had high political consciousness? The support of the broad masses of intellectuals for the Party and their love for their motherland and socialism are mainly shown in their endeavor to make progress in their professional work and in their creative labor. In order to have more time to gain professional proficiency and to do their work better, some comrades want to reduce some of their political activities. This is entirely different from shunning politics.

In socialist construction there are different responsibilities and requirements for different posts. We cannot expect intellectuals who are engaged in scientific research, cultural work, artistic work, and so on to participate in as many political activities and meetings as administrative and political cadres. We should see that making achievements in their professional fields and contributing their strength to the construction of the motherland have been their long-standing desires over the years, and much of their time has been wasted. At present, the Party's correct policy has opened up a vast field for the intellectuals to display their talents. Many comrades are seizing every second to work in order to make up for lost time. Of course, their desire and efforts should be supported and encouraged and should not be criticized or obstructed. Much less should we label them as "shunning politics" and dampen their enthusiasm. Just think of this: If our intellectuals do not concentrate their attention on their professional work, they will only be trained as ignorant and incompetent "armchair politicians," no matter how many meetings they are asked to participate in. What is the use of being "good in politics" in this way?

Of course, we also oppose the idea that intellectuals should "ignore what is going on beyond their immediate surroundings." As masters of their country, intellectuals should concern themselves with and participate in the management of state affairs. They should study Marxism, study the Party's principles and policies, and raise their political consciousness. However, what we should pay special attention to at present is continuing to eradicate the influence of "armchair politics," and protecting and developing the enthusiasm and initiative of intellectuals in endeavoring to gain professional proficiency and dedicating themselves to the Four Modernizations.

31

Wei Yin

AGAIN ON THE NEED FOR THE APPEARANCE OF 10,000-YUAN HOUSEHOLDS AMONG "NINTH CATEGORY" PEOPLE

"THERE MUST ALSO emerge 10,000-yuan households among the 'ninth category' people" was a sentence originally said by a person of "foresight" and not dreamed up by the author to try to please the public with claptrap. At present, this may sound harsh, but in the future, whether in "industry, agriculture, commerce, schools, or the army," people may not regard it as strange at all. It has already become a rule that whenever a "peak" opinion that reflects the truth comes into being, it will be regarded as heresy. In the United States, there was a Margaret Sanger, who was a forerunner in preaching birth control. More than seventy years ago, when she put forward her theory, she was immediately denounced as advocating heresy, and her propagation of birth control and contraceptive knowledge were regarded as an "obscene, salacious, lascivious, and filthy" act. Her work was then forbidden. Was not the old "contract system" once regarded as a dreadful monster? Why is it worshiped today? It is thus obvious that there is a process for the people to realize the truth. At present, when some people say that there must be 10,000-yuan households among the "ninth category" people, it sounds a bit harsh, and some people even ridicule it as a fantasy. This is also an inevitable thing.

Now, let's return to our subject. By saying that there is the need for the appearance of 10,000-yuan households among the "ninth category" people, we mean that it is a necessary thing, but at present it has not yet appeared, because there are still conventions and unreasonable decrees that block the way. Not only is it difficult to become a 10,000-yuan household, it is even difficult to become a 1,000-yuan household. Even deserved and reasonable rewards were usually treated as presumptuous income. It seems as if the "ninth category" people must remain poor for their lifetime. A little increase in prosperity may be considered as impermissible behavior. If lightly treated, their reasonable rewards may be deducted for this or that reason; and if seriously treated, they will run up against rumors and slander. How is it possible to become a 10,000-yuan household?

There was an engineer named Li Hengzhang in the electronic instruments plant in Gaozhi County, Heilongjiang Province. In accordance with the demands of his contract, if he could complete the task of designing two new products, he would be awarded 2,200 yuan. This was written in black and white. It is said that this award "lauded the intellectuals to the skies." In fact, what Li Hengzhang got

Yangcheng wanbao [Yangcheng Evening News], February 3, 1983, p. 2. Translation from JPRS 82955, February 28, 1983, pp. 47–48.

was but 2,000 yuan or so, and what is more, they had the contract as evidence. However, the people of this plant tried to break their promise and ironically satirized him. It seems quite difficult even for the emergence of a 1,000-yuan household among the "ninth category" people, to say nothing of examples from far away. In a public health center in nearby Guangzhou, there were two doctors who could work miraculous cures and bring the dying back to life. To be certain, they had quite a number of patients. The monthly income of the two departments where the two doctors worked amounted to 20,000–30,000 yuan. Owing to their special contributions, the hospital offered them each a monthly bonus of 270 yuan. This made some people breathless: How outrageous! The reason why we did not publicly report this in the past was because we feared being troubled with advocating the "reckless issue of bonuses." Since last July, this hospital has been forced to make a change and has decreased their bonuses to around 80 yuan. This is how things go. If the intellectuals cannot even get their reasonable reward, what is the use of talking about "10,000-yuan households?" The peasants can become "super 10,000-yuan households" by raising 40 dairy cows. The value of the inventive creativity of scientists is by no means less than 1,000 dairy cows. But what material rewards have they received in return? This is not reasonable! What a terrible thing it will be if we do not carry out reform.

We were informed recently by the press that Zhao Shouyi, minister of Labor and Personnel Affairs, pointed out, while being interviewed by reporters: "The people should be paid more for more work. It is reasonable to obtain a partial reward as a result of the wealth created through labor. This conforms to the distribution principle of socialism. It is wrong to obstruct, deduct by every means, be jealous of, or even suppress and attack those people who get more rewards for having a high level and strong capability and who have put in more labor and made greater contributions." Although it is not possible at present for the appearance of 10,000-yuan households, we can gradually develop them. But the "leftist" ideology that hinders distribution according to work must be reformed! All irrational rules and regulations must be reformed! In a word, if these are not reformed, it would be impossible for the state and people to prosper, and the appearance of 10,000-yuan households among the "ninth category" will be only a dream.

32

WOMEN REJECT RETURN TO HOME

THOUGH SOME PEOPLE have suggested that women should return to housework in order to leave more and better jobs for men, the idea has

Beijing Review No. 5 (February 4, 1985), pp. 9–10.

been rejected by both women and men in public opinion polls.

Lately some union officials have suggested that too many women are employed in types of work more suitable to men and that women should step aside to make way for unemployed or underemployed young men. They argue that women—especially women in their childbearing years—actually hinder economic development and result in lower productivity, poor quality, and inefficiency.

Women first began moving out of the house and into the workforce after the idea was put forth during the May Fourth Movement in 1919, the first democratic mass movement in the history of modern China. But the idea was not realized until the 1950s, when millions of Chinese women began to go to work.

In 1949 women made up only 7.5 percent of all workers in state-owned enterprises. The percentage rose to 21 percent in 1965 and 36 percent in 1983. In addition, one-third of China's scientists are women, and women have begun to take leadership roles in a number of fields.

But some have begun to suggest that there are too many women in the workforce today. Xing Hua, an official of the Beijing Trade Union, said, "It is because a woman is naturally more adept at housekeeping than a man that she should carry more of the family burden. But they must be worn out if they at the same time go to work. How can we say women are liberated under such a situation?"

To solve the problem, some have suggested that some working women, not all, stay at home, while giving their husbands or brothers double wages. They argue that under these circumstances, families would retain their same level of income, and women could run the house and raise children much better.

The suggestion is flatly rejected by 9 out of 10 people polled. In Nanchang, Jiangxi Province, 100 persons were randomly questioned last summer. Among 50 women, 46 said they were unwilling to leave their jobs, no matter what the situation. The other 4 said they would like to return home if their jobs could be taken by their sons or daughters. Of 50 men polled, only 6 said they would like to see their wives resign their jobs, if it meant higher wages for themselves.

This proves, said pollsters Bi Bingsheng and Fu Zhihong of the city's Women's Federation, that most people reject the idea of women returning home. "The idea reflects the feudalistic ideology that women are inferior to men and incapable of performing work that requires high intelligence or an aggressive manner. Women's liberation depends, in the final analysis, on economic status," said Bi.

However, the status of women is not only reflected in the employment rate, said union official Xing. She published her own opinion poll last year, indicating that 64 percent of the women workers at the Beijing Da Hua Shirt Factory favor her "phased employment" theory. The theory suggests that a woman worker take leave from her job when she is seven months pregnant and stay off the job until her baby reaches the age of three. Xing suggests that women on leave receive 75 percent of their normal salary and be allowed to return to work after the three-year period. "This will benefit children, women, their families and our society," said Xing.

Some of those polled, both women and men, felt the idea is a good one. It definitely seems to be more acceptable than the suggestion that women return to the home forever. It seems the vast majority are in favor of women playing a major role in modernization. However, said Zheng Zhaohong, a staff member of the All-China Women's Federation, the debate is beneficial. It urges us to solve our social problems, especially the time-consuming housework that takes up most of our spare time, she said. But housekeeping problems should not be solved at the cost of women's jobs. Instead, said Zheng, housework should be reduced by developing the service trades and socializing, modernizing, and professionalizing housekeeping.

FURTHER READINGS

Brodsgaard, Kjeld Erik. "The Democracy Movement in China, 1978–1979: Opposition Movements, Wall Poster Campaigns, and Underground Journals." *Asian Survey* 21:7 (July 1981), pp. 742–774.

Falkenheim, Victor C., ed. *Citizens and Groups in Chinese Politics.* Ann Arbor: University of Michigan China Monograph Series, forthcoming.

Falkenheim, Victor C. "Political Participation in China." *Problems of Communism* 27:3 (May-June 1978), pp. 18–32. (Also see the related discussion, "Participation in China," *Problems of Communism* 28:1 (January-February 1979), pp. 75–80.)

Goldman, Merle. *China's Intellectuals: Advise and Dissent.* Cambridge, Mass.: Harvard University Press, 1981.

Goodman, David S. G., ed. *Groups and Politics in the People's Republic of China.* Armonk, N.Y.: M. E. Sharpe, 1984.

Nathan, Andrew J. *Chinese Democracy.* New York: Alfred A. Knopf, 1985.

Rosen, Stanley. "Guangzhou's Democracy Movement in Cultural Revolution Perspective." *The China Quarterly* No. 101 (March 1985), pp. 1–31.

Seymour, James. *The Fifth Modernization: China's Human Rights Movement, 1978–1979.* Stanfordville, N.Y.: Human Rights Publishing Group, 1980.

Townsend, James R. *Political Participation in Communist China.* Berkeley: University of California Press, 1969.

Womack, Brantly, ed. "Electoral Reform in China." *Chinese Law and Government* 15:3–4 (Fall-Winter 1982–1983).

Womack, Brantly. "The 1980 County-Level Elections in China: Experiment in Democratic Modernization." *Asian Survey* 22:3 (March 1982), pp. 261–277.

D. Bureaucracy

WHEN THE AUTHORITIES embarked on an ambitious administrative reform program in 1982, they signaled their intention to improve both the efficiency and the responsiveness of state and Party institutions. The reforms, accompanied by a Party rectification campaign, ran headlong into entrenched local, unit, and factional interests. Yet national authorities persisted in their attempt to gain control over the bureaucracy and to increase its cost-effectiveness.

Traditionally, Party leaders have used rectification campaigns to increase their control over Party members, now numbering approximately 42 million, and the most recent attempt to discipline the Party was no exception. Stressing the need for politically reliable cadres, the national leadership launched an intensive effort to weed out leftists and other undesirables from among the Party's membership. Authorities also relied on more regular Party control measures such as reestablishing the discipline inspection system under the leadership of a national commission. Officials have improved state control over the bureaucray by strengthening the standing committee system of the National People's Congress, by popularizing and further developing the nation's legal system, by instituting a system of leader responsibility, and by investing state auditors with the authority to investigate economic abuses within the bureaucracy.

China's modernization program also required substantial improvement in the efficiency of the bureaucracy. Having acknowledged the patrimonial character of China's institutions, authorities sought to implement elements of a legal-rational regime. As a matter of policy, officials championed such principles as recruitment based on merit, increased specialization, reliance on chains of command, and following rules and regulations, all elements of a Weberian-type system which had been much criticized during the Cultural Revolution.[1] However, local- and intermediate-level cadres resisted plans to improve the efficiency of the bureaucracy when it cut into their vested interests.

Although, at least in theory, the CCP leadership has succeeded in binding together China's bureaucracies, in practice they are composed of various, sometimes competing, interests. Bureaus and sections within ministries compete with other units for resources and for programs. Provincial and local agencies defend their interests and attempt to expand their domains. In this system cadres interact with one another based, in part, on kinship relations, geographic identification, generational age, and mutual benefit.

The continued existence of factionalism and the reliance on networks of personal relations point to the essentially functional nature of these informal patterns of behavior. Apart from the value that Chinese society places on *guanxi*,[2] structural factors also help to explain the persistence of these relationships. First, because desired goods and services (such as housing) are in short supply, most people must go without unless they cultivate informal connections. Second, in socialist countries, because cadres depend solely on the state for their livelihood and are unable to diversify their incomes, they seek security in their jobs by forming informal relationships of mutual obligation with other officials up and down the bureaucratic hierarchy.[3] The result is that within bureaucracies in China, officials are divided along factional lines.

In Selections 33 and 34, official China denounces the existence of factionalism, which it blames on the Cultural Revolution. Although in Selection 33, "Commentator," an authoritative Party figure (perhaps Deng Xiaoping), argues that left uncurbed factionalism will undermine the Party's rectification campaign, he proposes only modest solutions: educating cadres to abandon their factional ways and transfering cadres with factional tendencies to other units. Incentives to control or eliminate factionalism, however, are missing.

The more general problem of forming networks to "grease the skids" in the course of policy implementation is addressed in Selection 34. Faced with the conflicting pressures of having to fulfill quotas, but being unable to obtain the required raw materials to do so, intermediate-level cadres are tempted to strike bargains of mutual benefit with suppliers in "under-the-table" relationships. Consequently, resources are misallocated and the prestige of China's cadres is brought into disrepute. To solve the problem, authorities propose to strengthen the work of the Party discipline inspection commissions, and in particular to warn senior cadres not to engage in "unhealthy tendencies." The weakness of the commissions in dealing with Party members is obvious, however. Commissions are instructed to "criticize, halt, and *even* take disciplinary action" against violators. Again, normative sanctions seem to be all that the Party can muster against its own membership. Senior cadres are reluctant to disturb relationships that may affect their peers, or that, at least in the short term, appear to be necessary to get the job done.

The pervasiveness of "all-purpose glue," which is useful to gain access to commodities in short supply , is the subject of Selection 35. All sorts of people, regardless of their station, need this fellow to get jobs, housing, and even a wedding car. Based on mutual benefit, the ties bind together both bosses and their subordinates, and peers. Without *guanxi*, one has to wait in line or go without.

The next selections (36 and 37), authored by *Renmin ribao* (People's Daily)'s well-known muckraking journalist Liu Binyan, are lively investigative reports of official corruption. They are unusual in China, where the media, tightly controlled by the Party, serves chiefly to publicize Party policies and to persuade the people to implement them. In recent times, however, some intrepid reporters have begun to criticize the incompetence or corruption of local leaders, and often they have met with harassment, detention, or obstruction in their investigations. Although Liu Binyan's work is the most famous of this genre, Party authorities have treated him with caution. Officials are willing to have cadre abuses exposed in an effort to correct malpractices, but they are fearful that the Party's reputation will be sullied in the process. The Party's treatment of journalists such as Liu serves as a bellweather of their intentions toward the press.

Liu's two reports have certain features in common. These accounts reveal the inadequacy of the control system to prevent abuses of power by cadres. Outside investigators are powerless to check the behavior of the "invisible" networks. (Liu's description of the networks as "invisible" contrasts with "Commentator's" assertion in Selection 33 that they are "never imperceptible.") Local cadres command considerable resources, including the protection of influential patrons at higher levels and their crucial position as distributors of scarce goods and services. In both cases, leaders use their control over the personnel system to build their network: They make decisions on recruitment, promotion, and disciplinary matters based on the interests of the faction.

Even in the 1970s and 1980s, Liu Binyan reveals, authorities could dredge up or fabricate pre-1949 events to suit their purposes to tarnish the reputations of others. In Selection 37, not content with evicting the long-suffering Guo from his house (they needed Guo's courtyard for their own building program) and spreading wild rumors about his family, city officials relabeled him a "capitalist" for good measure. This occurred at a time when central authorities had disavowed the practice of using class labels to arbitrarily punish the people. The adaptability of local officials is clearly revealed in this selection. Thus, their reaction to China's new legal system, designed in part to curb cadre abuses, is to turn the law into another tool for pursuing their interests. Judges and lawyers need housing too! In this case they turn a deaf ear on complaints about abuses in the Housing Bureau in exchange for preferential treatment of their housing needs.

If Beijing has sought to impose tighter control over the country's bureaucracies, it has also sought to improve their efficiency. In particular, officials have begun to tackle abuses of the state and Party personnel system. In the course of recent reforms, however, the press has revealed the existence of persistent problems, the subject of Selections 38–40. In Selection 38, an official of a prefectural personnel bureau complains that because senior military officials intervene in personnel decisions to protect their favorites, rational personnel administration is impossible. As a result, authorities cannot select cadres based on merit, a situation that produces waste and the misallocation of talent. Faction leaders, in particular, are guilty of tampering with the personnel system, and, by implication, Party officials are the leading culprits.

In 1983, faced with the prospect of losing their jobs in Guizhou Province's administrative reform program, local officials retired "in a rush" in favor of their children (Selection 39). Following the practice in many places of the sons of urban factory workers inheriting their father's jobs, Guizhou's local cadres sought to place their children in their old positions. The reasons for this move are not stated. However, administrative jobs that pay relatively well and are in short supply in Guizhou undoubtedly were attractive. In addition, appointing relatives to these posts would ensure the continuation of valuable insider connections. Local cadres refused to replace the unqualified children, however, for more than five months. Only when the provincial Party committee intervened did officials take any action.

Cadre resistance to the administrative reform of appointing younger people to official positions is the subject of Selection 40. Despite the 1982 requirement of the central government that local officials appoint younger leadership groups, the average age of newly appointed provincial cadres remained unchanged. Since the end of 1982, when this piece was written, however, younger provincial-level officials have won appointments.[4]

The selections in this section indicate that intermediate- and lower-level cadres have considerable scope for resisting the policy directives of China's senior leaders. The enormous variety of "local conditions" in China require vaguely worded central directives, which gives considerable discretion to local officials. Localities control their own extra-budgetary funds, giving them some leeway to pursue their own goals. And geographic remoteness prevents central officials from closely scrutinizing local activities. Protected by intermediate-level cadres, local officials can to a certain extent go their own way. In Selection 41, "Commentator"gives vent to Beijing's frustration and demands that local officials stop taking "countermeasures" to obstruct central policies. In a stinging attack on local officials, "Commentator" condemns unitism or departmentalism and especially deplores the failure of local officials to take an overall view. The harsh tone of the commentary indicates the pervasiveness of this phenomenon in China today•

Notes

1. Martin King Whyte, "Bureaucracy and Modernization in China: the Maoist Critique," *American Sociological Review* 38:2 (April 1973), pp. 149–163.

2. See Lucian Pye, *The Dynamics of Chinese Politics* (Cambridge, Mass.: Oelgeschlager, Gunn & Hain, 1981), for the argument that factionalism in China is a product of Chinese culture.

3. Richard Kraus, "The Chinese State and Its Bureaucrats," in Victor Nee and David Mozingo, eds., *State and Society in Contemporary China* (Ithaca, N.Y.: Cornell University Press, 1983), pp. 132–147.

4. William deB. Mills, "Leadership Change in China's Provinces," *Problems of Communism* 34:3 (May–June 1985), p. 29.

33

Commentator

RESOLUTELY UPROOT FACTIONALISM TO ENSURE HEALTHY DEVELOPMENT OF PARTY RECTIFICATION

THE CCP CENTRAL COMMITTEE's decision on Party rectification points out: "At present, factionalism, which developed during the ten years of domestic turmoil among a number of Party members and cadres, has not yet been overcome. They still maintain factionalism instead of Party spirit. They use their faction as the line of demarcation and appoint people through favoritism while elbowing out of their way those who hold different views; they form cliques to pursue selfish interests, seriously impairing the unity and solidarity of the Party and hindering it from carrying out its line, principles, and policies." This state of affairs "must be thoroughly changed in the current Party rectification." Resolutely uprooting factionalism is a task that must be completed in the Party rectification. It also constitutes a key issue for ensuring the healthy development of the Party rectification process.

Factionalism is a product of the "Great Cultural Revolution" and is absolutely incompatible with the Party spirit of the proletariat. Since the downfall of the "Gang of Four," especially since the Third Plenum of the Eleventh CCP Central Committee, our Party has made consistent efforts to get rid of factionalism and to strengthen Party spirit in connection with work in all fields while bringing order out of chaos and effecting a historical change. At present, the number of people still clinging to factionalism has indeed declined. However, factionalist thinking and activities still exist, not only in the grass roots, but also among the leadership; not only in enterprises, undertakings, and units, but also in Party and government organs; not only among young cadres, but also among old ones. Whenever our Party sets about on an important job and deals particularly with a matter concerning a change of personnel, it will almost certainly encounter disturbances caused by factionalism.

For example, in the course of the structural reform and the reorganization of leading bodies, people who stubbornly stick to their factionalist position refuse to follow the four major principles for promoting cadres and tend to choose those in the same faction. The Party central authorities have ordered that all "people of

Renmin ribao [People's Daily], February 14, 1984. Translation from FBIS Daily Report, February 15, 1984, pp. K1–K3.

the three categories,'' no matter which faction they belong to, must be completely expelled [*qingchu*]. As another example, when the central authorities decided to crack down on serious economic and other criminal activities, the people obsessed by factionalism even harbored criminal offenders who had factional relations with them and thus hindered the settlement of some cases. Moreover, although the central authorities repeatedly have called for correcting unhealthy tendencies, they continue to go against the central instructions and seek selfish interests for themselves and their factions by forming their factionalist networks. Furthermore, when the Party is engaged in building its third echelon and selecting reliable successors for the Party's cause, they arbitrarily place in reserve those erstwhile rebels who hold the same views as they do or who have protected them before. As we are improving and developing the democratic system of the Party and the state and trying to properly organize Party congresses and people's congresses at all levels, they even take this opportunity to carry out illegal activities in violation of the Party's organizational principles to manipulate and even sabotage the elections. All this shows us clearly that without thoroughly eliminating factionalism, we will not be able to consolidate and sustain stability and unity in domestic politics and ensure the implementation of the Party's principles and policies; nor will it be possible for us to create a new situation in socialist modernization.

Now, as the Party rectification is to be unfolded in an all-round way, will the people with serious factionalist ideas begin to mend their ways? Experiences of the Party rectification pilot projects prove that some of them have indeed pulled in their horns, but others are still brazenly engaging in factionalist activities. In places where factionalism holds sway, certain people continue to overtly or covertly draw demarcation lines according to persons and factions; they only rectify the faction opposing them, even reverse right and wrong in assessing merits and mistakes, and deal blows at good comrades; and they deliberately conceal the problems of impurity of ideology, work-style, and organization among people belonging to a faction with ties to themselves. In places where the ''people of three categories'' are hidden, some seize the opportunity to stir up factionalism, create confusion, and divert the aim of Party rectification in a bid for self-preservation. The facts are very evident: If we slacken our vigilance during this Party rectification, and fail to oppose factionalism in a resolute and clear-cut way, it will be impossible to reach the goal of Party rectification, and possible hidden dangers will remain.

Comrade Deng Xiaoping pointed out long ago: "Leaders must take a clear-cut and firm attitude to oppose factionalism.'' "It is necessary to transfer people who persist in factionalism from their original posts and criticize their mistakes. Such matters should not be delayed.'' The main reason why factionalism in some localities and units has not been overcome for a long time is not that the problems have not been discovered, but because leading cadres there are weak and incompetent. They themselves may also be influenced by factionalism or have too many misgivings and selfish calculations, so they can only adopt an ambiguous attitude and cannot resolutely handle the factionalism problems.

People who indulge in factionalism are mostly comrades who have ideological problems and who have not eliminated the influence of the Lin Biao and Jiang Qing counterrevolutionary cliques. For the most part, they bear in mind such exploiting class ideology as extreme egoism, anarchism, and feudal sectarianism. Therefore, in order to overcome factionalism, it is not enough to merely take passive and preventive measures; we must carry out active ideological struggles. Thus, Party organizations at all levels, particularly those in localities and units where factionalism is running rampant, must place ideological work for opposing factionalism and strengthening Party spirit in an important position. The ideological work must be directed at the expressions of factionalism in these units and must be carried out in a clear-cut manner. People who have serious factionalist ideas must be deterred from continuing to practice factionalism. Criticism and self-criticism should be conducted to expose and analyze factionalism to prompt Party members who still have factionalist ideas to make thorough self-criticism and have firm determination to correct their mistakes and change their position.

Necessary organizational measures and active ideological struggles supplement each other. We should resolutely remove from leading posts people who have been found to be stubbornly sticking to factionalism, engaging in illegal activities in violation of discipline, and resisting and undermining the Party's principles and policies. More disciplinary measures should be meted out to them when Party rectification begins in their units, according to the seriousness of their cases. As for a small number of "people of the three categories" who have agitated for factionalism and made trouble, once their bad practices are discovered, facts must be ascertained as soon as possible and these people must be immediately expelled from the Party.

Some comrades argue that it is not easy to ascertain whether a person is practicing factionalism or not although measures must be taken against factionalism.

This opinion is not right. Factionalism is never imperceptible. At present, factionalism's most conspicuous expression is in the naked identity of interests formed among people who "held the same viewpoints" during the "Great Cultural Revolution" or else with a faction who protected one during the period. Rivalry for power and interests and using powers in pursuit of private gains represent the core of factional activities. For the sake of preserving and seeking selfish interests, they resist and oppose the Party central leadership's line, principles, and policies. Most Party members and ordinary people can clearly discern these phenomena. Therefore, so long as we rely firmly on the masses, make serious investigations, and use the Party's principles and discipline and state laws as a yardstick to judge people's deeds, then we will clearly see who has factionalist ideas and will be able to correctly and effectively launch a struggle against factionalism.

34

Central Discipline Inspection Commission of the CCP

[August 6, 1981] CIRCULAR ON ENFORCING PARTY DISCIPLINE AND ELIMINATING THE UNHEALTHY PRACTICE OF UNDER-THE-TABLE RELATIONSHIPS [*guanxihu*]

1. Lin Biao and the "Gang of Four" very seriously devastated our Party's style of work ideologically and organizationally during the ten years of internal disorder of the "Great Cultural Revolution." This pernicious influence is still far from being eliminated, and many unhealthy tendencies are continuously corrupting many of our Party members, cadres, and even some Party organizations. One of the prominent manifestations of this is the widespread appearance of so-called "under-the-table relationships."

2. Different kinds of relations naturally exist in life as well as in work, such as comradely relations, work relations, the relations between the high and low levels, organizational relations, the relations in production coordination . . . and so forth. These relations should be based on principle and should promote progress in our work and the advancement of our socialist cause and should support public interests, not private gain. However, the so-called "under-the-table relationships" represent a relationship of an entirely different nature; in the course of economic transactions and contacts in work, office workers would unprincipledly give concerned units or individuals some money or items (scarce equipment or items as small as cigarettes and as big as machinery and equipment) or they would promise them certain benefits because without these means of "establishing contacts," the other parties would make things difficult, and in the end things that should have been done would not be accomplished. These kinds of unhealthy tendencies and evil practices of establishing contacts for private gain and of building up "under-the-table relationships" are actually acts of offering and receiving bribes in disguise under most circumstances.

3. These kinds of practices of bribery in disguise involving "under-the-table relationships" were originally a product of the old society, but even in the old society people looked upon bribery as a shameful act and called it ill-gotten gains. In the ten years of internal disorder during the "Great Cultural Revolution," Lin Biao and the "Gang of Four" seriously destroyed our Party members' fine traditions and their work-style in performing their official duties honestly and doing everything according to principle.

They ruined the lofty socialist atmosphere in society and turned the practices

Xinhua [New China News Agency], Chinese, August 6, 1981. Translation from FBIS Daily Report, August 7, 1981, pp. K2–K3.

of establishing contacts and ''under-the-table relationships'' into a means of getting things done. This decadent and philistine work-style of "plucking a feather from a flying wild goose'' and of ''greasing the skids'' is not only common among office workers in general but is also prevalent between enterprises, government offices, and mass organizations. These actions have an impact on certain Party organizations and even on certain leading cadres. Some Party organizations have taken no action to criticize, struggle against, punish, or pay any attention to these serious, unhealthy tendencies; instead they have assumed an attitude of tacit consent and support toward them, thus aggravating the problems to a more serious degree.

4. This evil practice of favoring ''under-the-table relationships'' has caused substantial damage to our Party organizations, the state organs, and the entire society. (a) It has caused state funds amounting to hundreds of millions of yuan to flow into the hands of small collectives and individuals through hundreds of thousands of loopholes, thus seriously undermining socialist economic construction. (b) This improper give-and-take practice with tacit understanding has gradually contaminated a considerable number of working cadres with the philistine work-style of using public office for private gain and pursuing personal comfort. Some of them have become corrupt and degenerate, losing the communist moral character. This evil practice is a very damaging corrosive agent. (c) It is imperceptibly and seriously undermining the lofty socialist atmosphere in the society and thus inevitably influencing the thinking of the younger generation and poisoning our next generation. (d) It has besmirched the Party's image and damaged its prestige among the masses. All these are facts, not exaggerations just to scare people.

5. The work-style of a Party in power has a bearing on its life and death. Discipline inspection departments at all levels should concentrate their main efforts on constantly being concerned with the ideological and political unity inside the Party, on raising the fighting strength of Party organizations, and on safeguarding the Party leadership and the Party's prestige. One of the important tasks of discipline inspection departments is to wage a resolute struggle against unhealthy tendencies. Unhealthy tendencies and evil practices are absolutely incompatible with the work-style of our Communist Party. The problem of ''under-the-table relationships'' is a more common unhealthy tendency today. The State Council has promulgated a ''Circular Concerning the Prohibition of Unhealthy Practices in Commodity Circulation.'' All Communist Party members must be exemplary in publicizing and implementing the stipulations of the circular and must end all improper acts or acts of bribery in disguise by establishing contacts outside the scope of commodity circulation.

6. The Central Discipline Inspection Commission calls on discipline inspection committees at all levels to follow the guidelines of the Sixth Plenum and Comrade Hu Yaobang's ''July 1'' speech about enforcing the Party's organizational discipline and constantly keeping ourselves politically pure and healthy by accomplishing the following tasks: (a) We should resolutely struggle against the unhealthy tendencies of favoring ''under-the-table relationships.'' All cases

will be investigated and handled as soon as they are discovered. Party members, cadres, and the masses will be mobilized and given support to combat these unhealthy tendencies. (b) The discipline inspection committees of higher levels should have more courage to criticize, halt, and even take disciplinary actions against violations of discipline and law by those key cadres who have no regard for Party discipline and the laws of the state. (c) Heavier punishment should be meted out to those who continue this kind of improper activity after the State Council's circular is transmitted to the lower level. Those who commit more serious offenses should be dismissed from the Party. (d) All money and things derived from corruption and bribery should be returned or compensation should be paid. (e) Individuals or organizations who obstruct inspection of this unhealthy tendency shall be sanctioned by Party discipline with no exceptions.

[Signed] The Central Discipline Inspection Commission of the CCP

July 20, 1981

35

Wang Minglu

UNHEALTHY TENDENCY

(Comedians' Dialogue—*xiangsheng*)

A. What line of work are you in?

B. Performer of comedian's dialogues.

A. How's that? You're a performer?

B. Unhunh.

A. Who set you up in it?

B. What's that supposed to mean? I've loved the arts since I was a child, then I tested into a theatrical troupe.

A. Come off it, who do you think you're kidding? Now tell me the truth: What strings did you pull?

B. I didn't pull any strings.

A. No strings and you became an actor? Hmm, let me see—the old doorman at the Arts Bureau is your uncle.

B. Take your old uncle! What're you fixing me up with an uncle for?

A. No strings and there's no way you could become an actor. Now take our neighbor's kid: he had everthing going for him—the fundamentals, the physique,

Tianjin yanchang [Tianjin], 1979, No. 2. Translated by Thomas B. Gold.

somersaults and handstands all perfect. His voice—tenor, baritone and bass all perfect.

B. Everything in order, I'd say.

A. But he failed when it came to looks.

B. The kid wasn't nice looking?

A. No. He was great looking – soft white skin, thick eyebrows, big eyes, double-fold eyelids.

B. Then what was wrong?

A. Nothing except he had a mole right here. (Points to his face.)

B. And that did him in?

A. Forget it, didn't make the grade. Now if a gorgeous kid like that couldn't get in, how could someone who looks like you make it? Let everybody have a look. I've seen thermos corks that were better looking!

B. Leave it to you to make such a comparison.

A. I'm really puzzled. If you didn't pull any strings, how could you be a performer? All right, so you're a performer but you haven't done a very good job. So switch jobs! I'll fix it up for you. I can pull the right strings.

B. Why would I want to switch jobs? I won't switch.

A. We're pretty good friends, so let's keep in touch. If something comes up, we can talk it over. I've got plenty of strings to pull. Need a house? Is the place you're living in okay? If it's a house you need, I'm your man.

B. (aside) I knew he could pull strings, but why would I want to switch homes? Nothing doing.

A. Now don't be shy.

B. What's there to be shy about?

A. Is your home comfortable?

B. Just fine.

A. What's fine about it? Don't give me that stuff. What are you keeping such a stiff upper lip for? Everybody knows that when your son got married he had no place to live so he took over your house and now you and your wife are living in the gutter.

B. What? You say we're living in the sewer?

A. Not really. But you did take a round cement sewer pipe about a man's height, pile up bricks at either end, put in a window and door, and the two of you are living in it. It's a modern earthquake shelter.

B. Well I've never!

A. One day four rowdy kids came and pushed it to the other side of the road. The next day your kids couldn't find you: "Hey Dad! He was here last night. What the? How'd you end up across the street?"

B. So what if I live in a cement sewer pipe? Should I be ashamed of it? Lose face? You should feel sorry for me. I used to live in two rooms but they were flattened in the earthquake. The Gang of Four wrecked the earthquake prevention and relief work. But now things are straightening out: this year they've built 3 million square meters of housing and they'll build another 4 million next year. All in all that's 7 million.

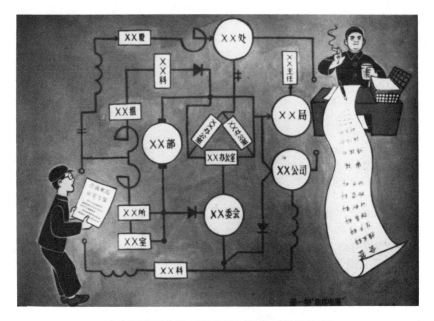

A DIFFERENT "INTEGRATED CIRCUIT"

Ling yige "Jicheng dianlu," by Jiang Peiyang

The poor fellow seeking approval has to negotiate his way through a maze of bureaus, offices, committees, companies, etc., to find the high and mighty "responsible person" authorized to grant approval. Note the typical depiction of the bureaucrat with his cigarette and teacup, writing endless reports.

A. Seven million, so what? You still need me. I'll fix it up for you. Otherwise, even if they build 8 million you won't get any. I've got connections in the Housing Bureau. I'll work it out for you, get you a flat of your own.

B. No thanks. Getting a house that way is dirty. Just now you said you could pull strings and fix it up for me. Well that's called an "unhealthy tendency." I know all about you Mr. Wheeler Dealer; all you ever do is pull strings.

A. What're you yelling for? Should I get you a loudspeaker so everyone can hear all over town?

B. Why are you afraid if someone else hears?

A. Idiot. Do you have to shout about pulling strings? Amateur. You've obviously never pulled strings before.

A. What's the good of being able to pull strings?

B. I can hardly begin to tell you. When other people line up to go shopping, you don't have to wait in line. I can buy things others can't buy. I can handle things others can't. Take an example—eating breakfast. Do you line up to buy donuts?

B. It's much easier to buy breakfast nowadays. On my way to work there are only ten or so people in line, so I can buy it quite quickly.

A. Quickly you say? When you buy a donut they make you buy a griddle cake too, just to get rid of them. Any donut you get was fried the night before. It sits out all night and gets leathery. You really have to gnaw and yank on it. "Ow, what a pain! Excuse me, could I try your scissors on this?"

B. You're getting carried away.

A. Well *I* don't have to wait in line.

B. How . . .

A. I can pull strings. When I eat donuts I insist on freshly fried ones. No matter how many people are lined up, I stride right to the front. "Elder Sister Xu, hem hem . . . " (*Puts out two fingers.*)

B. What's this mean? (*Doing the same.*)

A. Give me two.

B. What's this "Elder Sister Xu" business?

A. The person who fries the donuts is a female comrade named Xu—Elder Sister Xu.

B. Is she older than you?

A. No, she's just begun to work. A bit over twenty.

B. You're still a teenager then?

A. Whaddya mean teenager? I'm fifty-one!

B. Well then, what business does a fifty-one-year-old have calling a twenty-year-old "Elder Sister?"

A. You wouldn't understand. It's the established practice for pulling strings. When you pull strings, you must assume the role of someone's junior. The sweeter your words, the more honey you'll eat. Hahaha.

B. You'd stoop to anything. So you go down a generation just to get something to eat.

A. When Elder Sister Xu sees it's me, she gives me a look. "So you've come. You're late today. Wait a sec." After saying that, plop plop, she pulls off two pieces of dough. Oh boy, as big as steamed buns, and when they hit the oil they get as big as wok covers. She drops them in the wok and flips them four times but they're still not cooked all the way through. When she fishes them out, they're this big, golden brown, crispy and crunchy.

B. You just take them like that.

A. How's that?

B. Don't the other customers have any opinions about this?

A. Sure they do. At first some guy had words with me, but after a while it's okay. They're all used to it and I act very natural.

B. Hasn't anybody told you off?

A. Yes. One day an old lady was in line with a little girl. The girl called the old lady granny. "Granny, that fat slob comes every day, and he goes inside and says 'Elder Sister Xu' and puts out two fingers and walks off with two donuts. Granny, tomorrow you try saying 'Elder Sister Xu' and we won't have to wait in line either." The old lady said, "That'll be the day. Darling, saying 'Elder Sister Xu' wouldn't get us anywhere. Even if we called her Auntie we'd still have to wait in line. Let's not act like that man, my child. That's an unhealthy tendency.

Let him go wolf it down—I hope it gets stuck in his windpipe!''

B. She had you there. How about it? Did you sneak out the back way?

A. Ha! I go through the back door [euphemism for improper pull] every day, but that day I had to go out the front door. I deliberately went in front of the old lady and said, "Pardon me, ma'am, be careful not to get any grease on you. You think I'll get the hiccups from it, but really it's just the thing to cure a bellyache."

B. You were really asking for it, weren't you? Did the old lady let you get away with it?

A. She said nothing. But a stalwart young guy came over from the side and grabbed me. "Hey, hold on a minute. Xu, fry me up two just like you do for him, or else I'll smash your wok!"

B. Was he ever furious!

A. Furious? He was nothing compared to Elder Sister Xu. She didn't budge one inch. "Fry up two for you? Just look at you. I know your type. Have you got anything on him? He's got connections here." And that's the story—she and I are tied together.

B. Everyone who pulls strings is tied together.

A. When I thought about it, I realized Elder Sister Xu had hit the nail on the head. She had owed me one.

B. How so?

A. I was the one who managed to get that pair of polyester slacks for her. Fabric and labor only six yuan. Pretty cheap.

B. Oh now I get it. All this chatter and what you really do is sell cloth.

A. What would I want to sell cloth for? I don't sell cloth.

B. Well, those polyester . . .

A. I have connections. Little Zhao at the fabric store owed me one. When he's selling cloth if he thinks of me he'll mark it down, grade it as irregular and save it for me.

B. Then you exchange it for donuts.

A. What? Do you think Little Zhao gives me that fabric for nothing? I got him lard—more than four catties, without using meat ration coupons.

B. How'd you do that?

A. Markdown. Graded it as pig's head which doesn't require coupons. I took the meat and exchanged it for cloth, then exchanged the cloth for donuts.

B. Ahah!

A. If you know me and you're my friend, if something comes up, we can talk it over. Ask anybody in Tianjin about me—there's no one big or small who doesn't know me. I've got a nickname.

B. What is it?

A. All Purpose Glue.

B. Oh, so you're All Purpose Glue. Slip me five. We're two of a kind.

A. You're also All Purpose Glue?

B. No, fish glue.

A. What does fish glue have to do with anything?

B. Both of us have sticky fingers.

Everyone must be inoculated against this epidemic [details of disease and picture included].

Everyone must be inoculated against this disease [no details included].

Everyone must be beaten.

A GOOD THING BECOMES A BAD THING
Haoshi bian huaishi, by Fang Cheng

This is a story about the policy implementation process. At each bureaucratic level, the original, detailed policy loses information vital to successful implementation. Here the humor stems from a Chinese pun. "To inoculate" (*dazhen*) contains the same first character as "to beat" (*da*). Thus, when the policy reaches the basic level, the *zhen* has been lost; only the *da* is left. Note that the high official handing down the policy in the first panel is faceless, represented only by an arm.

A. You often hear someone say: "That guy sure knows how to manage, he can do everything." All purpose—that's me! I'm not only all purpose, I'm good at sticking by my friends—All Purpose Glue.
B. What rock did you crawl out from under?
A. What's that supposed to mean, hunh?
B. Do you have a real job?
A. Of course; how could I not have a job?

B. What line of work?

A. Backup.

B. You mean employee's benefits?

A. No, the union handles that.

B. In charge of procurement?

A. No, that's supply and marketing. I'm backup.

B. What kind of backup?

A. Backing up my own interests.

B. You do nothing at work except wheel and deal. Doesn't your chief ever criticize you?

A. Who ever said he doesn't criticize me? He can be really harsh.

B. I knew you'd take a lot of criticism. What'd he go after you for?

A. "All Purpose Glue, if you keep on like this, you're riding for a fall. Just what are you up to? Those pork chops you bought me last time were tough!"

B. You call that a criticism? Sounds like he's supporting your under-the-table dealings.

A. Ah me, the chief is just too hard on me. Always hits the nail on the head. My portion was tender but the chief's wasn't. I said, "I've learned my lesson. Next time I'll be sure and buy well-marbled meat." (*Imitating the chief*) "Forget about it! Come over here, come on." The chief called me into his office to speak with me alone. "All Purpose Glue, do me a little favor, okay? My wife's younger sister got sent down to the countryside nearly a year ago and hasn't been able to get back to the city. You've got to think of a way to get her back." I said, "Sure thing, Chief. I'll do everything in my power. You've given me a chance to atone for my crimes."

B. Atone for your crimes?

A. Don't you see? Once I get his sister-in-law back then afterwards I can get anything I want in the factory. I can walk on water.

B. Did you have strings to pull on this one?

A. No.

B. You could go and see Elder Sister Xu about it.

A. No good. Elder Sister Xu is only good for donuts.

B. Then exchange her for a donut!

A. Wouldn't work, even for ten of them.

B. So what did you do?

A. Asked around, sent out some feelers. You can get anything if you know how to ask for it. So then I got my answer: there's this young guy in our factory called Li. Well, his uncle is the Party secretary of the commune where the chief's sister-in-law had been resettled. I mentioned it to Li and he was absolutely sure there'd be no problem arranging it. He guaranteed he could get her sent back, but he didn't have time to work on it just then since he was busy with his own wedding. So he got me to help out with his nuptials first as a condition for the switch. As soon as the wedding was over, the chief's sister-in-law would be able to come back for sure.

B. Do you know how to arrange a wedding?

A. A snap. I arranged Li's wedding completely. I've got strings to pull. I bought his clothes, cabinet, sofa—I even arranged the entire wedding feast . . . , 16 tables all told.

B. Why set up so many?

A. Li has lots of relatives and friends. When it was all set up, the bride raised new demands.

B. What were they?

A. She absolutely had to have a car. If there was no car, she wouldn't leave her house.

B. That's a bad attitude to take. What's she being so extravagant for?

A. There was nothing Li could do about it. He called me over. I said, "It's nothing Li Baby, don't sweat it. All she wants is a car? I've got the strings, just a sec and I'll call over to the Janitorial Department."

B. What? You'd make the bride ride in a garbage truck?

A. I could clean it up and put down a carpet.

B. That'd never do. No way.

A. Bad idea? How about if I had the Construction Bureau send over a bulldozer?

B. What? Scoop the bride away?

A. Li said, "Don't joke with me, how about it?!" Well! I got an idea—Liu Zhi from our neighborhood drives in a motor pool.

B. What's the connection between you and Liu Zhi?

A. He owes me one.

B. He also owes you one? What's the story?

A. I got him his sick leave slips. A whole book of them.

B. Why so many?

A. I've got the strings. I'll get you a book of them. You fill in your sickness by yourself. They've already been approved.

B. You helped him play hooky?

A. Say what you will, it's sure made it easy for me to get a car. (*Dialing a telephone.*)

B. People sure know how to use each other.

A. "Hey, Liu Zhi. This is All Purpose Glue. Something's come up for Sunday afternoon at 2 and I need a car. A van would be best. Got to fetch a bride. What's that? Gotta be on the dot. Okay. I'll thank you again when I see you." (*Putting down the phone.*) "How about it, Li Baby? Just take it easy. The car will be there Sunday promptly at 2. Nothing for you to worry about. I'll go pick her up." Little Li had just left when "brrrrrg" the phone rang again. "Who do you want? All Purpose Glue? Speaking. . . ."

B. Always busy.

A. "What did you say? Oh, no . . . " (*cries*)

B. Are you okay?

A. My elder brother's wife's fourth maternal auntie's niece's eldest cousin-in-law's second maternal auntie's husband died.

B. You call him your relative?

A. Second Uncle was a swell old guy, especially since he owed me one.

B. He owed you one too?

A. He was the doorman at the hospital and he's the one who stole the sick-leave slips I gave Liu Zhi.

B. Ha! You'd stoop to anything.

A. It was really hard for the old guy. He had to get up in the middle of the night to stamp the official seal on them. People walking by outside scared him out of his wits.

B. Serves him right. He *was* stealing sick-leave slips, after all.

A. Second Uncle died old and lonely. He left no one. So I was quite busy with that. Had to call the funeral parlor right away to send a hearse.

B. Don't tell me you've got an in at the funeral parlor too?

A. I had strings to pull there. I really know my way around the funeral parlor and crematorium. If anything comes up, let's talk it over.

B. Nothing's up! Now who would want to keep in touch with a crematorium?

A. One call and the car was set to come Sunday at one to cremate Second Uncle. I had it all figured out. After I'd sent the hearse away I could go with Liu Zhi at 2 to get the bride. So once the wedding was over the chief's sister-in-law could come right back.

B. You sure had your work cut out for you.

A. Then Sunday, at 12, Liu Zhi called and said the car was out of the question. The motor pool had sent an urgent message that you needed their okay to borrow a car for personal use. Liu Zhi had his mind set. Couldn't he have said he needed it to take a sick man to the hospital? But no, he was completely up front. The dispatcher heard it was for a wedding and said nothing-doing; he'd never allow it.

B. Gotta think of something else.

A. I made another call for a car. I made a lot of calls. Either the guy was out or the car wasn't around. What could I do? If I couldn't pick up Li's bride, then the chief's sister-in-law couldn't get back from the countryside. Ha ha ha!

B. What's there to laugh about?

A. I got an idea. Didn't I say that the hearse was supposed to come for Second Uncle at one? Well, I could speak with the driver. Wouldn't they really get a kick out of fetching a bride?

B. It'd never work. The van says "Crematorium" on it.

A. I told them to send a new one that hadn't been lettered yet.

B. That's no good either. You'd put the bride and the stiff together?

A. A brand new hearse, put the corpse in the back, cover him up—nobody'd be the wiser.

B. You can solve anything.

A. The routing was perfect. Second Uncle lived over at Jin'gang Bridge and the bride was at Anding Bridge in Xiaowangzhuang. Li the groom was at Beiyang Bridge. All three bridges were right on the way.

B. Oh, now I've got it. At Jin'gang Bridge you load Second Uncle, then get the bride over at Xiaowangzhuang, then off to Beiyang Bridge and drop off the bride, then head for the crematorium.

Liu Qingtao

A. First I talked it over with the driver. He knew me. "All Purpose Glue, it's you again. You've been a very busy man this month. Damned if you haven't put away fifteen already. On average one every two days. Who's this we're burning today?" "My Second Uncle." "Who was it the day before yesterday?" "Fourth Aunt." "Oh, a lot of relatives." "No, come now! They were all people I owed favors. You've really got to help me out today." "Sure thing, don't mention it." "Let's stop the car over at Xiaowangzhuang." "Oh. Got relatives there?" "No, I've got to pick up a bride." When the driver heard that he said, "Have you been taking some drug? I load a stiff to fetch a bride?" "I told you I needed a lot of help, a lot . . . " I looked around. There was a carton of Phoenix Brand Filter Cigarettes on Second Uncle's table. I said, "I really appreciate this, I really do!" "None of that stuff . . . " (*Acts out the stuffing of the cigarette carton into the driver's pocket.*)

B. He put them in his pocket!

A. How about it? Just like he was stuck.

B. That's All Purpose Glue for you.

A. There was a union boss in Second Uncle's factory, a fat slob, real hard of hearing, insisted on going along.

B. That's part of his job.

A. We were busy loading Second Uncle into the rear of the van, then we got in and went off to Xiaowangzhuang to pick up the bride. When we drove up I called out, "Congratulations, congratulations . . . !" I knew one of the bride's sistersin-law. She's a girl who lives near our house. Her nickname is "The Dingbat." I spotted the Dingbat and she said, "Well look what the cat brought in! All Purpose Glue, what're you doing here?" "I came for the bride. C'mon, C'mon." It was still very quiet. There were three people in all. When they came out the sister-in-law saw the car and screamed like a Dingbat: "Hey, All Purpose Glue, what kind of car is this? Why are there blue and white stripes on it?" "It's a luxury car. C'mon and get in fast." I shoved her in and she saw the fat slob. "All Purpose Glue, how can there be somebody else in the car? Who's this fat slob?" "Er, uh, the Union Boss at Li the groom's factory."

B. Hah? Wasn't he Second Uncle's Union Boss?

A. I couldn't mention Second Uncle. We were smuggling him. I said, "Isn't that right Boss?" The slob was hard of hearing so he didn't hear too clearly. "Yes, yes, yes."

B. He'd say yes to anything.

A. The Dingbat was a real chatterbox and she hit it off with Fatso right away. "Sir, you must get real tired lugging around that fat body." "Whadya say?"

B. He didn't hear.

A. "You must get real tired!" "It's not so bad, not so bad. We were close to the Dear Departed for quite a number of years."

B. Uhoh, spilled the beans.

A. The Dingbat heard what he said. "Say, All Purpose Glue, what's this about a Dear Departed?.".."He meant me, my pet name is "Dear Hearted," didn't you know?

B. Fast thinking.

A. But the slob kept babbling on. "Our chief said don't worry about how much you spend on him." I said, "Sister-in-law, did you hear, the chief said don't worry about how much you spend for Li's wedding; do it up right." "We went all over Tianjin but he was simply incurable." The Dingbat picked up on that. "What's that about incurable?" "My good sister-in-law," I said, "in Tianjin slang 'incurable' means unbeatable. Li's wedding will be the tops."

B. An answer for everything.

A. The driver was sitting over there really amused. "All Purpose Glue," he mused to himself, "you're positively shameless, you are! In all the years I've been driving I've never seen anything like this. What a carload of action—tears and laughter all in one. Just like the parade that used to fetch brides in the old days. The joint's really jumpin!" He was supposed to stop at Beiyang Bridge, but went on his merry way straight to the crematorium.

B. How'd you get out of this one?

A. As soon as we got to the crematorium the bride realized what was going on. She was terrified and annoyed. "It was you who sealed my fate," she cried at her sister-in-law. "I said I didn't want a car but you insisted. You said it was a once-in-a-lifetime experience, so let's do it up right. This time we would go great guns—the beauty from the boudoir gets her first ride in a car! Well *now* look: the beauty from the boudoir has her first trip to the crematorium." The bride had a defect as well. When she got angry she'd have an epileptic fit. "We . . . "

B. What happened?

A. Out cold.

B. Shock.

A. The fat slob was scared out of his wits. "All Purpose Glue, now we have another one dead. Which one should we cremate first?" "You can't burn this one," I said. "The chief's sister-in-law hasn't come back from the countryside yet!"

B. Still worried about pulling the right strings!

36

Liu Binyan and Liu Guosheng

AN INVISIBLE MACHINE—A NEGATIVE EXAMPLE OF PERFUNCTORILY CARRYING OUT PARTY RECTIFICATION

What a Way to Carry Out Party Rectification

Have you ever seen such a scene? That at the plenary session of CCP members of the grain bureau, a person under investigation for having committed serious mistakes should pour out in public a stream of abuse against those who were investigating him, swaggering with arms akimbo? And this went on for two hours, with nobody trying to stop him. This very person was chief of the agricultural administration section under the grain bureau of Shuangya City, Heilongjiang Province. Some two years ago, he was informed against concerning the practice of extortion from the peasants.

An initial investigation discovered that there had been other offenses, too: He took advantage of his power to examine and approve applications for the purchase of grain, oil, and fodder to try to establish connections with influential people, and to do favors at no great cost to himself; he made use of his authority to handle and approve applications for grain rations from those who applied for registered permanent residence in the city to engage in bad practices for selfish ends. . . . That a chief of an agricultural administration section should have fifteen kinds of

Renmin ribao [People's Daily], February 8, 1984. Translation from FBIS Daily Report, February 10, 1984, pp. K5–K9.

authority in his hands, some of which even had a direct bearing on the subsistence of the citizens!

How could he be so bold? This section chief has himself answered the question. He threatened openly, saying: "Are there any exceptions in the cases of the leading members of the city in the transfer from registered rural residence to registered urban residence, and in the work arrangement of their own children and dependents? Yin Haijiang (secretary of the bureau CCP Committee) and Duan Lianxi (chief of the organizational section under the bureau) both did it!"

One day in the spring of 1980, an important figure of the city finance and trade office went personally to the grain bureau in a car to reprove the discipline inspection workers for investigating that section chief. At a meeting of the Standing Committee of the CCP Committee of the grain bureau, a decision was adopted to "expel that section chief from the Party and to remove him from his administrative office." However, the decision was later overruled by Yin Haijiang with his one vote. More and more problems concerning the section chief were revealed during the course of the investigation. Nevertheless, Yin Haijiang insisted on closing the case when only a few of the 200-odd incidents of transferring from registered rural residences to registered urban residences had been touched upon. Xia Zhongyi, deputy secretary of the Discipline Inspection Commission of the grain bureau, was chiefly responsible for the investigations into the case of that section chief. He had been engaged in public security and discipline inspection work for nearly four decades, but never had he witnessed two CCP committees of a higher and a lower level shielding a person who had committed grave mistakes. He left the bureau in anger and went to apply for an audience with the Central Discipline Inspection Commission. But he did not expect that, during his absence, he himself would become a target for investigation by Yin Haijiang and others.

All this took place at a time when the Party rectification of the grain bureau was under way (the grain bureau was one of the few units selected by the city CCP Committee for experimentation in Party rectification). In appearance, there was nothing to find fault with in the procedure of Party rectification: studying the documents, every individual CCP member comparing and examining himself against the requirements of the Party constitution, leading cadres taking the lead in practicing self-criticism . . . up to the reregistration of Party membership. But when the Party rectification came to an end, everything remained unchanged. The work team did not even know that there was an invisible but powerful political machine dictating everything.

The Secret of a "Setup"

Back in 1978, when the ferreting-out campaign was under way, some people told Xia Zhongyi that "a factionalist setup exists in the grain bureau," but he would not believe it. He had all along regarded the secretary of the CCP Committee of any unit as the personification of the CCP leadership. Now he has come to understand that he was taken in. Upon the exposure by the masses, Gao Yunwu, then the deputy secretary of the CCP Committee who was in charge of ferreting-out work, wanted to list Duan Lianxi, who had been a ringleader of the rebels and an organizer of atrocities of beating, smashing, and looting during the "Cultural Revolution," as a target for ferreting out.

Nevertheless, Yin Haijiang regarded him as innocent. As a result, Duan Lianxi, who had conducted inquisitions by torture and obtained confessions by compulsion, a killer of two innocent people, and elements who had engaged in beating, smashing, and looting were all left, and not ferreted out.

Shortly afterward, Yin Haijiang suggested the promotion of Duan Lianxi to chief of the organizational section. Again Gao Yunwu objected. At this juncture, his errors in economy, apart from his problems during the "Cultural Revolution," were also revealed. But he became chief of the organizational section all the same. Yin Haijiang was not satisfied with this, and he wanted to promote Duan Lianxi to be a member of the Standing Committee of the bureau CCP Committee and deputy chief of the bureau; to this end, he had submitted at least five reports to the city CCP Committee and had reserved a seat on the Standing Committee for Duan Lianxi beforehand. In fact, Duan Lianxi's actual strength had long surpassed that of the Standing Committee and the deputy chief of the bureau. Everything, big or small, was planned and decided by Yin Haijiang and him in private, and was then adopted by the CCP Committee.

What sort of a person was Yin Haijiang? What sort of relationship existed between him and Duan Lianxi anyway?

Yin Haijiang had been a worker, loading and unloading sacks of grain. As he was keen on adapting himself to the political climate, he became one of the chief leading members of the antirightist campaign in the grain bureau. Later, he became chief of the organizational section, a post that enabled him to personally grasp the authority of personnel administration. In appearance, he was a man of primitive simplicity, honest and kind, but in reality, he was experienced and astute, keen on political trickery, and good at attacking others. People's evalua-tion of the political work of cadre Duan Lianxi was: "Full of vigor and energy, he never attends to proper duties, but specializes in bustling about to establish connections."

When the "Cultural Revolution" broke out, Yin Haijiang took the side of the "upstairs faction" (rebels among political work cadres), headed by Duan Lianxi, and came under their protection. The "upstairs faction" had the personnel files of the cadres, workers, and staff in their control, and they could attack any of them at will by exposing the confidential personal history contained in the files. They had another advantage: they could refrain from doing any practical work, but specialize in seizing power, and in the practice of beating, smashing, and looting. The "downstairs faction," who were in charge of professional work, had to overcome all difficulties during the time of turmoil and to maintain the supply of rations for several hundred thousand people in the city; and, lacking experience in "struggle" and the desire to seize power, they could only suffer total defeat. From then on, those who were upright and professionally strong became objects of attack; they were depreciated and elbowed out, while a number of strong characters, who were keen on seeking personal gain, and professional "blockheads" were promoted.

What the Party rectification work team failed to see was such a fundamental problem—that in the grain bureau system there existed a factional setup formed by "people of the three categories" working hand in glove with those who had taken advantage of their power in seeking personal interests. Under the common aim of "first, grasping power; second, grasping the personnel; third, grasping money and materials," they colluded with each other, shielded each other, and made use of each other. And Yin Haijiang and Duan Lianxi were the very core of this factional setup.

On weekends and holidays, the jeeps in the streets of Shuangya City would shuttle to and fro, and in some of them were cadres of all levels attending dinner parties at the homes of "their own men." Now do not take this for only a demonstration of the unhealthy tendencies of "going in for eating and drinking extravagantly." Many personnel questions concerning promotion and demotion, appointment to, removal from, and transference between offices were the subject of bargains finally struck at the banquet tables.

In the acceptance for Party membership and in promotions, priority was given to those people belonging to the same faction, the "people of the three categories," and those who were degenerate in character, and those "dispelled from the Party, and removed from office" were no exception.

Once, Xia Zhongyi personally experienced such a great reversal in a personnel question. He and Lan Dianyin, a cadre of the Discipline Inspection Committee of the bureau, went together to investigate a person who was questionable in matters of economy. Lan Dianyin had all along been willingly bearing the burden of office, and had been bold in struggling, but she had not been given a raise since 1966. And it was also time for Xia Zhongyi himself to be promoted. Priority should have been given to cadres of discipline inspection work concerning consideration for a raise in salary. Nevertheless, they had never expected that they would not be given a promotion, while the target of their investigation, the person who was questionable in matters of economy, would be promoted and become deputy chief of the supply section!

In July 1981, a driver was transferred to the grain bureau. His name was Liu Shaoshan. The moment he arrived, he blared out: "I am invited here by your secretary, Yin Haijiang!" And it did not take him very long to use a whole tank of gasoline when he came to the car pool. When the car pool chief criticized him, he stopped showing up for work altogether for the following six months. He hired the car out to people for their private use, and when the car pool sent a man to collect the money for the hire, they said the money had already been paid to Liu Shaoshan. This very person used to commit economic errors when he worked in a market cooperative. And since he had been transferred to the grain bureau, he had colluded with profiteers, and engaged in embezzlement. But Yin Haijiang and Duan Lianxi were bent on promoting such a man. First, they wanted to transfer him to the labor and wage section, despite the objections of Gao Yunwu, the deputy secretary of the bureau CCP Committee. Further, they wanted to promote him to deputy secretary of the Nanshan grain administration station, which would be a post for a deputy section chief. At this juncture, the city procuratorate informed the grain bureau of the criminal case of Liu Shaoshan; that the grain bureau should nevertheless have insisted on giving him a raise. . . .

The reason for Liu Shaoshan's receiving favors was simply that he was a brother of a deputy secretary of the city CCP Committee. The appointments of several section chiefs in the factional setup of the grain bureau had all been his work, through connections with his brother and his cousin, who was in charge of the personnel administration of cadres in the city financial and trade committee. Those people in several bureaus of the city who wished to get promoted would all fawn on him, while he would offer official posts and make lavish promises wherever he went, and he was true to his word too! This meant that the relative of a person in power was enabled to indirectly exercise power outside his own realm, and the key link of the political power of the proletariat—the appointment and promotion of people—caused disorder within the Party's organizational line and cadre policy.

Without this arbitrary use of power, it would not have been so easy for Yin Haijiang and Duan Lianxi to operate their small factional setup.

From Politics to Economy

If you list the names of those who have been elbowed out or left out in the cold, you will find that most of them are intelligent, hardworking, and upright. Li Qihong, former chief of the planning and deployment section under the grain bureau, had been beaten to the point of disability before he was demoted and transferred to a grain administration station as a group leader. The deputy director of the organizational department under the city CCP Committee, who is in charge of the administration of cadres, told reporters: "That man is sufficiently qualified to become a section chief in the grain bureau."

But when some people in the grain bureau suggested the promotion of Li Qihong to deputy director of the grain administration station, Duan Lianxi went to the city CCP Committee to exert his pressure, and the suggestion fizzled out.

The Yin Haijiang-Duan Lianxi gang regarded every intelligent and upright person who would not "come over and pledge allegiance" as a threat to them. In 1975, the first flour mill in Shuangya City was put into production. There was not a single technical worker in the city, and they should have welcomed support and aid from other places. The provincial leadership had decided that a number of technical personnel of the flour mill at Qiqihar should be sent to Shuangya to support them; however, they were refused by Yin Haijiang and Duan Lianxi. Pang Bingquan, the sole engineer of the grain bureau, was the designer of the flour mill; actually, all the important designs and reforms here over two decades had been his achievements. However, Pang Bingquan was a person who had plenty of brains; besides, he was cruelly oppressed by Duan Lianxi and his gang and was naturally regarded as an alien element. Therefore, he was elbowed out and became a teacher, the only position in which he was able to apply his specific

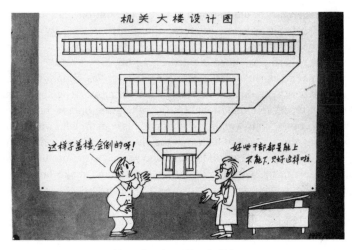

Plans for the office building

Cadre: Architect:
If you build it this way, it's   Quite a number of cadres only
going to topple over!   go up, they don't go down, so
                                          we have to build it this way.

DANGEROUS BUILDING
Wei lou, by Liao Bingxiong

technical skill. The flour mill was left in the hands of Qin Changqiu, who knew nothing about technology, but was one of Yin Haijiang and Duan Lianxi's gang.

Now, as a result of the arbitrary dismemberment and transformation of the equipment, and the confusion in operation, the losses have been most shocking. The electrical machinery that has been burned beyond repair amounts to over 100 sets. In not one year has the production plan been fulfilled. According to planning, in 1983 the mill should have handed over to the state profits of 640,000 yuan; however, only 230,000 yuan had been fulfilled by the end of October. There has always been a loss in the rate of flour output against wheat consumed in processing. In the first 10 months alone, it suffered a loss of 641 tons of flour in processing. The flour has long been of the worst quality, but it has been sold as being up to standard. The people of Shuangya have been using black and gritty, low quality flour for years.

"If we make do with the personnel, we shall have to make do with things as they are," is the conclusion drawn by a comrade who has been observing for a long time the factional setup in the grain bureau. Truly, if we do not break up such a factional setup, which is intolerable to the Party's principles and the socialist system, will it be possible for our industry to improve even if we have much better policies, more funds, and the most up-to-date equipment? And will the financial revenues be increased? Such factional setups are forever putrefying the atmosphere of our social life and are the most powerful source of spiritual pollution, which is impairing people's faith in our Party and in the socialist system.

Our readers who have read the report "Not Just for the Sake of Grain," carried in this paper on January 6 this year, are shocked and would like to know: How did it come about that there were such appalling economic losses? Now they can find the answer to it: The economic loopholes were caused by political ulcers, and the focus of infection was the social influence formed by those taking advantage of their power to seek personal gain in collusion with "people of three categories."

Even a deputy chief of the organizational department under the Shuangya City CCP Committee admits: The experiment in Party rectification in the grain bureau cannot be said to have been successful. However, this experiment was introduced to the whole province as a successful experience. But of course, this experience is not without significance, because it has revealed to people: If the Party rectification should be carried out perfunctorily, what dangerous trouble will it bring about in the future!

37

Liu Binyan

THE RIGHTS AND WRONGS OVER THE PAST THIRTY-EIGHT YEARS

A Reversal

Simply because of the size of China there are many unheard-of stories. A seventy-two-year-old man named Guo Jianying became a defendant; the No. 2 branch of the Xian Housing and Land Management Bureau, which twelve years ago occupied the backyard of Guo Jianying's house and robbed him of his property, became the plaintiff. On December 7, 1983, the branch bureau dragged in many people and sent dozens of armed men with a prison van to pull down a 12-square-meter asphalt felt shed in the backyard of Guo's house (142, Qingnian Street, Xian City). By order of Liang Ping, vice president of the Lianhu District Court, they brutally raided Guo's family!

There was a greater reversal: Another reason why the old man Guo became the defendant was that in 1946 he lent a large sum of money to the New Fourth Army, which was in a difficult position in southern Shaanxi at that time, to help it resolve a pressing need!

Renmin ribao [People's Daily], August 25, 1984. Translation from FBIS Daily Report, September 6, 1984, pp. K2–K7.

In 1958 the logic was such: Guo Jianying could take out so much money to support the revolution. Could he not be a capitalist? The answer was yes! This became a theoretical basis for "transforming" his private house. In 1966 this logic developed: How could a capitalist be willing to contribute so much money to support the revolution? It must be insincere support! So he was thrown in a "cowshed" on a charge of "passing himself off by political fraud." His family was in dire straits.

In 1972 a looter named Gu Laigen of the No. 2 branch of the Xian Housing and Land Management Bureau occupied the backyard of Guo's house by force. There he built a five-room, high-class house with an exclusive courtyard for Zhang Jintang, a section chief who held the power in the city materials bureau. During construction, the septic tank in the backyard was filled in, two brick toilets were destroyed, eight trees were felled, and Guo's property was confiscated. Ten years passed and China moved into a new historical period. But Gu Laigen was still able to ride roughshod. Supported by a friend named Shi Zhaoyi, who was chief of the financial section of the city Housing and Land Management Bureau, Gu Laigen had the house with an exclusive courtyard pulled down. He wanted to construct a building for the provincial timber company by expanding the area of construction to the north. This meant occupying nearly the whole courtyard. Guo Jianying was driven beyond endurance; encouraged by the line of the Third Plenum of the Eleventh CCP Central Committee, he rose in resistance against those people.

Unfulfilled Correction

Knowing that leftist mistakes had long infringed upon private legal interests and that many cases were related to housing property, Vice Mayor Li Tingbi, who has been in charge of Xian urban construction for many years, decided to investigate six families. An investigation group headed by Wang Jianpeng conducted a careful and practical investigation for four months and concluded that the social-ist transformation of the four private houses in 1958 was wrong. At a routine affairs meeting of mayors on June 16, 1983, mayors and vice mayors maintained that mistakes should be corrected and property rights should be returned to the owner. But Zhang Huaide, chief of the City Housing and Land Management Bureau, attending the meeting, objected and proposed that returning two private houses be postponed. Guo Jianying's house was one of them.

In the twenty-six years since 1958, Guo's family members increased and his children grew up. Since 1980 Guo's family has applied twice to build a house in the courtyard, but the Housing and Land Management Bureau did not approve their application. Guo's family had no choice but to build a 12-square-meter asphalt felt shed in the backyard for the youngest son to live in.

Although this wretched little shed was far from the construction site, Gu Laigen insisted that the shed was hampering the progress of construction. Guo's family maintained that the construction was in itself illegal and that the property ruined and taken away in 1972 should be returned. Vice Mayor Li

Tingbi supported Guo's family's reasonable and legal request. He instructed both sides to talk the matter over and suspended construction projects until the dispute was resolved. Having strong backing, Shi Zhaoyi and Gu Laigen turned a deaf ear to the vice mayor's instructions. They lodged a suit with the Lianhu District Court against Guo Jianying. Thus began a wrestling match with a great disparity in strength.

"Even If the Decision Is Wrong, It Must Be Carried Out!"

The superiority of the plaintiff was salient: I was a "unit" and an "organization" safeguarding "state interests," whereas the defendant was a family involved in private matters.

Guo Jianying, however, had a rare, favorable condition: President Li Xiannian issued two instructions with regard to his appeal. On many occasions, Comrade Ma Wenrui, first secretary of the Shaanxi Provincial CCP Committee, instructed that the Xian City CCP Committee should seriously implement President Li Xiannian's instructions.

Comrade Wang Feng, member of the Central Advisory Commission who participates in inspecting the implementation of policies and then-secretary of the Henan-Shaanxi-Hubei District CCP Committee, political commissar of the Henan-Shaanxi-Hubei Military District, and president of the district government, is the most authoritative person who can stand witness to the problem concerning Guo Jianying's loan. He instructed a responsible comrade to advise Comrade He Chenghua, secretary of the Xian City CCP Committee, not to violate Comrade Xiannian's instructions so as to avoid making mistakes.

On the night of December 5, 1983, Comrade Wang Feng, who was then at Xian, learned that the Xian City Court had decided to pull down the shed in Guo's backyard the following day. He called Secretary He Chenghua, telling him to delay the decision.

However, Secretary He Chenghua took notice then, and very resolutely. He told Li Tianshun, his personal secretary, to inform Guo Jianying: "Even if the decision is wrong, it must be implemented. In the future, if the verdict passed on you is reversed, I will have the building that has been constructed pulled down. But for now the decision must be implemented." The reason was that "the Party must not interfere in judicial affairs."

What Secretary He Chenghua said was contrary to the fact. Without interference by some Xian leaders, the case would not have been placed on file for prosecution. From the beginning, some comrades of the Lianhu District Court maintained that the case was a dispute over property rights, involved the problem of implementing policies, and should be handled by the Party and government departments concerned. They placed the case on file for investigation only after they had received instructions from some "city leaders." Also, only after the district court submitted the files to Secretary He Chenghua for approval was the judgment made.

With a high sense of organization and discipline, the district court and the intermediate court fulfilled their tasks exceptionally fast. Not only did they turn a blind eye to the plaintiff's violation of civil lawsuit procedures, but they themselves also violated procedures. They shortened the examination and approval process so as to enable Gu Laigen and his followers to continue the projects as soon as possible, as Gu Laigen and his followers had been waiting impatiently.

A Strange Investigation

In late December, Secretary He Chenghua wanted to implement President Li Xiannian's instructions. He formed a group to investigate Guo Jianying's case. To investigate what? First, to investigate the problem of Guo Jianying lending the money. The three investigations made over the past twenty years and more, Comrade Li Xiannian's instructions, and Comrade Wang Feng's testimony did not count. Second, to investigate the problem of transforming Guo Jianying's private house. The former investigation carried out by an investigation group of the city government and the conclusion made by the vice mayors of the city did not count.

By selecting the part of testimony that had been negated by a witness who possessed firsthand materials and by relying on testimony inappropriately obtained by a lawyer engaged by the Housing and Land Management Bureau, the city CCP committee investigation group tried to prove that Guo Jianying was forced to ''deliver'' the money to the New Fourth Army instead of willingly lending the money to the Army. For this, the investigation group distorted history and brought shame on the New Fourth Army. It asserted that the southern Shaanxi Party and Army adopted the policy of ''beating rich people'' and the method of ''canvassing votes,'' which in fact they never did. It even went so far as to say that because Guo Jianying informed against a guerrilla leader, the guerrilla leader was killed by the enemy.

It did so in disregard of the fact that since 1958, this allegation has been negated twice by a more reliable witness and that recently Comrade Wang Feng testified that the killing of the guerrilla leader had nothing to do with Guo Jianying.

In investigating private houses, the purpose of the city CCP Committee investigation group was no more than to negate the investigation carried out by the city government and to affirm the mistake in 1958, that is, that houses in a compound with an entrance or entrances commonly used by the dwellers were regarded as houses being rented. The purpose of this regulation was to make up the figure of 150 square meters, which was the minimum area fixed for ''transformation.'' So the site in Guo's backyard was ''transformed.'' Otherwise, occupation of Guo's backyard would have been unreasonable!

To be absolutely safe, it was necessary to alter the class status of Guo Jianying. In 1980, in line with Central (1979) Document No. 84, the Lanzhou Motor Transportation Company of Gansu Province, where Guo Jianying worked, determined Guo's class status as ''petty proprietor,'' which belongs to the category of the working people. But the city CCP committee investigation group maintained that the classification was a little biased toward the "right." So it began collecting materials concerning Guo Jianying in an attempt to prove that the classification had been carried out in a "minor key." It would be a good idea to determine Guo's class status as capitalist, as this would legalize the transformation of his private house in 1958 and would make unassailable everything done by the Housing and Land Management Bureau, by Gu Laigen, by the court, and by the city CCP committee.

This was how the principal leaders of the Xian City CCP committee implemented the "practical" spirit of the Third Plenum of the Eleventh CCP Central Committee and President Li Xiannian's instructions with regard to Guo Jianying's problem!

A Person Is Invincible If He Has the Power to Distribute Houses

In this drama, which was focused on Guo Jianying, the person named Gu Laigen played a very important part.

This Gu Laigen was a low-level cadre of the Housing and Land Management Bureau. Everyone knows that during the "Cultural Revolution" he commanded an attack on the city CCP committee and that he was a two-gun tyrant. But in his files, there is not even a single line recording his activities during the "Cultural Revolution"; nor can a trace of his several years' imprisonment be found (it was also struck off the table of contents). He often used the "house distribution tickets" he possessed to threaten or bribe people. He was good at using hard and soft tactics to force families out of the sites to be used for capital construction. Because of all this, many people dared not offend him, as he was quite useful to them.

In this affair, Gu Laigen demonstrated his power. He could instruct the Public Security Bureau to threaten Guo's family. He could hire some twenty gangsters to beat Guo's family and to carry out kidnappings. He could also control judicial departments. Why did Xu Pei, judge of the Lianhu District Court, side with Gu Laigen, ignore the most rudimentary legal proceedings, and shorten the process of examination? His purpose was to get a house, and indeed, he got one with two large rooms. Why did Yang Qingxiu of the city Intermediate Court overstep his authority to remove obstacles for Gu Laigen and to engage Liu so and so, lawyer of the legal advisory department? And why did Liu so and so, part-time lawyer, illegally open an introduction letter and take risks (because it was illegal) in investigating Guo Jianying's history and class status, which had nothing to do with the case? . . . Obviously, each had his own purpose.

What did Gu Laigen and his behind-the-scenes backer—Shi Zhaoyi, chief of the financial section of the Housing and Land Management Bureau—intend to have? The provincial timber company had long agreed to provide them with fifteen houses and a fund of 300,000 yuan. In addition, Gu Laigen got another thing: He and his wife were transferred back to Shanghai to work in a Shanghai-based Shaanxi office.

Dark Forces and Dirty Tricks

Now we can faintly see a "united front" encircling Guo's family. Oh, we nearly left out one important point. There were still two hatchet men.

The two hatchet men were Wei Zhijian and Zhang Jianxun. Wei was director of the neighborhood committee. Zhang Jianxun was dismissed from public employment in the 1950s because of corruption and moral degeneration. During the "Cultural Revolution," he was taken into custody and supervised by the masses because he beat a factory Party secretary so seriously that three of the secretary's ribs were broken. In the ten years of internal disorder, both of them trampled Guo Jianying's family underfoot to show that they were "revolutionaries" and to seek pleasure and material benefit. In recent years, together with their "worthy wives," they spared no effort in vilifying Guo's family. Nearly all they did yielded good results. Guo Jianying and his wife were old and were suffering from illness (unable to right the wrong, Guo Jianying's wife died of depression on April 27, 1984). Their two daughters, Guo Manli and Guo Yali, had to shoulder the task of lodging appeals. Is it not easy to frame cases against young girls? Wei and Zhang began to spread rumors about Guo's two daughters (although they were over thirty, they could not marry due to their father's case). When Guo Manli was nearly admitted into the Party, false charges were brought against her. When the city government sent persons to investigate matters concerning Guo's private house, rumors and slanders began to spread. Knowing that Guo Jianying and his two daughters were in Beijing visiting some central leaders, Wei and Zhang managed to get the number of Comrade Wang Feng's mailbox and sent their vilification letter directly to Comrade Wang Feng! Once a *Shaanxi ribao* [Shaanxi Daily] reporter visited Guo's family. Even during his several-minute stay in Guo's house, Zhang Yanqun, Zhang Jianxun's wife, lost no time in maligning the two girls in front of the reporter, saying: "Guo's daughters like to sleep around! . . ."

It was astonishing that what Wei Zhijian and Zhang Jianxun said about Guo Jianying's lending money to the Army, the transformation of his private house, and the classification of his class status was exactly the same as the conclusion made by the city CCP committee's investigation group!

We did not believe that the principal leaders of the Xian City CCP Committee had reached a tacit agreement with Gu Laigen, Wei Zhijian, and Zhang Jianxun. But objectively, they played the same role in determining the destiny of Guo's family! For example, the persons listed in the large number of vilification letters written by Wei Zhijian and Zhang Jianxun were all framed, but in fact these two villains did not have the power to do so. Guo Manli, Guo Jianying's second daughter, aged thirty-six, was a college graduate. She performed her work well and competently. It was natural to select her for a leadership position in the current structural reform. However, her promotion was postponed because of her father's case. The discussion of the problem of giving her full Party membership, scheduled last November, was also postponed. A person named Wang Jianpeng of the city government's investigation group had been selected for promotion, but not long afterward his name was struck off the list.

"Leftist" and Rightist Methods Applied in Different Ways to Different Persons

Comrades in charge of Xian City Party work should remember China's situation in the summer of 1946. Zhangjiakou and Andong were occupied by the KMT Army, and Yanan nearly fell. Our Army was making preparations for a retreat from Harbin, the largest city in the liberated areas. While our Party and Army were in an exceedingly difficult position and it was very hard to foretell the outcome of the struggle between the KMT and the CCP, out of his feeling of great reverence for our Party and Army, Guo Jianying, a peasant who never received education, lent to our Army a huge sum of money he had borrowed. People who do not understand the situation at that time can hardly estimate the significance and value of his act. Under Comrade Li Xiannian's command, the Fifth Division of the New Fourth Army made a breakthrough from Xuanhuadian in Hubei and went north. But the division ran out of food in southern Shaanxi, where it was intercepted by Hu Zhongnan's troops. A leader of the Army said to the peasants in southern Shaanxi: "Today you lend us a potato. In the future, we will repay you with a golden egg!" At that time, not everyone was willing to loan money or grain to the Army, and some people even swindled the Army's money which had been budgeted for buying materials! Having trust in our Army, Guo Jianying left Xian for faraway places to raise and borrow money. He finally succeeded in raising and borrowing a sum of 11 million francs. He risked his life to deliver this considerable sum to our Army.

After Liberation, he wrote this in his files, but some people said that he "demanded payment of the debt from the CCP." While "leftism" was running wild, Guo Jianying did not dare to demand repayment any longer. Without telling anyone, he reduced his own living expenses to repay, by monthly and yearly installments, the money he had borrowed to support the Chinese Revolution (according to documents Nos. 137 and 149 issued by the Ministry of Finance in 1957, the government should pay the debt it owes). He thought the matter would be over without demanding the payment of the debt and without asking to keep a record of his contributions. But unexpectedly, his contributions caused a great disaster to his family! During the "Cultural Revolution," his family were branded as "rebels" and had to borrow money to eke out an existence. Subsequently, not only the parents borrowed money from relatives and friends, but the children also borrowed money from their schoolmates. Although for ten years they never ate their fill and never bought vegetables, they still had to borrow money from others! The children's schooling, employment, marriage, and health were seriously affected, to say nothing of the political oppression and humiliation they suffered.

Of course, Guo Jianying is not a hero. But after all, he made some contributions to the victory of the Liberation War. Also, he was a victim of "leftist" mistakes. The CCP Central Committee has issued explicit policies and instructions with regard to his rewards and the way to treat him. But why does the Xian City CCP Committee still adhere to its ''leftist'' principles in handling his case? Why does the Xian City CCP Committee persist in its rightist principles in dealing with Gu Laigen and his followers, who have serious problems both in politics and morality and who rode roughshod in the ten years of internal disorder? Can creators and supporters of this affair be regarded as persons keeping abreast with the CCP Central Committee politically?

38

Chang Miao

PASSING ON NOTES TO INTERCEDE IS STILL A PREVAILING PRACTICE IN SOME AREAS

A Personnel Cadre Tells of His Dilemma

RECENTLY A CADRE of the Personnel Bureau of Southern Jiangxi Prefecture wrote us to tell of his dilemma. He said he had not done personnel work for long but was already frustrated by the thorny problem of making use of connections and pleading on others' behalf in personnel work. Personnel cadres find these things difficult to handle: First, a veteran comrade drops in to intercede for his friends or relatives; second, the family member of a leading comrade comes to ask for preferential treatment; third, an old classmate or old colleague visits to ask for a favor. On top of that, the number of informal notes written by leading comrades to plead for preferential job placement is increasing steadily. This year the province has assigned to the prefecture 809 army cadres transferred to civilian work. Of these, 357 have been assigned to work on the politics and law front, and the remaining 452 to work on other fronts. In regard to these 400–odd persons alone, informal notes written by leading comrades to plead in their favor, were more than 200. In some cases one note listed several persons and asked that they be taken care of. In other cases, several notes were written to intercede for one single person, and in individual cases the notes were as many as 10 or more. The intention of the notes was to have the cadres in question placed in the city, in commerce, foreign trade or units where more bonuses are awarded. How could all such demands be met? And job assignments for the college and university graduates every year result in the same harassment, causing the personnel cadres a lot of anxiety. As things now stand, cultivating connections poses a serious obstacle to the Party's policy of making

''Di tiaozi shuoqing feng zai yixie diqu rengran shengxing,'' *Zuzhi gongzuo dongtai* [Trends of Organization Work]. Reprinted in *Baokan wenzhai* [Digest of Newspapers and Periodicals] (Shanghai), No. 134, July 20, 1982. Translated by Ai Ping.

appointments according to qualifications. If this trend goes on unchecked, personnel work can hardly be done well. Some of the cadres engaged in doing personnel work are dissatisfied with the practice, but they can do nothing about it. Consequently they become depressed, including the one who wrote us the letter.

In regard to this matter, the Jiangxi Provincial Personnel Bureau sent people to Gangzhou Prefecture for investigation. According to reports by the prefectural personnel office and the prefectural office for placement of army cadres transferred to civilian work, what the cadre wrote about was basically true. In individual cases the problem was even more glaring. For example, there were altogether 379 notes written on behalf of the transferred army cadres, involving 521 persons. Of the total number of notes, 80 were written by leaders of the prefectural Party committee and commissioner's office, 15 were from army units, and 284 by people in other fields. The purpose was to help the transferred cadres find an ideal placement through connections and pull.

39

GUIZHOU CURBS RUSH RETIREMENT OF CADRES

SINCE AUGUST THIS year, work basically has been completed of the Party committees and governments at various levels in our province to check the unhealthy tendency of rush retirement of cadres and rush replacement of them by their children. According to statistics, by November 11, 99.2 percent of the more than 4,000 cases of rush retirement of cadres who are not qualified for retirement had been handled, and 98.4 percent of the 4,113 cases had been corrected of rush replacement of cadres by their children who are not qualified to replace them.

In the last ten-day period in August this year, the provincial CCP committee made a decision on resolutely checking the unhealthy tendency of rush retirement of cadres and rush replacement by their children, urging all localities to take this task as an important matter in the province's present endeavors to rectify the Party's work-style and to concentrate on comprehensively handling and correcting all cases in this regard within a definite time.

At the same time, it held a related meeting to unify people's understanding, to make a demarcation line on policy matters, to define the limits of cases to be sorted out and handled, and to study the measures to implement the decision.

The Guizhou provincial radio station issued the following short commentary entitled "The Key Lies in the Determination of the Leadership":

Radio Guiyang, November 30, 1983. Translation from FBIS Daily Report, December 2, 1983, p. Q1 (excerpts).

> Through several months of hard work, the work of the province to check the unhealthy tendency of rush retirement of cadres and of rush replacement by their children has now been basically completed. Of the numerous experiences summed up in the several months of our work in this respect, what counts are the facts and the determination of the leaders at various levels.

After the provincial people's government issued a document in March this year on checking the unhealthy tendency of rush retirement of cadres and of rush replacement by their children, because the leadership in some localities was not so mightily determined, by the end of July, over 5 months, only 82 cases of rush retirement and replacement had been handled throughout the province. After the provincial CCP committee made a decision on checking the unhealthy tendency of rush retirement of cadres and of rush replacement by their children, and held a special meeting on sorting out and handling all cases in this regard in August this year, the provincial CCP committee and government as well as the Party organizations and governments at various levels strengthened leadership over this work. In this way, rapid improvement was made in the whole situation. The question of the more than 4,000 people who are not qualified for retirement and of the more than 4,000 people who are not qualified for such replacement was solved in no more than 3 months.

This fact vividly indicates that the success or failure of doing something depends on the determination of the leadership. So long as our leaders at various levels are firmly determined and persistent and have the spirit of carrying the work through to the end at one stroke, they will surely achieve the planned results in their work.

40

Young Cadre Bureau of Central Organization Department

THE SLOW PROGRESS OF BRINGING DOWN THE AGE STRUCTURE OF LEADING BODIES CANNOT KEEP PACE WITH THE CADRES' NATURAL AGING PROCESS

WHEN REPORTING TO the Department leadership how things stand with the choice and promotion of young and middle-aged cadres by the

"Lingdao banzi manqinghua de jinbu bukuai, ganbushang ganbu nianlingde ziran zengzhang," *Zugong tongxun* [Newsletter on Organizational Work]. Reprinted in *Baokan wenzhai* [Digest of Newspapers and Periodicals] (Shanghai), No. 156 (December 21, 1982), p. 1. Translated by Ai Ping.

various provinces and municipalities, the Young Cadre Bureau of the Central Organization Department pointed out that right now the progress of bringing down the age structure of leading bodies still falls behind the cadres' natural aging process. Statistics show that compared with 1979, the average age of members of the standing committees of the 29 provincial, municipal and autonomous regional Party committees was, instead of going down, up by two and a half years at the end of 1981. Leading bodies of prefectural and county Party committees also rose by one year respectively. All this indicates that despite efforts made in the previous two years, the age structure of leading bodies which had already been too old in the past experienced little change.

According to statistics of the whole nation, truly qualified young and middle-aged cadres having been promoted to leadership positions above the county and bureau level totaled no more than 16,100 in number. Of this 84 were cadres promoted to the provincial level (under the age of fifty-five), 2,036 to the prefectural level (under the age of fifty) and 14,000 to the county level (under the age of forty-five). In some provinces and municipalities, quite a few cadres were promoted but among them the young and the middle-aged did not make a large proportion, mostly under 40 percent. The problem was the most pronounced at the provincial level, which fell behind the average of prefectures, municipalities, and counties and also behind the various commissions, departments, and ministries of the Party Central Committee and the State Council. In some provinces, those promoted, including candidates for major positions in the provincial Party committees, fell far short of the requirements set forth by the Party Central Committee in terms of age or other aspects. Generally attention was paid to the promotion of people just above fifty; it seldom expanded to include those around forty.

What merits attention is the existence of large numbers of dead angles and dead spaces at present. The task [of bringing down the age structure] has been stressed for quite a few years; however, some regions remain "untouched" up to now. A certain province, for example, has altogether 99 counties. But for several years not a single young or middle-aged cadre has been added to its 72 county Party committees as full or deputy secretaries or as members to 86 of its 162 prefectural level leading bodies. More important, 44 of the prefectural leading bodies do not even have reserve slates. Judging from the results of investigation, dead spaces remaining "untouched" as such account for 30 to 50 percent. The situation is quite serious.

The slow progress of lowering the cadres' age also gives rise to the problem of how to make the cadres professional and knowledgeable. Leading cadres at the provincial, prefectural and county levels have an educational background lower or much lower than the average cultural level of cadres in the whole country. What is more problematic is that over the last two years the provinces have all promoted in large numbers cadres with an educational background less than a junior high school graduate and they account for 41 percent of the number of those promoted.

41

Commentator

STOP TAKING COUNTERMEASURES, IMPLEMENT POLICIES

"THERE ARE POLICIES issued at the higher levels, but there are also countermeasures adopted at the lower levels." "You may have your policies, but we have our countermeasures."

These are quite popular sayings nowadays. Some people who are used to availing themselves of loopholes in policies and even distorting policies while engaging in unhealthy practices are acting precisely according to such sayings. They think themselves clever. The first thing to do to curb unhealthy trends is to stop this unhealthy trend of taking countermeasures against the policies of the Party and state instead of implementing them.

Policies are guiding principles for action formulated by the Party and the government to ensure fulfillment of a certain task. Policies stipulate what should be done, what should not be done, and how something should be done and how something should not be done to ensure fulfillment of the task. Reform of the economic system involves the destiny and future of the country and the nation. To ensure the reform's success, the Party Central Committee and the State Council have formulated a series of policies. The Party, the government, the army, the people, and the students throughout the country must all strictly follow and implement these policies.

Countermeasures mean strategies and methods to deal with or cope with something. Countermeasures were often adopted by two confronting armies, and they have seldom been seen in recent years. The saying, "The challenge of the new technical revolution and our countermeasures," was often heard some time ago. It uses a descriptive rhetorical means of personification also implying the "enemy" and "ourselves" and is put forward by one side that gives tit for tat.

Those comrades who brag about "you may have your policies, but we have our countermeasures" should think about who this "you" and "we" stand for and whom these countermeasures are against. To put it more bluntly, have you not regarded yourselves as the antithesis of the interest of the country as a whole? "We have our countermeasures." Have you not thus taken the stand of your unit, a small collective, to resist, interfere with, and even sabotage the implementation of policies? When a policy forbids raising prices at random, he may raise prices under disguise by changing the packaging and substituting secondary commodities for good ones. When a policy forbids indiscriminately issuing cash awards,

Renmin ribao [People's Daily], February 5, 1985. Translation from FBIS Daily Report, February 7, 1985, pp. K11–K13.

Local god of village A

Local god of village B

OFFICIAL NOTICE
Those wearing short
robes are forbidden
to pass

OFFICIAL NOTICE
Those wearing long
gowns are forbidden
to pass

Local god of village C

Local god of village D

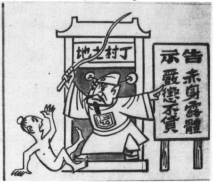

OFFICIAL NOTICE
Those wearing
clothes are forbidden
to pass

OFFICIAL NOTICE
Those who are naked
will be punished
severely without mercy

IT'S HARD TO BE A LITTLE GUY
Xiaogui nandang, by Liao Bingxiong

The ad hoc, arbitrary character of local policy is satirized here. Ordinary mortals
find it difficult to abide by the regulations of high and mighty local officials. As in several other cartoons (pp. 62, 64 and 72), the persistence of China's feudal past long
after "Liberation" is noted.

he may hand out material awards. When a policy forbids handing out material awards, he may "grant loans for buying things," which are supposed to be repaid by installments but in fact may take decades for repayment. Such measures are numerous, and they are used to deal with the country. Whenever a policy is formulated and issued at a higher level, some people will try hard to avail themselves of any loophole in that policy. They will strive to secure more benefits for their respective units and small collectives and will ignore the interests of the state as a whole. We can easily imagine what evil results these practices will bring.

What kind of people will adopt "countermeasures"? Most of them are leading cadres of some units or enterprises or people who have obtained their tacit consent. For the sake of their personal interest, and the interest of their respective units and small collectives, they may ignore Party discipline and state laws and violate policies. To put it frankly, they are blinded by a lust for gain. We would like to remind those comrades who are playing petty tricks: Wholehearted dedication to the struggle for building a strong and prosperous country and for the prosperity of the people is the fundamental purpose of Party members. He who violates this purpose is not a qualified Party member or a qualified cadre. Once our country and people are prosperous, personal problems and problems of any unit or small collective can easily be solved. In no way should we gain a little at the expense of the whole or gain a little only to lose a lot. If the interest of the whole is lost, the interest of the part is bound to come to nothing. Can there be any way out for us cadres if our reform of the economic system is interfered with and sabotaged and if our country fails to become strong and prosperous and our people fail to become prosperous?

Will we not then let our people and our martyrs down? Those who refuse to mend their ways after repeated admonition and education must be dealt with and punished according to Party discipline and state laws.

Stop taking countermeasures and earnestly implement the policies formulated by the Party and the state!

FURTHER READINGS

Barnett, A. Doak. *Cadres, Bureaucracy and Political Power in Communist China.* New York: Columbia University Press, 1967.

Burns, John P. "Reforming China's Bureaucracy, 1979-82." *Asian Survey* 23:6 (June 1983), pp. 692-722.

Harding, Harry. *Organizing China: The Problem of Bureaucracy, 1949-1976.* Stanford: Stanford University Press, 1981.

Lee, Hong Yung. "Deng Xiaoping's Reform of the Chinese Bureaucracy." In Ronald A. Morse, ed. *The Limits of Reform in China.* Boulder, Colorado: Westview Press, 1983, pp. 17–38.

Liu Binyan, *People or Monsters? And Other Stories and Reportage from China after Mao,* edited by Perry Link. Bloomington, Indiana: Indiana Univesity Press, 1983.

Oksenberg, Michel. "Economic Policy-making in China, Summer 1981." *The China Quarterly* No. 90 (June 1982), pp. 165-194.

Oksenberg, Michel, "Methods of Communication Within the Chinese Bureaucracy." *The China Quarterly* No. 57 (January-March 1974), pp. 1-39.

Schurmann, Franz. *Ideology and Organization in Communist China*. Berkeley: University of California Press, 1966.

Sullivan, Lawrence R. "The Role of the Control Organs in the Chinese Communist Party, 1977-83." *Asian Survey* 24:6 (June 1984), pp. 597-617.

Weng, Byron S. J., ed. "Studies on the Constitutional Law of the People's Republic of China." *Chinese Law and Government* 16:2-3. (Summer-Fall 1983).

II
POLICY
ARENAS

A. Industry

REFORM OF CHINA'S industrial sector has been dogged by conflict over both the formulation and the implementation of policy. At the macro level, senior leaders have disagreed over investment priorities, the extent of central control, and the need for a labor market. At the micro level, policymakers have disputed the extent to which factory managers ought to be responsive to market forces and to be autonomous from Party control.

Although China's leaders admit that previous rates of accumulation were excessive, they have failed to agree on such important issues as the relative priority to be accorded investment in heavy industry, such as steel or petroleum products, on the one hand, and light industry, such as consumer goods, on the other. Each sector has its advocates among senior leaders. Since 1979, for example, Politburo member Yu Qiuli has demanded increased investment in heavy industry, while Premier Zhao Ziyang has favored the rapid expansion of light industry.[1] The dominance of a given tendency has been determined to a large extent by the success or failure of previous policies, and also, in all probability, by the intervention of Deng Xiaoping.

Disputes among the leaders have also centered on the extent to which Beijing ought to retain central control of the economy. Some senior leaders, such as Politburo member Chen Yun, have advocated continued reliance on central planning. For them, the only alternative to central planning is the "anarchy" of the market, which is unacceptable. They viewed the 1980 attempt to decentralize planning with disfavor and were alarmed by the ability of provincial and local units to amass sizable "extra-budgetary" funds of their own.

Other leaders, notably Premier Zhao Ziyang, have advocated greater reliance on market mechanisms to improve efficiency. In their view, the rigidity of central planning has prevented units from being sensitive to local conditions and has prevented competition to increase productivity. Since 1984, authorities have accepted the need for substantially increased market control.

Finally, authorities have debated the need to reform China's cumbersome and highly inefficient employment system. Traditionally, a network of state labor bureaus, responsible to the Ministry of Labor and Personnel in Beijing, allocated labor to China's factories, government offices, commercial establishments, and other state-owned institutions.[2] The policy often resulted in serious overstaffing and the mismatching of skills, especially as local leaders used the system to build and to maintain networks of loyal supporters. Efficiency could be enhanced, some suggested, by abolishing the labor bureau system and allocating labor through a market.

The outcome of these debates has implications for the role of factory managers. Production for the market provides new criteria for evaluating industrial performance. It also fosters competition among industrial enterprises. Still, relaxed central controls provide managers with more flexibility to meet production targets. This is especially true in the area of personnel management: If managers could employ, reward, and discipline the work force, they could improve organizational effectiveness. Some Party leaders, however, have been reluctant to invest managers with this authority, fearing that it would undermine the Party's traditional, near absolute, prerogative to determine personnel matters (in practice based on political loyalty). (See Political Participation, Selection 10.)

The following selections, which include commentaries and editorials from the official press, investigative reports, a comic dialogue, and an analytical piece from Hong Kong, illustrate the extent of disagreement over the reform of industrial policy.

Determining the appropriate relationships among state, collective, and individual interests, while in theory fairly straightforward (the long-term interests of all units and individuals are the same), in practice has proved contentious. In what is now standard fashion, Selection 42 acknowledges that in the short term conflict exists among various interests in Chinese society. The Party must balance these interests and at the same time give priority to state accumulation. While admitting that in the past the rate of accumulation was too high, the editorial writer defends the need of the state to regain central control over local, ''non-key'' projects. The piece, reflecting the views of central planners, is a reminder that localities and departments must respect the interests of the state.

''Commentator's'' angry criticism of local leaders who take a ''one-sided view of the masses' interests'' (Selection 43) raises the apparently common problem of leaders who protect local interests at the expense of the state. In particular this takes the form of enterprises illegally retaining profits, some of which they use to pay higher wages (in cash or in kind) to workers. Although authorities disapprove of egalitarian distribution systems (''''eating from one big pot'' does not motivate workers to increase productivity), officials also disapprove of the ''indiscriminate'' payment of bonuses. In a stinging attack, ''Commentator'' condemns this economism as pandering to the ''excessive demand of the masses,'' who he then says are not really ''the masses'' at all, but simply ''a handful of backward people.'' The message is clear: Local units must consider the interests of the state as paramount.

Selections 42 and 43 are misleading, however, to the extent that they single out only *local* (enterprise and individual) interests as favoring increased rates of consumption at the expense of accumulation. The *central* leadership itself is divided on this issue, as Selections 44–48 demonstrate.

From 1979 to 1981, when senior leaders in Beijing disagreed on the nature of the policies needed to develop the economy, some policymakers turned to new magazines in Hong Kong, such as *Dongxiang* (Trends) and *Zhengming* (Contending), to articulate their positions. Veiled references to "the opposition," which characterized official media commentaries in China, were replaced in the Hong Kong leftist press by lively accounts that clearly drew the battle lines.

In Selection 44, *Dongxiang* China-watcher Ju Zhangyi outlines the 1979–1980 struggle within the central leadership between the "new economic group" and the "petroleum group." The position of each group is clearly identified: The "new economic group" favors increased managerial autonomy, greater reliance on markets, increased investment in light industry, and making better use of specialists and intellectuals, while the "petroleum group," centered around the Ministry of Petroleum, favors heavy industry, higher rates of accumulation, using mass campaigns to implement policy, and continuing to rely on amateurs and politicians. The dispute pitted reformers Deng Xiaoping, Premier Zhao Ziyang, Party Secretary General Hu Yaobang, and Vice Premier Wan Li against conservative Politburo members Li Xiannian and Yu Qiuli, Vice Premier Kang Shi'en, and Minister of Petroleum Song Zhenming. Selection 44 further illustrates the willingness of Chinese politicians to manipulate the news to their own advantage. The reformers publicized the Bohai oil rig disaster months after it had occurred in an effort to further pillory their opponents.

The reformers' position is reflected in Selection 45, a *Renmin ribao* (People's Daily) editorial broadly aimed at promoting light industry at the expense of heavy industry. The language of the editorial is moderate, however, because of the reformers' reduced influence in November 1981. Their policies, then under attack, were responsible for a steep rise in the rate of inflation in 1980. Reflecting the views of the "new economic group," identified in Selection 44, the reformers demand a reassessment of the role of heavy industry: It must "serve" light industry.

Heavy industry's defensive reply appears in Selection 46, authored by Liaoning Party secretary, Shen Yue. The Party must pay heed to the interests of the industrial Northeast, he says. He reminds readers of the substantial contribution that heavy industry makes to the state treasury, notes that heavy industry's rate of profit tax is higher than light industry's, and points out that light industry is dependent on the further development of "his" sector. Shen, leaving no stone unturned, finally quotes from Marx and Lenin to substantiate his claim that heavy industry is the "principal link" of the economy. It is precisely this single-minded pursuit of local interests that is the target of the editorial writer in Selection 42.

Selection 47 illustrates a strategy adopted by Shanxi's leadership to undermine investment in light industry in the face of a clear state council policy to protect light industry. The provincial leaders are caught between conflicting policy goals: protecting light industry, on the one hand, or increasing specialization through mergers (also approved by central authorities), on the other. Probably the chief concern of Shanxi officials, however, was to increase profits remitted to the provincial treasury, easily accomplished by taking over the collective enterprises. This sounds like simple pursuit of provincial interests ("departmentalism," "unitism," or "localism," in the idiom of Chinese politics) but the writer uses the much more damaging label of "leftism"—a serious error—to blast the provincial authorities.

In addition to disagreeing on investment priorities for industry, officials in China have disputed the nature of the labor allocation system. Some have favored continuing the "universal and unconditional" employment system (the "iron rice bowl"), while others have argued that it should be replaced by a system of contract labor (Selections 48–50).

Selection 48 addresses the issue at the macro level. State Economic Commission researcher Liu Xianghui argues that the "iron rice bowl" system of guaranteed life tenure suffers from a number of defects: In practice, it ignores both labor skills and the needs of production. It leads to overstaffing and the corrupting practice of sons inheriting their fathers' jobs. Liu favors a system of merit recruitment and tenure based on performance. He advocates both reform of the wage system and providing improved welfare benefits to encourage early retirement.

Although Liu fails to address the implications of his reforms for China's urban unemployed, now numbering an estimated 6 million,[3] he does suggest that women should withdraw from the labor force. He says: ". . . [T]hose who are incapable of doing complicated and heavy tasks in production" should be encouraged to do domestic labor." His position contrasts with the Women's Federation view, articulated in Selection 15 (Political Participation). Still, pulling some women out of the labor force may be a way to solve China's unemployment (and underemployment) problem, particularly if the "iron rice bowl" is abolished.

In 1983, South China's *Yangcheng wanbao* (Yangcheng Evening News) featured a debate on the merit of the "iron rice bowl" system (Selections 49–50). Emphasizing the advantages of the system in the past (it rewarded CCP supporters in the wake of the revolution), Selection 49 argues that the system has outlived its usefulness. Guaranteed employment for life tends to reward incompetence, undermines discipline, and destroys the motivation to increase productivity. Selection 49 may exaggerate the extensiveness of the system, however. Although "leftists further extended" the iron rice bowl system during the Cultural Revolution decade, at the same time, thousands of workers who were accused of political crimes lost their jobs.

In rebuttal, Selection 50 argues that critics of the "iron rice bowl" have identified the wrong culprit. The author points out in a slashing attack on managers that most of the ills attributed to the "iron rice bowl" are in fact the result of incompetent management, which, he argues, is guilty of subjectivism, bureaucratism, and corruption. Leading officials are the root cause of inefficiency, low productivity, waste, and low motivation. Selection 50 advocates improvement of the quality of managers, accompanied by wage reform within the fixed employment system.

The thrust of the criticism of the employment system suggests that managers do not now have enough authority to hire, discipline, and reward their employees. Under the proposed reforms, managers could dismiss workers hired on fixed contracts if their performance was not satisfactory. Selections 51–53, however, suggest that managers may have too much autonomy, or that they have abused their authority.

In Selections 51 and 52, *Renmin ribao* investigative reporter Dang Jizhi reveals the "very unusual things" that have transpired in a cement factory in Xian. This account indicates, first, that the manager of the factory has considerable power to assign subordinates to their positions. When "good guy" Hu was in charge, he appointed the experts to leading positions. When "bad guy" Li was in charge, he appointed his supporters to leading positions and dismissed the experts from their jobs. Indeed, fourteen years after the Cultural Revolution, leaders in this factory were still refighting it. Second, networks of personal relations linked the factory leaders to the city CCP committee and to the provincial Party committee.[4] When the city committee was "reorganized," heads rolled in the factory. The entire process of personnel administration here appears vulnerable to political maneuvering and is very unprofessional. The answer to Dang's rhetorical question, "Why does the Party permit this to happen?" is obvious. The Party itself is intimately involved.

The caricature of factory manager "Asbestos Tile Stone" completes the section (Selection 53). Caught in the middle between superiors (he deflects heat from them) and the masses (he absorbs heat from them), Mr. Stone is revealed to all as a political hack. Fear of making mistakes leads him to shun responsibility and to retreat to slogans, ritual, and a general paralysis. An opportunist, Mr. Stone has "no opinions, no views, and no thoughts." He simply passes the buck and cannot even take a decision on such an innocuous proposal as the provision of a day care center for his employees.

These final selections suggest that giving more power to factory managers, for example, to control personnel administration, would not necessarily result in reform. Insofar as they are corrupt and incompetent, additional power in their hands would only result in further abuses•

Notes

1. See Dorothy Solinger, "The Fifth National People's Congress and the Process of Policy Making: Reform, Readjustment, and the Opposition," *Asian Survey* 22:12 (December 1982), pp. 1242–1244.

2. See Lynn T. White III, *Careers in Shanghai: The Social Guidance of Personal Energies in a Developing Chinese City, 1949–1966* (Berkeley: University of California Press, 1978), pp. 100–114, and Martin King Whyte and William Parish, *Urban Life in Contemporary China* (Chicago: University of Chicago Press, 1984), pp. 37–42.

3. Derived from Feng Lanrui and Zhao Lukuan, "Urban Employment and Wages," in Yu Guangyuan, ed., *China's Socialist Modernization* (Beijing: Foreign Languages Press, 1984), p. 579. Until very recently, authorities in China invariably reported only the number of individuals "waiting for work," avoiding the term "unemployment." While the numbers of urban unemployed are now reported, many Western experts question the Chinese figures. For example, published statistics show that the urban unemployment rate

dropped from 5.9 percent (6.4 million) in 1979 to 1.9 percent in 1984 (see *Beijing Review* 36 [September 9, 1985], p. 9). On the other hand, in a confidential report to high Party officials written in March 1982, Hu Yaobang put the number of young people "waiting for work" at 14 million (*Issues & Studies* 19:2 [February 1983], pp. 78–85). Outsiders often put Chinese urban unemployment at three to four times higher than official government figures, and that of course does not include the 40 million or so (almost a third of the urban work force) that the government concedes are redundant labor in Chinese factories. See Tom Engle, "Reforming the Labor System," *The China Business Review* 12:2 (March–April 1985), pp. 40–44. See also Thomas Rawski, *Economic Growth and Employment in China* (Oxford: Oxford University Press for the World Bank, 1979), for a discussion of this problem.

 4. See Andrew G. Walder, "Communist Social Structure and Workers' Politics in China," in Victor C. Falkenheim, ed., *Citizens and Groups in Chinese Politics* (Ann Arbor: University of Michigan Center for Chinese Studies Monograph Series, forthcoming).

42

Editorial

THE WHOLE PARTY AND THE PEOPLE OF THE WHOLE COUNTRY MUST ATTEND TO THE OVERALL INTERESTS OF THE NATION

THE DEVELOPMENT OF socialist construction has raised a sharp question: in order to expedite the construction of the Four Modernizations, it is necessary that the whole Party and the people of the whole country should pay enough attention to the overall interests of the nation.

In our country, the interests of the state and of the people, between the overall situation and the local situation, and between immediate interests and long-term interests, are all basically identical. However, certain degrees of contradiction do exist between the state and the collective, between the state and the individual, between the collective and the individual, and between the central organs and the local units. It is precisely because of this that our Party has always attached importance to correctly handling the relationship between the state, the collective, and the individual, and also to correctly handling the relationship between the central authorities and the local authorities. In this respect, our Party has been educating the whole Party and the people of the whole country according to new developments in revolution and construction. At present, with regard to centralization and diversification, key construction projects and ordinary projects, accumulation and consumption, and other matters, there exist the problems of the interests between the state, the collective, and the individual, and the interests between the overall situation and local situation. We should guide the whole Party and the people of the whole country in correctly solving these problems both ideologically and practically.

In order to realize the goal of economic revitalization in the 1990s, and of the quadrupling of the general output value of industry and agriculture by the end of this century, from now on we should grasp well the construction of a batch of large-scale key projects. This is what the construction of the Four Modernizations depends on. In light of the current situation, the speed of development for the national economy depends on the general conditions of energy resources, on communications and transport, and on the raw materials industry. That is why we stress the importance of concentrating our efforts on boosting the construction of energy resources, communications and transportation, and other key items, so that other sectors can develop correspondingly. The present serious problem is that the key projects of the state have not met with resolute support and assurance, while the non-key projects have expanded drastically, and in many places new projects are springing up everywhere. If this problem is not solved well, the attention of the whole Party and the whole country is not centered on key

Renmin ribao [People's Daily], May 19, 1983. Translation from FBIS Daily Report, May 23, 1983, pp. K7–K9.

problems, efforts are diverted to grasp "sparrows," then the progress of the construction of the Four Modernizations will be hampered.

The prerequisite for building key projects is for the state to concentrate the necessary capital and funds. In the last two years the country's financial situation has taken a turn for the better. However, financial revenue has not increased rapidly. At the same time, proper arrangements have to be made in granting the necessary funds for the development of key projects, the technological transformation of enterprises, and the development of education and science. At present, the state still has financial difficulties, which are more serious among the central organs, and there exists quite a great contradiction between construction needs and the state's financial capability.

Aside from the factors of the low level of enterprises' operation and management and the poor economic results, the slow tempo of the increase of revenue is also due to the fact that the utilization and distribution of financial resources are too scattered. Examples are abundant: Increase in retention of profits of enterprises and in local revenue, but decrease in profits delivered to the state; inappropriate rise in consumption funds; in some places, the interests of the state are encroached upon, taxes evaded, and profits that should be delivered to the state are retained; some enterprises try every means to hold down the base figures so as to bargain with the state; and so on. This is a problem that has much to do with the overall situation of the nation. The whole Party and the people of the whole country should attach great importance to solving this problem.

People often use the terms the "great river" and the "small river" to symbolize the relationship of distribution between the state, the collective, and the individual. In the past, under the influence of the erroneous "leftist" ideology, the concept of "the small rivers will be full to the brim when there is enough water in the great river" was emphasized one-sidedly. Now some comrades emphasize just the opposite: "The great river will be full to the brim when there is enough water in the small rivers," demonstrating that only when the people are rich and the enterprises are rich can the state become rich. Which of the two sayings is more in conformity with the laws of nature, in terms of the relationship between "the great river" and "the small rivers," is not our primary concern. In any case, we think it one-sided to use the two similes to expound and prove the relationship of distribution among the state, the collective, and the individual. Because, whether there is one-sided emphasis on "water in the great river" or on "water in the small rivers," it is liable to violate the principle of giving simultaneous attention to the three components. In the past, because of defects in the economic system, the central authorities exercised too much and too rigid centralization, and the local authorities and enterprises lacked the requisite financial means for active operation. Besides, in terms of the people's livelihood, too much was owed to them, with the result that the initiative and activeness of various sectors were seriously damaged. This lesson must be borne in mind by all of us.

But it is absolutely not feasible to talk only of the affluence of the people and enterprises without respect to the affluence of the state. In handling the relationship among the state, the collective, and the individual, we should always adhere to the principle of paying simultaneous attention to the interests of the three components and oppose the trend of taking care of one component only. We should never permit the use of excuses to harm the state's interests and maintain the irrational interests of the enterprises or the individuals. In formulating the policy of distribution, we must follow an important principle, that is, the state will get the major part of the net income gained by the enterprises, and the medium and minor parts will go to enterprises and individuals respectively. The reason is evident: The state needs to carry on key construction projects, and the expansion of reproduction requires a material basis; without the concentration of requisite funds, vitalization of the economy is bound to fail, and the development of enterprises and the affluence of the people will lose their footing. We are concentrating our efforts on developing the key projects, and the aim of so doing is in the long-term interests of the people, and for the overall interests of the whole Party and the people of the whole country.

Enhancing economic results and strengthening of comprehensive balance have much to do with the overall situation in building the Four Modernizations.

What are the greatest economic results? From a macroscopic point of view, nothing is more important than the planned and proportionate development of production and construction. In the last two years enterprises have had more money in their pockets, and it is necessary, from a local point of view, for them to set up some urgently needed small-scale enterprises with self-raised money. However, in some places there have been repetitive items and aimlessly developed projects which have not taken into consideration the overall interests of the nation and which have made it difficult to control fixed asset investments outside the budget. In this way key items are pushed aside by ordinary items, and technological transformation is replaced by capital construction, with the result that the supply of raw materials and energy resources, and communications and transportation, have all become quite tense, which fails to conform to the requirement that the construction of key projects should be guaranteed. This situation should be changed in time, or else new readjustment will have to be enforced in a few years' time.

In dealing with economic work, leading cadres at various levels should pay enough attention to the overall situation; if the overall situation is disregarded and things of smaller importance are attended to, the result will be fruitless in the end. At the initial stage, after the founding of the country, Comrade Chen Yun reminded us that "comrades doing economic work are liable to give way to partial and local interests and departmentalism and neglect certain important issues. I want to remind our comrades that they should enhance their self-consciousness." How should we enhance our self-consciousness? The most important thing is to examine and evaluate our work in terms of the overall interests of the nation. Wrong acts should be immediately corrected if they are against the interests of the overall community. Every leading cadre and economic worker should center his attention on things concerning the overall interests of the nation, and should not confine himself to the narrow sphere of local interests.

43

Commentator

OPPOSE THE ONE-SIDED VIEWPOINT OF THE MASSES' INTERESTS

IN RECENT YEARS, the mass viewpoint and the mass line have been greatly restored in leadership work at various levels, and more and more comrades in the Party are showing concern for the masses' interests. This is an improvement. At the same time, we must also point out that there is still the one-sided viewpoint of the masses' interests among some of the comrades. If we do not pay attention to overcoming this situation, the economic construction of the state and the basic interests of the masses are bound to be seriously affected.

This one-sided viewpoint of the masses' interests is more prominently reflected in economic work. After the institution of the economic responsibility system by industrial and communications enterprises, the universal attention paid to economic results is good. However, under the banner of showing concern for the masses' interests, many of the enterprises have competed with the state for profit, and some have even taken advantage of the state. By means of selling their products domestically, some have kept two sets of books to keep more products than they are entitled to. Some have retained a great part of the profit and issued bonuses indiscriminately. Some have used the funds and raw materials of their own plant to manufacture such high-grade goods as TV sets and washing machines for distribution among the workers. They take only a token payment for these items and some do not take even a cent. On the question of state purchase and transfer of agricultural and sideline products to the higher levels in the countryside, some localities have paid more attention to partial interests and the masses' interests but not enough attention to state interests and overall interests. Some have not fulfilled the state target for transfer to higher levels but allow the communes and production brigades to produce and market their own products or distribute such products among individuals so that they can sell them in rural fairs. Moreover, they also want to transfer more and keep less of the unmarketable products. Some have shown one-sidedness in implementing the price policy, and they attach great importance to the forcing down of grades and prices. This is of course correct, but they are unconcerned about the effects of raising grades and prices and even represent the view of a parochial and backward section of the masses in asking the state for higher prices.

In certain state organs and units, some have also used the excuse of taking into consideration the welfare of the masses to trade small favors at the expense of the interests of the state. This one-sided viewpoint of the masses' interests has

Hubei ribao [Hubei Daily], December 27, 1981. Translation from FBIS Daily Report, January 19, 1982, pp. P4–P5.

basically violated the policy of taking into consideration the interests of the state, the collective, and the individual consistently advocated by our Party and our state. It has hindered the fulfilling of various state plans, affected the arrangements for the livelihood of urban and rural people, and led to confusion in certain aspects of economic life. It fosters the idea of "looking to money" among some of the people and even provides those lawless elements who seek private gain at public expense and who practice speculation and manipulation with an opportunity they can turn to their advantage.

After the Third Plenum of the Eleventh CCP Central Committee, the various economic policies carried out by our Party have properly manifested the policy of taking into consideration the interests of the state, the collective, and the individual. Therefore, they have not only promoted the rapid development of various socialist undertakings and enabled the national economy to recover from the crisis and return to the path of prosperity, but they have also provided more material benefits for the masses and greatly improved the life of urban and rural people. When correcting the former leftist mistake of neglecting the individual interests of the masses, some comrades have tended to go to the other extreme of neglecting the interests of the state. They therefore fail to see that the existing economic policy of the Party has already brought many advantages to the people. They still ignore the possibility of objective reality there and stubbornly want the state to give more individual benefits to the masses. Some have brazenly violated the policy of the Party and picked the pocket of the state to satisfy the excessive demand of the masses. These comrades think that they are representing the masses. Actually, they are not really representing the masses but are only representing the erroneous demand of a handful of backward people among the masses. They think that they are working for the interests of the masses, but actually, they are not. At the very most, they are only working for a handful of people in their own enterprise or unit. We must know that our state belongs to the people. If we harm the interests of the state, we will also damage the long-term interests and the basic interests of the broad masses of people.

We have always advocated showing concern for the livelihood of the masses and opposed bureaucracy because it shows no concern for the well-being of the masses. At the same time, we have also advocated arduous struggle and taking the overall situation into account and opposed putting personal material interests above everything else. To really represent the masses and show concern for the masses' interests, we must not only show concern for their immediate interests; the important thing is we must also show concern for their long-term interests and devote our energy to developing production. With the development of production the life of the people will gradually improve. We must not only show concern for the partial interests of our own locality or unit; the important thing is we must also show concern for overall interests and strive by every means to make more contributions for the state. Only when this great tree of the whole economy of the state is growing with vitality can the "branches and leaves" of various parts be luxuriant and green. We must not fix our eyes on the purse of the state and always depend on the state for money to carry out work; the important thing is we must also mobilize the masses to carry out work themselves and to work for their own welfare. Some good work can be carried out without money as long as we go deep into reality and help the masses to solve problems. In short, we must overcome the one-sided viewpoint of the masses' interests and uphold the correct and comprehensive Marxist mass viewpoint. If we can do this, we will certainly be able to do even more good work for the masses.

44

Ju Zhongyi

"NEW ECONOMIC GROUP" VERSUS "PETROLEUM GROUP"

THE "BOHAI No. 2" incident, which resulted in the deaths of seventy-two people and directly brought about a loss of some 37 million yuan, has finally come to an end. Before the opening of the National People's Congress (NPC), the highest authorities in Beijing adopted a resolute and ironclad policy to dismiss the petroleum minister, Song Zhenming, from his post and give the vice-premier in charge of the petroleum industry, Kang Shi'en, a heavy demerit. The response to these measures was encouraging both inside and outside the country as soon as the news was released.

"China is still prosperous!" The decision of the leadership in Beijing enables the people who think that China is hopeless to regain their confidence. In view of the handling of the "Bohai No. 2" incident, people mainly see the determination of the Beijing authorities to rectify the unfair system of rewards and punishments and slack discipline and to enforce Party discipline and state laws.

Important Background

In fact, this is only one side of the case. Recently, I met some friends within the economics circle in Beijing and learned that the "Bohai No. 2" incident had been handled against a background that is of great importance and cannot be ignored.

What is this background? On the surface the "Bohai No. 2" incident was an investigation into the causes of a serious accident. However, it was in fact an important confrontation between two different economic ideas and two different lines for economic development, and it was a critical trial of strength between the "new economic group" and the "petroleum group" in the Beijing leadership. The trial of strength ended with a victory for the "new economic group."

We must not underestimate this victory of the "new economic group." The significance that it bears in the history of Chinese economic construction is at least as great as that of the debate on the criterion of truth carried out in May 1978. It will have incalculable and deep influences on China's march toward the Four Modernizations.

Dongxiang [Trends] (Hong Kong), No. 24 (September 16, 1980), pp. 9–11. Translation from JPRS 76547, October 3, 1980, pp. 62–67.

The "new economic group" is a new term recently introduced in Beijing; the Chinese people are gifted in creating political terms. This term is a new name for the "practical group" in economic construction.

"New Economic Group"

Who are the heads of the "new economic group"? Its representatives in the administration of the State Council are Zhao Ziyang, Yao Yilin, and Wan Li; in the theoretical circles are Hu Qiaomu, Sun Zhifeng, and Xu Dixin; and inside the Party is Hu Yaobang. Of course, they are backed up by old revolutionaries such as Deng Xiaoping and Chen Yun.

In short, the "new economic group" advocates seeking truth from facts and working in accordance with economic laws. Specifically, where an enterprise is concerned, it advocates expanding the right of self-management, bringing the superior position into play, protecting competition, and promoting joint ventures. Regarding circulation, it advocates making appropriate use of readjustment by market supply and demand. Regarding economic planning, it demands scheduled, proportionate, and balanced development, stresses acting according to one's capability, and attaches importance to improving the people's material life. Regarding the labor system, it proposes adopting a more flexible policy and reviving and developing individual industrial and commercial households as a supplement to the state planned economy. Where employment is concerned, it demands that the state abolish its monopoly and unified distribution and advocates appropriate circulation of capable persons, open recruitment, and freedom in choosing jobs. Regarding personnel management, the "new economic group" opposes remaining laymen and encourages experts to dominate factories. All these measures thus in fact meet the demands of the present economic stage of China in a better way. These are bold measures that are practical and break out of ideological confinement.

The implementation of these measures has already accelerated, and surely will further speed up, the recovery of the backward Chinese economy and pushed forward the progress of the Four Modernizations. However, it is not easy for these measures to be implemented. There are certainly many kinds of obstacles in the middle and lower levels. Moreover, some people in the higher level in Beijing object to it, and the "petroleum group" is representative of this opposition.

We Cannot Underestimate the Capacity of the "Petroleum Group"

Besides the criticized petroleum minister Song Zhenming and Vice-Premier Kang Shi'en, the "petroleum group" consists of one or two people who hold a higher post and are more authoritative. Of course, they cannot triumph over the "new economic group" in a trial of political strength. However, they have been recognized as the economic authority for a long time and have taken up leadership posts in economic, financial, and state planning. We must not underestimate their capacity, since they are still enjoying traditional power.

The "petroleum group" advocates the traditional method of economic development that China has implemented over the past thirty years, especially following the tradition of the Daqing oil field. In other words, the "petroleum group" pushes forward economic construction by giving prominence to politics and by means of mass movements, and directs the economy with methods used during the war years. Where economic development is concerned, it gives prominence to heavy industry and neglects light industry and agriculture. It does not care about balance and one-sidedly goes after high quotas. Regarding finance, it advocates huge accumulation and pays no attention to improving the living standard of the people.

This economic ideology continued to dominate Chinese economic circles, even two years after the downfall of Jiang Qing and her accomplices. Later, when the work-style of seeking truth from facts was encouraged and discussions on criterion of truth were launched, people began to see its flaws. People recognized that extremely strict management and the idea of the "iron rice bowl" were in fact a chronic malady. They also realized that the "new petroleum group" was too fond of greatness and success but in fact did not know how things stood. They eventually saw the drawbacks of taking risks and letting laymen be masters of the house. We can see the absurdity when we refer to the ten-year planning of economic development put forward by Hua Guofeng at the first session of the Fifth NPC in February 1978. Over the past few years newspapers have disclosed the large number of abandoned and suspended construction projects. The reason for this was that the capital construction front was overextended, and construction was hurriedly carried out without adequate consideration and without adequate raw materials and preparation. All this was in fact the result of the direct or indirect influence of the economic ideology of the "petroleum group." The salient facts were the extravagance of the "1.7 meter" rolling works in the Wuhan Steel Mill, the selection of an improper location for the Baoshan Steel Mill, the suspended construction of the Shandong Heavy Iron and Steel Plant, the failure to make good the promise of supplying Japan with oil, and so forth.

Hu Qiaomu Sounded the Bugle

The confrontation between the two economic ideologies of the "new economic group" and the "petroleum group" began to develop immediately after the great debate on the criterion of truth in May 1978. In May of this year [1980] at a State Council meeting, Hu Qiaomu gave a report on "to act in accordance with the economic laws and speed up the achieving of the Four Modernizations." In his report, he systematically summed up experiences and lessons in economic construction over the past twenty years and acutely criticized the bad habits of paying no attention to objective laws in economic construction and blind leadership according to the officers' wills. He further stressed a series of guiding economic principles such as planned, proportionate, and balanced development and attaching importance to laws governing the market. This could be called the first relatively complete thesis on the new economic policy, proposed by the "new economic group" on an important occasion, which sounded the bugle to carry out economic development in accordance with economic laws. However, diverging points of view exist in the higher level of the PRC with regard to Hu Qiaomu's thesis. This important speech was published three months later in *Renmin ribao*, that is, on October 6.

Although the new economic plan has been formulated, there are many obstacles to it. There are conflicts between the higher, middle, and lower levels inside the CCP. The reason for this is that on the one hand it is difficult to turn the tide since people have gotten used to the situation that has been in effect for some time, and on the other hand some officials have been content to be laymen and labeled themselves as the "big rough and ready chaps," and this new economic policy is in direct conflict with their personal interests.

During this period, if people paid attention to the economic reports of the CCP provincial and municipal newspapers and journals, they would have discovered many contradictory phenomena. Some provinces and municipalities were still faithful to the campaign of learning from Daqing and conducted meetings on a grand and spectacular scale to select and award Daqing-model enterprises, while some other provinces and municipalities did not mention a single word about Daqing-model enterprises. This reflected the various responses of different provinces and municipalities to the new economic policy.

Zhao Ziyang and Wan Li Shoulder Great Responsibilities

Since the force of habit was very great and in order to be more precise, the "new economic group" headed by Deng Xiaoping and Chen Yun entrusted the high-ranking officers of the "practice group," Zhao Ziyang and Wan Li, who were famous for their emancipated minds and acute and decisive work-style, to carry out experiments on the new economic policy in some units in Sichuan and Anhui provinces. Zhao and Wan did their jobs well and to the satisfaction of the "new economic group." Experiments proved that this new economic policy could liven up the dull and rigid Chinese economic system, and it enhanced the activism of officers and workers of the enterprises; the rate of increase of production value became generally higher than that of nonexperimental enterprises. The market was livened up in a very short time, and the people's living standard was improved. The progress of Sichuan and Anhui aroused the people's attention. The reputation of "Ziyang (the red sun) shines high and Wan Li (10,000 *li*) is bright" spread like wildfire.

Practice is the ground for a great debate. The success in Sichuan and Anhui can be regarded as the first victory of the "new economic group."

However, the confrontation between the economic ideology of the "new economic group" and the "petroleum group" was not very apparent at that time because it was still not the principal conflict. At that time, the principal conflict within PRC political circles was a vigorous debate waged by the "practice group" and the "whatever faction" centered on adopting a correct attitude toward Mao Zedong Thought. The Third Plenum of the CCP Central Committee at the end of 1978 was the climax of this debate. On the other hand, the Chinese economy was at the brink of collapse at that time because of a poor economic situation and its being trampled upon by the gang of Jiang Qing. After the smashing of the "Gang of Four," the danger of economic collapse appeared due to construction of new projects without a prior and adequate understanding of the actual economic situation. The situation can be compared with one in which a person who has just recovered from a near-fatal disease participates in a marathon. Therefore, it became a pressing task for the economic sphere to solve the serious imbalance of economic development. Thus, the ideological confrontation between the "new economic group" and the "petroleum group" was neglected when people urged "readjusting, restructuring, rectifying, and improving" the national economy. As a matter of fact, the proposal and implementation of the principles of readjustment were a measure and a victory of the ideology of the "new economic group."

The Decision on Abolishing the Old Ten-Year Plan

The eight-character principle on readjusting the economy was officially put forward at the second session of the Fifth NPC convened in June 1979, and a period of three years was fixed for its achievement. In the wake of the implementation of the policy of readjustment, the flaws of the "petroleum group" in its planning for economic development in China were to a large extent exposed. People realized that they had been working not according to objective laws and their capability. Simultaneously, the conflict between the "new economic group" and the "petroleum group" became daily more acute. This April, the decisive level of the PRC finally came to a resolute decision. They decided to abolish the original ten-year economic plan and formulate a new one. At the same time, they decided to reassign Yu Qiuli from the position as chairman of the State Planning Commission to be in charge of the State Energy Commission, and appointed Yao Yilin concurrently chairman of the State Planning Commission. After Yao Yilin had taken up his post, he gave an important speech, stressing that the state must work in accordance with its own capability and make gradual progress in economic planning. He criticized the old method of planning solely by subjective opinions and without paying attention to objective laws. He also criticized blindly going after high quotas at a tremendous speed.

This was a critical fight that the "new economic group" won. And because it so happened that the oil rig "Bohai No. 2" capsized during this period, how to squarely analyze and handle this serious incident thus became another trial of strength between the "new economic group" and the "petroleum group."

Points of View

In accordance with the viewpoint of the "petroleum group," there were bound to be sacrifices in striving for progress. Thousands of people sacrificed their lives on the battlefield in order to win a great victory. In comparison, the lives of seventy-two would mean nothing in order to develop an oil field of strategic significance. We must enhance the revolutionary spirit of "fearing neither hardship nor death,'' and it is reasonable to pay a price when you are inexperienced in certain aspects. In light of this, the Oil Ministry and its subordinate marine exploitation bureaus should not shoulder great responsibility with regard to the capsizing of the "Bohai No. 2" platform.

In the opinion of the "new economic group," however, this was an extreme case of dereliction of duty. It violated objective laws and showed no respect for science and was an example of blind leadership by subjective opinions. Song Zhenming and others took the achievements of Daqing as their own and became giddy with success. They thought that they could apply past experience throughout their lives; they were arrogant and did not take others' advice. Thus, the once advanced petroleum ministry became corrupt and enforcement of rules and regulations became slack as laymen took over leadership and workers lacked adequate training. The "Bohai No. 2" platform was imported seven years ago. However, important materials such as the book on stability calculation had not yet been translated, and they even paid no attention to a report submitted by the first front team of the drilling platform. All this finally led to a shocking catastrophe. If we do not strictly handle this severe incident, we will not be able to enforce Party discipline and state laws and vigorously and speedily implement and push forward respect for science and the new economic policy, which works in accordance with objective laws.

Removing a Big Stumbling Block

The "new economic group" was resolutely determined to get rid of all obstacles and made a thorough investigation of the "Bohai No. 2" incident. They finally won a complete victory after a seesaw battle of more than eight months.

By examining the background, we can see that the handling of the "Bohai No. 2" incident is of great significance. It has removed a big stumbling block in the implementation of the new economic policy. It appears that it will continue to exert influence on the PRC's economic construction in the future.

45

Editorial

HEAVY INDUSTRY MUST READJUST ITS SERVICE ORIENTATION

WE HAVE SCORED significant results by resolutely implementing the policy of readjusting the national economy. The agricultural situation is

Renmin ribao [People's Daily], November 16, 1981. Translation from FBIS Daily Report, November 24, 1981, pp. K3–K5.

very good, and the development of light industry is rapid. The proportional relationships among agriculture, light industry, and heavy industry are more in harmony than before.

While we put emphasis on developing light industry, we must also readjust the service orientation of heavy industry so that heavy industry can better meet the needs of society. This is an important issue and one that is related to the overall harmonious development of the national economy.

Heavy industry, particularly machine building, has been declining since the beginning of this year. Part of this decline was predictable and normal. This was not the case with the other part. Some heavy industry products were unmarketable. Rather than producing and stockpiling them, it would have been better not to produce them at all. This decline was rational. Some heavy industry products are needed by society. Because the service orientation of heavy industry had not been readjusted properly, these products were not produced. We should have thought of ways of producing them.

With the emphasis on developing consumer goods production, misunderstandings have arisen in the minds of some comrades. They think, for instance, that the smaller the proportion of heavy industry to the entire national economy, the better. This is totally wrong. Heavy industrial areas should bring into play the advantages that heavy industry has to offer. They should also develop light industry according to their own characteristics. At present, in the country as a whole it is both necessary and correct to stress the development of consumer goods production. However, we must on no account neglect the place that heavy industry occupies in relation to the national economy or the role that it plays in it. One of the basic laws governing economic development is that the production of the means of production must be proportionate to the production of the means of consumption, that is, the primary category of production must be proportionate to the secondary category of production. There must be an appropriate proportional relationship between the two. They are interrelated and interdependent. Heavy industry provides consumer goods production with technological equipment, power, raw and other materials. The reason why light industry has advanced so quickly in recent years is precisely because heavy industry already possesses a fairly good foundation. Without heavy industry as a backup, the development of light industry cannot be sustained.

Heavy industry must be readjusted according to the normal proportional relationships within the national economy. To this end, we must clearheadedly recognize the changing conditions and accurately grasp the service orientation of heavy industry. Both the idea, as far as heavy industry is concerned, "of leaving the orientation unaltered, not easing off with production, and leaving the equipment untouched," and the idea of holding out while heavy industry tasks are not too overwhelming, even though this means that there is no work to do, are wrong. In the 1960s, the readjustment of the national economy proved to be effective. However, readjustment at that time failed to clear up leftist errors in economic work. After readjustment, heavy industry continued to develop along the same old path, leading to a total lack of coordination within the national economy, heavy industry becoming heavier, and light industry becoming lighter. In our readjustment this time around, we must ensure that the service orientation of heavy industry undergoes a corresponding change. Only when the service orientation has been properly readjusted can heavy industry play its correct role and make major advances.

In our readjustment of the service orientation of heavy industry, a matter of primary importance is that it should serve consumer goods production. The development of consumer goods production requires heavy industry to provide it with various kinds of machinery, raw materials, and other materials. With heavy industry changing toward serving consumer goods production, the metallurgical, machine building, electronics, chemical, and other such sectors will show a corresponding development. From this we can see that emphasis must be placed on giving greater play to heavy industry, so that the production of the means of production will be proportionate to the production of the means of subsistence and, on the basis of coordinating the national economy, we can thus strive for the development of heavy industry.

The readjustment of the service orientation of heavy industry must serve the technological transformation of the national economy. The various sectors of our country's national economy possess a fair abundance of technological equipment, but much of the equipment is still rather backward. The equipment of quite a few light industrial enterprises dates back to before the founding of the PRC or even to the 1920s and 1930s, while that of quite a few heavy industrial enterprises dates back to the 1940s and 1950s. According to incomplete statistics, there are at present 2,500 types of special-purpose equipment in the light industries, of which 600 need to be replaced and 900 need to be transformed in a planned way. These conditions bear testimony to the urgency of the task of technologically transforming the national economy as well as the arduous nature of the tasks which heavy industry has to shoulder. Heavy industry still has to carry out its own technological transformation and to strengthen its resources, transportation, and other such bottlenecks affecting the national economy. With continuous progress being made in the field of technological transformation, heavy industry will also continue to develop.

Readjusting the service orientation of heavy industry means that it must serve exports, provide more products of a high quality, and adapt to the needs of the international market. Our country has a fairly strong and large machine building industry and metallurgical industry, as well as an abundance of coal and other minerals. The entry of heavy industry products into the international market not only brings in more foreign currency for the state, but also enables us to see how our country's products fare on the international market.

The national economy is an integral whole. The readjustment of the service orientation of heavy industry is favorable to the development of the integral whole and will adapt the development of heavy industry to that of agriculture and light industry, thus promoting the day-by-day relationalization of the whole national economic structure.

46

Shen Yue

SOME QUESTIONS ABOUT GIVING FULL SCOPE TO LIAONING'S FAVORABLE CONDITIONS IN HEAVY INDUSTRY

LIAONING PROVINCE IS one of our country's important centers of heavy industry, being one of the earliest built with the support of the whole country. Over the past 32 years since the founding of the PRC, total capital construction investment in the whole province amounted to 34.7 billion yuan. Nearly 400 large and medium-size enterprises have been built. The gross value of industrial output increased by more than 3,800 percent over the initial period after the founding of the republic. The fixed assets of enterprises owned by the whole people amount to 11 percent of the national total and occupy first place for the whole country. Liaoning has a relatively complete assortment of various kinds of industry, but the proportion occupied by heavy industry alone is over 33.3 percent. The important task before us now during the further readjustment of the national economy is how to put into full play Liaoning's superiority in heavy industry in order to upgrade the national economy.

Fully Display the Leading Role of Heavy Industry in the National Economy

With the further readjustment of the national economy, heavy industry has been downgraded in planning, and its production has been on the downturn. As a result, some comrades have entertained the erroneous notion that since the readjustment of the economy called for the development of light industry, heavy industry should "stand aside." They even considered heavy industry as a heavy "burden." Indeed, in the readjustment of the national economy, should heavy industry even be developed? The answer is definitely in the affirmative. In readjustment work, that portion of heavy industry that should be suspended must be suspended, while that portion that should be developed must be developed so that the heavy industrial sector can maintain a definite speed of development. Over the past two years, owing to economic readjustment, that proportion of the national economy made up of light industry has risen while that of heavy industry has declined. This is a normal phenomenon and accords with the relationship between light industry and heavy industry. But we should not derive from this the conclusion that the lower the proportion of heavy industry the better, or even that

Hongqi [Red Flag] No. 22 (November 16, 1981). The author is secretary of the Liaoning Provincial CCP Committee. Translation from FBIS Daily Report, December 10, 1981, pp. S1–S7 (excerpts).

portion of the heavy industrial sector that should be further developed or that should be maintained at its present level should both be reduced in order to increase the level of light industry. The vigorous development of light industry is entirely necessary, but without modern equipment and raw materials, it is impossible to produce modern consumer goods. In discussing the theory of social reproduction, Marx said that the two big categories of social production should have a relationship of mutual dependence, balance, assistance, and restriction. When expounding on the theory about the conditions for realizing expanded reproduction with the gross capital of a society when things were balanced, Marx offered the following formula: The value of the products of the first category must be equal to the value of the compensated portion of the unchanged value of the two big categories and the value of the supplementary portion of the unchanged value of the two big categories. Based on Marx's exposition on the theory of expanded reproduction, Lenin pointed out the theory of the priority development of the means of production under the conditions of technological improvement. Our own practice has also amply shown that heavy industry is the principal link of the national economy and that the development of the national economy is inseparable from the priority development of the first category.

As for Liaoning Province, production of heavy industry products must be vigorously developed in order to ensure a definite speed of development of the national economy. The reasons are: (1) Liaoning is the center of heavy industry for the whole country. Many of its products are required by the whole country. It bears the important task of supporting the economic construction of the country. The original value of the fixed assets of its heavy industry and the gross value of its industrial output each made up about 11 percent of the national total, ranking first among the provinces of the country.

Failure to do a good job of promoting production of heavy industrial products of the province would affect not only the economy of the province but also the economic development of the whole country. (2) With heavy industry making up a big proportion of the economy of the province, the development of industrial production in the province depends to a large extent on heavy industry. A drop of 1 percent in the value of output of heavy industry must be compensated by an increase of at least 2 percent in the output value of light industry. Light industry cannot bear the burden of a fall in heavy industrial production, and if heavy industrial production fails to progress, the growth speed of industry as a whole will be affected. (3) Liaoning has many backbone enterprises of heavy industry. They are the economic lifeline of the country. They have enormous potential. If they are run successfully, they can make immense contributions. The state of national finances depends primarily on these big enterprises. Of the profits remitted to the state from provincial industries, heavy industry's share is 88 percent. Remittances from the four large steel plants and the six large oil refineries account for 62 percent of the total profits remitted to the state by the state-operated enterprises in the province.

Actually, if their profits were to fall, other enterprises could hardly make up for the loss. Judging from the situation in the first eight months of this year, a drop of 1 percent in the profits tax [as published] of heavy industry will require a growth of 7 percent in light industry in order to make up the difference. Heavy industry not only accounts for a large share of the economy but also provides huge profits. Last year, the profits tax [as published] generated from 100 yuan of output value were as follows: light industry, 21.86 yuan; heavy industry, 27.65 yuan; and among the heavy industries, petroleum industry, 43.37 yuan, and metallurgical industry, 33.78 yuan. Hence, if the production of heavy industry is increased, the financial revenue of the state will be enhanced and the national economy will be enlivened. (4) Heavy industry and light industry depend on and regulate each other. If heavy industry is not developed, light industry cannot be developed either. In the province as a whole, 45 percent of the raw materials for light industry are derived from heavy industry. Conversely, light industry also directly renders many services to heavy industry. The role of many small light industrial plants is to make accessories for large plants of heavy industry. Therefore, if heavy industry does well in production, light industry will have the needed raw materials, equipment, and supply of energy, and will thus be enlivened. At the same time, progress made in the production of consumer goods will naturally encourage heavy industry to reorient the direction of its services and reform the structure of its products. This literally will enable heavy industry to advance in the course of readjustment. (5) Heavy industry should be subjected to a concrete analysis and not be governed by a general rule. Among the products of heavy industry, some are of good quality, while some are of poor quality; some have been produced in abundance, while some have not. Even among the quality products, some products are still secondary in quality. For example, heavy industry in our province renders more services to itself than to agriculture, or to light industry, or to the domestic and foreign markets. Our supply of energy, such as coal, electricity, and crude oil, is not abundant or very impressive. As for the metallurgical industry, the production of ordinary steel products is excessive, while production of small steel products is rather scanty. According to an investigation made of the five industries and trades of metallurgy, machine-building, crude oil, petro-chemicals, and construction materials, currently the supply of over 150 varieties of "short-line" products lags behind demand. An increase in the production of these products not only can satisfy current demand but also can enliven the production of heavy industry. All the above illustrates that the large proportion occupied by heavy industry in the economy of the province is not a burden but represents wealth and affluence. It does not denote an inferior position but a superior position. Only in performing well the work of readjustment and production of heavy industry can there be any improvement in the entire national economy.

Correctly Shape the Direction of Services and Fully Tap the Hidden Potentials of Current Heavy Industrial Enterprises

Some comrades have shown a lack of confidence in letting heavy industry maintain a definite speed of development in the course of readjustment. Some have suggested "the direction should remain unchanged, the workers contingent should remain intact, production should continue and, generally, things should be carried out this way throughout the readjustment." These viewpoints are all erroneous. They illustrate that these comrades entertain conflicting views about the policy of further readjusting the national economy. Since the beginning of this year, the state has readjusted the production plans of certain departments of heavy industry. This is necessary. The proper and correct attitude to assume is to take advantage of this opportune moment, correct the direction of services, reform the structure of products, and actively take up the tasks of improving the quality of products and increasing their varieties and not just idly sit around and passively wait for development. In the course of readjustment, heavy industry should not remain idle. It has a lot of potential and certainly can accomplish much. If only the objective of socialist production can be clearly understood and the direction of the services can be truly rectified so that heavy industry will serve the people's livelihood needs, serve technological restructuring, and serve national defense and the export trade, then its development can surely be guaranteed.

Putting Heavy Industry's Superiority in Full Play; Providing Vigorous Support to Light Industry

Our stress on grasping heavy industry does not mean that we can dispense with light industry. On the contrary, light industry must be greatly developed. In Liaoning Province, simultaneously with firmly grasping heavy industry, the vigorous development of light industry is tantamount to giving fuller play to the role of heavy industry. In Liaoning, heavy industry occupies a large portion of the economy of the province. Our cities and towns are densely populated, and a large number of people are currently awaiting employment. The purchasing power of the people has all along been higher than the national average. Development of light industry will increase the production of daily-use consumer goods. It will help in meeting the livelihood needs of the people, make the market flourish, speed up currency circulation, stabilize commodity prices, provide jobs for those awaiting employment, and increase the revenue for the state.

Development of light industry is inseparable from the assistance provided by heavy industry. Production of the means of production should not only be for the purpose of meeting the production needs of the production department itself but also to meet the needs of those departments that produce consumer goods and require more of the means of production. The ultimate purpose of socialist production is to satisfy the livelihood needs of the people. The heavy industry of our province accounts for a large proportion of its economy, has a strong foundation, and is capable of supplying a large quantity of means of production for the production of consumer goods. This provides an advantageous condition for the development of light industry. Over the past two years, the heavy industrial cities of our province such as Shenyang, Anshan, Fushun, and Dalian have achieved notable results in their activities aiming at the target of "heavy industry helping light industry and light industry promoting heavy industry.'' The experience and methodology of these activities were mainly the following: (1) Organizing heavy industrial enterprises to provide the textile and electronics industries with advanced technical equipment and model tools, thus speeding up the steps in the technological restructuring of light industrial enterprises. (2) Organizing heavy industrial enterprises to provide the textile and electronics industries with large quantities of raw materials that are good in quality and conform with the prescribed specifications; a portion of steel products and petrochemical raw materials are provided to them from a fixed source of production and supply, thus building up firm cooperative relationships. (3) Organizing heavy industrial enterprises to assist light industrial enterprises to solve technological problems and overcome technological problems. (4) Organizing those heavy industrial enterprises that have the necessary conditions to directly manufacture daily-use consumer goods and that possess more or less similar production techniques and raw materials as light industries. (5) Transferring to the textile and electronics industrial system a portion of the heavy industrial enterprises that have become idle, or have no prospects for the future, or are fit for use in light industrial production, thus reinforcing the technical backing to light industry. (6) Organizing a number of heavy industrial and light industrial enterprises for economic cooperation centered on the production of key light industrial products; carrying out production cooperation on the ''one dragon'' thesis.

(7) Transferring from large heavy industrial plants technical personnel and management cadres to help certain light industrial enterprises to reinforce their technical capabilities and to reorganize and improve their operation and management. In general, the adoption of these measures has helped, on the one hand, to solve the key problems in light industrial production that have been long standing and, on the other hand, to open up a new service area for heavy industry. It is beneficial to coordinating the relationship between light industry and heavy industry and promoting the overall development of industry in general.

47

SHANXI FORCING COLLECTIVE, ENTERPRISE MERGERS

COLLECTIVELY OWNED ENTERPRISES are being merged by force into state-owned enterprises in North China's Shanxi Province, seriously jeopardizing the development of light industry and handicraft production in that province, *Economic Daily* [Jingji ribao] reported.

China Daily, February 7, 1985. From FBIS Daily Report, February 15, 1985, p. R5.

Thus far, 170 collective enterprises with total assets of 110 million yuan (U.S. $40 million) have been forced to merge into the province's state-owned factories. This accounts for more than 11 percent of the total assets of the second light industry (handicrafts and small merchandise industry) in the province.

This "commandeering" of collectively owned business already has adversely affected the supply of small consumer goods in the provincial market and has generated complaints from people involved in business, the newspaper said.

Shanxi began merging collective enteprises by compulsory order into state-owned enterprises several years ago, and it intensified the process in the name of "industrial specialization" after 1982. This was aimed at boosting the revenue of the local government because "the profits of such enterprises are not turned over to the state treasury," the newspaper said.

Such action was a violation of the State Council's regulation of "maintaining the ownership, leadership, and finance of collectively owned light industrial enterprises at their original status," *Economic Daily* commented.

If this "commandeering drive" goes on in Shanxi, the province's entire second light industry will collapse because "they will come to merge you into their system once you start making a profit," many employees of the province's collectively owned enterprises complained.

In a commentary on Tuesday, the *Economic Daily* said the action of "commandeering collectively owned light industrial enterprises in the name of economic reform" must stop immediately. It is the policy of the state to encourage and develop collectively owned industry, "which has not yet fully recovered from the leftist blows it suffered over the past decades," the commentary said.

Collective industry has an important role to play in the country's modernization drive, and the provinces should learn to protect these enterprises instead of jeopardizing their existence in the old "leftist fashion," it added.

48

Liu Xianghui

IDEAS OFFERED TO REFORM EMPLOYMENT SYSTEM

CHINA'S URBAN AND rural labor force exceeds present construction and production requirements. Although more than 37 million people were given jobs in the last five years, there are still many waiting for employment. Some 5 or 6 million new hands will join the labor force each year, resulting in a net increase of 3 million new labor force annually after deducting those who have retired or quit. In addition, a portion of the rural population will be shifted

China Daily, December 18, 1982. From JPRS 82672, January 18, 1983, pp. 83–85. The author is with the Investigation Research Division of the State Economic Commission. The article reproduced here is a summary of a longer article published in Chinese in *Renkou yanjiu* [Population Research].

to the cities each year, and they will have to be provided with jobs.

The fundamental solution is to develop production. For the next several years we have only some 30 billion yuan to invest each year in capital construction. At our present level of industrial technology, that will accommodate only some 2 million workers. However, since our economic development in the next few years will depend mainly on renovating existing enterprises and the introduction of advanced technology, it will further reduce the manpower requirement, thus providing fewer opportunities for those who make their debut on the stage of employment.

We have been practicing a system of universal and unconditional employment under which the state or society will take the responsibility to provide work for every able-bodied person. The percentage of employed of the urban and nonrural population has increased from 20 percent at the time of Liberation to more than 50 percent now. In some cities and towns the percentage has risen to 60 to 70 percent. There are now 34 million women working, one third of the total number of workers.

This system of universal and unconditional employment and other labor practices have brought many problems that cannot be easily solved.

The multitude of unemployed people will soon be too heavy a burden on the state and society. It will also affect the economic returns and efficiency of enterprises. The unemployed are arbitrarily assigned to various regions and departments regardless of actual production requirements. They are assigned simply for the sake of assigning, and the result is that five people are doing the work of three people.

Industries find it difficult to introduce advanced technology while government offices are swollen with functionaries. This sacrificing of the interests of production and construction for the sake of solving the problem of providing employment for the unemployed has led to a heavy drop in the speed of the growth of labor efficiency in recent years.

Basic Feature

The enforcement of universal and unconditional employment aggravated by lengthy terms of employment and the current retirement policy is also responsible for the drop in quality of contingents of workers and functionaries. In most enterprises and government offices, there are invariably many old, physically weak, and sickly workers and functionaries, while large numbers of young people wait for jobs. The policy of letting sons or daughters replace their retired fathers or mothers renders impossible the selection of candidates who are best qualified.

We must consider the most basic feature of our country, which is that we have a population of 1 billion now and 1.2 billion by the end of this century. To solve the contradictions involved in employment, it is necessary to earnestly implement the policy fixed by the Central Committee of ''coordinating employment placement by labor administration departments, employment placement through voluntary organization on the part of those unemployed, and employment placement sought by the individuals themselves.'' It is our tentative idea that the following methods and measures can be introduced:

1. Employment according to need and selection of best candidates must be strictly enforced in all enterprises. Procedures for examinations and employment on trial should be observed. The enterprises have the right to fire surplus personnel.

2. Leave for female workers and functionaries should be prolonged or increased to take care of their health needs. Maternity leave may be extended to about a year. A new system of voluntary leaves for child-rearing for a period of from five to ten years may be introduced under which the mothers may draw wages somewhat lower than their basic wages. It is estimated that the introduction of such a system may provide vacancies for 200 million prospective workers.

3. Requirements for enjoying retirement should be lowered, and duration of employment should be shortened.

4. Contingents of temporary workers should be expanded and flexible working hours enforced.

Emancipation

There are apprehensions about the abolition of the system of universal and unconditional employment. Some worry that it might affect social stability. Actually, if those who are incapable of doing complicated and heavy tasks in production are encouraged to do domestic labor and give up the positions to the young, society would become more stable and orderly.

Others maintain that encouraging women to give up their jobs to look after household duties is tantamount to asking women to return to the kitchen, which is counter to the idea of the emancipation of women. This is certainly a misinterpretation of the meaning of the emancipation of women.

For a long time we have been publicizing too much the principle of "no work in society, no food in the family," which helps spread the idea of despising doing household duties. Our policy of low wages but more employment also helps drive more people to leave their families to look for jobs. This increases the burden on state and society.

There are also worries about the livelihood of those who lose their permanent jobs through the implementation of the new employment system. In this connection, the state will surely install a series of social welfare funds for labor insurance and social relief.

49

Zheng Yonghui

WHY IT IS NECESSARY TO DO AWAY WITH THE IRON RICE BOWL SYSTEM

THE PRESENT FIXED-JOB system is commonly called the "iron

Yangcheng wanbao [Yangcheng Evening News], February 23, 1983. Translation from JPRS 83440, May 10, 1983, pp. 26–29.

rice bowl'' system, which is not a necessity in socialist countries, and especially is not a manifestation of the superiority of socialism. It is a product of the specific historical circumstances of our country.

The so-called fixed-job system means that the placement of staff and workers of the people-owned enterprises and public agencies is taken care of centrally by the state. Employees come, but never go. They can only be promoted, but not demoted, and they cannot be dismissed. In the early years after the founding of the People's Republic, the state adopted the policy of the "totally guaranteed" placement and employment of the staff and workers of bureaucrat-capitalist enterprises and former employees of the Guomindang state organizations, in order to resolve the unemployment problem left over by the old society. The Government Administration Council stipulated on July 25, 1952, that "all state- and private-owned enterprises must adopt the total guarantee policy with regard to the staff and workers who have become surplus owing to the implementation of production reform and rational enhancement of labor productivity. Their original enterprise units are to pay them their original wages (to be calculated into these enterprises' costs), and must not discharge them." This was entirely correct at that time. Later on, because of the needs for the development of the country's construction, the scope of "total guarantee" was further expanded in 1954, even the placement of persons released after serving a sentence was "guaranteed" by the state.

Based on our understanding, there was no fixed-job sytem and "total guarantee" policy in the Soviet Union, not even during the Lenin and Stalin eras; nor was there one in Romania, Yugoslavia, Hungary, Poland, Democratic Germany, etc. Instead, a contract work system was implemented under which people can come and go. Thus we can see that the fixed-job system was originated and developed under our country's specific historical circumstances. Of course, the drawbacks of this system became obvious already at the end of the fifties and the beginning of the sixties. In a 1958 report of the Sichuan provincial Party commit- tee approved and submitted to the Central Committee it was pointed out that the most distinct problem of the current labor system was that "the recruited workers and staff can come, but not go," and "no matter whether or not there is work, workers cannot be dismissed, and cannot be transferred to different types of work and different factories." In view of these facts Comrade Liu Shaoqi proposed in 1958 to reform the system. He proposed that, based on the conditions of our country, we should adopt two labor systems. The enterprises can hire or dismiss. They should use more temporary, less permanent workers. The new system of new factory-new employees and the old system of old factory-old employees should be implemented, aiming at gradually changing the present fixed-job sys- tem. In the meantime, the wage distribution system and labor insurance benefits system must be appropriately reformed. Comrade [Liu] Shaoqi's idea was imple- mented on a trial basis before 1966 in a number of places and obtained good results. Unfortunately, for various reasons, especially owing to the destruction wreaked by the "Cultural Revolution," his correct proposition was not realized. During the "Cultural Revolution," with the interference of the ultra-"Left" line, the scope of "total guarantee" was further expanded; thus the "burden" on the state became heavier and heavier, and the contradictions became more and more distinct.

Disadvantages of the "Iron Rice Bowl" System

The current "iron rice bowl" system violates socialist economic principles, is unsuited to the coexistence and development of various economic elements, and does not help in making our economy work. Our socialist economy is still a planned commodity economy. The enterprises need a labor force combined with the means of production to satisfy their economic and technical demands. They can make changes as the conditions of their production change, that is, the enterprises must have certain authority to adjust the labor force so that the labor force can be moved rationally within the enterprises. For example, our country is currently developing multiple economic elements. We especially need to develop commerce, service trades, etc. There is a need to rationally move the labor force among the enterprises of various ownership systems. However, because of the differences in welfare benefits between the fixed system and other employment forms, the people are attracted to strive for jobs in the people-owned units. Some unemployed people, including their parents, would rather wait for fixed-jobs with less daily pay than choose now available collective and individual jobs with more pay; thus they have imperceptibly increased resistance to opening all avenues for employment and have also encouraged the unhealthy tendency of "entering the back door." If we could open up this "forbidden zone" of the fixed-job system, all enterprises could recruit their own workers and choose outstanding ones for employment based on their production needs after going through relevant hiring procedures examined and approved by the responsible authorities. In this way, various economic elements would be more and more prosperous and flourishing because of the active mobilization of the labor force, thus helping to accelerate the development of the national economy and the improvement of the people's livelihood.

The present fixed-job system is unfavorable to the improvement of productivity. The enterprises cannot select, according to the changing situations of their production, their own workers both in terms of quantity and quality. People that the enterprises need cannot get in; those the enterprises do not need cannot get out. The enterprises are forced to accept staff and workers who do not meet their needs, so much so that they are unable to handle those who have violated the law and discipline and refuse to mend their ways despite repeated admonition. Thus the frontline personnel of the enterprises have been decreasing year by year, and rear-service personnel have been increasing. The enterprises have more hands than needed, and their burden is becoming heavier and heavier. Meanwhile, in the process of production, the enterprises require that their staff and workers continue to advance in depth and breadth their knowledge in production technology. But the "iron rice bowl" system fetters the workers' consciousness to master science and technology. A number of people do not strive to make progress, do not care about studying or working, and do not exert themselves. Everyone is holding on to his "iron rice bowl," feeling secure without fear of losing it. Furthermore, the fixed-job system is the reason why the workers cannot choose freely their occupation, develop their own special skills, and why their creative ability is fettered. All this has shown that this irrational fixed-job system is the main cause of the long delayed improvement of our labor productivity.

The present fixed-job system is also unfavorable to the enforcement of the socialist principle of distribution "from each according to his ability and to each according to his work." Once a worker gets his "iron rice bowl," no matter what economic results the enterprise achieves, his salary can only be raised, but not reduced, regardless of whether he does a good job or not, and of how much work he is doing. The enterprises have no authority to dismiss, still less to expel, those staff and workers who severely violate labor discipline, do not accept authority in their assignments, stay away from work over a long period of time without good reasons, and even commit crimes. This seriously dampens the enthusiasm of staff and workers of the enterprises and obviously runs counter to the principle of distribution "from each according to his ability and to each according to his work."

Do Away with the "Iron Rice Bowl" System, Substitute the Fixed-Job System with the Contract Hiring System

Since the fixed-job system's drawbacks are so obvious, we must reform it, comprehensively pushing for a contract hiring system that basically has the following characteristics and contents:

1) The enterprise and the worker sign a labor contract, free to get in and out. The enterprise may recruit and hire, selecting good workers for employment according to its production needs and following certain examined and approved procedures. The worker can choose his occupation according to his own technical skills and interests. In order to guarantee the quality of the enterprise's employees, there must be a probationary period after the hiring, and upon the completion of the probationary period, the enterprise and the employee sign the labor contract, which includes the employee's tasks, duties, salary, benefits, labor discipline, etc. During the probationary period if someone is found unsuitable to the set conditions, he can be dismissed.

2) The worker's pay and benefits can go up or down. The present irrational pay system must be done away with. Grading and grade evaluation, based on workers' qualifications and performance, must be implemented. Unified wage standards should be formulated by provinces and cities with appropriate salary grades, according to the workers' technical and professional level and the degree of their contribution. The salary for a worker hired by a new unit should be reassessed, based on the person's qualifications. The enterprises have the authority to adopt various wage forms, closely combining the quality of production management and economic results with the degree of the workers' contribution.

They can raise or cut salaries, moving them upward or downward. 3) A new social and labor insurance system is established to solve, with overall planning, the employees' retirement and other social insurance problems, to free the employees' mind of their fear of behind-the-back disturbances. This is the significant guarantee that the new contract hiring system gives. In fully bringing the superiority of the socialist system into play, we must uniformly enhance the social and labor insurance system concerning the contracted employees' retirement, job disability, unemployment aid, death, and aid for surviving family members of workers who die on the job. Dismissed or discharged workers can be given certain unemployment aid during the period of their unemployment according to the length of their continuous service. The sources of social insurance premiums are: one, from the current labor insurance premium in enterprise units and public agencies; two, from the enterprises' welfare funds; three, the monthly small amount of workers' mutual-aid fund. The enterprises are responsible for the workers' labor insurance to be transferred to the overall social planning. This is a significant reform. The government must establish appropriate insurance organizations, labor insurance companies, or present labor service companies to specially administer the contracted workers social insurance. In addition, the government must establish and improve the present organization of labor administration, that is, the labor service companies which must organize, adjust, take in, and send out in large numbers and train employed workers and gradually take up the responsibility of adjusting the distribution and redistribution of the labor force of the society. They will become the hub of regulating the labor force and taking over some functions from factories and enterprises, so that the enterprises can concentrate on production.

At the present stage of socialism, because the labor of the workers must be rewarded and the enterprises must consider the state's interests and the enterprises' collective interests, the combination of means of production of socialist society and labor force must be conditional, not unconditional. The contract hiring system is implemented by adopting the form of labor agreement, closely combining the means of production and the labor force, so that the workers must give equivalent labor (including various deductions) in exchange for equivalent pay by the enterprises. At the same time, the system can effectively ensure the workers' labor rights. The present fixed-job system, however, does great damage to this combination. It has brought about the phenomenon of "eating out of the same big pot." Some comrades do not understand the characteristics of socialist labor, mistakenly taking the "iron rice bowl" as the superiority of the socialist system and as the expression of socialist workers being masters of their own country. As a matter of fact, this has seriously hampered the evolution of our socialist society's superiority. With the implementation of the contract hiring system, this situation will greatly change. The workers, in the process of integrating with the means of production, will not only enjoy full labor rights, but will also have to take appropriate economic responsibilities and receive material benefits accordingly. This way, they can truly handle correctly the relationship among the state, the enterprise, and the individual.

50

Yi Duming

IN DEFENSE OF THE IRON RICE BOWL SYSTEM

WHAT DOES "IRON rice bowl" mean? As far as people know, "iron rice bowl" means that a person has a secure job, is unlikely to become jobless, and can feed himself without worrying about hunger. It seems that it is not a bad thing, but is absolutely worthy. Before Liberation, this writer was often jobless and suffered from hunger. Because there was no "iron rice bowl," I joined in the revolutionary ranks and engaged in revolution. The purpose of the revolution was to let the people of the whole country each have an "iron rice bowl." Many of our revolutionary comrades struggled all their lives so that the people of the whole country could each have an "iron rice bowl." (Of course, there were still nobler ideals.)

Recently, however, quite a number of people have gone so far as to complain about the "iron rice bowl." They think that production comes to a standstill and enterprises are at a loss, workers are disobedient and are not easy to direct, they lack discipline and their enthusiasm cannot be aroused, all as a result of the "iron rice bowl" system. It seems that all faults are to be attributed to the "iron rice bowl" and that the "iron rice bowl" is really guilty of unpardonable evils. As a result, many leading cadres in enterprises are inclined to deem hiring temporary workers who will never be allowed to become regular staff as an all-powerful magic weapon. They even maintain that temporary workers are much better than regular staff and workers because temporary workers have greater initiative, and once they are admitted as regular staff, they will no longer be obedient or enthusiastic. Views like these are numerous; this is really unjust. Consequently, the "iron rice bowl" has suffered unredressed injustice. In fact, the reason why certain enterprises cannot move ahead, or why they suffer losses, is that the leading groups are incompetent, that subjectivism and bureaucracy give rise to different opinions among staff and workers, making it impossible to bring their initiative into play. There are other reasons: the leading groups regard enterprises as their own private kingdoms and engage in irregularities such as practicing unhealthy tendencies or going through the back door, which result in serious waste; mismanagement results in low output, inferior quality of products, and enormous waste; leading groups are blind in setting production goals because they do not attach importance to scientific market research; or they are unable to arouse the enthusiasm of the workers because they do not implement the production responsibility system but "eat out of the same big pot." All of these have nothing to do with the "iron rice bowl." Why should they obstinately attribute

Yangcheng wanbao [Yangcheng Evening News], February 23, 1983. Translation from JPRS 83440, May 10, 1983, pp. 30–31.

these faults to it? As the saying goes: "One who does not know how to pole a boat complains about the winding river." It is really lamentable. Therefore, the writer wants to cry out for the "iron rice bowl system" with a heavy heart. I hope that the concerned authorities will rehabilitate it. I wish that the people of the whole country could each have not only an "iron rice bowl," but a "gold rice bowl."

51

Dang Jizhi

QIXIANZHUANG VILLAGE IN XIAN CITY TODAY

QIXIANZHUANG IS a well-known village in Xian, for it was a place where Comrade Zhou Enlai lived and carried out the struggle. Who could have imagined that in precisely the same city there would emerge another "village" called "Qixianzhuang" where a number of people of ability and political integrity are deprived of the opportunity to play their role. The "village" is the Xian City cement factory.

The Xian City cement factory was set up in 1970 with an investment of 8 million yuan from the state. For ten years it successively suffered losses. By 1979, the leading group of the factory had already been reorganized eight times, but none of the leaders in the group were able to score any achievements. At that time the factory employed, through an "under-the-counter relationship," Li Naiheng, a "cement expert" who knew nothing at all about cement. The factory appointed him to the post in charge of maintaining all the equipment in the factory. For fourteen and a half months he tried to fix the machinery but failed to make it turn out even half a *jin* of cement.

After he worked on the machines, people found that no electric switches had been installed or the machine turned the wrong way or rattled. What was to be particularly regretted was that he almost destroyed the key component of the mechanized horizontal kiln, the "stick with wolf's fangs" (the technical term is a rolling feeder). He worked on the machinery until March 1980, but still failed to put the factory into operation.

In the face of this difficult problem, the then Xian City CCP Committee publicly advertised the job vacancy. Hu Zhaoming, a scientific and technological worker who graduated from a cement specialty course in a university in the early 1960s, applied to be transferred from the city building materials department to the cement factory. He relied on the technical forces in the factory and spent only

Renmin ribao [People's Daily], April 6, 1984. Translation from FBIS Daily Report, April 25, 1984, pp. K12–K15.

thirteen days in overcoming tremendously great difficulties in fixing the machinery, repaired the nearly destroyed "stick with wolf's fangs," and made the machinery produce cement. This instance made the city CCP committee realize that we had people of talent and virtue right in our hands. The question was, why had we failed to employ them? After discussion, the city CCP committee decided to assign Hu Zhaoming to the post in charge of the cement factory.

The first thing this ordinary intellectual did after his appointment was to reduce the overstaffing and select and appoint people of talent and virtue to important posts. He assigned all those who had not much to do to posts in the first line of production, freed a large number of talented people, and formed them into a factory technology department. In this department were employed senior engineer Zhang Fawen, engineers Zhang Guan and Chen Bingkun, assistant engineers Chen Zhongquan and Wang Ming, and college graduates with specialized cement knowledge Wang Shouming and Hou Huiping.

When the factory was managed by people who knew their jobs, many achievements were scored. Zhang Fawen, an old engineer who was wrongly labeled a "rightist," gave up his holiday leave and led an experimental team to work day and night. He finally succeeded in calcining black raw materials, after which the factory yielded its first batch of high grade cement. Through experiments, he succeeded in substituting coal ash from power stations for slag in the material mix, thus finding a short-cut in overcoming the shortage of raw materials. Engineers Zhang Guan and Chen Bingkun installed a hammer mill, which no one in the factory had dared to touch and which had lain idle for a long time. Thus they overcame a major difficulty in production. Chen Zhongquan progressively transformed the packing line of the factory and thus ensured normal production in the factory. By the end of December the factory had turned losses into profits in one stroke. It yielded more than 22,000 metric tons of cement, kept more than 3,500 metric tons of high-grade burned cement raw materials in store, and put an end to ten years of losses. For the first time, its staff and workers received year-end bonuses. The city CCP committee decided to publicly praise the factory in the newspaper.

Hu Zhaoming achieved great success in his work. However, this also exposed him to retaliation. Motivated by jealousy, that unprofessional Li Naiheng, who had damaged the equipment, wantonly abused Hu Zhaoming. Those who were not capable of operating the factory and did not intend to work in a practical manner began to exercise their permanent "right to criticize." They made a mockery of Hu, spread rumors, and even sent "reports" to accuse Hu. Xu Xieling, a deputy chief of the city Building Materials Bureau who had obtained his post by overthrowing his former superior, stopped a commendatory article, already approved by the bureau Party group secretary, from being carried in the newspaper and deliberately laid obstacles before Hu so as to stop the factory from regular operation. Encouraged by Xu, Li Naiheng stirred up trouble everywhere: "Stop working, everybody. Just wait until Hu Zhaoming is expelled from our factory for failure to keep the factory running." In collusion with other people he insisted on rejecting cement products that had passed quality inspection and refused to let the products leave the factory.

As a result, the factory was jammed with surplus stock and the plant was forced to stop operation. Much stock deteriorated from the humidity or was even discarded.

While these people were stirring up trouble, the leading body of the Xian City CCP Committee was reorganized. Hu Zhaoming was faced with a still tougher situation. Soon after that, a strange decision was made: Hu Zhaoming was to return to the bureau to wait for a new post. As soon as Hu Zhaoming was moved from the factory, the technical section, which was regarded as his sphere of influence, was dismissed. Some members of the section were expelled while others stayed idle. More than twenty people were involved in the case.

Among other small-sized cement enterprises in the country, the Xian City cement factory had the best equipment, the newest plant building, and a big contingent of technical personnel and was known as the best of its kind in the country. However, the factory had the lowest output, and its losses accounted for more than half the total losses suffered by 144 cement factories in the country. This was nothing strange, or, one could say, it was an inevitable outcome.

Yang Yongmao, the responsible person of the factory who took Hu Zhaoming's place after he left, said: "I will never use them (referring to those technical personnel) even if I have to pay them for staying idle." When Hu Zhaoming had been managing the plant the technical section had already completed all the design work for the project for an annual output of 150,000 tons of high-grade cement, and the factory had bought a complete set of equipment, including a rotating kiln, tube mill, coal powder grinder, electric dust collector, and so on, which could have yielded economic results once it was installed and put into operation. However, the equipment has now become seriously rusted owing to long-standing exposure to the open air. The existing equipment, ranging from transportation and lifting facilities to crushing, clay baking, store house, and other facilities, was designed to meet the specifications for an annual output of 150,000 tons of cement. Nevertheless, since the rotating kiln has not yet been installed, the equipment in operation fails to run at full capacity, wearing out and bringing about waste of electricity, just like a stout horse drawing a small cart. The present annual output is a mere 20,000 to 30,000 tons. By the end of last year, the aggregate losses of the factory amounted to 4.17 million yuan, and the factory was on the verge of bankruptcy.

To our great surprise, now those activists in the "Cultural Revolution" who had been "driven" by Hu Zhaoming to work in the workshops have had good luck again. A man called Hu Qingzhou, who was formerly a worker under the house building system and persecuted a lot of people during the "Cultural Revolution," has now been promoted to be the chief controller in charge of production and was even elected as the factory's representative to participate in the national conference on cement production technology the year before last. Of course, he made a spectacle of himself at the conference since he knew nothing about production. Another man called Zhang Jingtai, who had been promoted for his merit in overthrowing his superior during the "Cultural Revolution" and was expelled from the Party and removed from the post of workshop chief after the Third Plenum of the Eleventh CCP Central Committee, has now recovered his former position and thus made a mess of everything again. He also made a lot of money from recruiting a number of casual laborers. Li Naiheng, the professional in "earning extra income," has even been "appointed" by the responsible person as the assistant factory manager despite his proven criminal activities of taking bribes from casual laborers.

As a result of the perverse acts of such people, the Xian City cement factory lost 1.1 million yuan from 1981 to 1983. It continued to muddle along in such a way. Until the end of 1983, the city authorities had no alternatives but to remove principal leaders of the factory from office because it had suffered too many losses.

People say that there are countless things that are quite unusual in the Xian City cement factory. For example, such a small factory, which only needs about 200 workers on the first line of production, often hires more than 100 casual laborers throughout the year. The secret of the matter is: The more laborers that are hired, the more some people benefit. They offered the official post of deputy director to engineer Chen Bingkun, head of a technical section, but they asked him only to take charge of the odd jobs of back-up services. When Chen questioned this, the reply was: "You ought to be satisfied."

Zhang Quan, Chen Zongquan, Wang Shouming, and other engineering personnel were forcibly transferred to workshops and were told with fine-sounding words: "You are being transferred to strengthen the first line."

Lin Yuexian, a supervisor of cement production of the provincial Building Materials Bureau, pointed at Zhang Fawen, an old engineer, and said: "Remember, you were once a rightist." Principal leaders of the Xian City cement factory also said: "These rightists are not reliable, as most of them were released from corrective training teams." Under the pressure of such flogging, Zhang Fawen could do nothing but apply for resignation.

The very Li Yuexian who brought disgrace on Hu Zhaoming suddenly became a member of the joint fact-finding team organized by the department for economic affairs of the provincial CCP committee. At the very beginning of an investigative report on Hu prepared by Li Yuexian, he wrote: "Hu Zhaoming comes from a landlord's family."

Hu Zhaoming was again transferred to the city's Building Materials Bureau, but he has been kept waiting for an assignment for three years. The production of the "Qixianzhuang village"—the Xian City cement factory—was at a standstill for three years; it failed to produce 200,000 tons of high-grade cement and to turn over 8 million yuan to the higher authorities. However, that deputy director of the city's Building Materials Bureau, by the name of Xu, who rose in the "Cultural Revolution," has been promoted three grades in succession in recent years. But Hu Zhaoming has still been refused the title of engineer on the excuse of "providing insufficient basis for supporting the title," and his salary raise was withheld.

To uphold justice, offices of the newspapers *Shaanxi gongren bao* [Shaanxi

Workers' News] and *Keji shichang bao* [Science and Technology Market News], breaking through all kinds of obstructions, made an in-depth investigation and published three articles to expose the matter last July, August, and September. Nevertheless, at this late date no reaction has been heard. What does the silence mean? People have to ask: "The Party Central Committee has time and again stressed the necessity of implementing the Party's policies among intellectuals, consolidating enterprises, and turning losses to profits. Should these Party policies still stand in Xian City? Should it carry them out?"

52

Dang Jizhi

SEQUEL TO "QIXIANZHUANG VILLAGE IN XIAN CITY TODAY"

More About "Several Unusual Things in Xian City Cement Plant"

FOLLOWING THE PUBLICATION of the report "Qixianzhuang Village in Xian City Today," I received a number of letters from the readers.

They raised such questions as: How can there be so many "very unusual things"? I would like to provide some more information to our readers.

When the people of virtue and ability in the "Qixianzhuang" (Note: This refers to the technical section of the factory) of the Xian cement factory were treacherously attacked in 1981 and were left idle for a long time, the inspiring spring breeze of the Twelfth CCP Congress once again stirred up their spirit. They broke through numerous barriers, on their own initiative undertook the task of designing the new production line of the Tongchuan City Dongfeng building materials plant, planned to increase the production capacity of the plant from 40,000 tons to 80,000 tons, and once again fully utilized their talent. But these events underwent a tortuous course: In early 1983, the agent of the Tongchuan City building materials plant came to discuss the problem of inviting Zhang Fawen and other engineers to help them in the designing of the new production line. When the agent contacted the Deputy Director Yang Yongmou, Yang said: "How can you trust people whom we are not even utilizing?" With the arrangements made by some influential people and through other means, the engineers were finally allowed to leave with the agent. After arriving at Tongchuan, the engineers settled down in the mountain valleys. Through nearly six months' painstaking work, the design task was completed on schedule. Although they

Renmin ribao [People's Daily], April 23, 1984. Translation from FBIS Daily Report, April 30, 1984, pp. K5–K7.

earned a sum of money for the cement factory, and although the director of the Dongfeng building materials plant went, in spite of the rain, to the Xian City cement factory to present a silk banner and a letter of thanks, Yang Yongmou refused to receive him and accept the things he presented. Is this not an unusual thing?

In October 1983, Li Naiheng was promoted to the post of deputy factory director. The first thing he did after taking charge of production was to hand over the crushing section of the raw materials workshop, including equipment and technicians, to the casual laborers for management. Not long afterward, the crusher was seriously damaged in an accident owing to the casual laborers' poor management. The damage to this large machine, which could handle a capacity of 130 tons per hour, affected the entire production line.

As a result, production at the factory was suspended for over half a month, and there was a decrease of at least 30,000 tons in the amount of stone crushed, which caused immense losses to the factory. After the crusher was repaired, instead of drawing lessons from the losses, the section was again handed over to the casual laborers for management. The staff members indignantly asked Li Naiheng: ''Why should the section be handed over to the casual laborers since so many of our workers have no work to do?'' Li replied: ''The casual laborers are obedient, and I insist in doing what I want!'' Is this not unusual?

By the end of 1983, the cement factory was still suffering from deficits, and it seemed that there was no hope for annual bonuses. In spite of the urgent circular on curbing price hikes of the means of production and the provision on checking the indiscriminate issue of bonuses, Li and his kind violated the state price policy about the planned allocation of cement and handed thousands of tons of cement to a shop run by young people, who were awaiting jobs, to sell at high prices. The illegally earned money was regarded as ''bonuses'' and issued. From December 9 to 30, under various pretexts, each worker received goods and cash equivalent to 114 yuan. By way of contrast, the units that came to pick up the goods according to quotas allotted by the state could not get any cement. Is this not very unusual?

In 1983, that very Li Naiheng contracted two projects with the casual laborers on the ''transformation of the production line.'' According to the 21 items of the two projects submitted, the casual laborers ''disbursed'' over 9,000 yuan for the building charges. However, after careful examination, 13 out of the 21 items were found to be fabricated. In light of the figures verified by the capital construction office, the casual laborers should have been paid only 3,700 yuan.

The extra money, amounting to over 5,000 yuan, should of course be recovered. Using the excuse that these casual laborers were ''honest'' and ''pitiful,'' Li Naiheng and Yang Yongmou refused to recover the extra amount paid. In addition, Li threatened Comrade Chang Yinchuan, a cadre of the capital construction office who took part in checking the figures, and said: ''How dare you involve me in the case? The accounts handled by you in the past must be checked immediately!'' Is he not very fierce?

In late February 1984, Shaanxi conducted a provincial inspection on cement quality with the participation of responsible technical people from various prefectures, cities, and counties. The inspection team took a sample from the cement produced by the Xian City cement factory and delivered it to the designated testing unit, the state-owned Yaoxian County cement factory, for a chemical analysis. The results of the examination proved the stability of the cement negative. Li Naiheng was deputy director of the factory in charge of production and technology, and his wife was head of the laboratory. Li knew the seriousness of the case and was thrown into confusion. Under the pretext that "the casual laborers took the wrong sample," he hatched a plot and demanded that another sample be taken for reexamination. Consequently, Li Naiheng personally took the so-called new sample and, together with one of the members of the inspection team, went to the Yaoxian County cement factory in their factory car to make the "reexamination." People may ask: How, in such a serious matter, can the sample be wrongly taken? Who is supporting Li Naiheng from behind in brazenly practicing fraud? Who is the man overriding the inspection team and permitting Li Naiheng to run wild?

Concerning the perverse acts of Li Naiheng the workers of the cement factory were extremely indignant and repeatedly reported the situation to the departments concerned at higher levels. They even went directly to the city CCP committee to make complaints. Since October 1983, the 1,100 tons of cement in the seven warehouses of the factory have not been delivered owing to the unstable condition of the cement, which has affected the progress of projects in many units.

From January to March this year, the output of cement was only 35 percent of the plan for the first quarter, causing a large deficit. The city authorities should be aware of this state of affairs.

It is incomprehensible that the city CCP Committee and the departments concerned did not take any measures to punish Li Naiheng and his kind, but promoted them and put them in important positions. Why? And why is Hu Zhaoming, who turned the deficits of this factory into profits, consigned to limbo for three years with no one taking an interest in the matter?

53

Wang Minglu

MR. STONE, FACTORY MANAGER

(Comedians' Dialogue—*xiangsheng*)

A. Let me perform something for you.
B. Uh . . .
A. I have a question to put to you in front of all these comrades.

Tianjin yanchang [Tianjin], 1980, No. 3. Translated by Robert N. Tharp.

B. What question?

A. What kind of work do you do?

B. I perform comedians' dialogues.

A. Oh my goodness: What a wonderful job! I have the greatest admiration for that kind of work!

B. Oh, is that so?

A. Just look! Let everyone look at this interesting job of yours—standing here with everything so neat and efficient. How about asking your leadership if you could use another person?

B. To do what?

A. If you need somebody, how about getting me transferred here to help you? Admit it—it's a great idea!

B. Uhhh . . . don't you have a job?

A. Yes . . . I have a job . . .

B. What?

A. Uhhh . . . I'm a "do nothing" [lit., *bugan*, a slip of the tongue for *ganbu*, "cadre"—tr.].

B. What? What?

A. (*flustered and stuttering*) No, no, no. I'm a . . . I do . . . I don't do . . . I'm a . . . I'm a cadre who does nothing, I . . . I mean a do-nothing cadre, I mean . . .

B. What's that? What're you saying?

A. Uh . . . uh . . . I . . . I . . .

B. Come off it! Why don't you just say you're a cadre and be done with it!

A. You didn't hear what I said. I really *am* a cadre, but I don't do anything! (*laughs insincerely*) Ha, ha, ha!

B. Ohhh! Ahah! *I* get it! You're a *sponger*!

A. Yeah, how 'bout taking me?

B. No, no! We've got our own spongers!

A. Just listen to you! How can you be so utterly rude!

B. Huh?

A. What's this about "sponging"? How could I possibly take money for nothing? Do you think this business of being a cadre is a bowl of cherries?

B. Oh no, I didn't jump to any conclusions.

A. Is our job all that easy?

B. Tell us what you actually do.

A. I'm the director of a factory. Ha, ha, ha! (*his hollow laugh again*)

B. A factory director!

A. Yeah!

B. Directing a whole factory must be really tough!

A. My God!!! What?!

B. Really demanding work!

A. Wow! This is it! All these years and you're the first person I've run into who has shown me any sympathy.

B. Right . . .

A. Oh wow! Just for what you said I must stand you to a treat. I invite you for dinner!

B. No, no, there's no need for that.

A. Oh, come on! No need to be polite about it! I'll take you out and treat you to steamed stuffed dumplings. You come up with six bucks and if it's not enough I'll kick some in! (*audience roars with laughter*) Look—I'm inviting you, and that's all there is to it. Okay?

B. Okay, if you insist.

A. Yeah, yeah . . . huh? What do you mean if I insist? I only meant you're great *in spirit*, sympathizing with someone like me—a factory director, sitting in an office, busy, busy, busy all day . . .

B. Busy with what?

A. So busy that both feet are beginning to turn upwards . . .

B. Oh boy . . .

A. I have to do everything! When a memo comes in from the higher authorities, I have to receive it . . .

B. Oh, you're the dispatcher.

A. . . . When the leadership comes out with new policies, I have to spread them . . .

B. You're the communicator.

A. . . . When we implement the Party line, I have to do the public readings . . .

B. You're the megaphone.

A. . . . When important resolutions come down . . .

B. You're the one that . . .

A. I . . . I'm going to quit! I can't take it any more.

B. Right. You can't . . .

A. Well! You don't have to stand there agreeing with me! . . . What's wrong with my work?

B. Well, isn't your job just receiving, dispatching, and passing things along?

A. Right! That's the way you have to do it. That's the way I understand a cadre's job, that's the way it has to be done, and doing it that way is the only way not to make mistakes.

B. What do you mean by "making mistakes"? Publicizing the Party's policies is the right thing to do. Even more important is that we must apply the policies to all the specific situations of local units, and then carry them out!

A. (*laughs insincerely again*) Ha, ha, ha! That's not the way I do it.

B. How do you do it?

A. Anything not in the documents, I don't talk about. Anything not in the documents, I don't do. Ha, ha, ha!

B. Well then! How do you go about "bringing into play the positive energies at the central and local levels"?

A. Uh . . . anybody who wants to do that . . . can go ahead and do it! Ha, ha, ha! Me, I don't make any mistakes.

B. (*aside*) He only cares about making mistakes . . . (*to A*) Let me put it this way. If something's good for the Four Modernizations . . .

A. Then I wait for guidance from Party Central!

B. If it helps promote "stability and unity.". .

A. I wait for guidance from Party Central . . .

B. If it would raise the living standards of the people . . .

A. Wait for guidance from Party Central . . .

B. Where do your own opinions come in?

A. I have no opinions.

B. Can you discuss your own views?

A. I have no views.

B. Tell the way you feel about things?

A. I have no feelings.

B. Do you have a head?

A. I have no head. (*audience roars*)

B. (*aside*) Wee, that's right, he has no head! That's right, that's right.

A. How can you say that? If I were a hollow cavity standing here, you'd be scared silly!

B. What I'm asking is, do you have a *brain*? If you don't have a brain, you're just a wooden man.

A. Then . . . you're made of plastic!

B. What do you mean I'm made of plastic?!

A. Well, you called me a wooden person!

B. Look at you! No opinions, no views, no feelings. You're as wooden as they come!

A. Come on now! If that's what you're saying, then I say you're half paralyzed.

B. What on earth does *that* mean?

A. What do you mean "what does it mean?"?! You called me as wooden as they come! Anyway, I was only giving you the secret of my success as a cadre for so many years.

B. What secret?

A. The way not to make mistakes is to have no opinions, no views and no thoughts. Just keep holding down your position. Ha, ha, ha! (*much applause by audience*)

B. Is your work worth anything when you do that?

A. Is it ever! Let me tell you the truth: if you hung around with me for a while . . . a guy like you . . . hah! When it comes time to "Oppose the Right." . . . hah! . . . I'd be the "Oppose," and you'd be the "Right"!

B. Uh, oh.

A. When it comes to "Rectifying Work Styles" I'd be Rectifying, and you'd be the Work Style!

B. Gee whiz!

A. In any Movement, I'd be the mov*er*—you'd be the mov*ee*!

B. All you can do is rectify me!

A. Don't I have to? A free thinker like you? Could we allow that? When a campaign comes, you'd have to be hit first . . . hee, hee!

B. Oh, hit me first, huh?

A. Yeah, but the same campaign would never touch me!

B. How's that?

A. Well, I have a characteristic . . .

B. What's that?

A. With subordinates I'm warm and friendly; with superiors I neither cringe nor talk back. I handle people by laughing and joking; I handle words by hemming and hawing. Ha, ha, ha, ha!

B. Why do you hem and haw?!

A. It's best to talk in half sentences.

B. Half sentences?

A. Yeah! That way, you can interpret it any way you wish! And if you get it wrong, it's your own fault! Ha, ha, ha, ha, ha!

B. Gad! You have me taking responsibility for everything!

A. Of course!

B. What if we—as subordinates, as workers—had complaints to bring to you, and wanted you to help us?

A. Fine! Happy to be of service!

B. Okay then, I'll get your reaction to this . . .

A. Good! Good!

B. Uh . . . wait a minute. We've been talking all this time but I haven't asked your honorable name.

A. Name's Stone. Ha, ha, ha!

B. And your first name?

A. Asbestos Tile. *(audience laughs)*

B. What???

A. Asbestos Tile Stone! Ha, ha, ha.

B. So you're the famous Mr. Asbestos Tile Stone!

A. Right, right. Ha, ha.

B. Then our names are alike.

A. What's yours?

B. Prefabricated Board. Alike, right?

A. Absolutely not!! Totally different!

B. What do you mean? They're both building materials!

A. Oh no they're not! Prefabricated board is nothing but sharp corners and angles and edges. Something you can't pick up or move around easily. It just stands around outside and trips people up. Everyone who sees you gets fed up with you! You're a nuisance!

B. And you?

A. Asbestos tiles are wholly different! They're round, you know. Turn 'em over and they're still round—always nice and round. Ha, ha, ha. When it's hot up top, we can bring down the heat. When the heat comes from below, we can absorb it. There we are in the middle, always cool and collected, peaceful and quiet, all seasons green. Ha, ha, ha, ha! We insulate from cold, we insulate from heat. Ha, ha. (*lengthy applause*)

B. Right! The whole reason we can't get our jobs done is because of you and your lousy layers of insulation!

A. Don't bother with the insulation levels! If you have a problem, just come to me.

B. Right, We *have* to come to you. You're well-situated—the Factory Manager!

A. That's right! Ha, ha.

B. Mr. Manager!

A. Yes? (*belches*)

B. I have a problem for you.

A. Fine, fine.

B. Our factory production hasn't increased for years. There's always a deficit. Aren't you worried about this?

A. Oh my goodness, my dear old artisan! What good does worry do? My worrying about it won't help, and there's no point in your getting excited either. Right? After all, you'll still get your pay at the end of the month! Ha, ha, ha!

B. (*exasperated*) What kind of thinking is this?

A. Just take your salary!

B. This has nothing to do with my pay! The point is that we *waste* too much in our factory!

A. Oh come on now! It's not just our factory. What factory doesn't have waste? Ha, ha!

B. Labor discipline is too slack!

A. Now listen to me. You just take care of yourself. Don't you worry about others, okay?

B. It's *got* to be taken care of. Look how people arrive late and leave early! It's extremely serious!

A. Okay, but what do you want *me* to do? Squat by the gate every morning and sign people in?

B. I didn't say you have to sign them in. But why don't you *catch* them?

A. Right. Good, okay. Good idea. I'll start catching at once. How about you? How many times have you been late this month? (*audience laughter*)

B. You're catching *me*? Oh, come on!

A. You see! You're not so happy when you're the one that's grabbed. You think others'll be happy to be grabbed? See? You're just asking for trouble! Offending a lot of people! Just asking to be hit with a poster campaign!

B. I'm not afraid of posters! I support justice!

A. Ohhhh!!

B. Too many people are doing private work at home!

A. Oh, come off it! What's wrong with a little private work? Everybody's doing it! Just as long as I don't see it . . .

B. Then you should look around!

A. Nah, be pretty awkward if I saw anything . . .

B. Oh, great! Now that's really something! . . . Listen, the Li boy and the Zhang boy have gotten into a fight . . .

A. So what? Young people always get into fights! Just make sure an old guy like you keeps a safe distance. Don't let them bump you. Ha, ha, ha . . .

B. You're not going to get involved?

A. Why should I get involved when they've only just begun? Wait'll one of them gets killed, then let the courts take over!

B. What a neatly passed buck!

A. But of course!

B. I . . . have another problem.

A. My goodness! Where do all your problems come from? People like you are really . . . "problematic." Ha, ha!

B. *I'm* problematic? Aren't you supposed to solve things?

A. If I can't solve them, I just have to pass them along. Ha, ha.

B. There're a lot of mothers with small children in our workshop, and it's very inconvenient for them to be taking the children with them to and from work . . .

A. (*feigning concern*) Oh, yeah, yeah, definitely . . .

B. . . . they can't find any child-care centers nearby . . .

A. Yes, yes, quite.

B. . . . and they have a lot of problems coming to work in the mornings and going home in the evenings.

A. Oh, I see!

B. How about our factory here setting up a child-care center?

A. Oh yeah, I see. Your idea is that our factory here should build a child-care center, yeah? Ha, ha, ha!

B. That's right.

A. Why don't you go to the Planning Section and draw up a plan? Ha, ha, ha, ha, ha.

B. You're passing the buck again. I won't let you pass it.

A. Oh so?

B. I've been to the Planning Section, and they agree—they told me to confer with you.

A. Oh . . . then better ask the Administrative Section . . .

B. They've already approved all the logistics. They have plenty of materials, and all they need is approval from . . . uh . . . all expenditures within the factory must be handled by the Director of Finance and Accounting.

A. Ahah, well you'd best go discuss it with him. Ha, ha, ha . . .

B. The Director of Finance and Accounting says they can afford it.

A. Then you better ask the Department of Production. Ha, ha, ha . . .

B. The Department of Production said that, in the interests of furthering the Four Modernizations, and of relieving the worries of parents, they vigorously support it . . .

A. Of course! Of course! This is a big thing for the factory. So, we must discuss it with the Party Secretary . . . ha, ha . . . and seek his instruction . . .

B. The Secretary's in the hospital.

A. So why don't you go to the hospital and ask him?

B. Now you're pushing me off to the hospital. Look, I already went to the hospital. The Secretary said that you're in charge of things. If you approve it then it'll be okay.

A. Oh, so that's what he said . . . uh . . . uh . . . That's what the Secretary said, huh?

B. Right, right, right. That's what he said. Let's see where you pass the buck this time . . .

A. Well, it's true that I *am* in charge of things. And your idea is, the Secretary said I should approve it, huh?

B. Right! Right!

A. My my. You really are an enthusiastic comrade. Let me give it some thought . . . This business of building a child-care center for the factory is . . . you know what I mean . . .

B. Yeah?

A. Under the present circumstances, we must, of course, go with the green light and stop with the red, right? What do you think?

B. Whaaat?

A. We all know the benefits to be derived from the building of a child-care center, right, comrade? But then, "it's better to be three minutes late than one second too early."

B. What's all this??

A. Speaking in the aggregate, with the concern of maintaining a living, we must expand the economy and ensure the source of supply, ha, ha, ha, right?

B. Huh?

A. The marketplace is thriving and prices have been stabilized. And as far as our factory is concerned, you know the route we must take—"Friendship first, competition second." Ha, ha, ha . . . (*audience laughter*) Uh . . . In this regard, though, nevertheless, otherwise, there's no doubt, if it weren't so . . . but do you understand what I'm saying? (*much audience laughter*)

B. What's all this nonsense?! You're only saying half sentences . . . What could I possibly understand? All we're doing is trying to settle the question of a child-care center.

A. Right! Right! That's right. I remember now. The question of a child-care center, right! You really are enthusiastic! Well, regarding the problem of the child-care center, how about this? What do you think of this?

B. What?

A. Of course, I know you're very sympathetic with working mothers, right?

B. That's right.

A. But . . . we must also consider the working fathers, right? (*audience laughter*)

B. What do you mean "working fathers"?

A. I mean the . . . partners of the working mothers! Ha, ha. We call them "working fathers."

B. No such term exists!

A. Even if it doesn't, we have to talk about it. If we don't, people will complain. They'll say we only concern ourselves with working mothers and ignore working fathers. There will be misunderstandings!

B. Nobody's going to say *that*!

A. Didn't you just say it yourself?

B. I was talking about a child-care center!

A. That's right! I remember now. A child-care center. Right, right. I remember now, there's a document from Party Central—you probably haven't seen it, have you?

B. What document?

A. Party Central says that the localities are prohibited from building storied buildings, halls, or guest centers.

B. Wait a minute, Mr. Manager! We only want a nursery!

A. "Storied buildings, halls and guest centers." That's what a child-care center is—you see the word "center" there, don't you? We have to follow the spirit of Party Central.

B. Oh, I get it. As long as the word "center" is there, we can't build it, eh?

A. Exactly! Exactly!

B. Mr. Director. Let's talk this over. When we've built it, we don't have to call it a "center," Let's call it a "room," okay?

A. What?

B. Or child-care "house," or child-care "depository." Or we can just call it "the child-care area."

A. Oh dear! Aren't you being too flexible about this? I couldn't do anything to deceive the leadership. Ha, ha, ha, ha. I couldn't do that . . .

B. Then what *are* you going to do?

A. Let's see now. This is beneficial to staff and workers, right? Let's wait a bit and get some guidance from Party Central, or maybe the Municipal Party Committee will have an opinion on it . . .

B. Wait a minute! Just one minute here! To build a child-care center you have to go to the State Council or something?

A. Right! That's right. Of course!

B. But, the manifesto of the Third Plenum of the Tenth Central Committee clearly said that in order to further the Four Modernizations we should relieve the worries of working parents. Right?

A. That's right. I know about that. But I've read the whole manifesto and never found one single place where it says our factory should build a child-care-center!

B. You think they have time to go one by one?

A. Exactly! That's what I'm saying. It doesn't mention us. So, we should wait a while and not be in a hurry. Not only that, we must deliberate about it. Weigh everything.

B. Weigh what?

A. Weigh the question of building a child-care center, that's what. We have to see if it conflicts in any way with family planning.

B. What kind of conflict could there possibly be?

A. Think about it! There are quite enough children as it is. Now if we go and build a child-care center, and conditions become much more favorable, the female comrades will be even more zealous in bearing children . . .

B. That's totally irrelevant.

A. What do you mean "irrelevant"? It's perfectly . . .

B. All we're trying to do is solve a difficulty.

A. I know. But it's only a temporary difficulty, and it's easy to solve!

B. How?

A. All you have to do is stop giving birth!

B. Me? Now I'm giving birth?

A. I'm just saying that you shouldn't bring up this question!

B. I'm only reporting a problem!

A. Oh! Do you have a problem?

B. Uhhhhh . . . all my talking has been wasted!

A. What . . . ? What . . . ?

B. Mr. Director, if that's your attitude, I have a complaint about you!

A. What complaint? Feel free to say it! Welcome, welcome! I welcome all complaints. *Please* give me your criticisms. Ha, ha, ha, ha!

B. I'm going to tell you even if you don't want to hear. You . . . cadres like you . . . I've seen through you! You're stumbling blocks to the Four Modernizations . . .

A. Oh, good, good! That's a good criticism. Ha, ha! We thoroughly welcome it when you can courageously come forward and criticize your leaders. Such a spirit is truly worthy of esteem. Especially now, with our all-out effort towards the Four Modernizations, you are *exactly* the type of talented person we are looking for. The next time they set up a May Seventh Cadre School [for thought reform—tr.] you'll be the first to go!

B. That's plain revenge!

A. Huh? How could it be revenge? Revolutionary work requires it!

B. I'm not afraid of you. Let me tell you, Mr. Stone—Mr. Asbestos Stone . . .

A. You flatter me, Mr. Prefabricated Board!

B. *That* he remembers! I've never met anybody like you before . . .

A. Well, *now* you have, huh? Ha, ha, ha, ha, ha!

B. No other cadres are like you . . .

A. Oh yeah? Then where did I come from?

B. (*aside*) He's got me there!

A. Of course!

B. There's no way I can discuss anything with you. I'm going to the higher levels . . .

A. Don't do that! No! Don't go to a higher level. The comrades up there are having a hard enough time of it as it is. They're busy from dawn to dusk! Don't go bothering them. If you have anything to discuss, discuss it with me. What's your problem?

B. I get nowhere talking with you!

A. On what?

B. Our yearly deficit . . .

A. Oh, we're waiting for guidance from Party Central on that . . .

B. The child-care center . . .

A. Go and see the Secretary . . . Ha, ha, ha . . .

B. Laxity of discipline among the workers . . .

A. Laxity among the workers? Go and see the Administrative Section! (*sounding exasperated*) Didn't I just tell you all this?

B. All you do is pass the buck. What the blazes are you worth in that position of yours?

A. Worth? What am I worth? I'm *terribly* useful. My job is important! I'm indispensable!

B. Doing what?

A. Picking up my salary on time.

B. Oh, still sponging!

FURTHER READINGS

Andors, Stephen. *China's Industrial Revolution*. New York: Pantheon Books, 1977.

Baum, Richard, ed. *China's Four Modernizations: The New Technological Revolution*. Boulder, Colorado: Westview, 1980.

Brugger, William. *Democracy and Organization in the Chinese Enterprise, 1948-53*. Cambridge: Cambridge University Press, 1976.

Field, Robert Michael. "Changes in Chinese Industry Since 1978." *The China Quarterly* No. 100 (December 1984), pp. 742-761.

Field, Robert Michael. "Growth and Structural Change in Chinese Industry." In Joint Economic Committee, Congress of the United States. *China Under the Four Modernizations, Part I*. Washington, D.C.: U.S. Government Printing Office, 1982, pp. 303-333.

Rawski, Thomas G. *Economic Growth and Employment in China*. Oxford: Oxford University Press for the World Bank, 1979.

Reynolds, Bruce L. "Reform in Chinese Industrial Management: An Empirical Report." In Joint Economic Committee, Congress of the United States. *China Under the Four Modernizations, Part I*. Washington, D.C.: U.S. Government Printing Office, 1982, pp. 119-137.

Shirk, Susan L. "The Politics of Industrial Reform." In Elizabeth J. Perry and Christine Wong, eds. *The Political Economy of Reform in Post-Mao China*. Cambridge: Harvard University Press, 1985, pp. 195-221 (also see the articles by Barry Naughton and Christine Wong, pp. 223-278).

Walder, Andrew G. "Industrial Organization and Socialist Development in China." *Modern China* 5:2 (April 1979), pp. 233-272.

Walder, Andrew G. "Organized Dependency and Cultures of Authority in Chinese Industry." *Journal of Asian Studies* 43:1 (November 1983), pp. 51-76.

Walder, Andrew G. "Some Ironies of the Maoist Legacy in Industry." In Mark Selden and Victor Lippit, eds. *The Transition to Socialism in China*. Armonk, N.Y.: M. E. Sharpe, 1982, pp. 215-237.

Walder, Andrew G. "The Remaking of the Chinese Working Class, 1949-1981." *Modern China* 10:1 (January 1984), pp. 3-48.

Watson, Andrew. "Industrial Development and the Four Modernizations." In Bill Brugger, ed. *China Since the 'Gang of Four'*. London: Croom Helm, 1980, pp. 88-134.

Wong, Christine. "Ownership and Control in Chinese Industry: The Maoist Legacy and Prospects for the 1980s." In Joint Economic Committee, Congress of the United States. *China in the 1980s*. Washington, D.C.: U.S. Government Printing Office, forthcoming.

B. Commerce

REFORM OF COMMERCIAL POLICY in post-Mao China has produced conflict among senior leaders and between them and local officials. Within the central leadership, official China has disagreed over the extent to which the economy should be regulated by administrative means (central planning) or by economic means (market mechanisms). In the implementation of commercial policy, especially of the policy to encourage individual entrepreneurs to set up small businesses, central leaders have run into opposition from local officials. While these issues do not exhaust the range of controversies in the commercial policy arena, they do illustrate conflict within and between levels in the administrative hierarchy and conflict at both the policy formulation and implementation stages.

In her study of post-1949 commerical policy, Dorothy Solinger identifies three major tendencies among China's central leadership: radical, which emphasizes class conflict; bureaucratic, which stresses state control; and marketeer, which seeks to maximize productivity.[1] Conflict has emerged among the tendencies on such issues as *the role of state organs and state-set prices* (bureaucrats and radicals favor a larger role for the state, while marketeers, endorsing free markets, favor a reduced state bureaucracy); *the nature of the distribution system* (radicals favor self-sufficiency, bureaucrats favor centralized distribution, and marketeers favor reliance on free markets); *the nature of planning* (bureaucrats favor centralized, top-down planning, while radicals and marketeers favor decentralized, bottom-up planning); and *the institutions of market control* (radicals favor using roving bands of peasants and workers to enforce market regulations, bureaucrats prefer using "market control committees," and marketeers favor minimal supervison and self-regulation).[2] Either alone or allied with one another, central leaders representing these tendencies have made China's commercial policy.

In the post-Mao era, after a brief struggle, the marketeers gained the ascendency. Gradually, authorities lifted the state monopoly on the purchase of most agricultural products and permitted them to be distributed in the market. Officials reduced the scope of mandatory production planning in favor of "guidance" planning. Then, in 1984, the Party adopted plans to further implement marketeer commercial policies in China's cities.[3]

Sharp controversy has surrounded the debate over the relative merit of regulating the economy directly by means of central planning or indirectly by relying on market mechanisms. Although pro-marketeers such as Premier Zhao Ziyang appear to have won the day, other senior leaders have criticized these policies. Thus Politburo member Chen Yun, addressing the September 1985 CCP National Conference, blasted the pro-market position. The primacy of the planned economy must be ensured, he said. For this reason, market regulation, which "involves no planning, blindly allowing supply and demand to determine production,"[4] must play a subordinate role.

When Beijing relaxed restrictions on the individual economy in 1979, and then positively endorsed it as a supplement to the socialist economy, many local leaders resisted the policy. Years of campaigning against "petty capitalism" had convinced many local officials that the policy was wrong. They used a variety of strategies to suppress or harass local individual entrepreneurs: denying them space, access to utilities or licenses, and levying heavy taxes and additional fees. Still, by July 1985, authorities reported that the number of individual industrial and commercial households registered in urban and rural areas throughout China had reached almost 10.65 million; these private businesses had over 15 million employees.[5] If some local leaders resisted the policies, others, jealous of the financial successes of the small businessmen, accommodated themselves to the new situation by reserving licenses and other scarce inputs for themselves and their kin.[6]

The selections in this section, drawn from authoritative editorials and commentaries, as well as reports of investigations conducted in China's leading cities, illustrate the range of conflict in the commercial arena.

Post-Mao policymaking has been characterized to an increasing extent by public discussion of different viewpoints, a practice unheard of during the Cultural Revolution decade. Then, authorities suppressed disagreements or used them only to teach by negative example. Nevertheless, in the forums recently published, leaders have circumscribed the scope of the debate to fit their needs. In particular, the Party has charged intellectuals to justify policy options in terms of current regime needs.

Selections 54 and 55 provide some indication of the debate over the role of central planning and reliance on the market in the regulation of the economy. In a recital of different viewpoints on the issue (in Selection 54), published in "the intellectuals' newspaper," *Guangming ribao* (Guangming Daily), Lu Zhenmao offers his readers little guidance. Written in the esoteric jargon of Chinese Marxism, this selection, like others in the reader, is initially concerned about the meaning of socialism under the reforms. Does socialism necessarily imply a "planned economy"? Although most Chinese economists, according to Selection 54, argue that some planned element is essential, others reportedly disagree.

For our purposes the most interesting part of Selection 54 is the discussion of the relative priority that ought to be given to regulation by planning or by market mechanisms. Lu identifies four viewpoints, ranging from giving planning the dominant role to giving market mechanisms priority "under planned guidance." The narrowness of the options considered here is immediately obvious. In each case, "planning" is a feature of the viewpoint. Not to anchor the positions with a reference to "planning" is apparently unacceptable in this discussion. The views expressed in the forum contrast with Chen Yun's position, referred to above, that regulation by the market is completely divorced from planning.

Pro-marketeer views characterize the editorial on rural commerce in Selection 55. Authorities propose that local state commercial entities be put on a profit-making basis, that planning be geared to meet "market demands," and that mandatory planning be replaced by guidance planning—all part of the marketeer platform. Indeed, the editorial writer gives the dominant role to reliance on market mechanisms. These views run directly counter to those proposed by Solinger's "bureaucrats," who would use market levers as a supplement to planning, preferring to rely on the "the plan" to regulate the economy.

Implementation of policies to encourage individual entrepreneurs at times provoked "willful opposition"[7] from local officials. Strong endorsements for the policy, authored by central leaders, appear in Selections 56 and 57. In the face of considerable opposition, authorities should encourage individual businesses, the editorial writer argues in Selection 56, as a supplement to the socialist economy. In such areas as tailoring, bicycle repair, photography, and restaurant operation, large state-owned institutions, which are centralized and bureaucratic, have been unable to meet popular demand.

Returning to a familiar theme, Selection 56 raises the question of whether the individual economy is really "socialist." Its answer, not surprisingly, is "yes," because individual entrepreneurs do not "exploit" the labor of others. The writer ignores the fact that entrepreneurs under the reforms may now hire labor. When does this become "exploitation"? Optimistically the writer suggests that the individual economy will exist "for a long time" in socialist China, and that it will not go bankrupt as in capitalist countries. The writer thus ignores the many individual cases of small business failures reported since 1983.

A further push for China's fledgling individual economy appears in Selection 57. "Commentator" argues that state-owned commercial entities should be run on profit criteria, should use the contracted services of individual entrepreneurs, and should compete with them to increase efficiency. Criticizing state commerce's "bureaucratic practice," the writer demands that it emulate the more productive individual sector.

These pieces contrast oddly with the investigative reports in Selections 58–60, one each from Beijing, Shanghai, and Guangzhou. Selections 58 and 59 deplore the murder and mayhem that surfaced in large urban markets as unscrupulous traders disrupted "market order." Unable to attack the policy of individual economy directly, opposition to it has taken the form of publishing lurid accounts of attacks on customers and market regulation cadres. (The fate of the latter was probably uppermost in the minds of the writers.) Not advocating a total ban on the individual economy, these writers demand that there be greater regulation and that the market be "cleaned up." Reflecting the position of Solinger's "bureaucrats," Selection 59 advocates strengthening the bureaucracy to control commerce and to suppress illegal activities. The revelation that "market gangs" control, Mafia style, the distribution of certain scarce commodities prompts these writers to demand that authorities step up administrative and policing measures. A marketeer might reply that the administratively set prices of these products are too low. Officials should raise prices, not step up "regulation," to weed out speculators and black marketeers.

The news from Guangzhou that 30 percent of individual entrepreneurs have gone bankrupt (Selection 60) raises implicitly the question of the role of local officials. Guilty of harassment and bureaucratic bungling, city administrators have attempted to curb small business activities. They have removed the businesses from prime sites; levied all sorts of taxes, fees, and fines; and withheld essential fuel and utilities. Although the reasons for this opposition are not stated, they probably include both a fear that the policy is "capitalist" and will be denounced at some later date and a desire to protect the profits of city-owned enterprises that are competing with the small businesses•

Notes

1. Dorothy J. Solinger, *Chinese Business Under Socialism: The Politics of Domestic Commerce, 1949–1980* (Berkeley: University of California Press, 1984), pp. 60–122.
2. Solinger, *Chinese Business Under Socialism*, pp. 72–74.
3. "Decision of the Central Committee of the Communist Party of China on Reform of the Economic Structure," *China Daily*, October 22, 1984.
4. *Beijing Review* 28:39 (September 30, 1985), p. 19.
5. FBIS Daily Report, September 19, 1985, pp. K13–K14 (*Xinhua* [New China News Agency], September 18, 1985).
6. See FBIS Daily Report, February 20, 1985, pp. K10–K11 (*Xinhua*, February 14, 1985).
7. See FBIS Daily Report, September 30, 1983, p. K16 (*Renmin ribao* [People's Daily], September 26, 1983).

54

Lu Zhenmao

A SUMMARY OF DISCUSSIONS OVER THE PAST THREE YEARS ON THE PROBLEMS OF PLANNED ECONOMY AND REGULATION BY MARKET MECHANISM

CORRECTLY UNDERSTANDING AND HANDLING the problem of the relations between a planned economy and regulation by market mechanisms constitutes a key problem in the reform of the economic system. Over the past three years, economic theorists and practical workers in our country have conducted extensive research and discussions on this problem. On some of the points a breakthrough has been scored, while on others further studies and deliberations are still necessary. The following is a summary of the basic views concerning certain of the major problems in the discussions:

1. The Basic Special Features of a Socialist Economy

The first view holds that the basic special feature of a socialist economy is that it is a planned economy. A planned economy is an important landmark that differentiates the socialist form of production from other forms of production, whereas a commodity economy cannot be so differentiated. Although commodity production has a history of several thousand years and has existed in various socioeconomic patterns, it cannot become a special feature differentiating a certain social production form from other forms and, in fact, has never determined the nature of any socio-economic system. When commodity production reaches the highest point of development, not only do all the products of labor become commodities but also the labor power of mankind becomes a commodity.

Marx himself never took the commodity economy as being a special feature of the nature of capitalism. On the contrary, he warned people of the following: that what differentiates the capitalist form of production from other forms of production does not rest on commodity production but rather on labor power becoming a commodity and on the manifestation of labor as wage labor. Hence, we cannot denote the special feature of a certain socioeconomic system with the criterion of whether or not it practices a commodity economy. Naturally, we cannot take commodity production and commodity exchange as the basic special features of a socialist economy.

Guangming ribao [Guangming Daily], May 29, 1982. Translation from FBIS Daily Report, June 8, 1982, pp. K6–K9.

A second point of view believes that the basic special feature of a socialist economy should be described as a commodity planned economy or, in other words, a planned economy with commodity relations. A planned economy is divided into two stages: a stage of commodity-planned economy and a stage of product-planned economy. The planned economy of a socialist society is a commodity-planned economy, while the planned economy of a communist society is a product-planned economy.

A third point of view contends that the special feature of a socialist economy is that it is a commodity economy with a plan. Under socialist conditions, a planned economy and a commodity economy are two sides of the same thing. True, the planned economy is an important special feature of the socialist economy, but commodity production and commodity exchange are not outside the socialist conditions; nor are they the heritage of the old society but, rather, they are intrinsic and inherent in a socialist society. Therefore, the basic special feature of a socialist economy should be described as a commodity economy with a plan.

A fourth point holds that socialism is a developed stage of the commodity economy. The process of productive force gradually developing to a high stage of socialization can be completed only in the full development of the commodity economy. A natural economy can only develop to the stage of a commodity economy and only when a commodity economy has developed to a high degree can it enter into mankind's high-grade social form that is devoid of commodity and currency. The stage of a developed commodity economy cannot be surpassed, but the stage of capitalism can be avoided. We do not take the capitalist road. We cannot but take the road of the developed socialist commodity economy. But the socialist commodity economy is a type of developed commodity economy that does away with labor power as a commodity.

A fifth view contends that neither the planned economy nor the commodity economy should be considered as the basic special feature of a socialist economy. The planned economy is spoken of as opposed to the state of anarchism of a capitalist economy, whereas a commodity economy is spoken of as opposed to a natural economy. Strictly speaking, this is not a problem of the same category or the same series. As a problem of the same series, then, one is "with a government," and the other is "without a government" or anarchic; one is planned, and the other is unplanned; and one is a natural economy, and the other is a commodity economy.

2. Relations Between the Commodity Economy and the Planned Economy

One point of view holds that a planned economy under socialism must rely on commodity production and commodity exchange. At present, the productive force of our country has not reached a high degree of development; the socialist public ownership system still retains two separate forms, namely, that of ownership by the state and that of ownership by the collective, while the production units of the state-run economy still possess to a certain extent different kinds of economic interests. Under such conditions, the existence and development of commodity production are objectively necessary. For this reason, under socialist conditions, a planned economy must be pursued on the basis of the public ownership system, while commodity production and commodity exchange must also be vigorously developed. At the same time, in exercising planned control over the whole national economy, the state must give sufficient thought to, and utilize, the law of value and resort to the use of such levers as profits, prices, interest rates, taxation, and so forth.

Another viewpoint contends that a socialist economy is a combination of a planned economy and a commodity economy. A socialist economy is a planned economy built on the foundation of the public ownership of the means of production. A planned economy demands that the reproduction process be subjected to meaningful social regulation, that is to say, to planned regulation, and that suitable proportionate relationships be maintained within the national economy, that production and demand be relatively balanced, and that the maximum economic effect be obtained with the minimum consumption of labor. At the same time, the level of development of the productive force of our country is still not sufficiently high. There still coexist the economy under the system of ownership by the whole people and the economy under the system of ownership by the collectives and the laboring masses. The disparity in the material interests of the individual and of the collective still exists, while commodity production and commodity exchange are very much in evidence. Therefore, under socialist conditions, the planned economy and the commodity economy are combined.

Another view believes that in a socialist economy the commodity economy is the real content, while the planned economy is the outside crust.

3. On the Intention of Regulation by Planning Mechanisms and Regulation by Market Mechanisms

One point of view holds that in reality regulation by planning mechanisms is carrying out planning by means of directives, that is to say, the state and planning departments at various levels issue directives to the lower levels designating targets that the units reponsible for the execution of the plan must firmly carry out and be sure to fulfill.

Another view holds that regulation by planning mechanisms should embody, on the one hand, regulation to be executed by means of the directive type of planning and, on the other hand, regulation to be executed through planning of a guiding nature and by the use of economic levers and the law of value. However, some comrades contend that in the future, under conditions of a normal development of the economy, regulation by planning mechanisms can considerably reduce the targets that are designated by directives, or eliminate the directive type of planning altogether and replace it by planning of a guiding nature. On the other hand, some comrades believe that a socialist economy cannot greatly reduce the targets designated by directives, far less eliminate altogether the directive-type of planning. The directive-type of planning is a basic landmark of the socialist planned economy. Its elimination will necessarily result in social production being in a state of anarchy.

As for regulation by market mechanisms, one view contends that in essence regulation by market mechanisms is regulation by the law of value. This is because regulation by market mechanisms is always connected with the commodity economy. The socialist economy is a planned economy that embodies commodity relations, but the law governing the relations of a commodity economy is the law of value. Hence, regulation by market mechanisms is principally the utilization of the regulatory function on production and circulation of the law of value and the utilization of the active role of the various economic levers that are related to value, so as to promote the smooth realization of planned control. Comrades holding this view further contend that irrespective of whether the law of value is consciously utilized in regulation, or whether the law of value itself spontaneously exerts the regulatory function, both belong to the sphere of regulation by market mechanisms.

Another view holds that in essence regulation by market mechanisms is regulation exerted spontaneously by the law of value and is realized principally through the spontaneous fluctuations of prices. It believes that in general regulation by market mechanisms should not be called regulation by the law of value, except when the law of value spontaneously exerts its role of regulation. At the same time, this view contends, regulation by market mechanisms should not be called regulation by price fluctuations, except when prices spontaneously exert their regulatory function. Comrades holding this view believe that conscious utilization by the state of the law of value when formulating plans is not regulation by market mechanisms, but is regulation by planning mechanisms.

4. Relations Between Regulation by Planning Mechanism and Regulation by Market Mechanism

The first point of view holds that under socialist conditions, regulation by planning mechanisms should be the leading factor, and regulation by market mechanisms should be supplementary. Since a socialist economy is a planned economy built on the basis of the system of the public ownership of the means of production, the law governing the planned development of the national economy becomes the principal regulator of socialist production, and the state must consciously and in a planned manner arrange for social production in accordance with the public's common interests. At the same time, since a socialist economy is also a commodity economy built on the basis of the system of public ownership, it must naturally be regulated by market mechanisms. Hence, in actual socialist life, the law governing the planned and proportionate development of the national economy and the law of value both play a regulatory role. But the two do not play an equal role. Rather, the regulatory role of the law governing the planned development of the national economy occupies the leading place. This is determined by the innate nature of the socialist economy.

The second view believes that in a socialist economy regulation by planning mechanisms and regulation by market mechanisms perform a mutually supplementary and mutually complementary role. A socialist economy is a planned economy based on the public ownership system and is also a commodity economy based on the public ownership system. Hence in a socialist economy, we should unify its planned character and its commodity character, that is, in regulation by planning mechanisms full use is made of the market mechanism, and in regulation by market mechanism planned guidance should be strengthened.

A third point of view contends that a socialist economy should practice planned commodity economy. Hence, in addition to the law governing the planned development of the nation's economy, the law of value also plays a role in the regulation of the national economy. These two laws exert their functions subject to the limitations of the basic laws of socialism. Thus, this objectively determines that what a socialist economy practices is planned regulation by market mechanism, in other words, full utilization of the regulatory function of the market mechanism but under planned guidance.

A fourth point of view holds that under socialist conditions, regulation by planning mechanism and regulation by market mechanism can be combined, or can work together in many different ways and forms. Irrespective of whatever form is chosen by a socialist state, it must be assured that coordination exists between the various departments of the national economy, between the various links such as production, circulation, distribution, and consumption, and between the two forms of regulation, namely, regulation by planning mechanisms and regulation by market mechanisms. Moreover, the principal role of regulation by planning mechanisms must be ensured so that regulation by market mechanisms can only play a supplementary role under the guidance of planning and within a general limit specified by planning to the end that the proportionate and coordinated development of the national economy is fostered and not hindered.

55

Editorial

STATE-RUN COMMERCE SHOULD TAKE AN ACTIVE PART IN REGULATION BY MARKET MECHANISM

IN RECENT YEARS, rural reform, which started earlier than reform in other fields, has proved a remarkable success and has effectively

Jingji ribao [Economic Daily], January 11, 1985. Translation from FBIS Daily Report, January 18, 1985, pp. K13–K14.

promoted the development of a market economy in the rural economic structure. The present situation in the development of the rural commodity economy is excellent, but there remain things that still need to be better coordinated. The recent national rural work conference decided to further reform the state's rural economic management system, especially the system of assigning farm produce purchase quotas in order to expand the scope of regulation by market mechanisms under the guidance of state planning and to promote the development of the rural commodity economy. This will be another major reform following the introduction of the output contract responsibility system in the rural areas and will be of great significance to the development of the rural economy.

The measures for increasing the functions of the market mechanism include the following points: In the field of production, the state will no longer lay down mandatory production plans for the peasants; and in the field of marketing, apart from a very small number of products, the state will not assign any mandatory farm produce purchase quotas to the peasants. Instead, state purchases will be based on contracts and transactions through the markets. This will mark a significant change. The peasants will change their production arrangements from the previous mode of being subject to state plans to a pattern that is oriented to the markets; and the state's planned management over agriculture will shift from the previous means of administrative control to a pattern that relies mainly on economic means.

After the market mechanisms are brought into fuller play in the rural economy, the requirements for peasant households as well as for the state and state enterprises to attain their set economic targets will become higher rather than lower. State-owned commercial enterprises and state commercial departments will be involved in market activities so as to ensure the fulfillment of the plans. The most important prerequisite for this is to formulate planned targets in light of market demands and the social production capacity so as to coordinate and integrate market demands and social needs and to ensure that the planned targets are based on a solid foundation. That is the only way to ensure a correct orientation in which state commerce can play a positive part in market activities.

When participating in market activities, state commercial departments must apply various economic levers and follow the law of value. With markets being opened wide, the economy will become more prosperous. Facts in the rural economy over the past few years have proved this point. However, there must be some means of regulation to give guidance to market activities. A particularly important means of regulation is the lever of pricing. With control over the markets being relaxed, prices will certainly move up and down. So the state must have the necessary material means to influence price fluctuations. For example, the state should hold a commodities reserve, which can be used to regulate supply and demand on the markets. The state can also use the state-owned commercial enterprises as a main force for regulating market activities. State commerce should not monopolize the markets, but it can act as an influential element on the markets.

In addition, it is necessary to widely adopt the contract system. The signing of purchase contracts between the state and the peasants can effectively bring the peasants' independent operations into line with the state economic plans. This also represents a good channel for state commerce to play a part in the market economy. With the state placing purchase orders with the peasants for major farm products at preferential prices and buying their surplus products at protective prices, this will effectively protect the peasants' interests and will ensure the stability of the markets.

Expanding the scope of market regulations in the rural economy is the most important step for further enlivening the rural economy. With the participation of state commerce in market activities as an influential economic force, the rural market economy will develop more soundly.

56

Editorial

APPROPRIATE DEVELOPMENT OF INDIVIDUAL ECONOMY IS A NECESSITY OF THE SOCIAL ECONOMIC LIFE

IT HAS NOT been long since individual economy began to resume its legitimate position in our country's economic life. Since the Third Plenum of the Eleventh CCP Central Committee, most of the people have enthusiastically welcomed the individual economy, but some people have watched it with suspicion, and a small percentage of people negate it with disgust. In short, what this "minor role" in our economy met on its emergence on stage was something far from applause. Today this paper carried a letter from a reader entitled "Individual Enterprises in Jinan Are Faced with Countless Difficulties in Carrying Out Their Business." We hope this will rouse people's attention to this problem. After reading the letter, some people may ask: Should we, in the end, allow individual economies to exist and develop in socialist China?

For this question, the Party's policy is explicit. From the Third Plenum of its Central Committee to its Twelfth Congress the Party constantly adhered to the principle of protecting and appropriately developing individual economy and confirmed that individual economy was a beneficial supplement to and necessary component of our socialist economy. The "Constitution of the PRC" fully affirms the necessity of the development of individual economy. The problem is that in actually carrying out this policy, some comrades have failed to free

Renmin ribao [People's Daily], January 9, 1983, p. 1. Translation from FBIS Daily Report, January 11, 1983, pp. K1–K2.

themselves from the influence of the "leftist" ideology and have adopted an incorrect attitude toward the individual economy.

For a fairly long period before the Third Plenum of the Eleventh CCP Central Committee, we wrongly regarded individual economy under a socialist system as being of a capitalist nature or as the soil that generates capitalism. We transcended the real level of development of our productive force and banned or merged most of the individual industrial and commercial enterprises. During the ten years of civil disorder, we wantonly "cut the tail of capitalism" and completely destroyed the individual economy. Now we begin to understand this problem correctly and are restoring the legitimate position of individual economy. However, there are still some people whose thoughts have failed to catch up with ours. Therefore, in order to develop individual economy, we should raise our understanding and correct our thoughts.

Is individual economy capitalist in nature? No. Our answer is explicit. What we call individual economy is the combination of the individual ownership of the means of production with individual labor, and the laborer supports himself by his own labor. Capitalism, however, is a combination of the private ownership of the means of production with wage labor, and the capitalist relies on the exploitation of laborers for his living. Individual economy has nothing to do with exploitation. It differs diametrically from capitalism. At present the individual workers in Chinese cities and towns in general earn their own living by labor and offer their own skills to the country. This has nothing to do with capitalism but is beneficial to socialism. Such an economy should be put under protection and support.

Will individual economy under the socialist system generate capitalism? No, it will not. Individual economy is an economy of small commodities. Along with the development of the productive force, some of its trades and enterprises tend to be replaced by socialized production, but as many of the individual trades and enterprises have distinguishing features and are flexible, they will be independent for a long time. In a capitalist society, individual economy may rise and become a capitalist economy or suffer bankruptcy. Things are different in a socialist society.

As socialist transformation has long been completed in China and a mighty socialist economy has been established, the way to capitalism is blocked for individual economy, which can only be affiliated to socialist economy. We should no longer have any doubt about its nature. It is precisely because of a misunderstanding of the nature of individual economy that some people regard it as being inferior and have created obstacles and tried to squeeze it out. If we do not correct these erroneous ideas, we will never be able to develop individual economy.

It is wrong to regard the developing individual economy as a makeshift measure. Some people have turned a deaf ear to and have refused to help solve the actual problems related to individual economy. In fact, restoring and developing individual economy is by no means an emergency measure, but a necessity of social economic life. For present-day China, the development of socialist mass production is not sufficient, commodities are not abundant and the circulation of commodities is slow, and the management is poor. Our retail shops should be small and should be situated in various parts of our cities for the convenience of the people rather than be excessively big or located densely in a few areas. As for service trades such as repair work, photography, washing and sewing, we require them to be spread even more widely everywhere and to be even more flexibly run for the convenience of the masses. In the future, we should encourage individual enterprises to run these service trades.

In the 1950s, there were quite a large number of individual industrial and commercial enterprises in our country's urban areas. This provided a great convenience for the masses. At present, despite the efforts in the past few years to recover it, the number of individuals and enterprises are still too few to meet the needs of the social economic life. It is imperative to adopt measures to promote the development of individual economy for a considerable period in the future.

57

Commentator

STATE COMMERCE SHOULD GIVE UP SOME OF ITS TERRITORY

THE TWO REPORTS carried by this newspaper today about Hebei Province reforming small retail businesses and the twenty-seven small stores in Chongwen District, Beijing, carrying out a contract system are worth reading, because they provide a useful reference aid to the present reform of the state-owned commercial system.

Along with the development of industrial and agricultural production, a richer variety and an increasing quantity of industrial goods and farm produce has poured into the markets. The development of commodity production and the development of commodity circulation through various channels will inevitably make an impact on the existing system of commercial operation and management. In the past, because there were not many commodities on the markets, state-run commercial organizations could monopolize almost all businesses. Now this practice can no longer meet the needs of the rapidly developing situation. It is imperative that the system of commercial operation and management be thoroughly reformed.

Last year some localities began to try adopting the contract responsibility system in some retail and catering shops. Among these shops, those that have continued to pursue this system have all overcome the drawbacks of "eating from

Renmin ribao [People's Daily], April 25, 1984. Translation from FBIS Daily Report, April 30, 1984, pp. K17–K18.

the same big pot'' and have changed the previous egalitarian practice in the distribution of earnings. They also have improved their service attitude and quality. The contract system should be adopted in all commercial enterprises. This should be a point beyond question. However, an unsettled question is on what basis wages and bonuses in these enterprises should be paid. If this question is not properly settled, the burdens are likely to be shifted onto customers.

As far as small shops, restaurants, hotels, and other small services are concerned, they should be allowed to adapt more flexible measures and to contract more business to collectives and individuals.

Individual workers or groups of workers should be allowed to directly handle the business of the whole enterprise on lease. During the lease they must bear responsibility for both profits and losses. These small shops are large in number, widely distributed, and there is a small number of workers in each of them. However, they provide services for the general public and have a large number of customers. After these shops are rented to individual workers, their business results will directly affect the personal interests of the workers. This can fully arouse the initiative of workers and can bring into full play the strong points of these small shops, such as handling a wide variety of goods, having long business hours, and providing services and delivering goods to the customers' doorstep. By doing so, workers can earn more and it will be more convenient for customers.

State-owned commerce should not continue to take on all commercial business; instead, it should give up some of its territory. On the surface it seems that its position is narrowed; in fact, what has been cut down is the ''bureaucratic practice'' in commerce. This will only cause state-owned commerce to improve its operations and the quality of service and to better play its leading role so as to enable commerce as a whole to develop rapidly.

58

Chen Xianxin

RESOLUTELY DEAL WITH "BLACK SHEEP" LURKING AMONG INDIVIDUAL BUSINESS HOUSEHOLDS

THE INDIVIDUAL ECONOMY in Beijing Municipality has made substantial progress this year, and the employment rate is more than double

Xinhua [New China News Agency], Chinese, July 14, 1983. Translation from FBIS Daily Report, July 20, 1983, pp. R2–R3 (excerpts).

that of last year. While the great majority of individual households are law-abiding and honest in business transactions, a handful of lawless elements, mingling with individual households, have engaged in economic speculation for exorbitant profits and in other criminal activities, greatly undermining social and market order. These lawless elements have been rude and unreasonable in making deals. They verbally abuse and beat up customers and even carry concealed weapons, threatening the lives of customers. Some set up stalls without a license and force customers to buy things from them when they examine and price the merchandise. They verbally abuse and beat up customers when the latter refuse to buy.

Since the beginning of this year a number of cases of violence and murder have been reported among individual peddlers as a result of disputes in business transactions. An investigation shows that many hoodlums and persons released from prison after serving their terms carry murderous weapons with them, threatening customers and market management personnel and undermining public order in the capital.

Most of these lawless elements, mingling with individual business households, operate without a license; many are persons released from prison without having been properly reformed; some are jobless youths; and others are workers and staff members holding jobs. They are "black sheep" among the individual business households who have given a bad name to the individual business households. There are more than 14,000 individual business households in Beijing Municipality; judging from market demands and people's needs, this number is far from sufficient. However, we must never let these "black sheep" carry on their business and commit crimes. Unless they are resolutely banned, the interests and safety of consumers and legitimate business operators cannot be protected and market order cannot be maintained; if this situation is allowed to develop, "northern overlords" and "southern overlords" will surface again. Public security organs in Beijing Municipality have recently taken measures to deal with the situation. Industrial and commercial administrative departments in Beijing have also made all-out efforts to check and outlaw peddlers operating without a license and individual households doing business against regulations. Various districts have also set up offices for the maintenance of order in the markets. All these measures and methods are necessary. But the broad masses hope that decisive and forceful measures will be taken to resolutely suppress the principal offenders committing violent crimes, severely punish criminals, outlaw peddlers operating without a license, and strengthen management of individual business households so as to maintain market order and public security in the capital.

59

Chen Yanyi

SHANGHAI BANS UNLICENSED BUSINESSES AND ILLEGAL TRADING

To Protect the Interests of Producers, Lawful Vendors, and Consumers

DURING THE LAST ten days of June, the Shanghai Municipal Government put together more than 2,500 people from departments of Business Administration, Public Security, Taxation, and Commerce and also neighborhood organizations in an all out effort to clean up the market. They investigated and dealt with over 2,500 unlicensed operations and other unlawful dealings, banned 15 illegal marketplaces, and cracked down on a number of local despots who had seriously disrupted the market. With this, public order on the market took a turn for the better, and the interests of the producers, peddlers, and consumers were secured.

Of late, supplies of aquatic products, fruit, vegetables, and some industrial products have been tight in Shanghai. In addition, Shanghai lacks an adequate work force for market administration. Availing themselves of this opportunity, a small number of individual peddlers illegally bought up state-controlled goods for resale and even bullied other peddlers to tyrannize the market, thus disrupting normal business dealings. Recently at Shiliupu market, the largest marketplace of farm produce and sideline products in the whole municipality, there emerged a market gang headed by a fish peddler by the name of Wang X and three others. They intercepted the supply of goods and resold them at a high price, and bullied and abused the suppliers and individual peddlers engaged in normal businesses. This year when the yellow croaker was in season, Wang X and his partners monopolized more than 40,000 catties of yellow croaker shipped in from Zhejiang Province. They sold the fish at a high price and also controlled the price of other peddlers. One eel peddler sold his goods at a price a bit lower than Wang's and had his booth smashed by Wang's gang. Recently the Public Security Subbureau of Nanshi District prosecuted twelve cases, including the case of Wang, of "market despots" who committed violence and crimes.

As for unlicensed individual peddlers, the Department of Business Administration in Shanghai, on the basis of regular checkup and suppression, recently launched a citywide crash inspection. They uncovered large amounts of goods that were unlawfully bought and sold, coupons, and smuggled commodities. The

"Shanghai qudi wuzheng jingying he weifa jiaoyi." *Renmin ribao* [People's Daily], July 6, 1983, p. 1. Translated by Ai Ping.

Public Security Bureau and the Business Administration Department have also beefed up their control of certain ship terminals and railway stations where unlicensed operations and unlawful dealings are comparatively more concentrated.

60

THIRTY PERCENT OF GUANGZHOU'S PRIVATE BUSINESSES HAVE CEASED OPERATION

REPORTER YANG GUOYAN disclosed that according to the findings of the industrial and commercial sectors in Guangzhou, 30 percent of the 18,500 individual industrial and commercial businesses in the city have suspended operations at various times. A survey made in North Chaoyang, Hungchiao, and Beijing Streets showed that 216 have closed down and 27 have suspended operations, making some 32 percent of the total. According to the individual businesses, one major factor accounting for the failure of businesses is the difficulty of finding suitable locations for their operations. It is no longer permissible to set up stands along the sidewalks of first, second, and third class streets. The original stands are being readjusted and relocated. However, many of the relocated individual businesses have, for lack of better alternatives, moved into side streets and alleys and been forced to pull up stakes because of the lack of business. Another factor contributing to the failure of individual businesses is the high payments they have to make and the heavy fines levied against them. An individual business has to make six or seven kinds of payment. Take Wang Qinjia, who operates a food store as an individual business on North Liberation Street, as an example: his monthly volume of business has been assessed at 800 yuan. Aside from taxes amounting to over 40 yuan per month, he has to pay 24 yuan for street maintenance, 7.5 yuan for street usage, 15 yuan for street cleaning, and 10 yuan for validation of the contract of hired help, as well as sanitation service fees and fuel costs totaling 90 to 100 yuan a month. He explained that with all those payments to make it would be most difficult to continue operations. The heavy fines imposed also present a serious problem. Because a person named Chen who operates a food store on People's Street was seven days late in paying the street usage fee in May, he was assessed a fine of 525 yuan. He stated that since he would not be able to pay the fine even if he sold all his assets, he had no choice but to suspend operations. Then, too, certain units other than the industrial

Yangcheng wanbao [Yangcheng Evening News], June 8, 1982, p. 1. Translation from JPRS 81886, September 29, 1982, pp. 95–96.

and commercial administration departments would often compel individual businesses to suspend operations, would impose fines, and would revoke licenses at will.

In addition, some individual businessmen have quit or suspended operations because of their failure to obtain fuel, materials, and water and electricity installations. Although food stores were originally allocated 120 *jin* of coal a month, only 20 to 25 *jin* is actually made available. As a consequence, many of the stalls are in a state of semisuspension.

It is obvious that unless a solution is found to these problems, individual businesses will continue on their downward trend. In the first quarter of this year, only 1,838 persons in the city applied for business licenses, a drop of over 30 percent compared to the same period last year.

It is the hope of the individual businesses that the concerned departments will unify their thinking, coordinate their planning and action, and take positive steps to resolve the difficulties. For instance, space may be set aside for putting up booths along the wide sidewalks on first, second, and third class streets to serve breakfast in the morning and snacks in the evening. As for such matters as the payment of fees and fines and the supply of materials and fuel, they should be handled according to the ''Temporary Provisions for the Control of Individual Industrial and Commercial Businesses'' issued by the municipal government so that the legitimate rights of individual businesses may be protected. The suggestion has also been made by the individual businessmen that an overall administrative office should be set up by the concerned departments of the city to deal with these problems and that the street maintenance fee should be used for the benefit of the individual businesses, and not in large part be spent on projects which have nothing to do with the individual businesses.

FURTHER READINGS

Bennett, Gordon, ed. *China's Finance and Trade: A Policy Reader.* White Plains, N.Y.: M. E. Sharpe, 1978.

Bennett, Gordon. ''Commerce, the Four Modernizations, and Chinese Bureaucracy.'' In Sidney L. Greenblatt et al., eds. *Organizational Behavior in Chinese Society.* New York: Praeger, 1981, pp. 94–111.

Chan, Anita, and Jonathan Unger. ''Grey and Black: The Hidden Economy of Rural China.'' *Pacific Affairs* 55 (1983), pp. 452–471.

Chinese Economic Studies 13:4 (Summer 1980).

Perkins, Dwight H. *Market Control and Planning in Communist China.* Cambridge, Mass.: Harvard University Press, 1966.

Solinger, Dorothy J. *Chinese Business Under Socialism: The Politics of Domestic Commerce, 1949–1980.* Berkeley: University of California Press, 1984.

Solinger, Dorothy J. ''Commercial Reform and State Control: Structural Changes in Chinese Trade, 1981–1983.'' Paper prepared for the 34th Annual Meeting of the Association for Asian Studies, Washington, D.C., March 1984.

Solinger, Dorothy J. "Socialist Goals and Capitalist Tendencies in Chinese Commerce, 1949–52." *Modern China* 6:2 (April 1980), pp. 197–224.

Solinger, Dorothy J. "The Fifth National People's Congress and the Process of Policy Making: Reform, Readjustment, and the Opposition." *Asian Survey* 22:12 (December 1982), pp. 1238–1275.

Solinger, Dorothy J. *Three Visions of Chinese Socialism*. Boulder, Colorado: Westview Press, 1984.

Wan Dianwu. "Commerce." In Yu Guangyuan, ed. *China's Socialist Modernization*. Beijing: Foreign Languages Press, 1984, pp. 351–402.

c. Agriculture

ALTHOUGH THEIR NEW agricultural policies were undoubtedly popular and succeeded in raising rural incomes, nonetheless, in their pursuit of decollectivization, China's post-Mao leaders faced several problems: How could the abrupt change of policy be explained to the people and to the Party rank and file in acceptable value terms? How could some local resistance to the policies be overcome? How could the negative consequences for other policy arenas, such as birth control, be managed?

Throughout the Maoist era, collectivization of agriculture was a cornerstone of orthodox economic policy. When Liu Shaoqi and his supporters authorized experiments with household farming (decollectivization) in the early 1960s, other leaders opposed them. Indeed, during the Cultural Revolution, radicals savaged the policy of household contracting and condemned Liu and his associates for attempting to implement it. By first reviving and then going beyond the 1960s policies, leaders faced a number of ideological problems. What possible justification could there be for the policies? Had the earlier condemnation been mistaken? Why were the policies appropriate now? The central issue required a reexamination of China's rural class policy, a feature of many of the following selections.

A second problem concerned attempts by local officials and envious neighbors to undermine or negate the new measures. Some local leaders attempted to sabotage the policies because they thought that they were "capitalist" and were, thus, fundamentally wrong. Others believed that the reforms would be short lived and, thus, ought not to be seriously implemented. Still others envied the largely material success of their neighbors under the new policies. For these reasons, some local officials and ordinary peasants resisted the implementation of the reforms.

Finally, the implementation of agricultural policy has had consequences for policy in other areas. As authorities have parceled out the land, they have inhibited the spread of mechanization. Encouraged to "get rich," peasants have pulled their children out of school to work on the farm. Birth control policies and PLA recruitment drives have also been affected.

This section highlights conflict that emerged in the course of implementing agricultural policy. It draws from press commentaries, survey data, and interviews with former peasant leaders carried out in Hong Kong and thus illustrates the richness of data sources more recently available for the study of contemporary China.

Selections 61–66 have in common the leadership's concern for ideological problems associated with the introduction of the new agricultural policies. These pieces also provide evidence of the shifting direction of elite concerns as first they experimented with a modest liberalization of marketing opportunities before introducing household contracting and a general decollectivization of agriculture.

In Selections 61 and 62 authorities take the first steps toward an ideological justification for the policies that followed. Selection 61 criticizes the previously legitimate policy of giving "bad" class labels to poor peasants who became rich through their own labor. Local authorities were now required to rehabilitate the peasants, return to them their property (which had been confiscated by the authorities), and restore to them their rights of citizenship. Just how devastating a "bad" label could be to a family's fortune as late as 1978 is indicated in the piece. Peasant Deng's sons were dismissed from their leadership posts, were no longer eligible for military service, and had difficulty finding suitable brides.[1]

The early worry of some national leaders was, then, to undo the damage caused by the arbitrary class labeling policy of the Maoist era. As authorities parceled out the land to peasant households under the new policies, however, additional worries emerged. In a strongly worded and authoritative piece, "Commentator" criticizes the notion that ownership of the land would be returned to individuals as a part of the reforms. Alarmed by the possibility that the old, pre-1949 ruling classes, landlords and rich peasants, would attempt to reclaim their position, "Commentator" asserts that collective ownership of the land would continue. The strength of the piece is that it indicates that the practice of dividing up the land along traditional lines was probably widespread. Interestingly, the article fails to discuss the difference between ownership of the land and control over its use. What difference does it make who owns the land if peasants have the right to its use for an extended period of time (up to fifteen years and beyond in some cases) under contracts that can be inherited?[2]

Selections 63–65 bring the debate up to date. In Selection 63, "Commentator" argues the now familiar position that peasants ought to be actively encouraged to "become rich through labor." The author, while admitting that 150 million peasants live in poverty, argues that living standards for everyone will be improved under the new policies as benefits "trickle down" from the newly enriched to the poor. Indeed, since 1980 when the new policies were implemented, average per-capita rural income has risen substantially.[3]

Rural class divisions will not reemerge, "Commentator" argues, because the new rich peasants will act as models to be emulated by their poorer neighbors, and because the rich will provide material and technical assistance to the less well off. These themes are continued in Selection 64, which indicates the extent of the shift in official thinking from the Cultural Revolution days. Selflessness and egalitarianism are replaced by the individual pursuit of wealth. While both Selections 63 and 64 raise the problem of class polarization, neither piece deals with the question of what the newly rich will do with their wealth.

The report of Politburo member Hu Qiaomu's visit to Fujian (Selection 65) indicates dissension within the leadership over the extent to which the pursuit of wealth ought to be official policy, and it demonstrates that the line between legitimate and illegitimate methods of becoming rich is exceedingly thin. Hu explicitly condemns the blind pursuit of wealth or what Selection 63 calls ''doing everything for money.'' This backpedaling serves to pacify more conservative elements among the leadership, who are concerned that the policies may be undermining socialism.

The ideological condition of suburban peasants is investigated in Selection 66. The survey, an example of the kind of social science investigation that is becoming increasingly common among Chinese academics,[4] raises a wide range of problems. Chinese peasants, not surprisingly, hanker after life in the cities: easier jobs, higher living standards, better services, more consumer goods, and a greater variety of entertainment make urban life attractive. Years of propaganda about the joys of rural living have failed to convince these peasants. Still, underemployment in the countryside is a serious problem, and the survey indicates that authorities would have little difficulty convincing the peasants to move to jobs in small towns and nearby cities.

The survey also reports a ''get rich'' mentality that has infected rural Party members around Shanghai. They are concerned for self and their families, and Party life has become ritualized. The survey thus seems to confirm the fears of ''Commentator'' in Selection 63 and Hu Qiaomu in Selection 65 that the blind pursuit of riches has undermined traditional Party values. Surveys such as this probably reinforced the view among some Party leaders that a Party rectification was necessary.

Finally, the survey highlights the view of Party members that informal networks are essential for getting ahead and getting along. ''One more friend is one more road'' for achieving one's goals. The need to cultivate relationships (see Bureaucracy section) thus extends to the grass roots.

If the new agricultural policies have created problems in the ideological realm, they have also prompted resistance by both ordinary people and local leaders. Selections 67–69 highlight the problems of specialized households, those peasants who have undoubtedly benefited the most from the new policies. In Selection 67 the reasons for Chen's bankruptcy are discussed (peasants must relearn how to assess the risks of producing for a market), but the role of local cadres in the fiasco is ignored. Did local enemies of the new policies encourage Chen's ''blind expansion''? Only with the connivance of local officials could Chen have amassed 150,000 yuan worth of debt. And, therefore, these same officials, in their own interests, must bail Chen out.

The role of local officials is explicitly addressed in Selection 68. Here village cadres, surprised by the relative ease with which peasant Yang was able to make a bankrupt brick kiln into a profitable business, took matters into their own hands when profits appeared to them to be ''too large.'' They demanded that Yang pay a management fee, and when this was refused, the officials disconnected the kiln's power supply and confiscated its land. Interestingly, at a time when national leaders were propagating "rule by law," these local leaders ignored the law. They were able to resist the intervention of county leaders, and only when the provincial Party secretary intervened was the matter resolved (in Yang's favor) by a court. This case indicates the fragility of both the contracts and the "rule of law" needed to enforce them. Only when the most powerful person in the province intervened did the village officials back down!

Not only local officials but ordinary villagers sometimes resisted the new policies. Although undoubtedly an extreme case, Liu's suicide (Selection 69) highlights the torment he endured as a result of his financial success. His neighbors' envy prompted them to take direct action (theft and poisoning) to level Liu's income. Liu obviously trusted neither the law nor local officialdom; instead he replied with a shotgun—vigilante justice. Indeed, where were the officials during this episode? It is likely that they gave tacit approval to the thefts and poisoning to teach Liu a lesson. It was legitimate for Liu to adopt the new policies, as long as he did not earn too much more than his neighbors.

In addition to the ideological problems and instances of resistance to the policies, decollectivization has had certain consequences for other policy arenas. While Selection 70 is a wide-ranging discussion of the process of implementing the new policies in a Guangdong village, it also indicates that household farming made practicing birth control more difficult. The link between having more sons and financial security is even more clear as a result of the policies. Selection 71 suggests that decollectivization has consequences for recruitment of peasant sons into the PLA. While this was previously attractive as a means of upward mobility, after decollectivization, peasant youths preferred to stay at home so that they could contribute to the family fortune.

The interviews also highlight some of the problems that we have discussed above and that are revealed in official sources. Selection 70 indicates, for example, that commune cadres, who acted as rural gatekeepers, were unwilling to experiment with the new policies until they received official approval from their superiors. Village officials, who stood to gain by the policies, acted as a buffer between higher levels and the village. They simply did not want to know whether the policies, very popular locally, were being implemented. The interview also indicates that "Commentator's" worries (in Selection 62) about peasants treating the land as their own were probably well founded. In the Guangdong case, peasants did precisely that. Interview data, then, provide valuable insights into and detail about the implementation process and help to substantiate material that has appeared in official sources•

Notes

1. For a discussion of class policy, see Richard C. Kraus, *Class Conflict in Chinese Socialism* (New York: Columbia University Press, 1981).

2. "Circular of the Central Committee of the Chinese Communist Party on Rural Work During 1984," translated in *The China Quarterly* No. 101 (March 1985), p. 133.

3. *Beijing Review* 29 (July 22, 1985), pp. 20–21.

4. See David S. K. Chu, ed., *Sociology and Society in Contemporary China, 1979–1983* (Armonk, N.Y.: M. E. Sharpe, 1984).

61

REHABILITATION OF "CAPITALIST" COMMUNE MEMBERS

THE PARTY COMMITTEE of Duoyue Commune in Meishan County of Sichuan Province recently rehabilitated and exonerated commune member Deng Shaocheng and his family, who were designated "capitalist upstarts" in the heyday of the "Gang of Four," and returned to him all his property confiscated at that time—a six-room tiled house, 1.5 *mu* of private plots, a bicycle, and 50 yuan in cash.

Under the influence of the revisionist line of Lin Biao and the "Gang of Four," which appears to be left but is right in essence, proper domestic sideline occupations conducted by members of Duoyue Commune were condemned as practicing capitalism, and unreasonable barriers were thus imposed on such sideline occupations. Labeled a typical case, Deng Shaocheng and his family became targets of criticism and struggle at mass rallies. His family was condemned as "capitalist upstarts," and a portion of his family's labor remuneration was also confiscated.

The label "capitalist upstart" not only harmed Deng Shaocheng's family economically, but also brought about extremely serious political consequences. His oldest son and second son were dismissed from their posts as production group leader and production team accountant respectively. Because his family was labeled a "capitalist upstart," Deng Shaocheng's third son was disqualified when he attempted to join the army. Furthermore, because of Deng Shaocheng's family label, even matchmakers could not find brides for his sons.

Having realized during the struggle against the gang that the previous treatment of Deng Shaocheng was a serious mistake, the Party committee of Duoyue Commune decided to openly admit this mistake and rehabilitate Deng Shaocheng and his family. Speaking at the rehabilitation meeting, Luo Guoxiang, Party committee secretary of Duoyue Commune, said: It was proper for Deng Shaocheng and his family to actively participate in productive collective labor and develop domestic sideline occupations. Instead of criticizing and condemning them, we must support and encourage them.

Commune members warmly support the action taken by the Party committee of Liya Commune in Zhengan County of Guizhou Province to rehabilitate poor peasant Huang Shaojun, who was once designated a "newly emerging rich peasant." In May 1977 some persons informed the Xinming Production Team of

Xinhua [New China News Agency], Chinese, January 17, 1979. Translation from FBIS Daily Report, January 19, 1979, pp. E20–E22 (excerpts).

Liya Commune that the income of Huang Shaojun's family exceeded that of other commune members and that Huang was a newly emerging rich peasant as well as an upstart in rural areas. Imbued with the fake left but real right idea advocated by Lin Biao and the "Gang of Four" that whoever becomes rich tends to be revisionist and that comfortable living means capitalism, some cadres of the commune then unreasonably confiscated Huang Shaojun's bank deposit of 890 yuan, one sewing machine, and some furniture and instructed all production brigades to launch mass criticism against him as a major target of struggle. Huang Shaojun was later designated a "newly emerging rich peasant and upstart."

After receiving the two important documents circulated by the Party Central Committee—"Xiangxiang Experience" and "The Question of Xunyi County"—the Party committee members of Liya Commune were deeply moved ideologically. Most of the comrades realized that under the pernicious influence of the "Gang of Four" Huang Shaojun was wrongly designated; what they criticized was not capitalism and who they struggled against was not a class enemy but a commune member of poor peasant origin. They decided to take immediate action to correct this serious mistake.

After a thorough investigation, the commune's Party committee now realizes that instead of stopping commune members from developing proper domestic sideline occupations in accordance with the Party's economic policies, the commune-level Party committees should vigorously promote and support such sideline occupations.

A *Xinhua* editor's note reads in full as follows: An extremely important condition to put into full play the enthusiasm of the peasant masses in our country is to pay full attention to the peasants' material interest economically and effectively ensure their democratic rights politically. Opposing the people, Lin Biao and the "Gang or Four" promoted a counterrevolutionary revisionist line that appears to be left but is right in essence, confused the two different types of contradictions, undermined the socialist collective economy, and suppressed the masses of commune members.

Commune members Deng Shaocheng and Huang Shaojun, who were designated as "upstarts" and "newly emerging rich peasants," are two good examples. The case of Huang Shaojun, who was designated as a "newly emerging rich peasant" after the "Gang of Four" was smashed, shows the depths of the fake left but real right influence of Lin Biao and the "Gang of Four."

Under no circumstances should we underestimate the pernicious influence and evil consequences of this fake left but real right revisionist line in the rural areas. All peasants who were victims of false charges, wrong sentences, and frame-ups must be rehabilitated. Only thus can we achieve stability and unity in the rural areas and give fuller play to the peasants' enthusiasm.

62

Commentator

UPHOLD COLLECTIVE OWNERSHIP OF LAND, UPHOLD THE DIRECTION OF COLLECTIVIZATION

THE GROWTH OF China's agriculture and the prosperity of its rural economy hinge on our continuing in the direction of collectivization and on adhering to the socialist road. The aim of the various forms of the agricultural production responsibility system is precisely to bring the superiority of the collective economy into full play and mobilize the enthusiasm of the masses of commune members. To achieve this end, collective ownership of the means of production must be resolutely safeguarded and the principle of distribution "to each according to his work" conscientiously implemented. We must never hestitate or waver in this respect.

For rural communes and their subdivisions, protecting collective ownership of the means of production mainly concerns keeping collective land intact and adhering to the idea of the land, the most precious means of production, continuing to be owned by the collective and owned collectively by the peasants. This has been long stipulated in explicit terms in the Party's policies and the government's decrees. The various important documents published since the Third Plenum of the Eleventh CCP Central Committee all took the adherence to collective ownership of such basic means of production as land as a precondition in the readjustment and reform of the rural economy. All the forms of the contract system— whether it is the system of fixing output quota contracts for each special line of production or the system of assigning responsibility to each laborer and linking remuneration with output or the system of fixing output quotas for individual households or the system of peasant households assuming full responsibility for task completion—are reforms in management and distribution methods and partially a readjustment in the relations of production for the purpose of making them suit the level of development of productive forces. But in no way do they mean a change in landownership.

At present, in the course of setting up the responsibility system in the places where the system of fixing output quotas for individual households and the system of peasant households assuming full responsibility for task completion are followed, there have emerged two kinds of misunderstanding among the cadres and commune members in regard to these systems. They are: first, some people mistakenly regard the implementation of the responsibility system as merely practicing the system of fixing output quotas for individual households and the

Renmin ribao [People's Daily], October 30, 1981. Translation from FBIS Daily Report, November 6, 1981, pp. K1–K2.

system of peasant households assuming full responsibility for task completion. Second, some people mistakenly regard the practicing of the system of fixing output quotas for individual households and the system of peasant households assuming full responsibility for task completion as "land being parceled out to peasant households for individual farming." In a few regions there have even emerged such false rumors as "land being returned to a household" and "identifying the land which was the property of one's ancestors." This led to some confusion in people's thinking. These misunderstandings and rumors must be clarified in good time. Illegal actions such as selling and renting the land assigned to individual peasants under contract and building houses, kilns, and graves on farmland must be resolutely stopped. The prompt solution of practical problems will help clarify the false rumors. These problems demand the serious attention of the various localities.

Ours is a country of vast territory with conditions varying from place to place. Since the forms of the production responsibility system are numerous and varied, in implementing them it is necessary to adjust to local conditions and trades. Whether to carry out production targets with unified administration under the production teams or to assign them to individual peasant households under a contract hinges on the actual conditions. The system of peasant households assuming full responsibility for task completion is one of the various forms of the responsibility system as well as a method of decentralized management under collective ownership.

The peasant households fully responsible for task completion under a contract have the right to use the land but not to own it. Moreover, they are responsible for protecting the land and other collective property. In the whole course, ranging from production to distribution, they should be subject to collective management and restrictions. This is fundamentally different from the conditions after agrarian reform and before the cooperative transformation of agriculture, but all these are moves on the socialist road. "Land being parceled out to peasant households for individual farming" was an individual economy in which production was carried out separately by individual peasant households under private ownership of land by the peasants. In our history, it once occurred where "land was returned to a household." It was in a time when, under the leadership of the CCP, the peasants seized back means of production such as land from the exploiting classes by overthrowing the "three big mountains." The current system of fixing output quotas for individual households and peasant households assuming full responsibility for task completion and the system of "land being parceled out to peasant households for individual farming" and "land being returned to a household" are two entirely different things. They must not be lumped together.

The recently convened National Agricultural Work Conference [1981] stressed the adherence to the direction of collectivization, solemnly declaring several changes that cannot be made: no changes should be made in the long-term implementation of the agricultural production responsibility system, in the numerous and varied forms of the responsibility system, and in the ownership of land. We deeply believe that the older generation of peasants who underwent the experience of being liberated and standing on their own feet and the younger generation of peasants who have had the experience of taking the socialist road can fully judge the actual state of affairs and distinguish right from wrong, and they will not believe such rumors as "land being parceled out to peasant households for individual farming" and "land being returned to a household." It cannot be denied that in the course of setting up the responsibility system there is a tendency to "return to individual farming," which has emerged in a few regions. Some places have gone as far as to seize land owned collectively and to wreck the collective property. This is the result of weak leadership and even the result of their refusing to have anything more to do with the matter. This is a setback in our practical work and runs counter to the Party's principles and policies.

At present, various localities are setting up and perfecting the production responsibility system. The leading organs must firmly grasp this work in a planned way and check up on the work. The cadres at all levels must go down to the grass-roots units, conduct investigation and study, find problems in good time, analyze the actual conditions, and correctly handle them. The vast numbers of rural cadres and commune members must bravely step forward and boldly and forcefully denounce and stop the illegal actions of a handful of persons who deliberately create or spread rumors and who encroach on collective ownership of land. The Party organizations at various levels and the government departments must all the more take a clear-cut stand in propagating and enforcing the policies and decrees, work out concrete measures, and support the peasant masses in upholding collective ownership of land and safeguarding collective ownership. The small number of persons who refuse to correct themselves after individual education and dissuasion must be seriously dealt with. Law must be enforced in the few verified cases of former landlords who seized the opportunity to settle old scores and to fabricate rumors to mislead people.

63

Commentator

ENCOURAGE THE PEASANTS TO GO ALL OUT TO BECOME WELL-OFF THROUGH HARD WORK

ENERGETICALLY SUPPORTING THE peasants in developing production so as to increase income, gradually get rid of poverty, and become well-

Renmin ribao [People's Daily], December 9, 1983, pp. 1–2. Translation from FBIS Daily Report, December 13, 1983, pp. K3–K5.

off is the starting point and end result of all rural work. China has 800 million peasants. Only when the peasants are really well-off and the rural economy thrives can the whole country be prosperous and strong. This is a simple and clear theory.

Some years ago, owing to the erroneous "leftist" influence, the peasants had the incorrect feeling that the Communist Party liked poverty and that the poorer a person was, the more revolutionary and glorious he would be. Some peasants even mistakenly thought that socialist society was a society in which the people "endured common poverty." Since the Third Plenum of the Eleventh CCP Central Committee, our Party has corrected its "leftist" mistakes, gradually cleared up such misunderstandings in its practice, led the several hundred million peasants in breaking free from spiritual shackles, and brought their initiative in production into full play.

In a short period of several years, a new situation has emerged in various aspects of agricultural production, the livelihood of the peasants has improved, and the problem of food and clothing for the 150 million peasants who had lived in poverty for many years has been basically solved. Facts have proved that the fundamental aim of our Party is to enable the peasants to overcome poverty and to become well-off. We are absolutely confident that we can lead the peasants in becoming well-off.

Although the livelihood of the peasants has improved over the past few years, we cannot say that they are already rich. Last year, the average income of each peasant was only 200 yuan, just enough to maintain the minimum standard of living and still very far from the requirement set by the CCP Central Committee for the peasants that they should be able to live a comfortable life by the end of this century. We must redouble our efforts, continue to bring into full play the initiative of the peasants in production, energetically develop rural commodity production, and enable the peasants to become well-off so as to make greater contributions to the country.

Most of our comrades can adopt a correct attitude toward the problem of the peasants becoming "well-off" and toward the problem of some peasants becoming well-off ahead of other peasants. They enthusiastically support the specialized households that have emerged in the rural areas and help them develop production so as to become well-off ahead of other peasants and to lead all the peasants in becoming well-off. But some people adopt a negative attitude toward the problem of some peasants becoming well-off ahead of other peasants, asserting that for some peasants to become well-off through hard work is an approach of dividing the peasants into "two opposing groups" and that this "is not the socialist road." This criticism does not hold water. The varying degrees of prosperity in the rural areas only reflect the fact that some peasants have become well-off and other peasants will become well-off later. This does not mean that the peasants are being divided into two opposing groups. We advocate the road of becoming well-off together, but it is only an illusion for the 800 million peasants to become well-off together on the same morning. With regard to the problem of egalitarianism in the rural areas, five years ago Comrade Deng Xiaoping explicitly pointed out: "People in some regions and enterprises, and some workers and peasants, are allowed to go ahead of others insofar as income and livelihood are concerned. When some people live better than others, they will certainly be the model producing great strength in and influencing their neighbors, and bringing along people in other regions and units." He also pointed out: "This is a great policy, a policy that can affect and bring forward the entire national economy." Practice over the past few years has fully proved the correctness of this exposition. To enable all the peasants to become well-off, we must adhere to the policy of letting some peasants become well-off first. It is just because of the implementation of this great policy that the days are gone when the peasants "eat from the same big pot," that they have been freed from their shackles, and that a new situation has vigorously emerged on the agricultural front.

Some people have branded the peasants who have become well-off as persons who "do everything for money." This is utterly wrong. "Doing everything for money" is bourgeois egoistic ideology that seeks private gain at public expense and is bent solely on profit. It has nothing in common with the peasants' mentality of becoming well-off through hard work. They are two completely different spiritual realms. Most of the peasants who have become well-off are activists who are good at organizing various production factors. They are educated and economically minded persons who have skills and can develop productive forces. They are the backbone in developing rural commodity production.

They are the model for becoming well-off through hard work, the pursuers and propagators of science and technology, and the activists in building the socialist cause in the rural areas. Many peasants who have become well-off not only keep making contributions to the country but also help the collective and other peasants open up all avenues to prosperity. Without reservation, they are willing to pass on their experience in becoming well-off and their management skills to others and to generously give part of their income to poor households. They also help run educational, health, and communications work and other public welfare work. They are shining with the splendor of the communist spirit.

Many regions have been able to quicken their steps in enabling the peasants to become well-off. This cannot be separated from the exemplary role of the peasants who have become well-off. They are advanced persons who are taking the road of becoming well-off together. Of course, there are individuals who indulge in dishonest practices, avail themselves of loopholes, and make a fortune by illegal means. There are some basic-level cadres who seek personal gain by abusing their rights and by illegal means. We must educate and deal with these persons and punish those who violate the law. We must solve negative phenomena emerging from capitalist ideology and the vestiges of feudal ideology through strengthening ideological and political education and by carrying out education using positive examples. We must strengthen the building of socialist spiritual civilization in the rural areas. It is not advisable to extend the concept of spiritual pollution to the rural areas.

At present, some peasants, including the peasants who have become well-off, still have doubts and misgivings. They enthusiastically support the Party's rural policy and are therefore afraid of a change in policy. They endured the sufferings of "having the tail cut off" and "upstarts being repudiated." Thinking that it is dangerous to be well-off, they are adopting the attitude of wait-and-see. Their initiative in becoming well-off through hard work has not been brought into full play. Some peasants are even afraid of carrying out exploitive production or long-distance transportation, which are permitted by policies. We must strengthen ideological education among the peasants and explain that the Party will not change its basic policy on the rural areas or its policy of letting some peasants become well-off ahead of other peasants. What must be changed is the superstructure that is not suited to rural economic reform, administrative methods that are harmful to the initiative of the peasants, and rules and regulations that hamper the further development of commodity production. This change is being carried out on a voluntary basis and is beneficial to the collective and the state and to the peasants' becoming well-off through hard work. To consolidate and develop the excellent situation in the rural areas, all departments and comrades doing rural work are required to emancipate their minds, improve their work, enthusiastically help the peasants overcome their shortcomings, and lead them in advancing faster along the road of becoming well-off together.

64

Zi Ye

HAVE THEY GONE "TOO FAR" IN GETTING RICH?

SOME PEOPLE HOLD that as some of the "two kinds of households" in the rural areas have acquired annual incomes of several thousand or above 10,000 yuan, "they have gone too far in getting rich." Therefore, consciously or unconsciously, they do not feel so happy about the peasants continuously getting rich through labor, and they are beginning to raise some difficult questions.

"Going too far in getting rich" is a confused concept. Can there be a limit to affluence? The Party Central Committee has proposed quadrupling the gross industrial and agricultural output value by the year 2000, enabling the people to live a relatively well-off life, which is only a new standard to be achieved in accordance with the actual power of our country. Even when this is achieved, it is

Renmin ribao [People's Daily], April 16, 1984. Translation from FBIS Daily Report, April 18, 1984, pp. K17–K18.

still not the limit of affluence. Time is marching on, and the people's living standard will become higher and higher. A few years or a decade or more from now, when people look back at those 10,000-yuan households of today, they will surely say: That was only an initial standard. In the old society, people were short of food and clothing, and they often lamented that "they had come to the limit of poverty." There is a limit to poverty, but there is no limit to affluence. The idea of going too far in getting rich never occurs to those people who are genuinely creating wealth through labor.

Communists do not generally praise wealth. We resolutely opposed the wealth of the exploiting classes in the old society and overthrew them politically and deprived them of their property economically through revolution. Even now we do not generally talk about getting rich. For example, we have all along opposed and resolutely cracked down on activities of getting rich through improper means in seeking ill-gotten gains, such as taking advantage of one's power in seeking personal gain, accepting bribes, graft and embezzling, speculating, smuggling and selling smuggled goods, and so on. Those who are saying that some people have gone too far in getting rich fail to draw a demarcation line between right and wrong, while regarding getting rich through hard work as something terrible. They are actually deviating from reality, deviating from the Party's policy on enriching the people. The "Gang of Four" approved of transition in poverty. At that time anyone getting rich was capitalism and whoever got rich must be overthrown. In some places, when an old lady raised a chicken, an old man grew a few tobacco shrubs, or some children raised a few rabbits, they were all regarded as the tail of capitalism, which was strictly prohibited. Among those people who hold that "some people have gone too far in getting rich," some of them are actually suffering from "wealth phobia," and they have not eliminated the pernicious effects of "being poor is glorious" in their minds.

There is an order of precedence in getting rich. When we let some people get rich first, it is precisely to bring the majority of people to become well-off too.

This should be said to be a general law of getting rich under the socialist system. Prior to the Third Plenum of the Eleventh CCP Central Committee, this law was denied and "common prosperity" was one-sidedly stressed, as if several hundred million people marching on in a row should be the correct road. The result was that the people never became rich, but suffered from long-term poverty. The Third Plenum of the Eleventh CCP Central Committee has precisely summed up this bitter lesson and drawn up the policy on enriching the people. Facts have proven that this is a policy warmly acclaimed by the people. Some people will become rich first, while the majority of people will follow suit. This has already become a reality in some places.

The implementation of the policy of letting some people get rich first began in the rural areas. At present the scope of its implementation is expanding. Apart from the peasants, we can make some enterprises, localities, coastal areas, workers, staff, and intellectuals get rich first. It seems that the policy of letting some people get rich first while bringing along the majority to get rich too is understood and accepted by more and more people and is achieving fruitful results in both urban and rural areas. If at this moment people should say that "some have gone too far in getting rich," it is not promoting but throwing a wet blanket on practical work and on the enthusiasm for production and faith in reform on the part of hundreds of millions of people. Therefore, saying such things should be criticized.

65

HU QIAOMU CRITICIZES DESIRE FOR WEALTH IN FUZHOU

THE ARMYMEN AND people in Fuzhou held a "double-support" [support the government and cherish the people, and support the army and give preferential treatment to servicemen's families] tea party in the Meifeng Building in Fuzhou on the afternoon of February 6.

Hu Qiaomu, member of the Politburo of the CCP Central Committee, spoke on behalf of the Party Central Committee and the State Council. He congratulated Fujian Province on its great achievements in economic construction in recent years. He also thanked the PLA units in Fujian for their endeavors in various respects. In his speech, Hu Qiaomu made reference to something he saw in a Fuzhou enterprise—a desire for "getting rich." He said that he had already pointed out to the responsible person of the enterprise that the formulation was improper, and the responsible comrade of the enterprise had pledged to correct it right away.

Then, he conveyed to the tea party the important instructions of the leading comrades of the Party Central Committee and the State Council on enriching the country and the people and serving the people. He said: The Party Central Committee and the State Council will not change their policy of supporting urban and rural people and enterprises in the country to become well-to-do by working hard, upholding the principle of more pay for more work, and opposing egalitarianism. However, we should not excessively and improperly publicize the 10,000-yuan households or 100,000-yuan households. If we have to publicize them, we should emphasize that they have become rich through legitimate methods and they have contributed to enriching the country and other people. We should overcome the unhealthy tendency among some people of putting money above all else, or even judging a person's social status by his income. Among Communists, government organizations, and socialist enterprises, we should firmly propagate

Fujian ribao [Fujian Daily], February 7, 1985. Translation from FBIS Daily Report, February 26, 1985, pp. K3–K4 (excerpt).

the glorious traditions of serving the people. We must sternly correct the mistakes of any organizations and individuals that resort to illegitimate means to sabotage socialist economic construction, abuse and undermine the banner of reform, and violate Party and government discipline and law to seek wealth. We should deal with them according to law and the seriousness of their cases. This is imperative not only for Party rectification and the improvement of standards of social conduct, but also for ensuring smooth economic development under the new circumstances of reform and opening to the outside world.

66
___

THE IDEOLOGICAL STATE OF RURAL YOUNG PARTY MEMBERS

An Investigation Report by the Xincheng Commune Party Committee, Nanhui County, Shanghai Municipality

IN THE PROCESS of studying and implementing the spirit of the Sixth Plenum of the Central Committee [June 1981], we conducted an investigation and analysis of the ideological state of the 245 young Party members of our entire commune. Through the investigation, we firmly believe that to strengthen the ideological education of young Party members is an urgent task.

I

Our commune has 796 Party members, of which 245 are young, making up 30.8 percent of the total. The basic situation of these young Party members is as follows:

THE GREAT MAJORITY JOINED THE PARTY DURING THE "CULTURAL REVOLUTION." There are 9 persons who joined the Party before the "Cultural Revolution"; 62 joined after the smashing of the "Gang of Four"; the remaining

Shanghai shi nanhuixian xincheng gongshe dangwei de diaocha baogao, "Nongcun qingnian dangyuan de sixiang zhuangkuang." *Dang de shenghuo* [Party Life], 1981, No. 5, pp. 48–49. Translation from *Sociology and Society in Contemporary China, 1979–1983* (a special issue of *Chinese Sociology and Anthropology*), edited and translated by David S. K. Chu (Armonk, N.Y.: M. E. Sharpe, 1984), pp. 170–176.

174, making up 72 percent of all young Party members, all joined during the "Cultural Revolution."

Among the young Party members, 133, or 54 percent, are aged thirty-one to thirty-five; 97, or 40 percent, are aged twenty-five to thirty; only 15 persons, or 6 percent, are under twenty-five years old. There are 68 women Party members, about 28 percent.

A MAJORITY HAS THE CULTURAL LEVELS OF JUNIOR HIGH SCHOOL AND PRIMARY SCHOOL. Only 9 persons, or 3.6 percent, have the cultural levels of college and secondary technical school; 26, or 10.6 percent, have a senior high school level; the remaining 220, or more than 85 percent, have only the cultural levels of junior high school and primary school.

OVER HALF [55.9 PERCENT] OF THE YOUNG PARTY MEMBERS HOLD VARIOUS LEADERSHIP POSTS. Among them, 37 persons [15.1 percent of the total] hold the "three posts" [sanzhi—Party branch secretary, brigade leader or factory manager, and chief accountant]; 15 persons [6.1 percent] hold posts in technical and professional work; 85 persons [34.7 percent] hold posts as production team leaders and as team and group leaders [in factories].

RELATIVELY FEW YOUNG PARTY MEMBERS ARE IN THE FIRST LINE OF AGRICULTURAL PRODUCTION. There are 36 persons, or 14.7 percent, who work for units of commune organizations and county-run enterprises; 106 persons, or 43.3 percent, work in commune-run enterprises; only 103 persons, or 42 percent, are in agriculture. But among them, only 39 Party members [or 15.9 percent of the total] are engaged directly in agricultural production.

A RELATIVELY LARGE PROPORTION OF YOUNG PARTY MEMBERS CONSISTS OF DEMOBILIZED SERVICEMEN FROM THE ARMY. Recruited for membership by the village production brigade Party branch were 126 persons, or 51.4 percent; 21 persons, or 8.6 percent, were recruited from commune-run enterprises and organizations; 98 young Party members, more than 40 percent, were demobilized army servicemen.

II

The mainstream and essence of young Party members are good and striving upward. They support the line, programs, and policies formulated by the Party Central Committee since the Third Plenum [December 1978]; particularly they have rather ample faith in following the two documents of the Central Committee on developing agriculture and implementing agricultural responsibility systems. But the following ideological trends and problems warrant the Party organization's attention:

1. DESIRING TO "ESCAPE FARMING" [TIAOCHU NONGMEN]. A mentality of looking down on farming and of leaving farming, "doing farming but not liking it" [wunong bu ai nong] is relatively common among young Party members. "Eyeing tall chimneys, the hearts are warm and cozy; holding iron rake handles, the hearts are ice cold"; in their hearts and souls they desire to "escape farming"

and become "farm escapees" [*tuononghu*] by getting hired into factories. Some say that agricultural production is without rhyme or reason, is endless, and is without regard to day or night; the life is most miserable and wearisome with the worst pay and conditions. Some others say that "in factories work takes less effort but the pay is high; one enjoys a good reputation and is well-known; it's easier to be in love and to find a partner." For the goal of casting off rake handles to work in factories, some are unwilling to be production team leaders, fearing that once a cadre it is impossible to get into factories; some try to make contacts everywhere, seeking channels through dishonest methods; some even make a scene. Recently, one woman Party member, a production team leader, wanted to marry someone in another brigade. Worried about being unfamiliar to the other brigade and unable to get a turn for employment in factories, she made a big fuss at a cadre meeting, obstinately demanding that her brigade leadership solve the problem of her entering a factory before she marries out. Commune members appraise these young Party members as "desiring life [to save effort] but not land."

2. HANKERING AFTER THE "LITTLE FAMILY." Some young Party members are unconcerned about the collective and major national affairs; talking of material benefits, pursuing ease and comfort, they care only about "privatization" [*sihua*—a play on the term *sihua*—Four Modernizations], pursuing the "modernization" of individual life. They want only to make their "own houses a bit larger, furniture equipped more completely, dowries more ample, and life more comfortable." Dissatisfied with the "three big items" already in their possession, some blindly pursue "televisions, electric stand-up floor fans, and big sofas" and other high-grade articles for daily use. Some consider only "hurrying to build a house, seize the time to get a wife, and get a son at an early date." Devoting his heart and soul to his little family after marriage, one young Party member was even unwilling to participate in regular activities of the organization, forgetting that he is a Communist Party member, adding, "It's all right so long as I guarantee not to break any laws."

3. ENGAGING IN IMPROPER "GET RICH" ACTIVITIES. Now that the goal is to liven up the economy, some young Party members, believing that it is permissible for some people to become wealthy first, make use of improper means to become "prominent" and "get rich." Some see money and get red-eyed with envy, and with their hearts pumping and hands itching, they leave the teams and villages without authorization to fish for money. Some even bought up state-controlled commodities in short supply and sold them illegally. Some produced agricultural by-products and engaged in illegal exchange of coupons and certificates. In the busy season, one young Party member went out of town without permission to peddle things and later advertised that he had "earned more than 50 yuan in one week." In order to make more money, some individual members even stole goods and materials from commune-run enterprises, thus creating very bad impressions among the masses.

4. UNWILLING TO BE "EXPOSED RAFTERS" [SPEAK OUT FOR JUSTICE].

Afraid to offend others, some young Party members behave according to "If you're nice, I'll be nice and keep on the good side of everyone." So long as their own individual interests are not hurt, they are only too glad to keep quiet, pretending not to see what is obviously wrong. Witnessing someone stealing the collective's construction materials, one young Party member from a commune-run factory was afraid to come forward to stop it. He even said, "The power above is great and the fists below are big; so what can I do?" Some members do not dare to fight against evil winds and noxious influences or against matters that infringe on the interests of the masses. They are unwilling to come out and speak for justice, believing that "One more foe is another wall, but one more friend is one more road," preferring to "plant more flowers" but not wanting to "cut down more thorns." In general, such thinking is rather prominent among young Party members.

III

The aforementioned ideological tendencies existing among young Party members are not new problems, however. That these ideological problems did not arouse our attention for a rather long time reveals, first of all, that we at the commune Party committee have not exercised effective leadership in ideological and political work, and that to varying degrees a lax and feeble state of affairs existed where we dared not launch criticism and self-criticism justly and forcefully against various ideological tendencies and mistaken words and deeds that existed among young Party members. Second, in many brigade Party branches the system of "three meetings and one class" has been unsound, in some cases becoming mere formalities where there still exists the phenomenon of the Party not caring about itself. Third, some basic-level Party cadres have taken the lead in unhealthy practices, thus influencing some young Party members.

Therefore, we are taking the following measures:

1. Organize cadres at the two levels of commune Party committee and brigade Party branch to earnestly study the documents of the Sixth Plenum of the Central Committee and the spirit of the conference on problems of the ideological front, to overcome the lax and feeble state of affairs, to inspire a revolutionary spirit, and to devote major efforts to strengthening ideological and political work.

2. It is necessary to take up the weapon of criticism and self-criticism, to solve in time the various ideological tendencies existing among the young Party members by using various ways to educate them to adhere to the "Four Basic Principles" and the lofty ideals of communism, to have a deep love for farming, to devote themselves to the "Four Modernizations," etc.

3. Vigorously enforce the Party's organizational life and strengthen the system of "three meetings and one class."

4. Intensify the education of young Party members who lag behind to impel their transformation. If education and assistance prove ineffective, individuals who do not meet the standards of Party membership should be dealt with appropriately by the organization.

67a

WELL-KNOWN FISHERY SPECIALIZED HOUSEHOLD CHEN ZHIXIONG GOES INTO DEBT

CHEN ZHIXIONG, a well-known fishery specialized household, has gone into debt. By last December his debts totaled 150,000 yuan. At present, with the help of the Gaoyao County CCP Committee and government in Guangdong, he has begun to rally his forces and continues to undertake contracted responsibility for specialized undertakings. He also has plans to repay the debts.

Chen Zhixiong is a native of Shayi Township, Shapu District, Gaoyao County, Guangdong Province, and has a family of nine, of whom eight are able-bodied workers. Since 1979, he has undertaken contracted responsibility for ponds that stretch more than one brigade or district, including Wenhuilang Lake, which yields a well-known fish called the Wenhui carp. He quickly became rich and caused a sensation throughout the county. Some people then criticized his practice of undertaking contracted responsibility for a pond that stretches more than one brigade and district. *Renmin ribao* [People's Daily] took up the issue. It has been six years since Chen Zhixiong began to undertake contracted responsibility. In 1979, he undertook contracted responsibility for 6 *mu* of ponds and earned a net income of over 6,000 yuan. In 1980, the pond that he undertook contracted responsibility for was expanded to more than 140 *mu*, and he earned over 10,000 yuan through both fish farming and Gorgon fruit production. After making money for two years, he became bolder. In 1981, he undertook contracted responsibility for over 430 *mu* of a pond that stretched over more than one brigade and thus earned a net income of more than 29,000 yuan through Gorgon fruit production and fish farming. In 1982, he continued to undertake responsibility for over 360 *mu* of ponds that stretched across more than one brigade, but suffered a loss of more than 28,000 yuan. In 1983, he again undertook responsibility for 2,200 *mu* of land at Wenhuilang Lake to alternately grow rice and breed fish, but again suffered a loss of more than 23,000 yuan. Last year he continued to undertake contracted responsibility for the 2,200 *mu* of land, but for many reasons there was a poor harvest for all his fish, rice, and Gorgon fruit. At the end of 1984, it was estimated that the total income from his operation would not exceed 50,000 yuan, which was less than the 80,000 yuan levy for his land fixed by the contract. His debts shot up to 150,000 yuan, of which 78,000 yuan was loans from the state and collective, over 46,000 yuan was private loans, and 30,000 yuan was accrued contract levy.

We have learned that the major reasons for Chen Zhixiong's losses were:

Nongmin ribao [Peasant's Daily], January 17, 1985. Translation from FBIS Daily Report, January 31, 1985, pp. K19–K20.

1. Blind Expansion of the Area of Contracted Land

The area of the land for which he undertook contract responsibility was increased from several *mu* at the beginning through several hundred to over 2,000 *mu*. He lacked the necessary labor, financial, and material resources and managerial knowledge for his undertaking. As a result, there was a reduction in the output of the products that he produced on a large scale. For example, the crop failure of his Gorgon fruit land alone caused a reduction in his income by over 100 yuan per *mu*.

2. Blind Management

In 1983, Chen Zhixiong grew 600 *mu* of a fine strain of hybrid rice and reaped 300,000 *jin* of rice worth 57,000 yuan. Last year he sharply increased the area of late rice land to 1,200 *mu*, but he did not have the technology to grow a fine strain of hybrid rice, and the crops failed on a large stretch of his land.

3. Poor Access to Information

The Gorgon fruit produced by Chen Zhixiong is unmarketable now and is stockpiled. This has tied up his funds. However, he has not lost his confidence despite these heavy debts, and he wants to continue to carry out specialized undertakings of a developmental nature by responsibility contracts to increase his income and repay the debts.

Recently, with the help of the Gaoyao County CCP Committee and government, he signed a contract with Huilong District to undertake the responsibility for fish farming in over 200 *mu* of barren pond. The county CCP committee and government also plan to help him in three ways: (1) help him find ways to sell his Gorgon fruit; (2) discuss with the creditors extending the terms of repayment; and (3) provide him with more technological and managerial guidance.

67b

Ji Yechang and Guo Pingzhang

ON THE LOSS SUFFERED BY CHEN ZHIXIONG

WHY DID CHEN ZHIXIONG, a man who was once called "an able man" by other people, incur losses and go into debt? This incident stirs deep thoughts by our rural cadres and the vast number of peasants.

When rural commodity production first began, Chen Zhixiong came to be regarded as an able man. He promptly discovered what was in short supply and

Nongmin ribao [Peasant's Daily], January 17, 1985. Translation from FBIS Daily Report, January 31, 1985, p. K20. This is a *Peasant's Daily* comment on the preceding document.

relied on his own skills in fish farming to bravely undertake contracted responsibility for fish farming on a large pond. The law of competition is that the better ones win and the inferior ones are eliminated. Under these circumstances, Chen Zhixiong, who once was a leader in carrying out commodity production, clearly lacked enough technological and managerial knowledge for his undertaking. There may have been many reasons for his losses, but the most fundamental was that he lost, or at least weakened, his contacts with the market and society. Despite lacking the necessary managerial competence, technological knowledge, funds, and material resources, he blindly changed the orientation of his undertaking and expanded its scale. As a result, he suffered failure.

Commodity production on a relatively large scale has just begun in our country's rural areas. This is still an entirely new field for our vast number of rural cadres and peasants. Many of them do not understand the law of value, know nothing about tax laws, and do not know how to analyze price trends, how to use funds and credit, how to sign contracts, how to engage in economic lawsuits, or even what commodities are, let alone the skill to keep up to date on the information and situation in all areas, the newest information, data on advanced technology, or modern scientific management methods. Therefore, our cadres and peasants should receive basic education about commodity production. If they fail to study, if they stick to old conventions, if they continue to view problems with old views and do things in old ways, or if they act brashly and rely on their luck, they will suffer setbacks.

The case of Chen Zhixiong's losses poses a question for rural cadres at all levels: If we say that in the past few years the criterion for whether a cadre has emancipated his mind has been whether he has been willing to hand over the production decisionmaking power to the peasants, then the criterion now for whether a cadre can create a new situation is whether he is able to teach peasants to carry out commodity production. Those who educate others should first receive education. Therefore, our cadres must study earlier, more quickly, and better than our peasants.

To greatly develop our country's commodity production, we should gradually expand the scope of the regulation of market mechanism.

68
—

HENAN'S LIU JIE HANDLES CASE OF BROKEN CONTRACT

As a RESULT of the direct intervention of Comrade Liu Jie, first secretary of the provincial CCP committee, the case of an arbitrarily torn up

Radio Zhengzhou, March 21, 1984. Translation from FBIS Daily Report, March 23, 1984, p. P1.

contract and the sabotaging of the production of a specialized household has been dealt with in Xinzheng County. Yang Naiyu, the specialized household engaged in running a brick kiln, and others have again gathered up their courage to vigorously develop commodity production.

In December 1982 several peasants in Huayangzhai Village of Guodian Township in Xinzheng County, Yang Naiyu, Liu Zhongyi, and others, contracted for the village's brick kiln which had been forced to stop production for three years because it suffered losses year after year. It was stipulated in the contract that they should pay 11,000 yuan to the collective during the three years of the contract. The signing of the contract was witnessed by the township government and registered in the county's notary office. After signing the contract, Yang Naiyu and others invested some 25,000 yuan to modify and improve the equipment of the factory, resulting in a rapid development of production. The total income for 1983 was 28,000 yuan.

Consequently, some envious persons in the village demanded that the contract volume be increased by 10,000 yuan annually and that the village committee charge (Yang Naiyu) and the others 10 percent for a management fee. Yang Naiyu and the others did not accept this, so some cadres of the village committee and production team, using the excuse that the original contract was unreasonable, disconnected the power supply to prevent them from carrying on production. Last November Su Xiaozeng, leader of the first production team, even went so far as to forcibly allocate the 15 *mu* of land belonging to the brick kiln to the masses. As a result, the kiln was forced to stop production.

After this year's Spring Festival principal leading comrades of the county CCP Committee and government personally went to the village to conduct an on-the-spot investigation and repeatedly communicated Document No. 1 of the CCP Central Committee to mediate in the matter. But some cadres of the Huayangzhai Village committee and the production team paid no heed and still intended to use various excuses to tear up the contract.

On March 9 Yang Naiyu and the others wrote a letter to Comrade Liu Jie, first secretary of the provincial CCP committee, to promptly investigate and handle the matter. Backed by the leaders of the provincial, city, and county CCP committees and conducting a thorough investigation, the Xinzheng County People's Court publicly tried the case and gave the following verdict according to the law.

1. The original contract signed by the two sides is absolutely legal and must be executed.

2. The Huayangzhai village committee and the first production team are to pay 1,500 yuan to those contracting for the brick kiln for their losses. Su Xiaozeng, who had a direct responsibility in the matter, has been fined 100 yuan.

3. It was wrong to allocate the land of the brick kiln to the masses. The land must be promptly recovered to be used by the kiln.

Yang Naiyu and the five other persons concerned were very satisfied with the verdict and promptly said that they would use 2,000 yuan to buy national bonds and 1,000 yuan to buy saplings to support forestry production.

69

THE WINDOW OF SOCIETY: XINJIANG SPECIALIZED HOUSEHOLDER COMMITS SUICIDE

ON NOVEMBER 2, 1984, Liu Guozhi, member of a specialized household in the 12th Company of the 69th Regimental Farm, committed suicide in (Huangzhou) by taking poison.

Liu Guozhi was honest, diligent, and competent. He signed a contract with the company for running an orchard, 30 *mu* in size. Through sweat and toil he reaped a large amount of fruit. However, when his whole family were sharing the joys brought about by the bumper crop, a calamity befell them.

On the evening of October 29, members of a household went to his yard. A dog disappeared. Dregs of fat and steamed buns were spread in water vats and on the ground. After the chickens ate them, they immediately died of poisoning. He was robbed of 200 to 300 kilograms of apples.

On the evening of October 31, some people again encircled the yard of Liu's house. They hurled stones at the doors and windows. Being driven beyond forbearance, Liu Guozhi fired a shotgun at the direction where stones were hurled. A pellet hit Tao Jinhe's left calf. Early the following morning, the eldest and second elder brothers of Tao Jinhe got Liu Guozhi into trouble and forcibly demanded medical expenses from Liu. At that time, Liu Guozhi gave them 100 yuan. That very evening, Tao Jinhe's fourth elder brother went to Liu's house again and cuffed and kicked Liu Guozhi. When Tao was about to leave, he said threateningly: There will be no end to this matter between you and me.

Liu Guozhi could not tolerate this insult and he said to his wife, crying: Other people robbed us of our fruit and beat me up. I cannot live on. Later, he said that he was going to the toilet. He did not return.

All listeners! At present, some peasants and peasant-workers in our region have gotten rich first on the strength of the Party's policies. However, some people in society have not worked hard but specifically have gained petty advantages at the expense of other people. They even committed blackmail and robbery. The death of Liu Guozhi, a member of a specialized household, was a tragedy brought about by those people with red-eye disease [jealousy] who robbed his house. However, this is not a time of turmoil today like the Great Cultural Revolution. Legal sanctions will surely be taken against those robbers. This matter is being investigated and dealt with.

Moreover, we *mu*st advise those who have gotten rich: When your legitimate

Radio Urumqi, January 15, 1985. Translation from FBIS Daily Report, January 17, 1985, pp. T2–T3.

interests are encroached upon, you must trust and rely on the judicial departments to resolve the matter. Liu Guozhi resisted at the expense of his life. It was not only useless but brought greater sorrow to his relatives.

70

DECOLLECTIVIZATION IN A GUANGDONG VILLAGE: AN INTERVIEW

The transcript below is taken from the oral account of a villager from Shaoguan Prefecture, northern Guangdong Province, interviewed in the summer of 1983 in Hong Kong. The interviewee had left his wife and children behind when he came out to Hong Kong in 1979, and returns to the village three to four times every year to see them. He most recently had been back to the village in February 1983.

His village, like almost all other villages in China, has divided the collective fields among all the families to be cultivated separately, almost as though the fields were private holdings. In the summer of 1983, I obtained accounts from twenty-eight interviewees regarding twenty-eight different villages in nine provinces*; and of these, fully twenty-six of the villages employ exactly the same system of household agriculture today. The village of this particular interviewee is unusual in only one respect. In almost every other village in my sample, the upper levels of the government had directed the peasants to divide the production teams' collective lands into family-operated small holdings. Only in the following account and one other village did the local peasant cadres and villagers decide to divide the lands on their own initiative.

Jonathan Unger

OURS IS A pretty rich village. In 1978, before all the recent changes in agriculture, the average guy could earn over a yuan a day in our agricultural production team. One reason is that there's lots of moneymaking natural resources in the hills. In particular, there are good timber forests up behind the village.

Interview by Jonathan Unger, University of Kansas, 1983.

*See Jonathan Unger, ''The Decollectivization of the Chinese Countryside: A Survey of Twenty-eight Villages,'' *Pacific Affairs* 58:4 (Winter 1985–86).

My dad used to be the team accountant. He was the only one of his generation who could read and write. Whenever documents came down, only my dad could read them, so he had prestige.

My kid brother became the head of the team in 1979, the same year that I took off for Hong Kong. Our family was financially strapped that year. Dad had died two years earlier, and the funeral had been expensive. My brother, moreover, had recently married, and you know how much that costs. And the three youngest kids in the family were still of school age. So our family was several hundreds of yuan in debt to the team. But my brother felt that, if given a chance, our household was capable of making a lot of money. For one thing, he himself was the strongest worker in the team. For another, his wife and my mom were strong and healthy, and the youngest kids would soon be teenagers and able to pull their own full weight in agriculture.

In late 1979, right after I arrived in Hong Kong, I read in the newspapers about the national leadership's support of a program in Sichuan Province which gave all responsibility for agricultural production to individual households [baochan dao hu]. So I wrote to my brother about it. In the village, there were no newspapers at all. So my brother pedaled out on his bike to find out more from an old friend of my dad, a cadre at the county capital, who told my brother all about the new Sichuan system.

My brother figured this new system would give him a good opportunity to do well financially. Moreover, there were several households in the team with little labor power and lots of little kids, who were thousands of yuan in debt to the team. My kid brother calculated that it's better to divide up responsibilities rather than always continue to have our living standard drained by those families.

My brother figured that the new household responsibility system was going to spread. He was gutsy and felt he would jump in and do it early. He didn't even tell the commune authorities. He just privately got the brigade Party secretary's approval, because the Party secretary was from our team. The brigade secretary said, "OK, but don't say I gave permission." You see, the new system would be to his family's benefit, too, since he had several strong healthy teen-aged workers in his household, but he didn't want other families pointing a finger at him, saying he was selfishly motivated.

For months the commune didn't find out anything. Our brigade is composed of five teams, each of which is a separate hamlet, and our hamlet is off by itself. The brigade, moreover, is the most remote of any of the seventeen brigades in the commune. It's at the very edge of the commune, up against the mountains, and there's a lake on the near side of it, so it's pretty isolated.

Throughout the 1970s, productivity in our team had been lower than it could have been, owing to the repeated know-nothing directives and campaigns that higher-level Party authorities kept forcing on the countryside year after year. By 1979, most of the families in our team were fed up and were quite ready to shift away from collective agriculture and all those directives. But about four households that were weak in labor were opposed to dividing up all the responsibilities. To pacify them, my brother said, "Ok, if you can't do all the work on your own, other households will help you.'' So we got their agreement and our new "household responsibility system" was kept safely secret till the harvest, when the team had to hand in the quota grain for sale to the state. Trucks came in to collect the grain, and saw the families sunning the grain separately. As a result, the next time there was a commune-level meeting my brother's name came up in quite unglowing terms. But my brother wasn't really punished, because by then documents favoring the household responsibility system had come down to the commune from on-high.

The new system worked in the following way. It gave each family full responsibility for the crops on a given piece of land, and the family had to hand in all of the crops to the team at harvest-time in exchange for team workpoints. The family couldn't decide for itself what to grow on the land; nor could it sell any of these crops on its own.

This new household contract system succeeded very well in our team. After handing in the team's grain quota, we still had left over for ourselves what previously would have been a whole year's grain production.

In 1980, my dad's friend in the county capital told my brother about yet a newer system of distributing fields [fentian] to each family and then letting them grow and sell crops all on their own. He told my brother that the new system had the support of top national leaders. My brother figured that our family could do even better under that system, so he called a team committee meeting. He told them that this new system of dividing the land was like Liu Shaoqi's baochan dao hu system of the early 1960s and that we would all gain financially from the switch. He said, ''We still can't eat as well as we'd like to, so why not go ahead with it?'' Since everyone in the team, including these four weaker families, had done well through his previous advice, they all said fine. We secretly divided the fields and other team assets before the New Year's of 1981. We were the first team in the district to take this step.

Like other places where the new system was being tried, the amount of land that each household received was determined partly on the basis of how many family members it had and partly on the basis of how many of these were able-bodied laborers. Moreover, to assure a fair distribution of land, every family received a fixed proportion of its share in good land, a fixed proportion in medium-grade land, and a fixed proportion in hilly land. To further ensure fairness, we held an open lottery to designate which families would be allotted which specific plots. Land distribution was too important to ever let any of the cadres get away with any cheating, and all of the cadres realized that.

As its share of good land, my brother's family received 4.8 mu [.8 acre] of rice-paddy fields. Along with the land, all the equipment that the team owned was distributed free of charge to the households. The team owned a lot of plow oxen, since there's grazing land on some of the hills—enough oxen to give one to every household. The team owned an old tractor, but with the fields divided it was near-useless, and everyone agreed it was best to let the old machine rust.

Under this new system, the yields increased yet again. With multiple cropping, my brother's family, in fact, is able to coax almost twice as much from his paddy fields as the team had been able to when we had collective production. With the help of all the family members, he gets by far the highest yields in the village. For the village as a whole, crop yields have increased by close to a quarter.

About half of our crop has to be sold to the state at the low price of 19.6 yuan per 100 kilos, as our family's share of the team's grain quota. But there's enough grain left over so that the family can now raise two breeding sows and four meat pigs, and on top of that fifty–sixty chickens. But because chicken is such an expensive meat in China, twice the price of pork, my brother is only willing to eat chicken when one of the flock gets sick and dies, or at New Year's, or when a very important guest arrives. Even though our village has become prosperous, diets there remain really frugal. The peasants in our area are like that.

Under that first, earlier system of household responsibility, when we still used workpoints to pay families, most of the families spontaneously had begun working the fields in small groups with other families. This cooperation almost always was among households that were closely related. Most of the families in the team are named Lin, and each of the five lineage branches of the Lin clan became a separate cooperating group. It was almost like pooling the land; nobody cared whose fields were tilled first and whose fields last. But once we shifted to the newest type of family responsibility system, this type of cooperation all stopped. You see, once the fields were divided on a long-term basis among the families and you could sell the crops on your own, each family wanted their own fields worked first. We were all less willing to cooperate with relatives. The only families who still till their land together are the three Zheng brothers. They're the only people of Hakka origin in the team, and there's always been a tiny bit of discrimination against them. So they feel especially close to one another. We others prefer to concentrate first and foremost on our own family's interests. We'll work our own land first, and only then look around to see if relatives need any help. The pay for such help has been tacitly pegged at the workpoint values of 1976—just a yuan per day—plus food, so it's really like doing your labor-short relatives a favor.

My brother is a real entrepreneur, and under the agricultural system he's made a bundle. The family earned 3,000 yuan in 1981 and more than 5,000 yuan in 1982. He has been able to make a lot of this money from the team's timber forests. He made a bid to the team to rent a part of a mountain in order to sell wood from it. These mountains still belong to the team, and by central government regulation you can't privately fell any team-owned timber trees. But a team can decide to cut down for firewood any species of trees that can't be used for timber. Before, it didn't pay to fell these, but my brother found out that under the new liberalized policies he could hire cheap workhands from very poor villages in Hunan Province. He already had contacts with these villages. Even in the 1970s, you see, the government had allowed us to hire Hunan people to help bring in our harvests. Now, he discovered, we're tacitly permitted to employ them privately year-long as hired hands. So my brother brought in seven or eight of them as lumberjacks, and pays them piecerate at 0.6 yuan per hundred kilos. He then sells the cords at 3.2 yuan per hundred kilos at the county capital, for a very nice profit. Most of the other folks in the team don't know how to find outlets for the wood, unlike my brother, who has good "connections" in town. So bidding for a mountain doesn't necessarily pay off for them.

All of the local industrial enterprises have been bid out for an annual fee to the highest bidders. Seven families, including my brother's and the three Zheng brothers, got together to make a successful bid for the team's small brick works. They agreed to pay 700 yuan to the team every year. Then they hired labor from Hunan Province to make the bricks and to cut the grass-fuel. We pay those Hunanese .02 yuan for every brick they make, then we turn around and sell the bricks at .05 yuan. It's been a good money-maker. So when another team in our brigade bid out its tile kiln, my brother jumped in and got a share in it too. He's still on the look-out for other investment opportunities.

On top of all his other income, my brother gets 100 yuan a month as team head. But he has very few duties, now that all the land is divided. Occasionally, there are meetings he's supposed to attend in the commune town or at brigade head-quarters. But if it's the agricultural busy season, he simply refuses to go. The brigade cadres have the same sort of priorities. None of them bother to stay at the brigade office, not even the public security chief.

Folks just want to concentrate on making money and improving their lifestyle. That's what people most aspire to these days. If you want to find a bride, it's easier if your family is prosperous. Where I come from, marriages are still arranged mostly through matchmakers, and until recently, people were most interested to find out from the matchmakers all about the other family's official class background and political standing. But not now; it's become a question of how much the family makes. Of course, if it's a matter of marrying a bride from a former landlord family, it's still good to be cautious—make sure their village is far away. And we're careful not only when it's a question of marriage. Though the documents from Beijing now say that there's no longer supposed to be any discrimination against the former landlords, we've gone through so many class-struggle political campaigns in recent decades that most folks are still afraid even to be friendly with such people. We fear the policies might just change again, and that we'd then be accused of friendships with class enemies.* People don't yet entirely trust that the government's new policies are here to stay.

Still, we're not really sure that the new economic policies won't be reversed. In fact, when the government publicly announced that it was okay to divide up all the land among the households, we were never told how long families would be able to keep the plots of land. Folks say, you *never* know what the future holds; the Communist Party always changes its mind. So the peasants feel, "I'd better make my money now, while the going is good." And they're careful about keeping their profits secure. For example, my brother won't put any of his money in the bank. He's afraid the government might later ask, how'd you make this money?

---

*Among the twenty-seven other interviewees, very few reported such fears. The majority claimed that in their own villages, once the government no longer supported the discrimination against bad class families, the various social distinctions that weighed against such households rapidly disap-peared.—J.U.

and take it away. Instead, he's put his money into new houses for his sons, all in a row, attached to his own house. He built five in 1981. He was already planning for the post-wedding situation of his sons, even though his eldest son was only three years old at the time.

Having sons is of central concern to everyone. In 1979, I had just married, and I heard that family planning would be enforced, so we rushed to have a kid that year. We wanted as many as possible. I've got three now, all sons, I'm glad to say. The penalties for having additional kids keep growing. In the countryside today, having a second child is okay—though if the first is a son, the authorities grouse about your having the second. The fine for the third is now 700 yuan, *if* your wife succeeds in giving birth. Starting in 1983, if the commune authorities catch up with a pregnant woman who already has two kids, they'll force her into an abortion. So the women hide in the fields at night, or hide out in the inner room of a relative's house, or run off to stay with someone in the city until they have the child. My brother is determined to have extra sons, and he feels he can afford the fines. His wife is now in her sixth month of pregnancy, playing hide-n-seek with the officialdom.

71

PLA RECRUITMENT IN RURAL FUJIAN: AN INTERVIEW

The following interview is part of a series conducted during the summer of 1982 in Hong Kong with a former brigade deputy leader from Fuqing County, Fujian. In 1980, his coastal village was composed of 12 production teams, or 1,300 people. By 1978–79, they had begun implementing variants of household contracting. Although the interviewee left Fujian in 1980, he makes frequent trips back to Fuqing County to visit his village.

One of the consequences of implementing the new "responsibility system" in agriculture was to make farming and other rural occupations more attractive. Peasants could earn much more than before and sometimes resisted sending their sons off to "waste" several years in the army.

IN OUR VILLAGE, PLA recruitment was usually carried out annually, at year's end. But this has varied over the years. In 1968 and 1969, under Lin Biao, recruitment was carried out twice a year. In 1970, only once, and

Interview by John Burns, 1982.

in 1971, there was no recruitment in our village at all. Then twice in 1972, once each in 1973–1974, twice in 1975, and once each in the years 1976 to 1979. Higher levels made the decision.

After 1978, peasants were not eager to enter the PLA. From this time onward, officers [in the PLA] were recruited from officer schools, and ordinary peasant recruits had no chance of being promoted to officer rank. Before 1978, ordinary soldiers had a chance to be promoted to become officers. Since 1978, peasants could only sign up for three-year hitches. This was unpopular, a waste of time because peasants saw that they would just be sent back to the countryside after the three years. Peasants always have the idea of leaving the countryside.

In 1979, as previously, when the central documents [relating to PLA conscription] arrived in the county, authorities set up a temporary conscription office [*bangongshi*]. They called a meeting of commune representatives, usually commune Party secretaries and military/security officials of the Party committee in the commune, and gave quotas of males to be recruited to each commune. (Women now enter the PLA through urban middle schools.)

These commune officials then called a meeting of brigade representatives. In our brigade these included me, our Party secretary, the militia [*minbing*] leader, the women's federation representative, the poor and lower-middle peasant association head, and the brigade clerk [*wentou*]. We brigade officials came to the commune temporary conscription office with a list of peasants, arranged by age (those seventeen to twenty-two years old), and class background. There were usually fifty to seventy vacancies for the whole commune in any one recruitment year. [This averaged about three vacancies per brigade in this commune.]

We brigade officials then read out the list of eligibles at a village mass meeting and asked these village youth to attend a special meeting with us. In our village there would be fifty to sixty males in this group of eligibles in any one year. We would ask them to volunteer [*baoming*], and, in years past, up to two-thirds of them would do so. We then sent to the commune a list of these thirty or so volunteers. A PLA doctor gave the volunteers a thorough physical examination, which in the past six or seven would pass (never more than ten). Prior to 1978, the commune sometimes couldn't fill the quota of fifty to sixty recruits owing to the poor health of local youth. We brigade officials would examine the political background of those who passed the physical exam, and if this was satisfactory we'd decide which ones should sign up.

In 1978, all the recruits wanted to join the army. But after 1978, they were mostly unwilling. Of course, some still were willing, especially those middle school graduates who could not get into university. This was a chance to escape the countryside. Still, sometimes the parents disapproved. Peasants said that sending a son off to the army would reduce their labor power, thus reducing their income. We would try to persuade them, pointing out that we would help the family if it got into difficulties. Fiancees of some recruits also sometimes disapproved. They didn't want their future husbands going off to be soldiers just as they were about to get married. We'd urge them to wait a bit. We'd point out that demobilized soldiers can be cadres, and isn't that good?

In 1979, there was only one suitable candidate, but he refused to go no matter how hard we persuaded him. The commune military/security official went to his house to persuade him to go. But the father and son each blamed the other. The father would way, "It's ok with me, just ask my son." The son would say the same. In 1979, only one person had passed all the tests, but fewer people volunteered then and in 1980. He wouldn't go to the mobilization meeting, claiming that the family needed the labor power at home. The result was that our village sent no one that year. The commune authorities criticized us for this, but there was little else they could do.

FURTHER READINGS

Burns, John P. "Local Cadre Accommodation to the 'Responsibility System' in Rural China." *Pacific Affairs* 58:4 (Winter 1985–86).

Chan, Anita, Richard Madsen, and Jonathan Unger. *Chen Village: The Recent History of a Peasant Community in Mao's China.* Berkeley: University of California Press, 1984.

Domes, Jurgen. "New Policies in the Communes: Notes on Rural Societal Structures in China, 1976-1981." *Journal of Asian Studies* 41:2 (February 1982).

Johnson, Graham. "The Production Responsibility System in Chinese Agriculture: Some Examples from Guangdong." *Pacific Affairs* 55 (1983), pp. 430-451.

Lardy, Nicholas. *Agriculture in China's Modern Economic Development.* Cambridge: Cambridge University Press, 1983.

Leeming, Frank. *Rural China Today.* New York: Longman, 1985.

Madsen, Richard. *Morality and Power in a Chinese Village.* Berkeley: University of California Press, 1984.

Mosher, Steven. *Broken Earth: The Rural Chinese.* New York: Free Press, 1983.

O'Leary, Greg, and Andrew Watson. "The Production Responsibility System and the Future of Collective Farming." *The Australian Journal of Chinese Affairs* No. 8 (1982), pp. 1-34.

Parish, William L., ed. *Chinese Rural Development: The Great Transformation.* Armonk, N.Y.: M. E. Sharpe, 1985.

Parish, William L., and Martin King Whyte. *Village and Family in Contemporary China.* Chicago: University of Chicago Press, 1978.

Perry, Elizabeth J., and Christine Wong, eds. *The Political Economy of Reform in Post-Mao China.* Cambridge, Mass.: Harvard University Press, 1985 (Part I, pp. 31-192).

Zweig, David. "Opposition to Change in Rural China: The System of Responsibility and People's Communes." *Asian Survey* 23:7 (July 1983).

Zweig, David. "Context and Content in Policy Implementation: Household Contracts in China, 1977-1983." In David M. Lampton, ed. *Policy Implementation in Post-Mao China.* Berkeley: University of California Press, forthcoming.

D. Education

AT FIRST GLANCE it might appear that the conflicts over educational policy that are revealed in the documents in this section have already been settled. On May 27, 1985, the Central Committee of the CCP issued the long-anticipated "Decision on Reform of the Educational System."[1] This Decision is meant to provide the basic guidelines for educational policy into the early twenty-first century. In many respects, however, the Central Committee document either ratified or extended familiar policies already in place; the most contentious issues remain. The highlights of the May Decision include: (1) the granting of increased autonomy to colleges and universities in a wide variety of areas, such as student recruitment, foreign academic exchanges, curricula reform, administrative appointments, and scientific research; (2) the expansion of technical and vocational education, leading to a tighter linkage between the educational system and the job market; and (3) the gradual development of a nine-year compulsory education system, with the most economically developed areas (about 25 percent of the population) to complete the task by 1990, those areas of medium-level development (about 50 percent of the population) "to make preparations for popularizing general, vocational, and technical education at the junior middle school level by about 1995," and economically backward areas to do the best they can, as economic conditions allow.

In a real sense, however, the appearance of the Decision and the related structural changes of June 1985 can be considered at least as significant as the Decision's actual content. Transmitting the Party's views on education in the form of a Central Committee document conveys the message that the leadership sees educational reform as one of the determining factors in the modernization program. It visibly suggests that education ranks with industry and science and technology—two of the Four Modernizations—as top priorities, since these two policy arenas were previously granted similar widely publicized Central Committee decisions (industry in October 1984 and science and technology in March 1985). Equally important, the Ministry of Education was abolished in June and replaced by the State Education Commission. The minister chosen to head this new commission was Li Peng, at the time one of only four vice-premiers of the State Council and expected to rise even higher. It was no surprise when Li entered the Politburo and the Central Committee Secretariat in September 1985. Li lost no time in noting the advantages the new commission had over the old Ministry of Education, emphasizing the increase in scope and power and the strengthening of leadership. He has ordered every department, ministry, and commission to assign a leading official to educational work and to increase their funding for education every year. Moreover, the placement of someone with Li's economics background in a position usually assigned to officials with strong ties to the academic world may aid in solving one of the thorniest policy problems that has plagued the education sector: convincing finance cadres that an investment in education is productive rather than consumptive.

The educational reform package closely resonates to Deng Xiaoping's overall strategy of modernization. Deng's educational line includes the total negation of the reforms of the Cultural Revolution, the stress on science and technology as a productive force rather than as part of the superstructure, and the downgrading of the political and social functions of education. Congruent with the general approach of encouraging some elements of society and some areas of the country to advance more rapidly than others, the educational system is becoming essentially bifurcated. A small ''elite'' sector has been created to train the first-class scientists and engineers necessary to meet the ambitious targets of the Four Modernizations program. Alongside the elite sector is a large ''mass'' sector that is expected to provide basic educational skills, with the possibility of additional vocational training, for the majority. The elite sector is heavily supported by central government investment; the mass sector is greatly dependent on local government, collective, and individual funding.[2]

Given the nature of the policy conflicts revealed in this section, the new Decision on education is not likely to end debate. In fact, some of the defects cited in these readings are likely to be exacerbated under the new reforms. This is particularly true for the most contentious issue, one which has long divided Chinese educators, viz., finding an appropriate balance between quality and quantity. Selections 73–76 address this question most directly. The debate over ''key'' schools (Selections 73–74) has existed since these schools were set up in the 1950s. Designed to train the nation's best talents as rapidly as possible, these designated schools are found at every educational level and are provided extra funding, allocated the best teachers, and expected to recruit the most outstanding students. In the assault on educational inequality during the Cultural Revolution, the ''key system'' was rescinded. Restored in 1978, key schools, according to their supporters, have made a major contribution to the raising of educational standards. To its detractors, the system has many flaws, with the strongest criticism reserved for key primary and secondary schools. The most common objections have concentrated on the social and psychological consequences of such a system. A wide gap is created between the relatively few who can attend these schools and the many who cannot. Whereas the best of the key senior highs can send virtually 100 percent of their graduates to a university, many ordinary schools have difficulty producing anyone who is of university caliber. The psychological demoralization of the ''losers'' who are shut out of the key system contrasts starkly with the self-satisfaction of the "winners." (See Selection 13.) The increasing trend toward vocationalization at the secondary level—by 1990 the plan calls for 50 percent of all students at the senior high level to be in vocational or technical schools, compared with the 1984 figure of 32 percent and the 1977 figure of 4 percent—is expected to reduce significantly the present intense competition to gain university entrance. Whether vocational schooling can be made attractive to Chinese youth, however, remains to be seen. As the May Decision admitted, "the decadent idea that vocational and technical education is contemptible . . . is deep-rooted."

Selections 75 and 76 deal with several related questions. First, in the drive to realize the Four Modernizations, is it rational to allocate scarce investment dollars to education prior to the development of production? For many economists an investment in education is seen as "nonproductive," but educators argue that economic construction can move ahead rapidly *only* on the basis of educational progress. While they agree that investment in education must take priority, educators differ among themselves on *where* the investment should be placed and *who* shall foot the bill. Once again, are investment dollars better spent on the elite sector, particularly the university level, or should greatest stress be placed on building a system of compulsory mass education to eliminate illiteracy? What percentage of the funding should come from the state, particularly the central government, and how much should the masses bear directly?

Selections 77–81, despite a variety of contexts, are all concerned with the advantages certain groups have in the distribution of educational resources and/ or the relationship of education to employment. The vocationalization of education has faced problems, at least in part, because such schooling has proved unpopular with the very people it is meant to serve. In the countryside, where the peasants themselves must pay a large share of educational costs, this is particularly the case. Selection 77 argues that the major obstacle to the establishment of agricultural middle schools is not the peasants, but rather local Party and government officials, as well as local educational personnel, since their children are the only ones who can possibly "quit agriculture." Although this argument is perhaps only partially true—the children of local officials and educational personnel clearly are best placed to test into an urban university, but it does not necessarily follow that peasants prefer vocational to academic schooling—it provides an example of the central government's attempt to pressure the "rural elite" into giving up some of its advantages. Moreover, it reflects the regime's overall strategy of rural development, which cannot succeed unless it prevents the flight of talented personnel to the cities.

Selection 78, from a forum on the causes of the high dropout rate in the countryside, reveals one important reason for this phenomenon. With many jobs at the discretion of local leaders, the linkage between educational level and employment prospects is at times tenuous. Selection 79 is an example of a common phenomenon: the difficulties women have in competing with men for schooling, employment, and so forth. In fact, despite the press campaign against the mistreatment of women and the more active role currently being taken by the Women's Federation, a number of Western scholars have argued that Deng's modernization program has already led to a decline in the independence of women.[3]

Selection 80 shows how the "privatization" of education—which includes the expansion of university places for those who have not passed the national entrance examination but can obtain outside funding, as well as the establishment of private schools—is likely to benefit further the children of cadres and intellectuals, who already are very much favored under the current system. As the national entrance examination becomes less important in choosing university students, the opportunities for the use of "connections" (*guanxi*) seems certain to increase. Selection 81 reveals how the low status of teacher training institutes and the dearth of educated personnel in China's backward areas combine to limit the number of qualified teachers at the basic level. Despite recent directives forbidding the transfer of teaching personnel to other lines of work, and the granting of free tuition, room, and board to students of teachers' colleges, the more open labor mobility market being created by the new economic reforms should make it difficult to solve this particular problem•

Notes

1. FBIS Daily Report, May 30, 1985, pp. K1–K11 (NCNA, May 28, 1985).

2. Stanley Rosen, "Recentralization, Decentralization and Rationalization: Deng Xiaoping's Bifurcated Educational Policy," *Modern China* 11:3 (July 1985), pp. 301–346.

3. For example, Margery Wolf, *Revolution Postponed* (Stanford: Stanford University Press, 1984); Beverly Hooper, "China's Modernization: Are Young Women Going to Lose Out?" *Modern China* 10:3 (July 1984), pp. 317–343; Elisabeth Croll, "Chinese Women: Losing Ground," *Inside Asia*, February–March 1985, pp. 40–41.

72

Wang Zhixin

EDUCATIONAL WORK NEEDS TO OVERCOME A HARMFUL TENDENCY

OVER A LONG period of time our educational work has been affected by a harmful tendency, namely, laying lopsided emphasis on promotion rate. The practice deviates from the educational policy of the Party and is detrimental to our endeavor to educate and bring up the entire younger generation. This tendency, according to my recent investigation in a number of places, has not been effectively reversed.

Affected by this tendency, some localities have overemphasized the key schools to the neglect of schools in general, which, in turn, concentrate their efforts on "key classes" at the expense of the majority of ordinary classes. Some schools have even gone so far as to conduct year after year the so-called "bake-again classes" to retain at school students who have failed in the college entrance examination but still have had fairly high test scores for "bake again" lessons, thus reducing the chances of admission into colleges and universities of graduates of the current year. It is the opinion of the masses that key schools have pooled together the teachers who are most proficient and students that have the highest test scores. They get the most investment and the best equipment and therefore have the highest promotion rate. The ordinary middle schools, though in the majority, can only have a handful of their graduates pass the entrance examination, and some of them even have "their heads shaved clean" (that is, none of their graduates have been admitted into institutions of higher education). This seriously dampens the initiative of teachers and students in ordinary schools.

Of course, it should have been a correct leadership method to direct more effort to running a number of key schools with success so that they could produce (good) experience, (good) teaching material, and (good) teachers to bring along the ordinary schools to improve and move forward together. But the problem now is that many localities are arbitrarily creating key schools. In the words of the masses, "The key schools are overemphasized and the ordinary schools belittled." The experience of the key schools is too expensive for the ordinary schools to imitate, thus distancing the former from the latter. Under such circumstances, the key schools lose their significance even though they have a high promotion rate.

Because of the lopsided emphasis on promotion rate, the division of those majoring in humanities and those in science courses begins in the first year of senior high school in some places. Those who major in humanities are exempted

"Jiaoyu gongzuo yao kefu yige youhai qingxiang." *Renmin ribao* [People's Daily], March 12, 1983, p. 3. Translation from *Chinese Education* 17:2 (Summer 1984), pp. 122–125.

from taking physics and chemistry, and those who major in science courses, geography and history. What is more, quite a few schools even remove from their curricula such courses as music, painting, and physical culture, for they are not included in the entrance examination. (Of course, it is another matter if no qualified teachers for these subjects are available.) Thus, the cultivation of students centers around the entrance examination rather than the training of high quality, talented people. Education in the elementary and secondary schools is designed to lay a groundwork for the students. If they are not required to study geography and history, how can they be educated in patriotism?

Owing to the lopsided emphasis on promotion rate, many places do not give lessons according to syllabi starting from Grade Four in elementary schools (the five-year program) and Grade Two in junior and senior high schools, especially in the graduating classes. Willfully they chop off the contents of regular textbooks by chapters and sections and cram the students instead with a variety of ''reference materials,'' ''test papers for knowledge inspection,'' etc. They assign to the students an excessive amount of homework and frequently give tests and examinations, forcing the students to mechanically memorize everything they learn. Confused and disoriented, the students are completely exhausted.

Also owing to the lopsided emphasis on promotion rate, many schools cut short their summer and winter vactions for students of the graduating class; they force the students to give up Sunday (as a holiday), exempt them from doing physical labor, and stop their recreational activities. They seldom organize such events as visiting factories, field trips to the countryside, social investigations, spring outings, camping, etc. It is even more difficult for the League and Young Pioneer organizations whose function is to conduct communist education among the youngsters to carry out their activities and play their role.

Students brought up in the above manner are dull of thinking, narrow in their field of vision, unclear about the purpose of study, and lacking in the spirit of collectivism. Their studies only cover a small range of knowledge; what they have learned is unsystematic and insubstantial, still less applicable. And the students' health also suffers. In some places as many as 38 percent of the candidates who sat in the college entrance examination last year were nearsighted, and the ratio was even higher in the cities. A lot of college teachers are of the opinion: ''Some students got high scores in the entrance examination, but they cannot retain their drive and lack a solid foundation in basic knowledge. We have to offer them make-up lessons in Chinese grammar after they enter the college.'' Obviously, the practice of laying lopsided emphasis on promotion rate is detrimental to an all-round development of the younger generation and impedes the progress of the entire educational undertaking.

A myriad of factors account for the lopsided emphasis on promotion rate. It is not only a problem of educational thinking but also involves to a large extent the educational system and the system of employment and labor. Therefore the main responsibility does not rest with the teachers. Some local authorities set the targets for promotion from the top to the grass-roots level, and some even make public the name list of schools in the order of their promotion rates; they regard the promotion rate as the sole criterion to judge the quality of education. And some parents blame the school and the teacher for their children's failure to pass the college entrance examination. Therefore, in reversing the tendency of laying lopsided emphasis on promotion rate, we must repeatedly educate the whole Party and the broad masses of the people in the Party's educational policy and hold discussions on the purpose of elementary and secondary education so that all of us can truly understand the dialectical relationship among moral education, intellectual development, and physical training; direct our attention to the students as a whole; and make solid efforts to improve elementary education. We educators and teachers in vast numbers should acquire a good grasp of the law of education, execute the teaching plan, and teach every course successfully.

73

KEY ELEMENTARY AND SECONDARY SCHOOLS SHOULD NOT BE ABOLISHED

Letter from a Member of the Jilin Provincial Education Bureau

OF LATE, NEWSPAPERS and radio stations at both central and local levels have aired different opinions over the issue of key elementary and secondary schools. Some newspapers carried articles that concentrated on the "drawbacks" in running key schools and demanded that they be abolished so as to "let all elementary and secondary schools compete." As a pedagogic study and discussion, the move was beyond reproach. According to the report of some newspapers, however, a few provinces and municipalities even went so far as to declare the abolition of key elementary schools and the method of having key middle schools enroll the better qualified students. As we all know, it was Vice-Chairman Deng who first proposed that key elementary and secondary schools be run after the smashing of the "Gang of Four." For this purpose the Ministry of Education convened a special conference, issued relevant documents, and has not yet made any decision concerning the abolition of the key school system. Under such circumstances, publishing in the newspaper the decision to abolish key schools has thrown people into confusion. Some people called or wrote to demand that the educational departments quickly declare the abolition of key

Zhang Shuhan, "Buneng quxiao zhongdian zhongxiaoxue." *Renmin jiaoyu* [People's Education], No. 1 (January 1982), pp. 32–33. Translation from *Chinese Education* 17:2 (Summer 1984), pp. 96–99.

FROM MIDDLE SCHOOL STUDENT TO UNIVERSITY STUDENT

Cong zhongxue sheng dao daxue sheng, by Dai Xingde and Wang Hui

Source: Zhongguo qingnian bao [China Youth News], June 21, 1983, p. 4.

University entrance is highly desired by youths and their families. In part owing to a traditional respect for learning, state policy has greatly enhanced the value of higher education by virtually guaranteeing a good job to graduates. Those who do not make it to the university are not assigned jobs by the state. This cartoon depicts the arrogance of those who gain university entrance and the willingness of their parents to spoil them.

schools, and some schools of non-key status asked for backbone teachers from key schools. There were also people who even considered a redistribution of the facilities owned by key schools. Thus a tension has been arbitrarily created between society and the educational departments, and between key schools and schools of non-key status. And the teaching order in many schools has been affected. All this undermines stability and unity and hampers the readjustment of educational undertakings. Personally, I believe our current endeavor to run key elementary and secondary schools indeed involves quite a few problems, and conscientious efforts should be made to address them. However, all this boils down to a question of how experience should be summed up and how further efforts can be made in order to run the key schools better; under no circumstances should we thereby arrive at a conclusion that key schools should be abolished. This is because:

First, China is now in the stage of readjusting its national economy, and it is impossible for the state to increase its educational spending all of a sudden, especially since the "Gang of Four's" sabotage has seriously sapped the vitality of our educational undertakings. Over the last ten years, appropriations to the elementary and secondary schools in our province have not been made in the full amount. Only 25 percent of middle school teachers now on the payroll are up to the job, and only 35 percent of the elementary school teachers are competent. This being the case, it would be better to properly muster a part of the limited manpower, financial, and material resources for the advancement of a portion of the schools. Otherwise, if we were to spread the resources evenly among all schools, then none of them could make progress. Furthermore, if the key schools can move forward, they will bring along other, ordinary schools in improving their educational quality. This is why we say running key schools is a matter of strategic significance. With regard to whether we should call them key schools, central schools, or experimental schools, it is only a question of form and not essence. Right now work in the schools has been put on the right track, and readjustment of educational undertakings is being made in a planned way. What is needed is continued stability, and it is also better to keep the educational policies steady. Some problems in educational work should be studied carefully, and major changes should start with pilot projects and then gradually be put into practice. Under no circumstances should we issue an order in the morning and rescind it in the evening.

Second, the crucial problem of elementary and secondary education at present lies in the ideology of running schools. If the key schools are not operated under a correct ideology but focus their efforts on a few "topnotch" students, they will not necessarily have a good performance. On the contrary, an ordinary school, if operated under a correct ideology and in accordance with the laws of education, may perform better than the key ones. Shuguang Road Elementary School in Nanguan District, Changchun Municipality of our province, is an ordinary school, but its students' qualification rate in the graduation examination tops all other schools of the municipality. This serves as a good example. It is natural for the various schools to differ from each other in terms of school facilities, teacher quality, and student capacity. Behind the differences are a host of factors, both social and historical. Leading departments at all levels and the mass media should look squarely at such an objective fact and encourage the elementary and secondary schools to proceed from their respective realities and make great efforts to move ahead so as to train more qualified personnel for the Four Modernizations program. They should not advocate the practice of arbitrarily bringing everyone to the same level and abolishing the key school system. Simply abolishing the key schools cannot resolve the current problems regarding school operation.

Third, the state is focusing its efforts on making elementary education, and not

THE REWARD

Jiangli, by Zhai Xin, fifteen years old, from
Guiyang No. 9 Middle School, Guizhou Province

Source: *Zhongxue sheng* [Middle School Student], No. 3 (March 1983), p. 81.

A wry view, from a middle school student, of parents training their children to
perform well by offering monetary incentives.

junior high education, universal. As far as our province is concerned, graduates
of urban elementary schools, in fact, have all been admitted into junior middle
schools. Judging from the planning of educational undertakings, however, we can
enroll all the graduates into junior middle schools but are unable to solve the
problem of distributing them evenly. Some residential areas in Changchun have a
population of several hundred thousand but do not have junior middle schools.
This has created an impassable barrier to the policy of assigning elementary
school graduates to middle schools according to the zones where they live. The
heart of the issue is still whether or not the school can proceed from reality, make
down-to-earth efforts to improve its educational quality, and truly implement the
Party's educational policy.

Five years have elapsed since the smashing of the "Gang of Four." Led by the
Party Central Committee and governments at all levels, the educational front has
made fairly rapid progress in the work of rehabilitation and consolidation during
the period, especially since the Third Plenum. In the course of forward movement, some problems have cropped up that we cannot ignore. It is the unshirkable
duty of the educational departments to solve them. Nevertheless, some of them
are not problems of education itself. For example, confronting the young students

is the problem of employment. It is a matter of education and also a social issue. Aside from enrollment into institutions of higher education, the middle school graduates all have to wait for job assignments. With thousands upon thousands of people trying to squeeze their way through a single-plank bridge, how can they be expected not to compete with each other for admission into colleges and universities? We must analyze in a realistic way the numerous causes for the problem. We should not simply lay blame on the schools or try to find a way out by abolishing the key schools. Rather, we should broaden our field of vision and try to figure out some fundamental solution to the problem. In my opinion, the two educational systems and two work systems proposed by Comrade Liu Shaoqi previously still bear immediate significance today; they are the fundamental method to solve the problem. The educational departments should prepare the young students for job assignments in terms of syllabus, teaching materials, and school system. More importantly, the whole Party and society must pay attention to the structural reform of secondary education to bring the educational system in line with the employment system. Only by doing so can problems involving general education be solved.

74

ACCELERATE THE BUILDING OF KEY UNIVERSITIES

[*Renmin ribao* Editor's Note] The June 9 issue of *Zhongguo jiaoyu bao* [China Education News] published a suggestion, under the joint signature of Kuang Yaming, honorary president of Nanjing University; Liu Dan, honorary president of Zhejiang University; Li Shusen, honorary president of Tianjin University; and Qu Bochuan, honorary president of Dalian Engineering College, to accelerate the building of a group of key universities. The following is a summary of the article.

THE CHARACTERISTIC OF modern scientific and technological development is the high degree of specialization and the comprehensiveness of the subjects of study. Almost all the famous institutions of higher learning in the world are multi-subject universities. China's higher institutions are mainly divided into liberal arts and science universities, multi-subject engineering colleges, and single subject colleges. Looked at today, such a setup is not completely compatible with the laws of scientific and technological progress and the developmental tendency of higher education, or the most effective and

Renmin ribao [People's Daily], June 11, 1983, p. 1. Translation from JPRS 84047, August 4, 1983, pp. 5–6.

economical way to train personnel.

China's higher institutions today are growing more comprehensive and multi-subject in nature. This development takes three forms: (1) Adding some science and a few liberal arts majors, the multi-subject engineering colleges are developing toward multi-subject universities (with some special emphases), such as Qinghua University, Central China Engineering College, Shanghai Jiaotong University, Tianjin University, and Dalian Engineering College. (2) Moving toward integration, some universities are launching interschool cooperative activities. Zhejiang, Hangzhou, Zhejiang Agricultural and Zhejiang Medical Universities, for instance, have formed an interschool cooperation committee, preparing to integrate. (3) Some new universities, such as Xizang University, are multi-subject universities. This tendency is favorable to accelerating the development of higher education and training high-level personnel and is compatible with the developmental laws of science and technology and higher education, and should be affirmed and encouraged.

It is suggested that among the 700-plus universities throughout the country, several dozen large ones with good foundations, strong faculties, superior teaching qualities, a high scientific research level, and the capacity to train high-quality Master's and Ph.D. candidates as well as undergraduates, be selected as the strategic focuses in the building of higher education and be listed among the key construction projects of the state. With additional investments, more school buildings, and more books and modern equipment, these schools will be propelled to expand their recruitment of undergraduate and graduate students and to launch scientific research work. It is estimated that, in the 7 or 8 years before 1990, these universities will be able to train, in all fields, several hundred thousand high-quality undergraduates, tens of thousands of Master's candidates, and several thousand Ph.D. candidates and to cultivate numerous professorial-level leading scholars of all kinds. This will not only provide personnel for the economic construction of the 1990s, but will also supply qualified teachers to other higher institutions in the country and lay a solid foundation for the development of China's higher education as a whole.

75

Fei Xiaotong

CLOSE ATTENTION SHOULD BE PAID TO THE DEVELOPMENT OF INTELLECTUAL RESOURCES

I HEARTILY SUPPORT Premier Zhao [Ziyang]'s statement on developing education, science, and culture in his government work report at the

Renmin ribao [People's Daily], June 25, 1983, Translation from JPRS 83966, July 25, 1983, pp. 19–21.

First Session of the Sixth National People's Congress. He exhorted us: "Close attention should be paid to the development of intellectual resources in the future." He also said that education and science constitute a necessary prerequisite for the economic upsurge. He called on us to go all out to enhance the people's scientific and cultural level, ideological consciousness, and moral standards, which all constitute a strong motive force for socio-economic development as a whole and for the building of socialist material and spiritual civilization.

I, and all the comrades in the group I belong to, eagerly hope that a solid foundation for the development of intellectual resources will be laid within the tenure of the current Chinese People's Political Consultative Conference. In order to realize this desire, we hold that we must grasp two vital points: (1) increase intellectual investment; and (2) effect compulsory elementary education.

Intellectual investment provides material conditions for developing intellectual resources, and this calls for the state to place more money in undertakings for cultivating the people's intelligence, or to increase its educational spending. We deeply understand the fiscal difficulties of the government. However, we do not think that intellectual investment can be made only after surplus financial resources are achieved on the basis of economic prosperity. This idea does not conform to the proposition that intellectual investment constitutes a prerequisite for economic prosperity. Since it is a prerequisite, it should be given first priority. The problem is not whether we have the strength to increase intellectual investment but whether we have the determination to do so. In my opinion, conditions exist at present to allocate in the first place a proportion for educational spending when the state budget is drawn up. In other countries, educational spending generally accounts for over 15 percent of the state budget. In our country, in 1982, educational spending only accounted for 10 percent. Can we say that the reason why the proportion of educational spending cannot be increased is that proportions of investment in other fields are to be fixed up first, and that no sufficient room can be left for education?

Many of our comrades understand the difficulties of the department in charge of financial affairs. Some of them have even suggested issuing education bonds. We believe that the people throughout the country are willing to further tighten their belts for the purpose of providing better education for their children. This is a fine tradition of our Chinese nation—parents are willing to work hard like oxen and horses for better educational conditions for their children.

According to the last census, people who are illiterate and semi-illiterate throughout the country total more than 235 million. That is to say, almost one out of every four people in our population cannot read and write, or cannot do so well. What a startling figure this is! It also lays bare the serious trauma caused by the ten years of turmoil. We must have a spirit of sleeping on brushwood and tasting gall to remind ourselves every minute that we should not eat and sleep easily if this figure is not eliminated. We hold that on the one hand we should take immediate action to wipe out illiteracy, and on the other hand, we should resolutely effect compulsory elementary education.

| Beijing | Shanghai | Inner Mongolia | Tianjin | Xinjiang | Nanjing |

GRADUATION ASSIGNMENT

Biye fenpei, by Ma Conglan, Anhui Province

Source: Zhongguo qingnian bao [China Youth News], June 21, 1983, p. 4.

Students at China's best universities are recruited on the basis of one national, unified entrance examination and, theoretically, can be assigned anywhere in the nation upon graduation. Those assigned to the largest cities have the biggest smiles. Assignment to a more backward area like Inner Mongolia brings sorrow, while assignment to the distant province of Xinjiang brings tears.

The popularization of compulsory elementary education is clearly prescribed in Article 19 of the new Constitution we adopted last year, but we have not seen any concrete measures of this thus far. At present, more and more people have come to realize that modernization will not be possible if there are not sufficient scientific and technological personnel. But how can we rapidly train more professionally competent personnel? In our opinion, there must be a solid foundation for cultivating talented people, that is, a high cultural level of the people throughout the country. In a previous period, impetuosity seemed to exist with regard to the issue of cultivating able people. Therefore, attention was mainly paid to key schools and key classes. But practice has shown that key schools and classes cannot cultivate a large number of talented people; rather, they may greatly frustrate the enthusiasm for study of most students who cannot enter key schools and classes. This can be seen more clearly in the countryside. There, the number of "drifting students" is continuously increasing. The so-called "drifting students" refers to students who discontinue their schooling before graduation. They think they have no hope of entering secondary schools or universities, so they would rather have a job earlier. This is one of the reasons for the appearance of new illiteracy. We hold that attention should be paid to developing intellectual resources throughout the country rather than cultivating a small number of elites. The raising of standards should be based on popularization. The pressing matter of the moment is to effect compulsory elementary education as prescribed in the Constitution.

By compulsory education we mean that a law should be laid down stipulating that children throughout the country have the right to receive free elementary education and that all parents have the duty to send their children to school.

People who do not fulfill this duty must be punished. At present, all developed countries have established this system. We are determined to build ours into a socialist country with a high degree of civilization, so we must not allow ourselves to lag behind other countries in this field. We should also notice that there are only seventeen years from now to the year 2000. Results must be achieved within five to ten years rather than in a century. Otherwise, more difficulties will emerge in the modernization drive in future days.

It takes ten years to grow trees, but one hundred years to rear people. Increasing intellectual investment, eliminating illiteracy, and bringing about compulsory education all seem to require money, but in fact they are all of vital and lasting importance. We would rather live more frugally to ensure that future generations of our Chinese nation will have better and better education. Recently, I was glad to learn from press reports that leading comrades of the Party have realized the strategic importance of strengthening education. We who have been engaged in educational work for many years will of course do our utmost to work in our glorious posts so as to justify the trust and expectations of the Party and the people.

76a

Zhou Zuyou and Ma Li

CORRECT OUR GUIDING IDEOLOGY IN RUNNING RURAL SCHOOLS

An Investigation into the Structural Reform of Rural Secondary Education in Jinhua Prefecture

JINHUA PREFECTURE IS an area that got a head start on reforming rural secondary education over other places in Zhejiang Province. Within the prefecture it was Jiangshan County and Jinhua Municipality that moved ahead of others. Jiangshan County already has in place a variety of multi-level reform programs, including (1) the establishment of a new agricultural technology school run by the county with a first-year enrollment of 164 students; (2) the setting up of 8 senior high agricultural vocational training courses on the subjects of agricultural technology and forestry by 4 complete middle schools, half the number of complete middle schools run by the county; other senior high schools offer elective courses in agricultural vocational training; (3) the experimental

"Duanzheng nongcun banxuede zhidao sixiang." *Renmin ribao* [People's Daily], July 3, 1983, p. 3. Translated by Ai Ping.

establishment this year of agricultural vocational training courses in four junior middle schools with the expectation gradually to spread them to the 72 junior middle schools across the county in order to provide junior high graduates not admitted to senior high school an additional year of agricultural vocational and technological training; (4) the establishment of 12 agricultural junior middle schools to enroll higher primary school graduates so that they can learn a professional skill during their 3 years of study. In contrast, however, there are still quite a few counties in Jinhua Prefecture that proceed at a snail's pace, and their efforts to reform the structure of secondary education run into stiff resistance.

From the Expectation of "Quitting Agriculture" Switch to the Expectation of "Going in for Agriculture"

Some cadres and educational workers told us that the purpose of the peasants in sending their children to school was to get them admitted into college, and admission into college was for the purpose of quitting agriculture. This was the biggest single resistance, they asserted, that confronted the structural reform of secondary education and the endeavor to develop vocational and technological education.

Is it true? The answer is no.

When setting up the first county-run agricultural technological school in the whole prefecture, Jiangshan County was worried that no one would apply for the entrance examination. Contrary to their expectation, those who applied for the examination were ten times more than the number to be enrolled. Quite a few parents begged to have their children attend the school at their own expense. Chen Guixi, an old peasant of Shuangqikou Commune, had contracted to take care of the tea plantation owned by the production brigade. Because of that, he specially asked his eldest son, Chen Hongyan, to quit his job as a substitute teacher with a monthly income of 29 yuan in order to enroll in the tea training course offered by the agricultural technological school.

We also learned from teachers of Luodian Middle School of Jinhua Municipality that the local history of growing flowers goes back several hundred years. This spring Luodian Middle School began preparations for starting a training course specializing in flower growing. They heard that some parents were so worried about their children's opportunity for promotion to colleges that they could not sleep at night. After investigation, however, they found only two persons who were anxious about this: One was the deputy chief of the district and another was a primary school teacher. The school repeatedly solicited the opinions of the parents and students. It turned out that of the ninety-eight students who studied in the two Senior Grade One classes, thirty-nine signed up of their own accord for the flower growing course. After the semester began, there were also a number of students of the regular course who asked to be transferred to the specialized course.

We have also heard stories about parents sending their children to agricultural technological schools. Last spring, Ye Shaoquan, from a household of Jinhua Municipality specializing in raising dairy cows, sent at his own expense his eldest son, a senior high school graduate, to receive training at Shanghai No. 11 Animal Farm for two months. This spring he again sent his son to study at the animal husbandry course of the newly set up agricultural technical school run by the municipality. The peasants observed: ''In the past we sent our children to school in order to get them to quit agriculture and find other ways to make a living. Now when we send them to school, our purpose is for them to master technology and truly go in for agriculture so that production can be boosted, our families can get rich, and the country can become prosperous.''

Switching from the expectation of ''quitting agriculture'' to the expectation of truly ''going in for agriculture'' indicates a change in the peasants' understanding about rural education after the installation of the various forms of the production responsibility system in the countryside. It also represents the new demands peasants set on secondary education in the rural areas. Many commune members have the opinion that many graduates of regular high schools have three inadequacies upon their return to the countryside, namely: inadequacy in terms of their frame of mind, unwillingness to settle down to agricultural undertakings; inadequacy of knowledge, lack of agricultural technology, and inability to handle even such work as plant protection and accounting; inadequacy of physical strength, incapability of doing technological work or taking up jobs that are heavy and dirty. Therefore it is their urgent demand to reform the structure of rural secondary education. Of course, this does not mean there are absolutely no more people who desire to ''quit agriculture.'' However, the resistance to the reform in no way comes from the peasants as some comrades have alleged.

Where Does the Resistance Come From?

Then where does the resistance actually come from? It comes from the incorrect guiding thought of some of the Party and government cadres and educational workers in running the schools.

Laying lopsided emphasis on promotion rate has become a serious deviation. Typical of this is the situation in Dongyang County. In their pursuit of a higher promotion rate, they have over the last few years focused their attention on regular high schools. They directed great efforts to running senior high continuation schools to help senior high graduates who had failed the college entrance examination review their lessons and virtually neglected vocational education in agricultural technology. Ganqi Agricultural School, though listed as a key middle school of the whole province, was neglected by all authorities ranging from the provincial through the prefectural to the county level. The whole school did not have a single teacher who had graduated from an agricultural or forestry college, and the school had always vacillated in its direction. Comrades of Dongyang County remarked: ''The agricultural middle school has fallen apart under the pressure of seeking promotion rate.''

Responsible comrades of the county education department had this to say:

"With regard to the guiding thought of education, some leading cadres are not soberminded. On the one hand, they are seriously out of touch with realities in the countryside, lacking the knowledge of how educational efforts are related to the development of rural economy; on the other hand, they take a one-sided view of talent and use college admission as the sole criterion to judge people. Mistakenly, they regard those who pass the college entrance examination as talented and those who fail as untalented. Therefore, they desperately seek to raise their promotion rate."

The educational department of Quzhou Municipality formerly planned to have its thirteen districts each convert a middle school into an agricultural vocational school this year. But the Municipal Party Committee disagreed. Consequently only Dazhou District of the whole municipality was willing to convert one. Dongyang County was prepared to convert No. 2 Huqi Middle School into an agricultural vocational school, and they, too, met with the opposition of the Huqi District Party Committee and the commune Party committee. Up to now many localities still use the promotion rate as a gauge to evaluate the performance of a school in disregard of all other aspects. Some comrades believe that aside from mistaking the desire of a few for the wish of the majority, the reason these leading comrades behave themselves in such a way is mainly because they want to have their own children get admitted into college and then quit agriculture. Therefore, in making a success of the educational reform in rural areas we face the urgent task of straightening out the guiding thought of leading cadres at all levels and the educational departments in running schools.

76b

THE WILL OF THE "OFFICIALS" AND THE WILL OF THE MASSES

IT IS MAN'S social being that determines his thinking. Since the Third Plenum of the Eleventh Central Committee of the Party, the situation in the countryside has undergone a drastic change, and so have the peasants in the way they view and weigh certain things. Take, for example, the education of their children. In the past, the peasants expected their children to "study well" so that they might enter the city and "quit agriculture." Now things have changed: The peasants are willing to send their children to school at their own expense so that the children can learn agricultural science and technology and, after schooling,

" 'Guan' yi yu min yi." *Renmin ribao* [People's Daily], July 3, 1983. Translated by Ai Ping. This is a *People's Daily* comment on the preceding document.

can stay at home to start some ambitious projects. Investigation of Jinhua Prefecture in Zhejiang Province clearly indicates the peasants' intention at present.

Obviously, the structural reform of rural secondary education, in which a sizable number of regular middle schools will be converted to agricultural vocational middle schools, is a move that conforms to the prevailing trend and goes along with the will of the people. However, the work has run into obstructions at quite a few places. One excuse of the obstructors is the peasants do not like it. Investigation of Jinhua discloses the crux of the matter: It is actually some Party and government cadres in the countryside as well as comrades from the educational department who fall behind the peasants in outlook and it is they who intend to have their children "quit agriculture." This "official" will runs counter to the will of the people and should be quickly corrected so that it can catch up to the will of the people.

77

Shi Wen

IT IS NOT A RESPECTABLE THING TO RELY ON THE INFLUENCE OF ONE'S DAD

CURRENTLY IN THE countryside not only is it a common occurrence for high school students to drop out, but there are also a lot of children who do not go to school at all.

Why do the parents show no concern for the children's education and give them no support, and why do the students take no interest in studies? By talking many times with the students (including those who graduated and those who dropped out) as well as their parents, I find this is directly related to the fact that some places, when recruiting young professionals, do not judge a candidate by his own qualifications but by the influence of his dad.

In our place the newly recruited elementary school teachers and medical personnel are mostly the offspring and relatives of the commune cadres. And technical personnel newly recruited by the commune- and brigade-run businesses and institutions—including those of agriculture, agricultural machinery, forestry, animal husbandry, and sideline industries—are mostly the offspring and relatives of brigade cadres. Sometimes an examination is given, but it is not those better qualified but those having more influential fathers who are recruited. If this problem cannot be solved, the students' enthusiasm for study will certainly be

"Kao laozide quanshi bu guangcai. *Heilongjiang qingnian* [Heilongjiang Youth], 1982, No. 8, pp. 15–16. The author is with the Agricultural Machinery Section, Hailun County. Translated by Ai Ping.

affected. On seeing this, some commune members and their children develop the idea that it is of no use to have more studies. Consequently, more and more students drop out from the schools.

To solve the problem of rural high school students discontinuing their studies, I am convinced, it is imperative to stop the practice of judging a candidate for new recruitment not by his cultural qualification but by his dad's influence. It is suggested that the county government set up an examination commission for the recruitment of rural professional and technical personnel so as to ensure the quality of recruits in the countryside. It should establish dossiers to keep a record of the cadres' job performance, recruitment, and promotion, and to strengthen administration. Those who are found to be engaged in under the table deals or malpractice should be strictly punished in the same way as those who violate the college entrance examination system. Only by doing thus can people feel it is worthwhile to pursue studies.

78

WHY IS THE ENTRANCE EXAMINATION SCORE REQUIRED TO ENROLL IN WORKERS' TRAINING SCHOOLS HIGH FOR GIRLS AND LOW FOR BOYS?

A Group of Young Women in Jilin Wrote to This Newpaper to Express Their Doubts

Comrade Editor:

When reading the special column ''Oppose Discrimination against and Maltreatment of Women and Effectively Protect the Rights and Interests of Young Women'' that your newspaper has recently started, we young women here are all very pleased. Incidents of viewing men as superior to women and discriminating against young women now abound in society. Enclosed herewith is a ''Notice on Test Score Requirements for Admission to Technician

---

''Jigong xuexiao luqu fenshuxian weihe nü gao nan di.'' *Zhongguo qingnian bao* [China Youth News], April 12, 1983, p. 1. Translated by Ai Ping.

Schools in Jilin Province'' published on the advertisement page of *Jilin ribao* [Jilin Daily] on August 12 last year. As you can see, there is great disparity between the minimum test score requirements many municipalities and counties set for female and male candidates respectively. We do not deny the fact that some factories and types of work need to have more male workers. But using such widely different test score requirements as an excuse to shut out large numbers of young women is really something we cannot accept. It is hoped that you can publish the notice in your special column and let everyone have a look at this living example of viewing men as superior to women.

Sincerely,

A group of young women in Jilin

Notice on Test Score Requirements for Admission to Technician Schools in Jilin Province

The unified examination, grading, marking, and recording of scores of candidates for technician schools in our province has been successfully completed, and the admission process will begin toward the end of August. The Provincial Labor Bureau will make an overall arrangement for the admission work and implement the principle of conducting an all-round screening—morally, intellectually, and physically—and enrolling the better qualified. In compliance with policies and regulations, appropriate preferential treatment should be given to candidates with a minority background or from remote border areas, three-good students, outstanding student cadres, candidates with outstanding athletic records, young returned overseas Chinese, children of returned overseas Chinese, and youth with a Taiwan origin.

In light of the sizes of enrollment of different municipalities and counties, types of work and specialties, and test scores of the candidates, we have determined after study the minimum test score requirements for male and female candidates in various municipalities and counties as follows:

City or county	Minimum passing score	
	Male	Female
Changchun city	240	275
Jilin city	210	260
Yongji county	290	310
Huadian county	215	255
Siping city	200	280

(Continued)

	Minimum passing score	
City or county	Male	Female
Hunjiang city	265	260
Yanji city	270	295
Tumen city	260	240
Yanji county	235	250
Dunhua county	330	320
Liaoyuan city	215	295
Baicheng city	180	180
Qianguo county	220	280
Fuyu county	280	295
Tonghua city	190	230
Helong county	300	330
Antu county	280	320
Wangqing county	230	—
Hunchun county	270	280

Jilin Provincial Labor Bureau

[*China Youth News*] Editor's Comment:

The phenomenon pointed out in the letter written by a group of young women in Jilin is not confined to that province; it happens in other regions and units as well. It is a problem of a universal nature. Right now there is much unfair treatment of young women. They are discriminated against in the recruitment of new workers or the enrollment of new students, they are harassed in marriages and love affairs, and they are ill-treated when they give birth to girls, . . . If things continue this way, can a woman still maintain her own independent personality, rights, and social status? Therefore we must put a stop to the idea of viewing men as superior to women.

*   *   *

In the 1950s and 1960s we combated in the countryside the phenomenon of unequal pay for men and women doing equal work. Now the problem of discrimination against young women in school admission and job placement has surfaced in the cities. The same cause is probably at the root. Aside from ideological reasons, there can be, of course, some practical problems involved. For example, there are different types of work and different needs. People can appreciate this. But there are a lot of discriminatory cases arising from matters beyond the needs of types of work. For these cases we have no choice but to trace the root cause to ideology.

79

THE CHILDREN OF CADRES IN HENAN PROVINCE ATTEND COLLEGE COURSES "AT THEIR OWN EXPENSE"

Tuition Can Be Subsidized If You Have Connections

THE MAY 11 issue of *Henan ribao* [Henan Daily] carried a report by its reporter Chen Xun entitled "An Investigation of Children of Cadres Attending College Courses 'At Their Own Expense.' " According to the report, eight children of cadres from the Design Institute under the Henan Provincial Textile Department, having failed the 1983 college entrance examination, found their way into the Zhengzhou Institute of Light Industry through their connections. They enrolled "at their own expense" in the Machinery Specialty. The length of schooling was four years, and every student had to pay 1,700 yuan in tuition. Of this the student paid 600 yuan, and the balance was picked up by the Design Institute. During the rectification campaign, some comrades raised the question: "Can this be regarded as an unhealthy trend?" Others said: "By rectifying the Party work-style we mean that consolidation must be carried out side by side with reform. Whether they mean business this time depends on the action of the leading Party group of the Textile Department!" In compliance with the requirements set forth in the Party Central Committee's decision on the rectification campaign, the Party leading group of the Henan Provincial Textile Department conducted an investigation and found the reports of the masses to be true. The group immediately stated explicitly that all the tuition subsidized by the Design Institute should be reimbursed by the students' parents, regardless of whose children they were. Based on their different financial conditions, from 10 to 20 percent of their wages should be deducted every month for the reimbursement.

Chen's investigative report also noted that, judging from Henan Province, the number of college courses offered at the students' "own expense," instead of decreasing, has been on the rise since the State Council issued the rectification document. And it has aroused strong feelings among the broad ranks of the people. In 1980 the whole province had only 7 institutions of higher education that offered college courses at the students' "own expense." Right now there are altogether 14 colleges and universities offering such courses, and the enrollment has gone up from some 600 to more than 1,800 at present. The length of schooling

"Henan ganbu zinü shang 'zifei' dazhuan ban." *Baokan wenzhai* [Digest of Newspapers and Periodicals] (Shanghai), May 22, 1984, p. 1. Translated by Ai Ping.

varies from 2 to 5 years. And almost every course involves full-time studies. The reporter looked into the files of students attending the Zhengzhou Industrial Institute "at their own expense." Altogether 5 specialties enrolled 180 students, of whom 83 were children of the faculty and staff of the Institute itself and all others were the offspring of cadres of agencies directly affiliated with the provincial government and other units. One of the agencies subsidized as much as over 30,000 yuan for the tuition of 11 cadres' children attending the specialty of electrical engineering. This state of affairs has already posed a serious obstacle to the normal teaching in the Institute.

80

Xian Renqun

HOW IS IT THAT GRADUATES OF A TEACHER-TRAINING SCHOOL CAN BE ASSIGNED IN SUCH A WAY?

An Urgent Appeal

OURS IS ONE of the prefectures educationally most backward in Shandong Province, and we are seriously shorthanded in teaching staff. However, in the job assignment for graduates this year, a large number of the graduates from Dezhou Teachers Training School, the only teachers training institution in our prefecture, were transferred to other areas of work. This provokes extensive complaints from the rural areas, where teachers are urgently needed.

Among the graduates from Dezhou Teachers Training School majoring in language, ten were assigned to work for the Dezhou Prefectural Party Committee and the Dezhou Administrative Office, sixteen stayed in Dezhou to work for offices directly affiliated with the Prefectural Party Committee and for the city itself, and more than twenty went to other localities. What was actually left for the twelve counties under the prefecture were only some twenty graduates.

The Prefectural Party Committee and the Administrative Office contacted Dezhou Teachers Training School for recruits even before the students had graduated and asked the school to recommend outstanding students. Consequently, the students were active everywhere, trying in every possible way to get themselves transferred out of teaching, into other lines of work. Thus, students who were unable to get a transfer are not reconciled to teaching; still less are they willing to teach in the countryside.

"Zen neng zheyang fenpei shizhuan biye sheng." *Renmin ribao* [People's Daily], August 9, 1984, p. 7. Translated by Ai Ping.

Dezhou Teachers Training School is devoted to the training of teachers for Dezhou Prefecture. It is not right to transfer its graduates to other fields of work. We strongly demand that the departments concerned take action to correct these unreasonable job assignments so that graduates from the Teachers Training School who have been transferred to other areas can return to teaching.

Xian Renqun
Education Bureau, Dezhou Prefecture, Shandong Province

FURTHER READINGS

Bastid, Marianne. "Chinese Educational Policies in the 1980s and Economic Development." *The China Quarterly* No. 98 (June 1984), pp. 189–219

Chen, Theodore Hsi-en. *Chinese Education Since 1949: Academic and Revolutionary Models.* New York: Pergamon Press, 1981.

Chinese Education. Quarterly translation journal, published by M. E. Sharpe, Armonk, N.Y.

Comparative Education No. 1 (Spring 1984), special issue on Chinese education.

Hawkins, John N., ed. *Education and Social Change in the People's Republic of China.* New York: Praeger, 1983.

Hayhoe, Ruth, ed. *Contemporary Chinese Education.* Armonk, N.Y.: M. E. Sharpe, 1984.

Lo, Billie L. C. *Research Guide to Education in China After Mao, 1977–1981.* Hong Kong: Centre for Asian Studies, University of Hong Kong, 1983.

Pepper, Suzanne. "Education and Revolution: The 'Chinese Model' Revised." *Asian Survey* 18:9 (September 1978), pp. 847–890.

Pepper, Suzanne. *China's Universities.* Ann Arbor: Center for Chinese Studies, University of Michigan, 1984.

Rosen, Stanley. "Recentralization, Decentralization and Rationalization: Deng Xiaoping's Bifurcated Educational Policy." *Modern China* 11:3 (July 1985), pp. 301–346.

Unger, Jonathan. *Education Under Mao: Class and Competition in Canton Schools, 1960–1980.* New York: Columbia University Press, 1982.

E. Literature and Art

IT MIGHT SEEM odd at first to include a section on "culture" in what is essentially a reader for students of political science. However, as has been frequently noted, literature and art have long had a political function in China. As true in traditional and Maoist China as in post-Mao China, the cultural arena is used to wage political struggle, thus avoiding the disruption that would ensue were the struggle to be waged directly within the top leadership.[1] In contrast to the West, where the separation between literature and politics is commonly taken for granted, major pronouncements on literary policy in China often come from the country's top leaders. Nor should this apparent convergence between literary and political authority—which can be traced back to Confucian China—be seen merely as a standard feature of communist regimes. As Perry Link has observed, Russian leaders such as Khrushchev have seemed more willing than their Chinese counterparts to admit their lack of expertise in literary matters, thus accepting, to a certain extent, an autonomous sphere for literature.[2]

Because of this close association between literature and politics in China, shifting currents at the top of the political system are quickly manifested down below in the form of warm or cold "winds," indicating a tolerant or restrictive environment for writers and artists. It is important to realize that the relative stability of the post-Mao economic policies of the reformers—including the strong support given to scientists, engineers, and other technical intelligentsia—has not prevented unpredictable winds from repeatedly buffeting the cultural intelligentsia. One observer has counted eleven wind shifts from the death of Mao down to 1984.[3] Indeed, a recent speech on literature and art by Party Secretary-General Hu Yaobang confirmed that central leaders are well aware of the direct relationship between their words and the literary climate:

> Anything said by our central comrades now is likely to stir up a big wind. When things are put one way, some comrades are likely to say: "Ah, it is liberation. Liberation. Things can be fixed easily." When things are put another way, some comrades will say: "Ah, it is bad. It is tightening up controls. Tightening up controls. The situation is not good.". . . So we really do not dare to talk.[4]

The five selections in this section reveal the differing viewpoints of creative artists and conservative literary bureaucrats (Selections 82 and 83), the attempt of an editor of a key literary journal to influence the temperature of the wind (Selections 84 and 85), and the caution writers must exercise on controversial subjects, until they are given the proper cues from above (Selection 86). Viewed another way, they represent the different levels of literary politics. Selections 82 and 83 are concerned with policymaking at the top of the system, with setting the basic guidelines of literary freedom; within these guidelines, and subject to the support of local leaders, editors may exercise some influence on this process, limited though it might be. Selection 86 demonstrates the weakness of those on the bottom—the writers—who often must await the arrival of the winds wafting their way down these various levels before plying their trade.

Selections 82 and 83 can be seen as two entries in the perpetual conflict between individual artistic freedom and state-imposed artistic constraints. It is important to note both the *authorship* and the *timing* of these two documents. Selection 82 represents a deathbed plea by Zhao Dan, a famous and popular actor, admonishing the Party that "literature and art is the business of writers and artists," that it "has upon it the strong stamp of individuality," and that it "should not be and cannot be bound by restrictions." Zhao Dan's prominence as a pre-Liberation film actor, combined with his terminal illness, gave some weight to his criticism of Party control. Nevertheless, the publication and wide dissemination of his speech in the national press in October 1980, followed by a brief campaign against Party interference in creative activity, was only possible because the autumn of 1980 was a high tide for reform. Ironically, indeed inevitably, Zhao's call for the separation of art and politics was used *politically* by the Party reformers against their more conservative opponents.

Selection 83, on the other hand, is the product of a different mind and a different time. Written by a "Commentator," it does not reflect the views of an individual like Zhao Dan, but of an authoritative voice in the Party. By September 1983, the wind had shifted several times since Zhao's appeal. For writers and artists, winter had come early. Although the "spiritual pollution" campaign[5] began officially only in October, the head of the CCP's Propaganda Department, Deng Liqun, was already presenting speeches in September inveighing against the existence of such pollution in the ideological realm. Indeed, the specific references to Stalin's formulation that those who do political and ideological work are "engineers of the human soul" are a prominent feature in Deng's September speeches, in Selection 83, and in the subsequent rhetoric of the campaign. Thus, it seems reasonable to conclude that Deng had an important role in writing this commentary.[6] If Zhao Dan is appealing to the Party to ease its demands on writers, protesting that "we artists had always found the term 'system' alien," Deng Liqun is appealing to writers to "completely grasp the ideological system of Marxism."

Contention on this issue within the Party remains as visible as ever, as recent events have shown. The thermometer reached a record high at the Fourth Congress of the Chinese Writers' Association, which met from December 29, 1984, to January 5, 1985. Hu Qili, a member of the secretariat of the CCP Central Committee and widely regarded as a rising star, spoke on the relationship between the Party and the country's literature and art workers. Critical of past attempts to interfere with writers, Hu emphasized the importance of "freedom of creation" for such mental workers. As he put it, "writers must be able to think with their own minds and must have ample freedom to choose material, themes, and artistic methods and to express their own feelings, emotions, and thoughts. . . ."[7] The Party and state were enjoined to provide the necessary conditions to ensure such freedom.

This particular heat wave was interrupted by a sudden cooling trend. A nationwide congress of all literary and art workers—the first since 1979—had been planned for June 1985, but had to be postponed because of continued ideological skirmishing within the CCP. Once again, the link between art and politics was demonstrated. The Party reformers had been hoping to use the June meeting to show their political strength and gain momentum prior to a plenum of the Party Central Committee in September, at which major personnel changes were expected to be announced. The inclement political weather in June brought out Deng Liqun, who provided some embellishments to the freedom of creation concept. First, he pointed out that while writers can write what they please, publishing houses and editorial departments, representing the Party, can refuse to publish unacceptable works. Second, the writers themselves must avoid "distorted" concepts of freedom. They must understand the Marxist view of freedom, which is based on inexorable laws, and see the necessary link between freedom and discipline. To put things in perspective, it should be noted that Deng's address was presented to those involved in propaganda work in far off Sichuan Province and was published only in the provincial Party newspaper. Thus, although some clouds had appeared in the sky, the forecast did not necessarily include rain. In fact, only a month later, Deng was eased out as director of the Propaganda Department (although he remained in the Central Committee Secretariat).[8]

Selections 84 and 85 ostensibly are entries in a debate over the relative merits of a popular movie. It seems likely, however, that the publication of No. 84 should also be seen as an attempt by the leading journal of literary criticism—*Wenyi bao*—to mobilize support for a controversial film and to discredit conservative opposition to a more "liberalized" intellectual atmosphere. Originally a novella, the film—*At Middle Age* by Chen Rong—won several major awards upon release. The story concerns the trials and tribulations of China's middle-aged, hardworking intellectuals. Perhaps the clearest message is that the political demise of China's radicals has failed to improve the living and working conditions of intellectuals and that at least some among this dedicated group have strong doubts that the situation will improve. Even as a novella the story attracted its share of criticism, most notably for "spreading a dark cloud" over socialist life.[9] Such stories—*At Middle Age* is merely among the best-known and most highly regarded of a certain genre—inevitably have become part of a forty-year-old literary debate, dating back to Yan'an. Is the function of literature to "praise brightness" or "expose darkness"?[10]

The discussion of *At Middle Age* in *Wenyi bao* began in April and May 1983, with articles assessing the quality of the movie, primarily in terms of its faithfulness to the novella. Selection 84, by Xu Chunqiao, is a critique of an entirely different order; it "totally repudiates" the film. The editor's note preceding Xu's broadside points out the various prizes the film has won, makes it clear that Xu's article was unsolicited, and invites readers to comment on Xu's piece (rather than the movie). Predictably, the journal received many comments, with the one by Yan Gang (Selection 85) the only one published in full. Excerpts from twenty-one other articles were published over the next few months. An editor's note in August pointed out that *all* of the contributions received thus far criticized Xu's views. An editor's note in September, the final installment in the "debate," noted that Xu received support only from a tiny minority.[11]

It is worth noting that the use of "straw men" to expand the boundaries of tolerance is recorded elsewhere in this volume as well. The cartoon in the political socialization section entitled "Enough to Blow Your Hat Off" celebrates even more directly a similar incident. In May 1979, the widely circulated *Masses Cinema* printed on its back cover a color photograph of a Chinese actor and actress portraying Cinderella and her prince, kissing. In August, the editors printed a letter from a Party cadre in outlying Xinjiang Province who fumed: "A foreign poisonous weed is attacking the Party and Chairman Mao!" Reading like a self-parody of the deposed "Gang of Four," this letter drew a large volume of caustic rebuttal, enabling the magazine's editors to score a point for tolerance.[12]

Finally, Selection 86 reflects the caution of writers who find the new rich peasants the most exciting figures in the Chinese countryside. Recognizing the complexity—"half angel and half demon"—of these characters, they find it impossible to portray the Chinese countryside realistically without incorporating these currently uncategorizable elements into their stories. Writers, who have often been burned politically, want it to be clear that their topics are acceptable•

Notes

1. Merle Goldman, "Culture," in Steven M. Goldstein, ed., *China Briefing, 1984* (Boulder: Westview Press, 1985), pp. 21–36.

2. Perry Link, "Cultural Reform After Mao," paper presented at the conference "To Reform the Chinese Political Order," Harwichport, Massachusetts, June 18–23, 1984, pp. 45–46.

3. Link, "Cultural Reform," p. 57; for more detail on "winds," see Perry Link, ed., *Stubborn Weeds: Popular and Controversial Literature After the Cultural Revolution* (Bloomington: Indiana University Press, 1983), pp. 1–28.

4. Hu Yaobang, "On Some Questions Concerning Current Literature and Art Work—April 11, 1985," FBIS Daily Report, October 4, 1985, p. W1 (*Zhengming*, October 1985).

5. Deng Xiaoping defined spiritual pollution at the Second Plenum of the Twelfth Central Committee in October 1983 as "disseminating all varieties of corrupt and decadent ideologies of the bourgeoisie and other exploiting classes and disseminating sentiments of distrust toward the socialist and communist cause and to the Communist Party leadership." See Thomas B. Gold, " 'Just in Time!' China Battles Spiritual Pollution on

the Eve of 1984,'' *Asian Survey* 24:9 (September 1984), p. 952.

6. On Deng Liqun's role at this time, see Stuart Schram, '' 'Economics in Command?' Ideology and Policy Since the Third Plenum, 1978–84,'' *The China Quarterly* No. 99 (September 1984), pp. 437–448.

7. FBIS Daily Report, December 31, 1984, pp. K4–K6 (NCNA, December 29, 1984). Hu Qili entered the Politburo in September 1985.

8. FBIS Daily Report, June 7, 1985, pp. K1–K5 (*Sichuan ribao* [Sichuan Daily], May 26, 1985); *Los Angeles Times*, June 20, 1985, p. 25; *Far Eastern Economic Review*, July 25, 1985, pp. 12–13. The most recent crackdown on literary freedom was the ban on the publication of all books, magazines, and newspapers that are published without official government approval. The justification for the crackdown was provided by a widely published speech on ideology and culture by the same Hu Qili who had cheered China's writers with his comments a year earlier. See *Los Angeles Times*, January 20, 1986, pp. 1, 13.

9. Perry Link, ed., *Roses and Thorns: The Second Blooming of the Hundred Flowers in Chinese Fiction, 1979–80* (Berkeley: University of California Press, 1984), p. 262.

10. Anthony J. Kane, "Literary Politics in Post-Mao China," *Asian Survey* 21:7 (July 1981), pp. 775–794.

11. *Wenyi bao* (Literary News), April 1983 to September 1983.

12. Perry Link, *Stubborn Weeds*, p. 27.

81

Zhao Dan

WHEN CONTROL IS TOO TIGHT, THERE'S NO HOPE FOR LITERATURE AND ART

[Modern Chinese Literature *Editor's Note*] *China's renowned film actor Zhao Dan died on October 10, 1980, at the age of sixty-five. Just prior to his death, he followed the* People's Daily *forum on the Party's leadership in literature and the arts with keen interest. His deathbed article, which follows, shows his concern over the issue of strengthening Party control in this area. It is an eloquent appeal for carrying out the "Double-Hundred" policy and the democratization of literature and art, both of which were key terms in many of the speeches at the November 1979 Fourth Congress of Writers and Artists, including those by a representative of the Party.*

THE *PEOPLE'S DAILY* is holding a discussion on "improving the Party's leadership over literature and art and enlivening the cause of literature and art." I was pleased to see the words "improving," and "enlivening," but I couldn't help feeling heavyhearted when I read the Editor's Note, which said in part, "The Party must improve its leadership over literature and art and strengthen it through improvement. In this respect we are unshakable." I don't know how broadly the "we" should be interpreted. I only know that some of our artists—people who have been unflinchingly loyal to the Party's cause—will feel apprehensive as a conditioned reflex whenever they hear about "strengthening the Party's leadership." This is because their experience with political movements has told them that every strengthening process brings great suffering and flagrant interference until "overall dictatorship" is attained. The memory is still fresh and that peculiar feeling is still there. Let's hope there won't ever be "strengthening" of that nature again.

In my opinion, strengthening or improving Party leadership means for the Party to better implement policies in literature and art and translate them into facts. Specifically it means how the Party can firmly carry out the "Double-Hundred" policy.

Should the Party exercise leadership over the actual creation of literary and art

Renmin ribao [People's Daily], October 8, 1980. Translation, with permission, from *Modern Chinese Literature Newsletter* 6:1 (Spring 1980). Translated by Betty Ting.

works? How should this leadership be exercised?

The Party should supervise the formulation of the nation's economic plans and the implementation of industrial and agricultural policies. But there is no need for the Party to tell the people how to grow crops, how to make stools, how to sew trousers, or how to prepare food. There is no need for the Party to instruct writers how to write and actors how to act. Literature and art is the business of writers and artists. Tight control by the Party will only stifle all hope for its development and will destroy it. The Gang of Four controlled literature and art down to the last detail. They even gave instructions as to what kind of belt an actor should wear and where a patch should go on a costume. So tightly did they control everything that only eight theatrical productions were left for 800 million people to see. Shouldn't this negative example put us on guard?

Which writer became a writer because the Party ordered him to be one? Did Lu Xun or Mao Dun write because the Party told them to? Did they write what they wrote because the Party told them to? Who ordered Marx to write what he wrote? Life and struggle—historical progress—combine to shape a given culture and produce its artists and theoreticians, "with a variety of artistic excellence that lasts several hundred years." No Party or faction, no Party group at any level, no Party branch, can control the character and style—the philosophical outlook—of the arts. Insistence on tight control is inviting trouble, expending energy for nothing, and bringing disaster on the arts.

Leaders in charge of literature and art at every level claim that they are the ones who "persist in the Party's policies in literature and art and uphold the revolutionary literary and artistic ideology," as if the professional writers and artists were only a crowd of dim-sighted, insensitive people. Otherwise, why is it that thirty years after the founding of the People's Republic and sixty years after the May Fourth New Culture Movement, when there are already several million proletarian literary and art workers in the country, almost invariably a nonprofessional who knows little or nothing about the arts is appointed to be in charge, from the Central Committee down to the province, prefecture, county, commune, factory, and mine level? It seems that leaders at the top cannot feel at ease unless this is so. It is a logic that confounds me no matter how much I think about it. What's more, when high-ranking leaders are nonprofessionals, when power is concentrated at those levels, and when the nonprofessionals constantly change their minds as they learn to become professionals, the million-strong contingent of writers and artists must also follow their every changing step. Also, there are some leaders who refuse to learn to become professionals, because once they do so they may well lose their positions as leaders. Life is advancing at such a rapid pace that even professionals are having a hard time trying to keep up with the changes and reflect them well. Added to this are the multitudinous interferences that constantly intrude, with the result that even the presently well-received works of literature and art are no more than portrayals of obvious facts and phenomena that people discuss in street conversations.

Should literary and art associations and groups arbitrarily make a certain ideology their sole guiding principle? Should they make what is said in one piece of writing their guidelines for creative work? We must think about this and discuss it seriously. In my opinion we can do better without them. Throughout history the arts never flourished when only one school of thought prevailed and all the rest were banned.

Deputies to the Third Session of the Fifth National People's Congress and the Fifth People's Political Consultative Conference held lively discussions on the question of "system." We artists had always found the term "system" alien. We were to discover gradually that we may care very little about "the system," but "the system" always keeps a tight control over us, forcing us to deal with it seriously.

In which countries is there such a huge proportion of nonprofessional cadres in the field of literature and art as in our country? In our society we don't talk about who supports whom because, except for the peasants and youth (and a small proportion of the elderly and women), you may say that each of us has an "iron rice bowl." But why must we have so many non-artist cadres supervising the artists? Some of these non-artist cadres could have made more meaningful contributions at other work posts. But now a huge number of "master swimmers" are all crowded into one swimming pool so that there is "standing room only." Every cadre who "supervises the arts," in order to faithfully discharge his duties, feels compelled to express his opinion about a creative work. Each takes a different view and it is hard to reach a consensus. Take, for example, the film *Lu Xun*. Since my first screen test in 1960, I have grown or shaved off a mustache more times than I remember. In the twenty years that have passed, in a big country like ours we should have been able to finish filming at least three to five features on Lu Xun, done in various styles, set in different periods of his life, and told from different angles. Yet now even talk about filming it has dwindled to almost nothing. This is not merely a matter of wasting the artistic life of one actor. This continued delay in making the film in fact affects the emergence of a new generation of Lu Xun-type writers and artists.

A work of literature or art has upon it the strong stamp of individuality. It is not something that you can approve by vote. You can comment on it, criticize it, encourage it, applaud it. Viewed in historical perspective, literature and art should not be and cannot be bound by restrictions.

Convention is not truth. Bad conventions cannot be regarded as hard and fast rules. The custom of stringent screening at every level will never produce good works. Not a single fine, vibrant work of literature and art since ancient times has ever been the result of screening! Every time a dispute arose over a film, I couldn't help speaking my piece. Sometimes I tried to hold my tongue. But nothing can frighten me any more. I feel only that I've jabbered long enough, and what good will it really do?

(September 1980 on my sickbed)

82

Commentator

LITERARY AND ART WORKERS MUST SERIOUSLY ESTABLISH THE COMMUNIST WORLD OUTLOOK

IN HIS "Government Work Report" to the Sixth National People's Congress, Premier Zhao Ziyang distinctly affirmed achievements on the literary and art front, but he also directly pointed out surface defects that must be rectified. People now place high hopes on our literary and art workers. To further promote our country's socialist literature and art, efforts should be made to strengthen the ideological construction of the ranks of writers and artists and to help them firmly establish the communist world outlook.

Generally speaking, our country's literature and art workers are mental workers who strive for the people and the socialist cause and are intellectuals of the working class. The majority of the ranks are young literature and art workers who grew up during the ten years of internal disorder. Owing to the disruption and destruction caused by the counterrevolutionary clique of Lin Biao and Jiang Qing, many of our young literature and art workers missed the chance to systematically study Marxism-Leninism-Mao Zedong Thought. As for the middle-aged and old literature and art workers, although they have long been nurtured in Marxism, some of them still do not know how to use well the Marxist stand, viewpoint, and method to analyze and study new conditions and problems arising from practical life. Therefore young, middle-aged, and old literature and art workers should all make further efforts to study basic Marxist theory systematically and to establish the Marxist world outlook. We must clarify the fact that our socialist society emerged from the womb of the old society only recently. All kinds of old ideas and habits of the exploiting classes still abound. They will breed and spread should the chance arise. In addition, the introduction of our open-door policy has inevitably brought corrosive influences of bourgeois ideology from abroad. At present, ideas of bourgeois liberalization and "putting money above everything else" have been reflected in the realm of literature and art to a certain degree. Facing such a new and complex situation, we cannot but firmly take the Marxist viewpoint as a guide in our literary and artistic creation. Only by so doing will we be able to maintain a correct direction and avoid being controlled by all sorts of erroneous tendencies and ideas so as to make greater contributions to building a socialist spiritual civilization.

Since the Third Plenum of the Eleventh CPC Central Committee, a surging

Guangming ribao [Guangming Daily], September 21, 1983. Translation from FBIS Daily Report, October 5, 1983, pp. K2–K4.

REVIEWING A MANUSCRIPT
Shengao, by Fang Cheng

The "big stick" is a standard symbol of literary control.

ideological emancipation movement has unfolded under the leadership of the Party Central Committee. The great achievements of this movement are that the spiritual shackles that long yoked the people have been frustrated, and that the people's thinking has been led onto the scientific track of Marxism. The ideological line is, in the final analysis, conditioned by the people's world outlook. The so-called personality cult and the "two whatevers" express idealism and metaphysics and are categorically antagonistic to dialectical materialism in terms of world outlook. They oppose the practice of seeking truth from facts and the subjective conforming with the objective; they also regard Marxism-Leninism-Mao Zedong Thought as an eternal dogma and deem Comrade Mao Zedong's fragmentary sayings a panacea. Repudiation of the personality cult and the "two whatevers" has freed a number of comrades from the ideological yoke of idealism and metaphysics and has led them onto the correct track of Marxism.

This success is very important. However, a very small number of people have gone from one extreme to the other. In criticizing mistakes made by Comrade Mao Zedong in his later years they have gone so far as to doubt the correctness of Mao Zedong Thought; and in opposing taking a dogmatic attitude to deal with Marxism they have gone so far as to doubt the guiding significance of Marxism's scientific tenets. Instead of replacing idealism and metaphysics with dialectical materialism and historical materialism, they replace one kind of idealism and metaphysics with another kind of idealism and metaphysics. Such a situation has also emerged within certain literary and artistic circles. Though the influence has extended only to a very few people, it should not be ignored.

In recent years, some comrades in literary and artistic circles have highly praised the theory of irrationalism that has spread in Western countries. This theory holds that literary and artistic creation is purely a kind of ''unconscious'' activity or even a kind of ''subconscious'' activity. It is said that good and attractive literary works can be created only in a state of unconsciousness and by virtue of distinct impulse, and that if the artistic creation is guided by or not freed from rational knowledge, it is inevitably foredoomed to failure. Such a theory is very harmful and runs counter to the world outlook and views on literature and art of Marxism. Literary and artistic creation has its specific characteristics. Thinking in terms of images is different from abstract thinking; it needs both intuition and imagination. Compared with scientific research, it is guided by rational knowledge in a more round-about and concealed way. All this only shows that artistic thinking is guided by theory in a specific way, but it never means that artistic thinking should not be guided by rational knowledge. Man's initiative is always guided by a certain goal. If there is no guidance of rational knowledge it is impossible to make any artistic creation. Lin Biao and Jiang Qing preached that the ''theme of literary creation must go ahead of the rest'' and ''leaders must give a hint first.'' They advocated that literary and artistic creation must start with subjective thought. Such an absurd theory must be criticized and repudiated. However, when refuting the theory, we should on no accout go to extremes and negate all guidance of rational knowledge. One characteristic of socialist literature and art is that it should be guided by Marxism. Writers and artists of socialist countries must of their own will observe everyday life and inspire their creation by means of the ideological weapon of Marxism. If they work with irrationalism, then they are bound to discard all guidance of rational knowledge. In this case, where is the guidance of Marxism? For this reason we should in no way blindly praise the philosophic and literary theory of irrationalism, but we should firmly protect our ideological front from the attack of this erroneous ideological trend.

The main access to the establishment of a communist world outlook is through study and practice. We must conscientiously study the works of Marx, Engels, Lenin, Stalin, and Mao Zedong and make ourselves masters of their scientific tenets. Meanwhile, we must conscientiously study the important documents issued after the Third Plenum and the recently published *Selected Works of Deng Xiaoping*, which are the concrete application and development of Marxism-Leninism-Mao Zedong Thought in China in the new period, and are also the correct guideline for building socialist literature and art. Of course, book learning is far from enough; we must also study in practice. We must progressively plunge into the thick of socialist modernization being carried out by broad sections of workers and peasants in order to know the life, thinking, feelings, will, and wishes of the masses of people and to identify ourselves with them in our thoughts and feelings. We must integrate theory with practice and use the Marxist

This . . . this . . .      Brilliant idea . . .
very enlightening

Specialist
on judging
flowers

FLOWER JUDGE
Ping hua, by Liao Bingxiong

Note that the official flower judge (flowers stand for literary works) has a big mouth, but no eyes. The real expert, eagerly taking notes, has eyes to judge quality; however, he lacks the freedom to express his views.

stand, viewpoint, and method to sum up historical experiences and to study newly emerged conditions and new problems. And no matter what, we must accurately and completely grasp the ideological system of Marxism and seriously use it to study the historical heritage and the present state of affairs. Thereby, the ideological level of our contingent of writers and artists will be further enhanced.

The literary and art workers of our age shoulder the noble task of building socialist spiritual civilization, so the Party and people have to set higher demands on them to foster their world outlook. As engineers of human souls, we must make our own souls become more pure and noble. Meanwhile, as igniters of the "spiritual torch," we must stand on a higher plane and see farther ahead than ordinary people when we have an insight into everyday life. An ancient saying goes: "The best poetry can only be cultivated by those who have the widest vision and the richest knowledge." Our literary and art workers should not be mediocre "artisans" who have good craftsmanship but are simpleminded, and still less should they be greedy "merchants" who put money above everything else. They should be honest and true spokesmen of the masses of people who have good morality, creative thinking, rich historical and cultural knowledge, and excellent artistic skill. All departments in charge of culture should strengthen and improve political and ideological work and adopt practical measures to help literary and art workers study, master, and use Marxism, organizing them to plunge into the thick of the new life of socialist modernization. Our goal is to raise the ideological level and artistic quality of spiritual food, scale new heights in literature and art, and create the most prosperous socialist literature and art. We must regulate the ideological trend in literary and artistic circles and help them cultivate a correct world outlook. This is the ironclad guarantee of a flourishing literature and art of our socialist country.

83

Xu Chunqiao

A MOVIE WITH SERIOUS DEFECTS
Criticize the Movie *At Middle Age*

[*Wenyi bao* Editor's Note] Since the movie *At Middle Age* has been shown, it has won acclaim from audiences, the Distinguished Film Prize of 1982 awarded by the Ministry of Culture, the Golden Rooster Prize awarded by the Chinese Movie Professionals Association, and the Hundred Flowers Prize awarded by *Dazhong Dianying*. In Nos. 4 and 5 of this publication, articles commenting on both the achievements and the shortcomings of this movie were published. We have now received an article from Comrade Xu Chunqiao that totally repudiates this film. Xu's article is published as follows, and comments from our readers are solicited.

SINCE THE MOVIE *At Middle Age*, a film script of the novel under the same title written by Comrade Chen Rong herself, has been shown, strong repercussions have been touched off in society, especially among intellectuals. As to the question of right or wrong, of course there are so many contradictory views that it is difficult to decide which is right.

In a sense, this movie extols the fine qualities of middle-aged intellectuals like Lu Wenting who work diligently and industriously, loyally and resourcefully for the sake of socialism and for her own job, and it expounds the importance of

Wenyi bao [Literary News], No. 6 (June 1983). Translation from JPRS-CPS-84-009, January 25, 1984, pp. 53–59 (excerpt).

middle-aged intellectuals as the hard core in the construction of the Four Modernizations. It has a certain practical significance.

However, because the writer has an obviously erroneous understanding of the guiding ideology in artistic creation, serious problems thus exist regarding important political principles in this movie, which lead to very bad social consequences.

1. In a letter in April 1888, Engels said: "In my opinion, the meaning of practical significance is to represent typical characters realistically in typical surroundings besides a realistic description of details." These words of Engels emphatically laid stress on the representativeness and truthfulness of literature and pointed out that only typical literature is realistic literature. Then, are the characters and surroundings in *At Middle Age* typical, or is the life reflected in this movie realistic? No! The writer of the movie unilaterally exaggerated the dark side of life. The essence of life is replaced by the subjective sentiment of the writer, which makes characters and surroundings in the entire movie deviate from life in order to serve the needs of the movie's theme. As a result, in the selection of the details of life and in the creation of the characters' images, it shows obvious falseness.

Let us talk about the characters in the movie first. Although Lu Wenting is enthusiastically responsible in her job and works very hard, yet in her life she is always passive. Apart from her work, she seems unable to move a single step and is faced with one difficulty after another. She always feels that she has no way out or that she is in a dilemma. Whenever she encounters something sad, Lu Wenting merely wants to solve her problem with tears: We find her in tears when her child is ill, when Yuan Yuan can eat only the sesame seed cake instead of having a regular lunch, and when she sees her husband becoming old and feeble. She does not handle difficulties in her life positively and optimistically, but instead adopts a compromising and timid attitude toward them. She attributes all indispositions and difficulties to the antithesis between work and marriage. It seems that one cannot marry if one wants to work or one cannot work efficiently if one wants to get married. This is an absolutely wrong view and an absurd explanation of life that is contrary to reason. Fu Jiajie, Lu Wenting's husband, has adopted an attitude of letting things slide and of self-mockery. The dinner with the Jiang Yafen couple is the best example of this. Why doesn't the writer show how they make a stand against destiny or challenge difficulties rather than let them wander and worry amidst perplexities and puzzles?

Obviously, when the writer was creating the image of Lu Wenting and her husband, she stressed that they are not fairly treated in society and thereby are caught in a dilemma, which eventually leads to a horrible tragedy. The writer failed to consider the main ideological trend in the spiritual attitudes of middle-aged intellectuals of this generation. Lu Wenting does not reflect the attitudes and ideals of life that the middle-aged intellectuals should have. Therefore, even though Lu Wenting is enthusiastic, responsible, and diligent in doing her work, people still think that the reason Lu Wenting works that way is that she proceeds from the humanitarianism of a medical doctor and does it with the conscience of an ordinary person. In so doing, this movie has seriously weakened the image of the middle-aged intellectuals as well as that of Lu Wenting. This is why we say that the image of Lu Wenting (including Fu Jiajie) is not typical. Turning now to the surroundings that appeared in the movie, it is easy to see that they are untrue and atypical. From the historical point of view, since the smashing of the "Gang of Four" and especially after the Third Plenum of the Eleventh CCP Central Committee, everything in our country has been marching toward the right track. Although dark sides of one kind or another still exist in some places, gloom ɪd darkness do not extend over the whole society. Darkness is being driven out ᶜ v light. "In our country, the dark side is always illegal and temporary." "It wiˡ eventually be repudiated and overcome by our Party and our people" (Hu Yaobang). And the movie *At Middle Age* has, taking Lu Wenting as its core, described a situation in which the intellectual is being left out in the cold, the bureaucratic work-style of the leadership is serious, and the dark corners cannot be illuminated by the Party. The writer has emphatically exaggerated such an isolated case to let people see the dangerous and disastrous circumstances encountered by intellectuals in this society and thereby feel suffocated.

Exaggerated and untrue depictions are also adopted by the writer to describe the living conditions of Lu Wenting. A family of four of an intellectual who has been working nearly twenty years lives in a small room in which one is almost unable to turn around. We do not say that such conditions do not exist, or perhaps it may be true in Lu Wenting's home or in the hospital where she works, but is it true in China as a whole?

In order to express the hard life, the heavy family burden, and the tremendous work load of intellectuals in our time, the writer does not allow Yuan Yuan to have a pair of white sneakers, so he has to color them with a piece of chalk. On the surface, it seems to be very true and touching. However, after careful deliberation, this exaggeration of the details of life obviously has a trace of the sham. Because Lu Wenting has to walk through many busy streets to and from work, how much time does she need to buy a pair of sneakers? If she really does not have time, why doesn't she give money to Yuan Yuan to buy a pair himself? Moreover, Jia Jia is put in the child care center with no one to take care of her while she is suffering with acute pneumonia and is repeatedly calling "Ma, Ma" with a miserable voice. The scene that immediately follows shows her being sent to the hospital for medical treatment. After she is back home, she does not have time to cook and she goes to buy sesame seed cakes. All this in such a tense atmosphere! Lu Wenting's housework is so heavy and her tears are so touching! We say there is no child care center that would ignore the life of a child; nor is there any child care center that would let a child who is suffering from acute pneumonia lie in an empty room and let matters slide.

2. Maxim Gorki said, "Literature is the history of life and the feeling of the times." Then, does the movie *At Middle Age* reflect the essence and the flavor of the life of the times? We can understand this question from the departure of Liu Xueyao and his wife.

The historical background for the departure of the couple was the latter part of the 1970s, which was a period when order was brought out of chaos and our

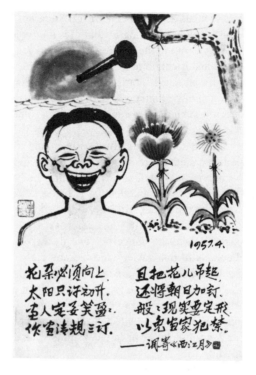

花朵必须向上
太阳只许初升.
画人定要笑盈:
依官诗规三订.

且把花儿吊起,
还将朝日加钉.
般:现实要定形.
以免皆家犯禁.
——调寄《西江月》

SKETCH FOR DOGGEREL
Dayoushi hua, by Liao Bingxiong

Translation:

Flower blossoms must face upward
The sun can only be rising
A person painted must be bubbling with smiles
These three rules are indispensible in art

Might as well hang the flowers
and nail the rising sun in place
All of reality must fit the mold
In order that artists stay in bounds.

(*To the tune of "Western River Moon"*)

This cartoon dates from April 1957. Because of this and similar cartoons, the cartoonist was labeled a rightist in June 1957; the label was finally removed in 1979.

country was revitalized after the "ten-year calamity." It was with such a historical background when everything in our country was about to move toward the right track, when hope was at hand, and when the light of an early dawn was illuminating the land that Liu Xueyao left.

Then, what really did force the Liu couple to leave? What attitude should the writer adopt toward this departure?

The couple departed because the "ten-year calamity" is still entangled in their minds. Owing to "overseas connections" and to the fact that they suffered from attacks and setbacks during the Cultural Revolution, therefore, even though our country is being vigorously developed, they do not believe that their motherland, which once brought misfortunes on them, will give them happiness and a world that will make the best use of everyone. Liu Xueyao said explicitly: "When can the light shine upon the entrance of my home? When can it shine upon my children?" This is why they place their own future, their own fortunes, and their own hope of extricating themselves from the unfair treatment received in their own motherland on Canada, a capitalist country. In Canada, they will be better off politically, economically, and materially than in our country; otherwise, they would not desert their motherland.

If Liu Xueyao and his wife left during the "ten-year calamity," it could be attributed to the crime of the "Great Cultural Revolution." However, they left at a crucial moment when we are sounding a bugle call for the Four Modernizations in our country, after the smashing of the "Gang of Four." Who is to blame?

It is easy to see that Liu Xueyao and his wife are cowards in life and typical representatives of the capitalist class who seek personal fame and gain and hanker after material comfort. At the time of their departure, they suffered no political persecution, or spiritual setbacks, except low wages (but higher than the average person's) and an inadequate dwelling. It can be said without the slightest exaggeration: Their condition at that time was better than 80 percent of the Chinese people. It was at that time when their motherland was in need of them, when their motherland was in difficulties, that they laid aside their work and abandoned their own motherland. The feeling of reluctance at the time of departure and the sentiment expressed by Liu Xueyao that "as I have lived most of my life, how many years can I stay in this world and why should I leave the ashes of my remains on the soil of a foreign land?" are but Liu Xueyao's sophistry by which the writer wants to absolve and forgive them for their ugly and despicable souls.

The farewell dinner party is a great example of the essence of the ideology of the Liu couple. Liu Xueyao uses satiric and ironic remarks to attack the society and mock our era. He does not cherish any hope at all for our country but rather pours out endless grievances by saying that "what we eat is grass, but we have no milk." He really does not know that in reality there are people who are even unable to eat that kind of "grass."

Such a pitiful creature in life and such a movie that betrays the motherland and the people must be held in contempt by the people. Yet the writer has given high-sounding excuses of one kind or another to absolve them of their desertion.

In creating these two characters, the writer was basically wrong in her thinking. This is why both the essence and the effect bestowed upon the images appear to be passive. The crucial point here is that the writer does not throb with the pulse of our times; nor does she understand the political flavor and the characteristics of the essence of the historical times that are being developed and pushed forward.

Both Lenin and Comrade Mao Zedong said that proletarian literature must become a part of the revolutionary cause of the proletariat and serve the political purpose of the proletariat. It must have an explicit ideological purpose. At the present stage, the ideological purpose our literature and art serves is to eulogize and praise new people and new deeds in the construction of the Four Modernizations and to resist and expose the ugly things in our lives. The writer of the movie *At Middle Age*, however, not only fails to resist and negate the ugly things but instead expresses sympathy for them, beautifies them, and gives them her support. Under the guidance of the erroneous ideology of the writer, it is easy to see who is to blame for the desertion of Liu Xueyao and his wife.

3. Literary works must pay attention to social effect. Then, what kind of social effect should it be? Comrade Hu Yaobang said: "Literature and art must reflect the spiritual sparks of our country and our people. It must, at the same time, serve as a spiritual light to enable 900 million people to have an even higher spiritual state, a loftier ideal, and a still better revolutionary quality and style in order to push our history forward. This is the issue that we have to pay attention to." Has the movie *At Middle Age* attached importance to these issues or has it led the people, through the "spiritual sparks" of Lu Wenting, to an even higher spiritual state, a loftier revolutionary ideal, quality, or style? It has not.

First, the keynote of *At Middle Age* is its spirit of depression. It is a tragedy. Lu Wenting's life experience and fate have painted the entire movie and the entire society with a dim and dusky tint. We do not see any future, brightness, or hope from the character of Lu Wenting. What we have seen is merely Lu Wenting's repentance and her painful reminiscence of the past at her bedside in the hospital and Fu Jiajie's most sorrowful cries beside her. The only way out and the hope that people have caught sight of from the painful life and the tragic fate of Lu Wenting may perhaps be the same as that of the Liu couple—going abroad; otherwise their fate will be just as miserable as Lu Wenting's. Even if Lu Wenting does not think so, the audience thinks this way. Knowing the hopeless fate of Lu Wenting, people have associated it with their own future and their own fate. The movie gives people a sense of fear and horror and a feeling of being permanently in a hopeless and painful predicament. After stepping out of the hospital, Lu Wenting is still faced with the heavy burden of life and family. Nowhere does the movie give us a hint that the fate of Lu Wenting may turn for the better. Intellectuals cannot thus be inspired with enthusiasm; nor can they thus be encouraged to make active progress and overcome difficulties; instead, the character of Lu Wenting gives them the impression that the life of this generation is hopeless and their fate is far from fortunate. They therefore are terrified and heavyhearted because their surroundings are too perilous.

Second, the attitude of the movie toward difficulties is avoidance and despair, rather than a search for solutions.

Third, the movie, which has weakened the image of the Party and of socialism, gives rise to a dissatisfaction with the reality of our society. What are the reasons for Lu Wenting's tragic fate? The reasons are the difficult life, the heavy work load, and the heavy family burden. This is not a matter of a particular family or a particular unit but a universal issue that remains to be solved step by step. Moreover, our Party and our country are not making efforts to improve the condition of intellectuals and to pay attention to science and technology. We have achieved successes. Given this historical background, the writer picks Lu Wenting as a typical example. What effect will this have? In this movie, we cannot see the Party's strength or the concern and warmth shown by the Party. The writer has attributed the tragedy of Lu Wenting to the Party's indifference and laissez-faire attitude toward intellectuals. She has also attributed the desertion of the Liu couple to our society and our social system. The direction of the writer's attack is quite obvious, that is, our Party and society have ignored the welfare of intellectuals and have always looked down on science. Socialism can only stifle real talents and not allow intellectuals to display their abilities. The hope of Liu Xueyao and his wife lies in a capitalist country. And the Lu Wentings who remain in our country accept their fate. Even if it is not the intention of the writer to demonstrate an ideology of this kind, it has already caused such a social effect. It is very clear that it has rendered the same result as that of *Unrequited Love*, but with a different approach.

84

Yan Gang

AN ARGUMENT IN FAVOR OF THE MOVIE *AT MIDDLE AGE*

A Countercriticism against "A Movie with Serious Defects"

AT THE END of last year, the preview of the movie *At Middle Age* was shown by the Changcheng Film Corporation and *Dazhong dianying* to solicit comments. I was very much perplexed in taking a look at this film that, before its completion, the corporation had once been ordered to delay. I really cannot understand why comments on this film have been so diametrically opposed and why the making of a film should be subject to ups and downs until a final approval could be made. What does this situation indicate? What will happen if this film is not appropriately made? Thank goodness, the film is true to the original story, which has been a success. It has become an ode with a deep feeling toward the middle-aged intellectuals cultivated by the Party. Since the movie was

Wenyi bao [Literary News], No. 7 (July 1983). Translation from JPRS-CPS-84-009, January 25, 1984, pp. 60–67 (excerpt).

shown, praise has come from old and young, inside and outside of the Party. However, it is difficult to cater to all tastes. Some of our comrades are extremely discontented because this movie "has serious problems in many important political principles that lead to very bad social consequences" and because it is "the same in nature as the movie *Unrequited Love* even if different in approach." (Xu Chunqiao, "A Movie with Serious Defects," see *Wenyi bao*, No. 6 of this year [Selection 83, above].)

Two years ago, someone said that the movie *At Middle Age* "had brought pressure to bear on the Party" and that "it is the second *Unrequited Love*." Now, Comrade Xu Chunqiao has repeated such a view. Why are there so many different views on this film? According to Xu Chunqiao, it is because it involves problems of "many important political principles." This really scares us. In my opinion, differences lie in the fact that everybody has his own guide to judge literary works. There is a guide to history and also a guide to aesthetics. Of course, it involves problems of "important political principles," but it is primarily a question of how to understand the realism of literature. With regard to realism, Comrade Xu Chunqiao made many remarks in his article. He repeatedly emphasized the authenticity of surroundings and characters. It is said that his guide is also Engels' theory of "realism." However, since his understanding of the mutual relations between both the bright and the dark sides in our real lives is a mechanical comprehension and his analysis of theme and characters of this film is oversimplified, therefore, in talking about authenticity and the representativeness of realism, he has stretched its meaning and tried every means to have an innocent person pronounced guilty, and thereby a film that is perfectly fine is criticized as if it had no saving graces. As a result, it is he himself who has deviated from Engels' theory of realism.

With regard to the so-called "serious problems that exist in many important political principles" in the movie *At Middle Age* and that are raised by Xu Chunqiao, some specific aspects have been mentioned throughout his article. On these specific aspects, he has held to extreme views that deviate from the reality of life and work. Therefore, the political label that he put on the movie *At Middle Age* is entirely subjective and unilateral and is imposed by force.

1. In the first place, Comrade Xu Chunqiao asserted categorically that Lu Wenting is a person who is hypocritical, untrue, and not typical. In his opinion, although Lu Wenting is diligent and responsible in doing her work, "she proceeds from the humanitarianism of a medical doctor and does it with the conscience of an ordinary person." He believed that Lu Wenting "has adopted a compromising and timid attitude toward difficulties of one kind or another but does not make a stand against destiny; nor does she challenge difficulties." Therefore, "this movie has seriously weakened the image of the middle-aged intellectuals of this generation." After taking a look at this movie, people feel that they are "hopeless" and that "they can never be extricated." All in all, in the eyes of Xu Chunqiao, Lu Wenting has become a pitiful creature who resigns herself to humiliation and adversities. Since the movie *At Middle Age* has managed to pick a character like this as a positive image to be eulogized, it is not only

untrue but is also not typical; not only does it distort intellectuals but it also damages the prestige of the Party. Therefore, it must be negated. But I feel these views are really very arbitrary and do not conform to the real conditions in the movie.

It is not the movie *At Middle Age* that distorts the image of intellectuals. It is Xu Chunqiao who misrepresents Lu Wenting, an intellectual.

Lu Wenting is not an ordinary woman who is mediocre and incompetent; nor is she a heroine with elegant manners; rather she is a middle-aged woman specialist who is imbued with the traditional virtues of a Chinese woman, gentle and cultivated, pliable and tough. Her lofty deeds of silently dedicating herself to the country make all visible or invisible pressures around her lose their weight. Her unusual spirit of forbearance makes all unreasonable appearances around her become intolerable. Her mental state and her lot are common among intellectuals in our country at present. However, Lu Wenting is absolutely not a generalized or a conceptualized image of intellectuals. Lu Wenting is Lu Wenting who is a doctor and a wife having a specific lot and a specific personal character. The difficulties faced by Lu Wenting are many-sided and involve a variety of aspects, including ideology, love, livelihood, theory, and health. Facing one difficulty after another, Lu Wenting, a professional backbone of society holding a "low post" and receiving "poor wages," is merely a stem of thin grass. She has "a professional burden outside and a household burden inside her family." She has to "support and wait upon her parents and bring up her children" and to "endure the sufferings of life and make enormous sacrifices." What she does yearn for and makes an all-out effort to achieve is to become a good doctor, a good wife, and a good mother. The movie *At Middle Age* opens up the tragedy of Lu Wenting who cures others and saves the lives of others at the miserable moment when she herself is critically ill. It is a fade-in, but it is deep in its meaning, which is exceptionally passionate and touching.

Lu Wenting collapsed. It is better not to say that she is knocked down by a merciless disease but rather by an unjust destiny. However, she has not been knocked down. She can "endure" and she is "tenacious." She has, after all, held out until after the Third Plenum of the Eleventh CCP Central Committee. In the face of adversities, Lu Wenting does not behave in as "compromising and timid" a way as Comrade Xu Chunqiao has described. What should she do to qualify herself as uncompromising and untamed? Can she be allowed to argue strongly on just grounds or to report to the Party Central Committee? Can she be allowed to ignore her patients and put aside the scalpel to lie down? No, that would not be Lu Wenting. Comrade Chen Rong does not want to create an image of a heroine "who fights against destiny." Based on her discoveries in her life, she wants to create an image of intellectuals that she deems to be more rich in artistic appeal— a lofty image of endurance and tenaciousness—so as to arouse the sympathy and respect of the people and make society pay close attention to the conditions of middle-aged intellectuals. This Lu Wenting we see on the screen today is just this sort of image. Under unjust treatment, Lu Wenting is poor but virtuous, hardworking and unconcerned about personal grievances, impartial and selfless, cautious and conscientious. She fulfills her duty wholeheartedly and unswervingly. Her loyalty and enthusiasm in carrying out her duty and her softness and virtuousness in getting along with her husband and children can be said to be exerted to the utmost. This is Lu Wenting, and this is "Lu Wenting's character"! In the movie *At Middle Age*, because Comrade Pan Hong's success-ful performance is authentic, exquisite, and full of artistic appeal (her two eyes are so lifelike!), "Lu Wenting's character" becomes more vivid and touching. We do not see from the image of Lu Wenting the slightest flavor of vulgarity and pettiness. It is a kind of lofty moral strength that has supported her and prevented her from complete collapse at a time when she is about to fall down. She is selfless so as to devote her own youth to the sacred cause of the people without reservation. The selfless sacrifice she made for work and the spirit of giving no thought to remuneration make a vivid display of the communist style of behavior. Lu Wenting's communist style of behavior is the result of the long education carried out by the Party. To extol the selfless Lu Wenting is to extol our Party. The theme of the movie *At Middle Age* is to extol. It extols the generation of intellectu-als, who are cultivated by the Party. Although they have experienced repeated hardships, the artistic intent of the movie *At Middle Age* is represented by the lofty sentiments about endurance of humiliation in carrying out important mis-sions, steadfastness tempered in difficulties, and soaring aspirations which are most touching. Can all this be explained merely by applying "humanitarian duties" and "the conscience of an ordinary person"? How can the conclusion that "the image of the middle-aged intellectuals of this generation has been seriously damaged" be drawn?

2. Comrade Xu Chunqiao continued that so far as the character of Lu Wenting is concerned, even if she herself is typical, her surroundings are not true or typical. He said: "After the Third Plenum of the Eleventh CCP Central Commit-tee, everything in our country has been marching toward the right track. Al-though dark sides of one kind or another still exist in some places, gloom and darkness do not spread over the whole society." Comrade Xu Chunqiao felt that the movie *At Middle Age* had tried its utmost to play up the "tragic ending" by exaggerating the "fabricated life," "paid attention only to the dark side to the neglect of the bright side," and "failed to reflect the essence of life." As a result, it makes people feel that "the surroundings are too perilous." Comrade Xu Chunqiao asked at last: Our Party and our country are now making efforts to improve the conditions of intellectuals and successes have been achieved. "It is with such an historical background that the writer picks Lu Wenting to play a typical example. What will the effect be?"

This involves the question of how literature reflects the essence of society, of how to treat the dark side of society, the theme of tragedy, the social effect of literary works, and so forth. In Comrade Xu Chunqiao's opinion, to write it is necessary in essence to stress brightness, and to write about brightness it is not advisable to "pay attention" to the dark side of life. Because the movie *At Middle Age* "pays attention" to the dark side, therefore it "fabricates stories" at great length. It depicts Lu Wenting as miserable and pitiful and socialism as dim and gloomy.

In my opinion, it is not only a misunderstanding but also a groundless fear, which, in the final analysis, is the reflection of social statistics and vulgar sociology in literary critiques. Xu Chunqiao does not believe that Lu Wenting does not have time to buy a pair of white sneakers for Yuan Yuan; he does not know that it is just a portrait of what Chen Rong, the writer, has seen and experienced. Xu Chunqiao feels that what Liu Xueyao said at the farewell dinner party is to "attack society and mock our era" and that his leaving the country is a "betrayal of his motherland," but he does not know that this is just a symbol of Liu Xueyao's dejection and an unreserved revelation of his contradictory state of mind. He is grumbling. Only some of his remarks are excessively ironic. Of course, it is absolutely true that he can stay at home. The writer clearly knows that she would be much more on the safe side if she wrote it this way; however, she did not. Sighing over the drain of a large number of intellectuals at that time, she wrote straightforwardly with a bitter hatred. Liu Xueyao and his wife's going abroad is written to awaken people and to set off Lu Wenting. Writing in this way, the objective effect of the work proves to be more thoughtful. Xu Chunqiao felt that the movie *At Middle Age* had exaggerated Lu Wenting's fate, which is excessively tragic and perilous. As a result, it makes people feel that there is only one way out, that is, "to follow the example of the Liu couple—going abroad." However, Lu Wenting herself has no thought of going abroad, and she does not. Moreover, while she is ill, it is not that she does not want to do her work, but that she is unable to do her work. It is not the writer who "fabricated" such a tragic character and story; it exists in our lives and it happens day after day. Can the examples of Jiang Zhuying and Luo Jianfu offer an explanation? Are examples like this still enough, or is it still necessary for writers to take great pains to "play up" and to "exaggerate"? What are the "dangers" in Lu Wenting's fate? The dangers lie in the fact that the repeated injunctions of the Party Central Committee on policies with regard to intellectuals have not been effectively, quickly, or evenly implemented. Is this not the hard fact? True, the fate of Lu Wenting is very miserable, which is enough to attract the attention of those who come to the rescue. In fact it has already shaken intellectual circles. Yet misery is not hopelessness. I believe that the movie does not "end in an aesthetic mood." Lu Wenting, who is weak and thin, does not "lean in Fu Jiajie's arms to march toward the rising sun," but as in the original novel, it is Fu Jiajie who takes every care to support his wife with his hand as they "march toward the rising sun in the cold wind." All in all, even if Lu Wenting dies at the final curtain, I think her spirit will never die and her image and voice will remain, and she will still be a good teacher and a helpful friend in encouraging middle-aged intellectuals of this generation to dedicate themselves to the construction of the Four Modernizations.

As to the question of "paying attention" to the dark side of society, it is true that the movie *At Middle Age* really "attaches importance to it." However, the movie *At Middle Age* really has a "dim" and "dusky" tint that is spread over art by life rather than over life by art. The reason why the movie *At Middle Age* does not make people feel hopeless is that it is not entirely "dusky." On many occasions it mentions that hope is like the "rising sun," touches upon the deep affection that Lu Wenting cherishes for her career and for the laboring people, and vividly describes Lu Wenting's disposition and spirit as well as the profound meaning of the tragedy of Lu Wenting. The profound meaning of the tragedy of Lu Wenting lies in the fact that middle-aged intellectuals are overloaded with labor but are underpaid, that they are the mainstay in work but are minimized in life, that they are of great importance in the construction of the Four Modernizations but underestimated in politics, that the policy on intellectuals is being implemented but has encountered difficulties, and so forth. Comrade Chen Rong knows very well that she herself has taken an "adventurous" road, but she is willing to "venture" and to take up the responsibility of authentically reflecting the present state of life.

The only way to develop literary and artistic creations is to face life outright and confront social contradictions squarely. Of course, this is a way which is not very safe. Yet, only because it is not very safe can brave warriors be ready to take up the cudgels for a just cause. Comrade Chen Rong has come that way. The movie *At Middle Age* was written in 1979. At that time, there was still prejudice in society against intellectuals. How bold and courageous was Comrade Chen Rong to recount specifically the loftiness and misfortune of female intellectuals.

What a pity there are still not many writers who advance bravely on a path that is not very safe. Some writers who fear dangers look for safe ways and they have found them. No uniformity should be imposed, because ideals vary from person to person, but it is hoped that their works will not deviate too far from social contradictions.

As to the question of the social effect of the movie *At Middle Age*, I do not want to say much about it. I want only to refer to a few matters at present. Two years after the publication of the novel *At Middle Age*, the middle-aged Jiang Zhuying and Luo Jianfu died. What a pity they died. After feeling deep regret, people are surprised at the fact that they did not do their best for intellectuals. They began to pay attention to improving the condition of middle-aged intellectuals. However, cases of despising, squeezing, and attacking middle-aged intellectuals still occur from time to time. On April 16 the Party Central Committee approved and distributed the "Report on the Physical Condition of the Middle-aged Intellectuals." On May 18, *Renmin ribao* [People's Daily] reported that a chief engineer in Fushun was dismissed without any justification. A few days later, the same newspaper again reported that an expert who had forecast the Tangshan earthquake was being oppressed. A few days ago, a meeting on intellectuals was convened by Beijing Municipality to eliminate ultraleft ideology on the question of intellectuals. Like many other important social questions, the question of intellectuals is accompanied by both hope and struggle, brightness and of course darkness. This is reality and this is life! Nowadays, people like Lu Wenting and the "Marxist old lady" still exist. Therefore, the movie *At Middle Age* is not out of date.

The presentation of the movie *At Middle Age* has been warmly received by the masses of intellectuals and the masses from all strata. Some old comrades said with a heavy heart after going to the movie: "We went too far in our bad treatment of intellectuals in the past!" Some leading comrades with a sense of responsibility expressed appreciation after going to the movie. They felt that this film has a practical significance and reminded the departments concerned to pay attention to resolving the difficulties encountered in the actual lives of middle-aged intellectuals. Lu Wenting enjoys immense popular support, and the movie *At Middle Age* is very helpful in speeding up the implementation of policies with regard to intellectuals. This is the social effect of this movie. This is a good effect that is very rare in literary and artistic creations! So long as Comrade Xu Chunqiao can study realism without deviating from reality, I think he will eventually understand how a work of genuine realism can help our society march forward without a feeling of "despair."

85

Gao Hongxiang

CAN THOSE FROM "10,000-YUAN HOUSEHOLDS" BE EXTOLLED AS NEW SOCIALIST PERSONS?

A New Problem in Portraying Rural Characters

THE NO. 4 issue of *Wenyi qingkuang* [The Situation in Literature and Art] this year published an article by Xiao Rong, in which the author said that she had more than once heard those who write stories about the countryside mention with interest the new type of figure emerging against the rural background: They are more clever and shrewd than ordinary peasants and are also kind of crafty. They know how to manage their business and are adept at scheming and trickery. They have more of an economic color than a political color and are marked by a certain tint of adventurism. Some people call them "half angel" and "half demon." It is the opinion of many writers that overlooking this type of figure in portraying village life would render the realities colorless. However, it is very difficult to characterize them effectively.

The difficulty is twofold: First, to what category should we assign them? Are they the so-called "new socialist people"? In real life it tends to be the "10,000-yuan households" or "specialized households" that are being praised. Nevertheless, judging from their success in triumphing over and supplanting others on the

" 'Wanyuanhu' neng zuowei shehuizhuyi xinren gesong ma?" *Baokan wenzhai* [Digest of Newspapers and Periodicals] (Shanghai), May 8, 1984, p. 3. Translated by Ai Ping.

market by every possible means, they reveal themselves to be ruthless and heartless; they refuse to concede to anyone, either relatives or friends. If we sing the praises of these persons as the new people of socialism, will we possibly create some confusion over the standards of social morality in our literary writings?

Second, what proper limits should we set for the portrayal of this type of figure? It can be said that they are the "compound" of different kinds of ingredients. On the one hand, their desires, goals, and the means they use can be reasonable and permitted by policy but, on the other hand, they can also be improper and even totally illegal. Some writers depict peasant-run enterprises in this way: "They take advantage of the wind of economic reform; they avail themselves of the loopholes in the planned economy; they conduct unhealthy under-the-table deals." They pay some price, including a certain degeneration of their morality. What a painful thing it is! The half "angel" is the brilliance of the peasants' talent, which is brought into play by the agricultural policy. The half "demon" is a variant of the small peasant mentality generated in rural areas of the old society, which has surfaced under the unhealthy social trends. Some writers hope literary critics can step up their efforts to explore and comment on these problems in relation to the realities of life.

FURTHER READINGS

Chinese Literature, quarterly, Beijing.

Croizier, Ralph. "The Crimes of the Gang of Four: A Chinese Artist's Version." *Pacific Affairs* 54:2 (Summer 1981), pp. 311–322.

Duke, Michael S., and the *Bulletin of Concerned Asian Scholars*, eds. *Contemporary Chinese Literature: An Anthology of Post-Mao Fiction and Poetry*. Armonk, N.Y.: M. E. Sharpe, 1985.

Gold, Thomas B. " 'Just in Time!' China Battles Spiritual Pollution on the Eve of 1984." *Asian Survey* 24:9 (September 1984), pp. 947–974.

Goldblatt, Howard, ed. *Chinese Literature for the 1980s: The Fourth Congress of Writers and Artists*. Armonk, N.Y.: M. E. Sharpe, 1982.

Goldman, Merle. *Literary Dissent in Communist China*. New York: Atheneum, 1971.

Hamrin, Carol Lee, and Timothy Cheek, eds. *China's Establishment Intellectuals*. Armonk, N.Y.: M. E. Sharpe, 1986.

Kinkley, Jeffrey C., ed. *After Mao: Literature and Society in China, 1978–1981*. Cambridge, Mass.: Harvard University Press, 1985.

Kraus, Richard. "China's Cultural 'Liberalization' and Conflict Over the Social Organization of the Arts." *Modern China* 9:2 (April 1983), pp. 212–227.

Lee Yee, ed. *The New Realism: Writings from China After the Cultural Revolution*. New York: Hippocrene Books, 1983.

Liang Heng and Judith Shapiro. *Intellectual Freedom in China After Mao*. New York: Fund for Free Expression, 1984.

Link, Perry, ed. *Roses and Thorns: The Second Blooming of the Hundred Flowers in Chinese Fiction, 1979–80*. Berkeley: University of California Press, 1984. (*At Middle Age*, by Chen Rong, is translated on pp. 261–338.)

Link, Perry, ed. *Stubborn Weeds: Popular and Controversial Chinese Literature After the Cultural Revolution*. Bloomington: Indiana University Press, 1983.

Liu Binyan. *People or Monsters? and Other Stories and Reportage from China After Mao*. Bloomington: Indiana University Press, 1983 (edited by Perry Link).

McDougall, Bonnie S. *Mao Zedong's Talks at the Yan'an Conference on Literature and Art*. Ann Arbor: University of Michigan Center for Chinese Studies, 1980.

Modern Chinese Literature, semi-annually, San Francisco State University.

Panda Books, Beijing, offers translations of contemporary Chinese literature (for example, Jiang Zilong, *All the Colours of the Rainbow*; Wang Meng, *The Butterfly and Other Stories*; and so forth).

Siu, Helen F., and Zelda Stern, eds. *Mao's Harvest: Voices from China's New Generation*. New York: Oxford University Press, 1983.

F. Population

OF ALL THE policy arenas under consideration in this volume, it is arguably China's population policy—specifically, the "one-child-per-couple" campaign—that has garnered the most attention in the West. Much of this attention has been owing to some disturbing and tragic, albeit unintended, consequences of this campaign, such as forced abortion and female infanticide. But China's attempt to hold its population to 1.2 billion by the year 2000 merits particular study by students of Chinese politics because it reveals the complexities of policy implementation. First, by disclosing the substantial differences between urban and rural implementation, it provides further confirmation of the dangers of overgeneralization in policy analysis. The "one child" policy has proved very successful in the cities, but policy success remains impossible without an improvement in rural implementation. The 1982 census revealed that 77.6 percent of the population lives in the countryside, but in 1981 over 90 percent of the 20.7 million infants born were from rural areas. Records over the years show that the birthrate and the rate of third and greater births in the rural areas are 50 percent higher than comparable rates in the cities.[1]

Second, it demonstrates the difficulties of fashioning a detailed, national policy applicable throughout the country, even in so crucial an area as population control. Although the one-child program is a centrally directed goal, a national birth-planning law that would stipulate economic incentives for the one-child family and disincentives for more than two births has never been passed. The first draft of such a law had been drawn up in 1979; by September 1980, when the National People's Congress was in session and the Party Central Committee issued an Open Letter on the subject (Selection 86), an eighth draft of this law was circulating at the grass-roots level for comment and reaction. As Pi-chao Chen has written, solutions to a series of nagging problems would have to be found before such a law could be passed. First, in the face of the likelihood of widespread noncompliance in the countryside, could the law's punitive provisions be enforced? Assuming they were enforced through coercion, what consequences would follow? Second, should special provisions for national minorities—particularly the Muslims—continue? Is there a danger in allowing the minorities, who make up 6.7 percent of the population, to increase this percentage over the coming decades? Third, the draft law calls for generous economic and other benefits to couples who pledge to have only one child, by accepting a one-child certificate, until the child is fourteen years old. Meeting that financial commitment requires substantial budgetary outlays, including extraordinary increases in the next two to three decades. Would the very success of the one-child policy prevent the state from investing in other projects that promise high return, even assuming that these funds can be found? Fourth, various interest groups have remained skeptical regarding the one-child policy. The army is concerned with the consequences of recruiting from a shrinking military labor pool, which would add to the difficulties they already face following the introduction of the production responsibility system. The Women's Federation has reacted to the resurgence of discrimination against women, particularly when the child allowed turns out to be a girl.[2]

The lack of such national legislation suggests a third observation: The importance of basic-level cadres in the implementation of any policy and the dilemmas central authorities face in eliciting compliance at the basic level in the rural areas. Many studies have commented on the ambivalence of rural cadres, who are local people generally sharing the values and attitudes of those they lead, and whose continuance in office depends on support both from superiors above and fellow villagers below.[3] The Party's population policy focuses sharply on the pivotal role of rural cadres. Implementation has been decentralized in two ways: first, it is left to the localities to generate family planning regulations consistent with central directives and local conditions, and second, it is up to the localities to establish and maintain the organizational structure charged with implementing the policy.[4]

In its dealings with rural cadres, the Party Center has used both normative and coercive methods in pursuit of family planning goals. The normative approach is best seen in the Open Letter of 1980. Central leaders are appealing to the most politically conscious activists in the localities—Party and Youth League members—to convince those less advanced in their thinking to support the one-child policy. While the reasons for the policy are spelled out, and some of the benefits (in terms of schooling, health care, employment and so forth) to be awarded to one-child families are suggested, penalties for noncompliance are not stated. Nor, for that matter, are the localities told how to fund the benefits they are to provide. The problem is seen as essentially ideological, in terms of "patiently persuading" the masses to "transform (their) prevailing social traditions." Indeed, the Chinese media, in its analysis of resistance to the one-child campaign, has been virtually unanimous in stressing that "feudal ideas"remain the major factor impeding successful implementation. Since nonideological causes are treated more as incidental than as integral parts of the problem, education and propaganda, rather than some more active central intervention—particularly one that would mean the expenditure of scarce state funds—remains the preferred solution.[5]

But the "appeal" to local leaders to take the lead in family planning should not be seen merely as a "request" from higher levels. The Center knows that local people are unlikely to comply with an unpopular policy if their cadres have not already adopted it first. Thus, pressure has been put on rural cadres to abort pregnancies, sign a single-child pledge, accept sterilization, and so forth, in advance of their neighbors. The introduction of the "cadre job responsibility system" in 1982 and 1983 tied a cadre's income to his/her family planning work. Each local leader was assigned about ten to twenty households, and that leader had to sign a contract with higher levels of government stipulating cash rewards or penalties, depending on the marriage and birth patterns of those under his/her jurisdiction.[6]

Despite such efforts, what emerges most forcefully is the limits on central power. Since family planning regulations are enforced through local funding with local personnel, higher levels cannot force them to be adopted, or if adopted, carried out.[7] The issue of funding is a crucial one. The Center is well aware of the value of economic incentives and disincentives. These were particularly effective in urban areas, where the state ownership system made the award of free medical care and schooling, preference in housing and job allocation, and monthly cash payments a relatively straightforward, albeit costly, matter. In the countryside, such rewards—or economic penalties, such as reduced work points, private plots, grain allocations, and so forth—were much less clearly defined, since they had to be funded from rural collectives rather than by the state. Not only did rural collectives vary widely in their resources, but the production responsibility system was decollectivizing the countryside at precisely the same time these collectives were expected to take on additional and onerous responsibilities in the course of monitoring the complicated birth planning system.

With the Center unable to exercise the same influence over rural cadres as they have in the urban areas—neither threats of demotion nor economic incentives or disincentives are particularly potent given current rural conditions—violations of national policy guidelines have not been uncommon. When the Center has forced the issue by putting maximum pressure on rural cadres, as in 1982 and 1983, widespread problems of female infanticide and forced abortion have been acknowledged in the Chinese press. Drawing back in the face of these tragic consequences, in April 1984 the Central Committee issued Document No. 7, "strictly prohibiting all forms of coercion and commandism" and "establishing planned parenthood more rationally and sensibly and on the basis of mass support." Couples in the rural areas who had "practical difficulties" and who wanted two children were to be given "special treatment."[8] By the summer of 1984, state family planning officials began to list an increasing number of conditions under which couples might have a second child. Provincial authorities followed suit and published their own detailed regulations granting exceptions to the one-child policy.[9]

The production responsibility system, which has contributed so much to increasing agricultural production, has proved particularly detrimental to the population program. The relationship between these two fundamental Party goals—high agricultural output and population control—is a classic example of policy conflict. As Tyrene White has described it, the system of full responsibility (*da bao gan*) has hindered the one-child program in four ways. First, division of land generally has been based on the amount of household labor power—the more family members the more land allocated. More land commonly means more income. For young couples already influenced by traditional values and family pressures, such economic logic may appear unassailable. Second, under *da bao gan*, brigade cadres receive parcels of land along with other peasants and are assigned production quotas. Since their income from the collective comes primarily from cultivating their allotment of land rather than from an administrative salary, as had been the case previously, administrative duties of all types, including family planning work, tend to be neglected. Third, local welfare funds, which are used to pay benefits to holders of one-child certificates, often have less money than before. Unlike the old system, under which collective income would be distributed only after the production team had removed funds for welfare and various expenses, individuals and households now are entitled to receive directly all the income from their production, from which they must pay the agricultural tax and contribute to the welfare fund. One result has been the depletion of welfare funds prior to providing all the promised benefits. Fourth, the responsibility system has not only posed problems for the dispensing of rewards, but also for the enforcement of penalties. In the past, team or brigade cadres rewarded those using contraceptives or holding one-child certificates with extra work points or other benefits, and they punished violators by deducting work points and denying tangible benefits. Now that income flows directly to the peasants, there may be no work points to reward or deduct and few tangible benefits to offer. As China moves into the crucial second stage of rural reform—the large-scale commercialization of rural production—local cadres may have no basis for determining household income beyond the value of contractually stipulated quotas. But this "within-quota" income will likely constitute an increasingly lower percentage of total household income; thus, cadres who persist in enforcement may find that such penalties fail to deter offenders. The responsibility system has therefore demonstrated the economic value inherent in labor power, further undermined the commitment of local cadres to family planning work, and disrupted the system of rewards and penalties on which compliance largely depends.[10]

A variety of factors—the persistence of traditional values, new rural economic policies, the noncompliance of basic-level cadres, and so forth—appear to be hindering the government's one-child policy in the countryside. In an effort to determine more systematically the elements that lead to success in the Party's population policy, social scientists have been mobilized to conduct detailed empirical studies on fertility and birthrate in a variety of localities throughout the country. Although the micro studies published in the open press tend to report investigations in localities that have, minimally, performed above the national average, some of the studies have provided important data on peasant attitudes. Particularly valuable are the analyses that incorporate a number of sociological variables, including the effects of socio-economic status, cultural-educational level, and social ideology on marriage and childbearing.[11] Selection 87, an inquiry into the reasons for unplanned (extra-quota) births in nine counties and two municipalities of Shaanxi Province, is a good example of this approach.

Several of its findings confirm the problems of policy implementation we have cited. For example, the authors note that some rural cadres are less than enthusiastic in promoting family planning, that the existing economic reward/punishment system has been partially negated by the effects of the production responsibility system, and that those violating family planning regulations by giving birth to a second child feel no pressure; in fact, their neighbors tend to support them. Interestingly, the survey concludes that "long-term social psychological reasons determined by socio-economic conditions (e.g., the desire for old-age support) and customs and habits" accounted for 81.6 percent of the self-reported reasons for extra-quota births, while short-term reasons (e.g., the need for stronger labor capacity) only accounted for 15.5 percent of the responses. This fits in with results from several other surveys. A study done in rural Hubei Province found that 51 percent of the 808 peasants questioned claimed that they wanted additional children for old age support, 25 percent were concerned about perpetuating the family line, and 21 percent wanted more labor power.[12] While survey data is consistent in showing that concern for old age security is the most important factor in the desire for additional children, particularly males, the interpretation of these findings is more problematic. Officially, these concerns are commonly blamed on feudal, Confucian ideas, which can be eradicated through propaganda and education. However, since there is virtually no state-financed old-age support in the Chinese countryside—another contrast with urban China—the continuing need for male children, while indeed similar to bygone days, very much reflects current economic realities•

Notes

1. JPRS 85041, May 7, 1985, pp. 56–66 (*Renkou yanjiu* [Population Research], January 1985); Erika Platte, "China's Fertility Transition: The One-Child Campaign," *Pacific Affairs* 57: 4 (Winter 1984–85), pp. 646–671. The one-child campaign, which was launched in 1979, marked the fourth time since the founding of the PRC that the government has attempted to restrict the country's birthrate. Earlier initiatives had begun in 1953, 1962, and 1971. Family planning was treated in an increasingly urgent fashion during the 1970s. By mid-decade the government was trying to require urban couples to stop at three. In 1977 it was announced that rural as well as urban couples must cease childbearing at two children. The promotion of the one-child policy was formally announced in January 1979, although a moderate goal of compliance by 20 percent of urban couples and 5 percent of rural couples was considered acceptable. Before the end of the year, the government position had changed from encouragement of the one-child family to insistence that almost all couples stop at one healthy living child. Undeniably, these birth planning efforts have yielded results. In 1970, one out of five babies were firstborn. Since then the proportion has risen to almost one out of three in 1977, and to almost one out of two—47 percent—in 1981. On these points, see Hou Wenruo, "Population Policy," in Liu Zheng, Song Jian, and others, *China's Population: Problems and Prospects* (Beijing: New World Press, 1981), pp. 55–76; Judith Banister, "Population Policy and Trends in China, 1978-83," *The China Quarterly* No. 100 (December 1984), pp. 717–722; Pi-chao Chen, "Birth Planning and Fertility Transition," *The Annals of the American Academy of Political and Social Science* 476 (November 1984), p. 137.

2. Chen, "Birth Planning," pp. 134–135.

3. John P. Burns, "The Election of Production Team Cadres in Rural China: 1958–

1974," *The China Quarterly* No. 74 (June 1978), pp. 273–296; William L. Parish and Martin King Whyte, *Village and Family in Contemporary China* (Chicago: University of Chicago Press, 1978), pp. 96–114; Richard Madsen, *Morality and Power in a Chinese Village* (Berkeley: University of California Press, 1984).

4. Tyrene White, "Implementing the 'One-Child-Per-Couple' Population Program in Rural China: National Goals and Local Politics," in David M. Lampton, ed., *Policy Implementation in Post-Mao China* (Berkeley: University of California Press, forthcoming).

5. Jeffrey Wasserstrom, "Resistance to the One-Child Family," *Modern China* 3 (July 1984), p. 359.

6. Banister, "Population Policy," pp. 722–727.

7. White, "Implementing the 'One-Child . . . .'"

8. FBIS Daily Report, July 10, 1985, pp. K2–K3 (*Renmin ribao* [People's Daily] Overseas Edition, July 5, 1985); JPRS 85068, July 9, 1985, pp. 27-34 (*Renkou yu jingji* [Population and Economy], February 25, 1985); JPRS 85071, July 22, 1985, pp. 51–53 (*Jihua shengyu* [Planned Birth], April 12, 1985).

9. Jim Mann, "China Eases Rule Limiting Rural Couples to 1 Child," *Los Angeles Times,* May 12, 1985, pp. 1, 18; JPRS 85027, March 18, 1985, pp. 97–98 (*Shenyang ribao* [Shenyang Daily], December 22, 1984); FBIS Daily Report, December 17, 1984, p. P3 (Radio Changsha, December 13, 1984); FBIS Daily Report, September 5, 1984, pp. S1–S2 (Radio Harbin, August 29, 1984).

10. White, "Implementing the 'One-Child . . . .'"; also see Chen, "Birth Planning," pp. 136–137; "Rural Take-Off: Raising the Stakes," *China News Analysis* No. 1277 (January 15, 1985).

11. Translations of four local empirical studies, including Selection 87, can be found in David S. K. Chu, ed., "Chinese Demography, 1978–1984: Theoretical and Empirical Studies," *Chinese Sociology and Anthropology* 16:3-4 (Spring-Summer 1984), pp. 90–144.

12. Cheng Du, "An Investigation of Rural Birthrates in Hubei Province," *Renkou yanjiu,* 1982, No. 5; translated in Chu, "Chinese Demography," pp. 107–116. For additional survey data, see White, "Implementing the 'One-Child . . . .'"; and Chen, "Birth Planning," p. 138.

86

Central Committee of the CCP

OPEN LETTER CALLING ON PARTY AND YOUTH LEAGUE CADRES TO TAKE THE LEAD IN HAVING ONLY ONE CHILD [PER COUPLE]

[September 25, 1980]

Beijing, September 25 [1980]. Xinhua News Agency Dispatch—The Central Committee [CC] of the Chinese Communist Party [CCP] has issued an open letter to all Communist Party and Communist Youth League [CYL] members concerning the question of controlling China's population growth. The complete text follows:

To All Comrades of the Chinese Communist Party and Communist Youth League Throughout the Nation:

In order to strive to limit the total population of China to within 1.2 billion by the end of this century, the State Council has already issued the call to the people of the whole country, advocating one couple giving birth to only one child. This is a matter that affects the rate and the future of Four Modernizations construction, affects the health and happiness of future generations, and is a vital measure that is consistent with the long-term and immediate interests of the people of the whole country. The Central Committee urges all Party and CYL members, especially cadres at all levels, to take practical action to take the lead in heeding the State Council's call and, moreover, to actively, responsibly, and patiently conduct publicity and education among the broad masses.

Since the founding [of the People's Republic of China], owing to progress in health work and the improvement of people's living conditions, the population mortality rate, especially infant mortality rate, has declined greatly, [and] the life expectancy has been greatly extended. However, we did not appropriately control the birthrate, thus allowing the population to grow too quickly. In the old China

"Dang zhongyang haozhao dang tuanyuan daitou zhisheng yige haizi." *Renmin ribao* [People's Daily], September 26, 1980, p. 1; *Zhongguo qingnian bao* [China Youth News], September 27, 1980, p. 1. Translation from "Chinese Demography, 1978–1984: Theoretical and Empirical Studies." A special issue of *Chinese Sociology and Anthropology* 16:3-4 (Spring-Summer 1984), pp. 83–89, David S. K. Chu, guest editor.

Editor's note: A flurry of birth control related activities, discussions, and directives were reported from many parts of China following the publication of this open letter. See English translations, e.g., *China Report: Political, Sociological and Military Affairs*, FBIS/JPRS 76672, No. 131 (October 22, 1980); 76736, No. 134 (October 31, 1980); 77179, No. 157 (January 15, 1981).

during the 109 years from 1840 to 1949, the whole nation's population only increased by a total of 130 million. In the 30 years since the founding of the PRC, however, more than 600 million people have been born; taking away those who died, there has been a net increase of 430 million persons. Such a rapid population increase has caused the people of the whole country to face greater and greater difficulties in having food, shelter, housing, transportation, education, health, employment, etc. This has made it very difficult for the whole nation to change within a short time the features of being poor and underdeveloped. Particularly serious is the fact that China's population grew the fastest during the period from 1963 to 1970; at present persons thirty years old and under make up about 65 percent of the total population. From now on, an average of more than 20 million persons every year will enter the age of marriage and reproduction. If the control of population growth, in the widespread advocacy of one couple having only one child, does not commence now using the time of the next 30 to 40 years, especially the next 20 to 30 years, then, based on calculations of the current average of 2.2 children per couple, China's total population will reach 1.3 billion after 20 years [2000] and will exceed 1.5 billion after 40 years [2020]. This will greatly increase the difficulties of achieving the Four Modernizations, creating a serious situation where it would be very difficult to have some improvement in the people's lives.

The most effective method of solving this problem is to carry out the State Council's call—each couple having only one child.

In terms of each family and household, additional people, before they are able to earn a living, means more expenditures [and] more grain, thus affecting the improvement of a family's [standard of] living. A quick computation makes this clear. After they are able to earn a living, on the one hand, they make contributions to society; but, on the other hand, they also consume goods and materials produced in society. In terms of the nation, if the labor productivity of industry and agriculture is still very low and the production of goods and materials is still not abundant, then the rate of population increase will directly affect the funds and accumulation necessary for modernizing construction. Excessively rapid population increase will reduce the accumulation of funds; reducing and slowing population growth will increase the accumulation of funds. Besides the family needing to increase the cost of upbringing, increasing population also requires the state, in order to solve their education, employment, and other problems, to raise educational expenditures, investment of equipment, outlays for social and public utilities, etc. Please think about it. How great a functional role can be obtained by using the amounts of money saved from these aspects to develop the economy and cultural-educational undertakings!

With excessively rapid population growth, it is very difficult to raise the people's standard of living. In terms of the supply of grain and food, to guarantee food grain, industrial grain, and other grain rations of urban and rural people, in the future the average annual per capita grain rations should reach a minimum of 800 *jin*. If an additional 100 million population is born, it is necessary to produce an additional 80,000 million *jin* of food grain. With our present average cultivated land of about 2 *mu* per person, if the population increases to 1.3 billion, then the per capita average cultivated land will diminish to one *mu* plus. Under the present conditions, on such a limited amount of land, it is extremely difficult to produce an average 800 *jin* of grains per capita as well as sufficient quantities of economic crops. Moreover, excessively rapid population growth not only increases the difficulties of going to school and obtaining employment, but also will cause excessive depletion of energy, water, forest, and other natural resources, worsen environmental pollution, and cause productive conditions and the people's living environment to deteriorate greatly, thus making it difficult to improve them.

That being the case, is the call of one couple having only one child realizable? As long as everyone makes a concerted effort, it is possible to obtain this goal. During the nine years between 1971 and 1979 when our country made great efforts to control population growth, cumulatively some 56 million fewer babies were born. Since 1979 several million young couples have heeded the Party's call by voluntarily giving birth to only one child. In the year 1979 alone, some 10 million fewer babies were born than in 1970. The facts prove that our people are reasonable [and] do take the situation as a whole into consideration; not only are they able to understand and sympathize with the country's difficulties, but also are capable of considering the interests of the future generations.

Some comrades worry that with only one child per couple, some new problems will appear in the future—e.g., aging of the whole population, insufficiency of the labor force, the number of males exceeding females, increasing numbers of old people to be supported by each young couple. Regarding these above-mentioned problems, some have stemmed from misunderstandings [and] some can be solved.

The phenomenon of population "aging" will not occur within this century because at present approximately one-half of the total national population is below the age of twenty-one, while elderly people above the age of sixty-five consist of less than five percent. At the fastest, the phenomenon of aging will arise only after some forty years. We are fully capable of adopting measures in advance to prevent the occurence of this phenomenon.

At present our country has a labor force of approximately 500 million. It is estimated that after twenty years, it will increase to 600 million. By the early twenty-first century, the labor force will still grow by more than 10 million per year. After thirty years [2010], the problem of population growth, which is most acute at present, will be mitigated, [and] then a different population policy can be adopted. It is not necessary, therefore, to worry about the problem of an insufficient labor force.

After Liberation, our population statistics over the years have demonstrated that the ratio of males to females has been more or less the same, with boys numbering slightly more. Since the advocacy of one child per couple, concerned departments have made investigations in some districts of the sex ratio of first-born children. The findings are also that boys number slightly more than girls. Working the same [as boys], girls grow up [and] can do some specialized work very well, and are more able to do domestic work. Also, a husband can be allowed to reside with the woman's family. The people of new China, especially the younger generations, must overcome the old ideology of male superiority over females [*zhongnan qingnü*]; if only a girl is born, she should be brought up well in the same way.

After forty years [2020] of the practice of one child per couple, some families may experience the problem where the elderly lack people to care for them. Many countries have this problem; we must attentively think of ways to solve it. In the future when production is developed and the people's lives are improved, social welfare and social security will certainly increase and improve continuously. Gradually, care for the aged can be achieved so that the lives of the elderly will be secure. To respect, love and protect, and provide for the elderly, to allow them to live their later years well, are the responsibilities that children should bear and also a fine tradition of Chinese society. The people of our country must promote this good social custom. The behavior of not providing for, or even mistreating, parents must be criticized; those that violate the law must also be punished.

When promoting one child per couple, it is also necessary to emphasize appropriately late marriage [*wanhun*] and late reproduction [*wanyu*]. The [minimum] age for marriage stipulated by the Marriage Law [1980] is not late. For the sake of study and work, however, appropriately late marriage must still be advocated and, even more so, properly delayed reproduction must be stressed. If young women begin reproduction at age twenty, five generations will be born within 100 years, [whereas] if reproduction begins at age twenty-five, only four generations will be born within a century. Consequently, late marriage [and] particularly delayed reproduction are both of great significance for reducing the magnitude and slowing the rate of population growth. Appropriately delayed reproduction also has many benefits for the young women themselves.

In order to control population growth, the Party and government have already adopted a series of concrete policies. Considerations and allowances [i.e., preferential treatment] are to be given to single children and their families with respect to admission to child-care centers and [primary] schools, in seeking medical services, employment, admission to [secondary and higher] education, and in assignment to urban housing and rural residential land [for building houses]. The policy of equal pay for equal work for men and women must be implemented earnestly. Major efforts must be launched in scientific research work on reproductive physiology, eugenics (i.e., not to give birth to babies with deformities) and birth control technology, to train a large contingent of qualified technicians, to do well work in guidance on birth control techniques, in women and infant health care, and in childhood education, in order to guarantee the safety of birth control techniques and reduce the number of babies born with congenital [and] genetic diseases. Concerned departments must speedily adopt effective measures and produce high-quality contraceptive drugs and devices to meet the needs of the masses.

Planned birth involves the immediate interests of every family and household; it is necessary to give priority to ideological work, to adhere to patient and meticulous persuasion and education. Some people indeed have practical difficulties in complying with policy regulations; they may have approval to have two children, but not three. According to policy regulations, [enforcement] for minority nationalities can also be relaxed. Birth control measures should rely mainly on contraception, the methods to be voluntarily selected by the masses.

The realization of the one child per couple [policy] is a major task of transforming prevailing social traditions. The Central Committee requires all Communist Party and CYL members, especially cadres of various levels, to be concerned with the future of the country, to be conscientious about the interests of the people, to be responsible for the happiness of future generations, to understand thoroughly the significance and necessity of this task, [and] to be exemplary. Party cadres must take the lead in overcoming feudal thinking in their own heads, discarding the mistaken idea that without giving birth to a boy one cannot carry on the tradition of continuing the family line. Young comrades must begin with themselves, while old comrades must educate and supervise their own sons and daughters. Every comrade must actively and patiently work on the masses around him; every comrade engaged in planned birth work must become a propagandist, to help the masses solve ideological and practical problems, and moreover, resolve not to resort to coercion and commandism in violation of law and [Party] discipline, [and] also to persuade others to do the same, so as to implement correctly the call of the State Council and to enhance the realization of the socialist Four Modernizations.

Central Committee of the
Chinese Communist Party

September 25, 1980

87

Zhao Liren and Zhu Chuzhu

A PRELIMINARY INQUIRY ON THE PROBLEM OF UNPLANNED (EXTRA-QUOTA) SECOND BIRTHS

SINCE NOVEMBER 1981, we have investigated in succession the circumstances of 932 cases of unplanned [extra-quota] second births [*jihua wai ertai*] in 9 counties and 2 municipalities distributed in the Guanzhong Plains, northern plateau, and southern mountainous region of Shaanxi Province. The cases under investigation were chosen at random, and 87 percent were rural families.

The resurgence of births in China in 1981 was marked by a decline in the

"Jihua wai ertai wenti chutan." *Renkou yanjiu* [Population Research], 1983, No. 3, pp. 36–39. The authors are with the Population Research Office, Xian Jiaotong University. Translation from "Chinese Demography, 1978–1984: Theoretical and Empirical Studies." A special issue of *Chinese Sociology and Anthropology* 16:3–4 (Spring–Summer 1984), pp. 117–130, David S. K. Chu, guest editor.

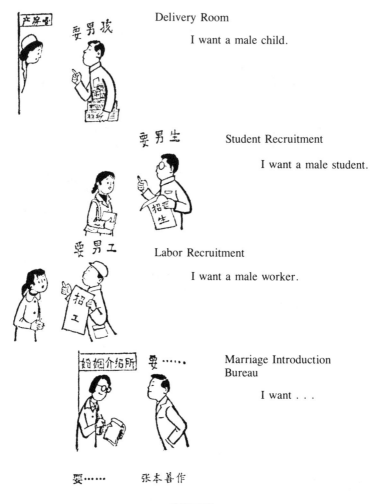

Delivery Room

I want a male child.

Student Recruitment

I want a male student.

Labor Recruitment

I want a male worker.

Marriage Introduction Bureau

I want . . .

I WANT

Yao, by Zhang Benshan

Source: Zhongguo qingnian bao [China Youth News], April 9, 1983

multiparity birthrate [*duotailü*] and a drastic rise in the rate of unplanned second births, resulting in unplanned second births outnumbering multiparity births.*

*In demographic research and in the context of current Chinese policies on population control, the notion of parity, i.e., the number of live children a woman has borne, is critically important. Generally, demographers define a multiparous woman as one who has had more than one child. In Chinese usage, however, given that the policy goal now strives for one child per couple, multiparity births (not multiple births as it is sometimes incorrectly rendered) refers to the third or greater number of births by a woman. The Chinese distinction between extra-quota, unplanned second births (and their birthrate) and multiparity births (and their rate) has implications for both demographic analysis and policy implementation. — D.S.K.C.

Therefore to bring under control the extra-quota second births becomes the key to population control at present. The aim of this investigation was to find the objective and subjective causes for the unplanned second births and explore ways to bring them under strict control.

An Account by the Peasants Themselves

Listed in our investigation form were 16 items, including age when giving birth, sex of the first birth, cultural levels of parents, family size and structure, etc. The factors contributing to the extra-quota second births can be summed up as follows:

1. The reasons for unplanned second births as accounted for by those investigated can be seen in the following [Table 1]:

Table 1

Self-Reported Reasons for Extra-Quota Second Birth (in percent)

	Need to have a boy								
Stronger labor capacity	For old age support	To perpetuate family line by male heir	Hope to have both son and daughter	Want to have two children regardless of their sexes	Want to have a girl	Contraception failure	Desire of grandparents	Since others have given second births, so do I	Special reasons
(1)	(2)	(3)	(4)	(5)	(6)	(7)	(8)	(9)	(10)
9.1	27.5	13.9	9.8	17.4	11.4	3.6	1.6	2.8	2.6 [98.7]

The reasons may be divided into two categories. The first category consists of long-term social psychological reasons determined by socio-economic conditions and customs and habits that have been in existence over a long period of time. This category includes columns 2, 3, 4, 5, 6, and 8 listed in Table 1, accounting for 81.6 percent of the total. Another category may be called short-term reasons, including columns 1, 7 and 9, which account for 15.5 percent of the total. The situation of column 1, i.e., wanting an extra-quota second birth because a boy has stronger labor capacity, is even more pronounced after implementation of the production responsibility system in the countryside. It is worth noting, however, that this item only accounts for 9.1 percent. We found that in the countryside there are loud voices that give insufficient labor as their reason for wanting second births. In fact, upon further investigation, the situation is not so. Because saying "wanting a second child due to insufficient labor" is considered reasonable, more people do so. As a matter of fact, social reasons such as the desire to perpetuate the family line with a male heir play a big role, but these can only be detected through in-depth investigation.

2. The frame of mind of those giving unplanned second births. With different intentions, they gave extra-quota second births. Their frame of mind after the second births may be summed up as follows [Table 2]:

Table 2

The State of Mind of Those Who Had Extra-Quota Second Births

Feeling sorry for being punished economically but with no regret for giving second births (1)	Willing to take punishment and rejoicing in achieving what they wished (2)	Feeling regret for being punished and unable to achieve what they wished in second births (3)	Feeling pressure for violating regulations concerning family planning (4)
54.8%	17%	21%	7.2%

Taking things as a whole, currently those who have given unplanned second births in rural areas do not feel any pressure. The 7.2 percent in column 4 are almost all city dwellers. Despite the different situations in columns 1, 2, and 3, none of those who had extra-quota second births regretted their own reproductive behavior. The reasons for such a frame of mind are: First, they believe that under the system of production responsibility they are able to bring up their children by doing more work and producing more without adding to the burden of the state. With perfect assurance, they tend to have this to say: "I give birth to my child and I'll bring him up on my own without costing the state a penny. In the past I worked eight hours a day, and now I work two hours more and can produce enough food for the child." They do not think that they have brought any disadvantage to the state with their reproductive behavior, with the result that they do not feel any dishonor. Second, many families do not suffer a decline in income because of second births. Generally a family of four is assigned responsibility for 7 to 8 *mu* of farmland. The farming can be done with the labor of one man and, at most, some supplementary work by a woman. Therefore, to have one more child in the family does not bring down its income. Of the almost one thousand families we investigated, family size for the majority consists of households of four to five persons. Four-person families make up 67.3 percent of the total; five-person families, 13.2 percent; and families of six and more, only 19.3 percent. Small families have fewer contradictions. With the man doing farm labor, the woman can stay at home to take care of the children, and family income is not greatly affected. Third, people in general tend to be sympathetic and supportive toward those giving extra-quota second births so as not to make the latter feel isolated and feel the pressure of public opinion. Fourth, for a variety of reasons, some of those who have extra-quota second births display an attitude of resistance. Some even think that the more punishment [for birth control violations], the more precious the child will be. When the child grows up and knows the hardship his parents went through, he will be more filial.

Summation and Analysis

We made a comprehensive analysis of the 923 cases of unplanned second births in connection with the economic conditions of the families, the sex of the first births, the interval between the births, and the parents' cultural level.

(1) Changes in the Income of Families Having Unplanned Second Births. [See Table 3]

Table 3

Comparision of Economic Income between 1981 and 1980

Localities	Number of families	Income increased Number of families	percent	Income decreased Number of families	percent	Income remained at the same level Number of families	percent
Yang County	12	—	—	12	100.00	—	—
Nanzheng Country	86	2	2.33	80	93.02	4	4.65
Mian County	65	6	9.23	56	86.15	3	4.62
Chenggu County	48	6	12.50	41	85.42	1	2.08
Danfeng County	37	4	10.81	27	72.97	6	16.22
Yanchuan County	21	—	—	20	95.24	1	4.76
Mizhi County	48	39	81.25	4	8.33	5	10.42
Wubao County	48	43	89.58	—	—	5	10.42
Jingyang County	324	108	33.33	187	57.72	29	8.95
Jintai District of Baoji	55	21	38.18	29	52.73	5	9.09
Shuiliu Commune of Xian	22	1	4.55	18	81.82	3	13.63
Total	766	230	30.03	474	61.88	62	8.09

As some of the localities were hit by natural disasters in 1981, 474 families, 61.87 percent of the total number of families we investigated, suffered a decline in their income. Some 230 families, 30.02 percent of the total, earned more, and 62 families, that is, 8.09 percent, kept their income at the same level. Hit by natural disasters, the proportion of families in the counties of Yangxian, Nanzheng, Mianxian, Chenggu, and Yanchuan and Shuiliu Commune in Xian that had suffered a decline in income came up to more than 80 percent of the families we investigated. Only in Mizhi County and Wubao County in northern Shaanxi, the families that had increased their income accounted for 81.25 percent and 89.58 percent of the total, respectively. This shows that we cannot simply link income with population growth; especially, we cannot link the unplanned second births directly to the ups and downs of income. For families that suffered a decline in income, having a second child would not bring much pressure to bear on their family economy. And for families that had an increased income, they developed the attitude of not fearing punishment. The peasants, having become affluent, always want to have one more child to make things more lively; the viewpoint of having more sons means more fortune has gained ground. It seems that income does not have much influence over extra-quota second births. Families that earn either more or less are both susceptible to second births.

(2) The Relation Between the Unplanned Second Birth and the Sex of the First Birth.

Table 4

Sex of First Birth

Localities	Number of births	Sex of first births			
		Male	Percent	Female	Percent
Yang County	75	37	49.33	38	50.67
Nanzheng County	91	29	31.87	62	68.13
Mian County	86	36	41.86	50	58.14
Chenggu County	50	18	36.00	32	64.00
Danfeng County	50	27	54.00	23	46.00
Yanchuan County	20	8	40.00	12	60.00
Mizhi County	51	17	33.33	34	66.67
Wubao County	48	19	39.58	29	60.42
Jingyang County	333	155	46.55	178	53.45
Jintai District	99	38	38.38	61	61.62
Shuiliu Commune	17	8	47.06	9	52.94
Total	920	392	42.61	528	57.39

From Table 4 we can see that of the 920 children of first births, girls made up a larger proportion than boys. This shows that some people gave second births out of their desire to have sons. Nevertheless, this proportion is not large. At the same time, many people wanted to have a girl because their first child was a boy. [They say:] "A daughter is one the parents can confide in. She cares for the elderly and is thoughtful. And she can handle needlework." It is also the common wish of the people to have two children regardless of whether they are boys or girls. For example, some people have this to say: "It is difficult to burn a single piece of firewood; nor is it easy to bring up a single child." They are worried that the fewer the children, the less filial they will be. This is normal social psychology. Therefore, whether the first birth is a boy or a girl, as we see it, is not the basic reason for second births.

Data from the investigation also show that the effect of the sex of the first birth on the second birth varies with different localities. In areas where the level of birth control work is comparatively high, baby girls occupied a higher percentage of first births in families giving extra-quota second births. Mian County and Nanzheng County and others are cases in point. Following the gradual rise of the level of family planning work and the continuous decline in the number of extra-quota second births, this factor will play an increasingly bigger role.

(3) The Interval Between the First Birth and the Unplanned Second Birth.

Among the 922 cases investigated as listed in Table 5, 43.28 percent had second births within two years, and 67.03 percent within three years. And those who had second births when their first born children were only one year old accounted for 15.47 percent in Yang County, 30 percent in Yanchuan County, 15.68 percent in Mizhi County, and 20.41 percent in Jintai District of Baoji. Adding them to those who gave second births within an interval of two years, the percentage would be 61.89, 65, 58.82, and 53.06 for the above localities, respectively. Such high proportions reveal the seriousness of the phenomena of giving births ahead of schedule and beyond quota, the high proportions of early marriages and early births, and an increase in the number of people who became pregnant again after having obtained single–child certificates. To implement late marriages and late births as required by the documents of the Party Central Committee, we have to make arduous efforts. Evidently, the short interval between the first and second births was a major feature of the resurgence of child births in 1980 and 1981.

(4) The Relationship Between Unplanned Second Births and Parental Cultural Level.

We investigated a total of 1,645 persons (including one or both spouses). Of the total, 12.27 percent were illiterate and 89.52 percent had an educational background of junior high school and under. Because of the ten years of turmoil, the actual cultural levels of these married young couples are far behind the record of their formal schooling. The low cultural level and high illiteracy rate pose a great obstacle to the implementation of family planning. Among those giving unplanned births, illiterates accounted for more than 35 percent in Nanzheng and Yanchuan Counties and over 20 percent in Mian and Wubao Counties. Having a low cultural level and not having knowledge about contraception and hygiene are among the causes for blindly getting pregnant and extra-quota births prevailing in the countryside. Our statistics also show the unplanned second birth givers

Table 5

Interval between First Birth and Extra-Quota Second Birth

Localities	Total Number of 2nd births	After 4 years and more		within 3 years		within 2 years		within 1 year	
		Number of births	Percentage	Number of births	Percentage	Number of births	Percentage	Number of births	Percentage
Yang County	84	19	22.62	13	15.48	39	46.42	13	15.47
Nanzheng County	90	28	31.11	23	25.56	35	38.89	4	4.44
Mian County	78	29	37.18	22	28.21	21	26.92	6	7.69
Chenggu County	50	16	32.00	13	26.00	19	38.00	2	4.00
Danfeng County	50	23	46.00	12	24.00	12	24.00	3	6.00
Yanchuan County	20	4	20.00	3	15.00	7	35.00	6	30.00
Mizhi County	51	11	21.57	10	19.61	22	43.14	8	15.68
Wubao County	48	11	22.92	13	27.08	19	39.58	5	10.42
Jingyang County	335	131	39.10	90	26.87	92	27.46	22	6.57
Jintai District	98	29	29.59	17	17.35	32	32.65	20	20.41
Shuiliu Commune	18	3	16.67	3	16.67	10	55.55	2	11.11
Total	922	304	32.97	219	23.75	308	33.41	91	9.87

mentioned above are generally in the age bracket of twenty to thirty, the peak fertility period, adding to the difficulty of bringing extra-quota births under control. In addition, the low cultural level is also directly related to the small producer's viewpoint on birth. In the eyes of small producers, using hoes and pulling carts do not call for a high level of culture; what is needed is strong physical capability. Therefore, they want to have more children, especially more boys. As there are large numbers of educated youth awaiting job assignments in Chinese cities and towns, the peasants feel even more strongly that sending children to school cannot reap benefits. Consequently, the promotion rates for elementary and junior high schools in the countryside tend to go downward. As the population grows, the school attendance rate falls, and the low school attendance rate reduces the quality of the population, which in turn brings up the birthrate. This deserves our serious attention.

Conclusion and Suggestions

Based on a comprehensive analysis of the above conditions, we can arrive at a general conclusion.

The current rise in second births is mainly owing not to economic reasons but rather to social and psychological reasons. The impact of economic and cultural levels on women's fertility rate varies with different localities. Under China's conditions today family income, sex of the previous births, and parental educational background are factors, among other things, that have a larger influence over multiparity births (that is, three births and more). As regards second births, however, the above analysis shows no pattern of regularity if judged by the increase or decrease of income alone. Those who have improved their living standard want to give second births, and so do those who are worse off than before. Therefore, it is not primarily direct economic causes that contribute to the increase in births, but rather social and psychological factors, particularly ideas such as raising children to support old age, perpetuating the family by male heirs, the worry of no insurance with a single child, etc.

All of these factors will remain over a long period of time and, correspondingly, there will long be the desire for second births.

To effectively hold down second births under the current conditions, we offer the following suggestions:

(1) Step up Propaganda and Education Work to Gradually Raise People's Self-Consciousness for Practicing Family Planning.

Whether or not we can effectively check the desire for second births in rural areas mainly hinges on the level of family planning work, the consistency and effectiveness in implementing the family planning policy, and other conditions. Progress is determined primarily by how propaganda and education is done. To hold down second births we must create a powerful public opinion so that the people can understand that advocation of one child for one family is the only feasible short-term measure to forestall a population explosion in China in light of our national conditions, strength, and the overall situation. Only by doing thus can we hold down the total population to under 1.2 billion by the end of this century. We must help the people to self-consciously cultivate a general social practice of having one child as glorious and to bring the pressure of public opinion to bear on those violating the state policy of family planning. We must conduct education in socialist spiritual civilization and patriotism as the central content of propaganda work for family planning. Consistent and thoroughgoing efforts should be made to disseminate knowledge about population theory so as to gradually change people's old, traditional point of view on birth. Attention must also be paid to the consistency and effectiveness of the family planning policy. By consistency we mean we cannot waver in the policy of advocating one child for one family. By effectiveness we mean all policy measures should be practical and feasible and be applied right to the point. If we can raise the level of family planning work and strengthen the consistency and effectiveness of policy, we can effectively check the increase of second births even though various factors for having second births still objectively exist.

(2) Simultaneous with the effort to install and perfect the various forms of production responsibility system in the countryside, we must take steps to implement family planning measures of economic restriction and reward. Implementation of the production responsibility system in the countryside has greatly mobilized the initiative of the commune members and enhanced the production of agriculture, but it has also created new problems and generated new circumstances for family planning. Some cadres are fearful that the policy of family planning might be modified and thus are unwilling and even dare not push for the family planning program. Because of changes in the forms of distribution, some previous stipulations on rewards and punishments are no longer applicable. As fines imposed on extra-quota births involve too many cases, they lose the meaning of economic sanction. After institution of the responsibility system of contracting for both land and labor, some people desire to have more children to augment their work force, thus entitling them to more farmland under their responsibility. In some places the contracted land was distributed according to the number of people and, as a result, those who violated the family planning requirements benefited and those who had fewer children felt that they suffered losses. Economic sanctions have no effect on some people, who assert: "As we can afford to pay the fines, it's up to us how many children we want to have." In light of this, preferential treatment for a single child, we believe, should be made concrete and put into effect; it should be embodied in the various policies of the production responsibility system such as allocating to the single-child families more contracted farmland and residential land. To carry into effect the stipulations about rewards and punishments, some regions direct attention to both kinds of production [i.e., material and human] simultaneously and sign contracts for both at the same time, namely, they enter into contract for the three major targets of grain, money, and births together. This is a good experience. In some localities the scope of contract terms is expanded to tie family planning to the economic interests of cadres and the masses at different levels so that punishment will begin with the leadership for the failure to implement the population plan. We must install and perfect the family planning program network at all levels and make solid efforts to resolve the compensation and subsidies for cadres working part time on the program.

(3) On the basis of enforcing the new marriage law, we must promote late marriage. As the [1981] Marriage Law actually advances the age requirement of marriage two to four years earlier, the phenomenon of early marriage and early birth has become a major factor contributing to the resurgence of childbirth in China. In light of this, we should educate the young people so that they can properly put off marriage to later years.

(4) Impose population tax. Now population in China is like a flood about to break a dam. To bring the unplanned births under control, it would be feasible to impose in the next few decades a head tax on extra-quota births. Starting from the unplanned second birth, a progressive head tax can be imposed on the third birth and above. At the same time, we can continue enforcing restrictive measures and sanctions against serious violators of family planning set down previously by Central and local authorities so that extra-quota births will not become legitimate after taxation. This still falls under the category of strengthening ideological education with the assistance of necessary economic measures.

The population tax collected by the state can be used to support population and education investment for family planning. This not only will improve the quality of our population but also not add much to the burden of the state finance. Using a population tax to make up the deficiency in education outlays is precisely a practice of taking it from the people and using it in their interests. It will tap new financial resources for us to make compulsory education universal across the country.

(5) Enlarge social insurance for the elderly. It is inappropriate, in our opinion, to generally criticize as feudal ideology the peasants' attitude toward raising children for old age support. In the final analysis, the problem of providing social insurance for the elderly can only be solved when social productive forces have developed and there are more collective welfare facilities available. As we understand it, a large portion of unplanned second and greater births in rural areas come from the consideration of old age support. Such thinking has not only a component of feudal ideology but also points sharply to the social problem of how we should provide for the old people. We should make use of the superiority of the socialist system and we should try to have organizations at all levels, especially the departments of labor and civil affairs, seek a common understanding and join efforts to gradually expand social insurance for the elderly, and resolve some practical problems. Following the growth of the collective economy, material conditions for providing social insurance for the elderly will become increasingly available. We can also try the method of allowing the state, the collective, and the individual all to contribute a share so that the insurance company can insure peasants. In 1981 Baoji Prefecture was hit by a flood. The insurance company made huge payments to cover the damage and thus enjoyed a very high reputation. Obviously we can undertake to provide social insurance for the elderly.

By employing the above measures as major approaches to comprehensive control, especially with education in spiritual civilization and patriotism as the centerpiece of the family planning program, it is entirely possible to generate powerful public opinion to bring under strict control unplanned second births while actively advocating one child for each couple.

(July 1982)

FURTHER READINGS

Aird, John S. "Population Studies and Population Policy in China." *Population and Development Review* 8:2 (June 1982), pp. 267–297.

Banister, Judith. *China's Changing Population*. Stanford: Stanford University Press, 1985.

Banister, Judith. "Population Policy and Trends in China, 1978–1983." *The China Quarterly* No. 100 (December 1984), pp. 717–741.

Chen, Pi-chao. *Population and Health Policy in the People's Republic of China*. Washington, D.C.: Smithsonian Institution, 1976.

Chu, David S. K., ed. "Chinese Demography, 1978–1984: Theoretical and Empirical Studies." Special issue of *Chinese Sociology and Anthropology* 16:3–4 (Spring-Summer 1984).

Coale, Ansley J. "Population Trends, Population Policy, and Population Studies in China." *Population and Development Review* 7:1 (March 1981), pp. 85–97.

Croll, Elisabeth. *The Politics of Marriage in Contemporary China*. Cambridge: Cambridge University Press, 1981.

Davis-Friedmann, Deborah. *Long Lives: Chinese Elderly and the Communist Revolution*. Cambridge, Mass.: Harvard University Press, 1983.

Keyfitz, Nathan. "The Population of China." *Scientific American* 250:2 (February 1984), pp. 38–47.

Liu Zheng, Song Jian, and Others. *China's Population: Problems and Prospects*. Beijing: New World Press, 1981.

Mosher, Stephen Westley. "Birth Control: A View from a Chinese Village." *Asian Survey* 22:4 (April 1982), pp. 356–368.

Orleans, Leo A. *Every Fifth Child: The Population of China*. Stanford: Stanford University Press, 1972.

Orleans, Leo A., and Ly Burnham. "The Enigma of China's Urban Population." *Asian Survey* 24:7 (July 1984), pp. 788–804.

Platte, Erika. "China's Fertility Transition: The One-Child Campaign." *Pacific Affairs* 57:4 (Winter 1984–85), pp. 646–671.

Tien, H. Yuan. "China: Demographic Billionaire." *Population Index* 38:2 (April 1983), pp. 1–43.

Tien, H. Yuan. *China's Population Struggle: Demographic Decision of the People's Republic of China*. Columbus: Ohio State University Press, 1973.

Tien, H. Yuan, ed. *Population Theory in China*. White Plains, N.Y.: M. E. Sharpe, 1980.

Wasserstrom, Jeffrey. "Resistance to the One-Child Family." *Modern China* 10:3 (July 1984), pp. 345–374.

White, Tyrene. "Implementing the 'One-Child-Per-Couple' Population Program in Rural China: National Goals and Local Politics." In David M. Lampton, ed. *Policy Implementation in Post-Mao China*. Berkeley: University of California Press, forthcoming.

Wolfgang, Marvin E., ed. *China in Transition* (special issue of *The Annals of the American Academy of Political and Social Science, November 1984*—articles on population by Sidney and Alice Goldstein, Lee-Jay Cho, and Pi-chao Chen, pp. 90–141). Beverly Hills: Sage Publications, 1984.

APPENDIX:
ORGANIZATION CHARTS

The Party

The *National Party Congress*, theoretically the supreme decision-making body of the Party, consists of about 1,500 delegates, who are nominated by senior Party leaders and elected by provincial and other local Party congresses. The Congress is supposed to meet every five years (it last met in 1982). Based on nominations from senior Party leaders, it elects the *Central Advisory Commission*, composed of veteran cadres and headed by Deng Xiaoping, the *Central Commission for Discipline Inspection*, headed by Chen Yun, and the *Central Committee*. The Central Committee, composed of 210 full, voting members and 130 alternate, nonvoting members, handles Party matters between Party Congresses. Based on nominations from senior Party leaders, the Central Committee elects the *Politburo*, which consists of 20 full and 2 alternate members, the *Standing Committee of the Politburo*, which consists of 5 of the Politburo members (Chen Yun, Deng Xiaoping, Hu Yaobang, Li Xiannian, and Zhao Ziyang in 1986), and the *Secretariat*, which consists of the Party secretary-general (Hu Yaobang), and 10 secretaries. These bodies are charged with the day-to-day running of the Party and with making major policy decisions affecting the Party. Real power within the Party is centralized in the Standing Committee of the Politburo. The Central Committee also elects a Party *Central Military Commission*, headed by Deng Xiaoping, which is charged with overseeing Party matters within the People's Liberation Army.

The State

The *National People's Congress*, theoretically the supreme state decision-making body, consists of about 2,700 delegates nominated by senior Party leaders and elected for 5-year terms by provincial and other local people's congresses. The National People's Congress elects the *president* and *vice-president* of the People's Republic; the *State Council*, which is the executive arm of government, headed by the premier (Zhao Ziyang), and composed of numerous ministries, commissions, and subordinate organizations; the state *Central Military Commission*, headed by Deng Xiaoping (its membership in 1986 duplicated the Party Central Military Commission); and senior members of the *Supreme People's Court*, and the *Supreme People's Procuratorate*, which acts as a prosecutor's office. The people directly elect only delegates to the basic- and county-level people's congresses.

Chinese Communist Party Organization

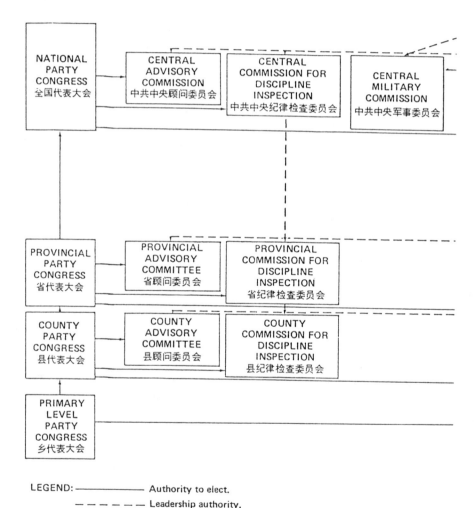

LEGEND: ─────────── Authority to elect.
        ─ ─ ─ ─ ─ Leadership authority.

SOURCE: Constitution of the Chinese Communist Party, 1982.

中国共产党组织表

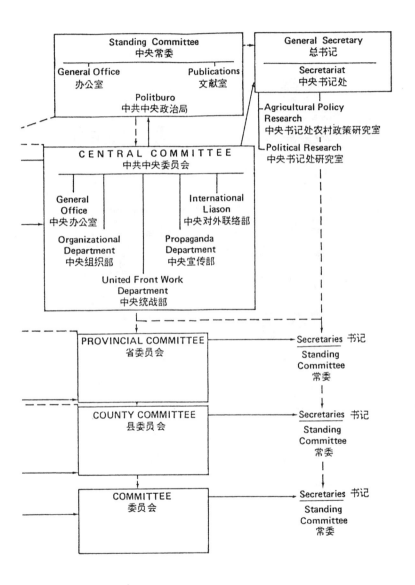

State Structure of the People's Republic of China

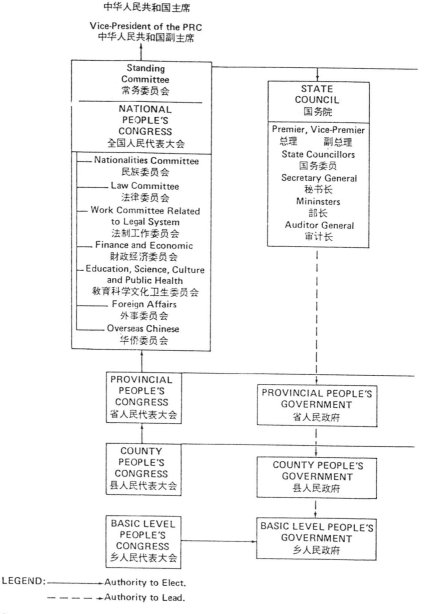

Source: Constitution of the People's Republic of China, 1982; and Zhongguo shouce (Hong Kong: Ta Kung Pao, 1984).

中华人民共和国政府结构

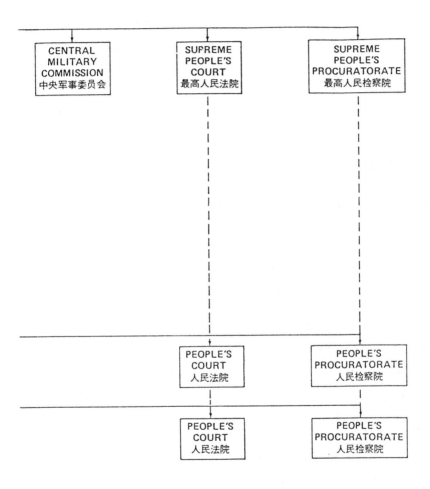

GLOSSARY

Bohai No. 2 incident. In 1979, Chinese oil rig No. 2 collapsed in the Bohai Gulf, killing 72 workers. Authorities blamed incompetence in the Ministry of Petroleum and disciplined several senior leaders.

CCP. Chinese Communist Party.

Chen Jingrun. Well-known middle-aged mathematician. Member of the Institute of Mathematics of the Chinese Academy of Sciences. Severely criticized during the Cultural Revolution, he is now a model of how the Party treats non-Party intellectuals.

CYL. Communist Youth League.

Democracy Movement. From late 1978 to 1981 young political activists published critical articles in unofficial publications in many of China's major cities calling for more democracy, the rule of law, and human rights. Authorities, after first using the "Democracy Movement" to criticize the Cultural Revolution and Mao Zedong, suppressed it in 1981.

Double hundred policy. The policy of "letting a hundred flowers bloom and a hundred schools of thought contend," formulated in 1956–57, generally meant less Party control of literature and art workers.

Everyone eating from the same big pot. The policy of paying approximately equivalent wages to all workers regardless of their productivity. Equalitarianism.

Four basic principles. As outlined in China's state constitutions, these principles are adherence to socialism, the dictatorship of the proletariat, rule by the Chinese Communist Party, and subscribing to Marxism-Leninism-Mao Zedong Thought.

Four Modernizations. First outlined by Premier Zhou Enlai in 1975, they include modernizing industry, agriculture, science and technology, and national defense.

Four principles for promoting cadres. Authorities should promote cadres who are revolutionary, young, educated, and specialists.

Gang of Four. The "gang," arrested soon after Mao's death in 1976, included Jiang Qing (Mao's widow); Wang Hongwen, a worker from Shanghai and CCP vice-chairman; Yao Wenyuan, a vice-premier of the People's Republic; and Zhang Chunqiao, another vice-premier.

Iron rice bowl. The policy of giving security of tenure in employment, widespread throughout China.

Jiang Qing. See "Gang of Four."

Jiang Zhuying. Scientist and Party member who died in middle age from overwork. Member of Institute of Optical Mechanics of the Chinese Academy of Sciences in Jilin Province.

Jin. About 1.1 pounds.

Key (point) school/class. Mostly urban schools and classes in which the most and best resources and the brightest students were concentrated. Students from "key" middle schools had a much better chance of achieving a place in a university.

Lai Ruoyu (1910–1958). Prominent CCP member, active in the labor movement, and former chairman of the All-China Federation of Trade Unions.

Lang Ping. Champion athlete, member of the World Championship Chinese Women's National Volleyball Team.

Li Lisan (1899–1968). Early CCP member, active in the labor movement. Denounced by Mao for concentrating on revolution in the cities, rather than in the countryside. Former Minister of Labor, and vice-chairman of the All-China Federation of Trade Unions. Reportedly committed suicide during the Cultural Revolution.

Lin Biao (1907–1971). Minister of Defense from 1959 to 1971, and designated "successor" to Mao Zedong, Lin allegedly attempted to stage a coup d'état in 1971. He died in an airplane crash while fleeing the country. His crimes were later linked to those of the "Gang of Four."

Lu Xun (1881–1936). Leftist writer, active in the May Fourth Movement. A leading modern essayist and social critic.

Luo Jianfu. Scientist and Party member who died in middle age of overwork.

Mao Dun, penname for Shen Yenping (1896–1981). Leftist writer, former chairman of the Chinese Writers' Union and a former Minister of Culture.

May Fourth New Culture Movement. In this 1919 urban protest movement, intellectuals demanded a popular culture, including writing in the vernacular, which would make culture accessible to the common man.

Mu. One sixth of an acre.

NPC. National People's Congress.

Ninth category people. Derogatory term to refer to intellectuals, particularly during the Cultural Revolution years. Intellectuals, as "ninth category people," came after the other eight "bad" categories: landlords, rich peasants, counterrevolutionaries, bad elements, rightists, renegades, enemy agents, and capitalist-roaders.

"One dragon" thesis. In industry, the "dragon" system grouped a number of enterprises according to product or service.

PLA. People's Liberation Army.

Penghu, Quemoy and Matsu. Islands off the coast of Fujian, currently occupied by the Guomindang (KMT).

People of three categories. People who joined in the beating, smashing, and looting during the Cultural Revolution; close associates of the "Gang of Four"; and cadres who persistently resist the policies adopted since 1978. These people were identified in 1982 as targets for dismissal from office.

PRC. People's Republic of China.

Production responsibility system. In agriculture, the system of household contracting, which operates on the principle of linking income to output.

Question of Xunyi County (Shaanxi). Subject of Central Committee document No. 42, issued in July 1978, authorities criticized the coercive and commandist behavior of some cadres in Xunyi County as they implemented agricultural policy.

Red and expert. Red means to become politically qualified and expert means to become professionally qualified. Closely associated with Mao Zedong, the expression is also used in Dengist China.

Special economic zones. Established by a State Council directive in 1978, the four special economic zones in Guangdong and Fujian provinces are expected to attract foreign capital, improve the international balance of payments, help in the development of native industry, and bring advanced technology to China.

Specialized household. In agriculture, a household that specializes in producing one commodity, most of which it turns over to the production team for an agreed upon price.

Spiritual pollution campaign. Initiated in October 1983 at the Second Plenum of the Twelfth Central Committee. On that occasion, Deng Xiaoping defined "spiritual pollution" as "disseminating all varieties of corrupt and decadent ideologies of the bourgeoisie and other exploiting classes and disseminating sentiments of distrust toward the socialist and communist cause and to the Communist Party leadership."

10,000-yuan households. Peasant families whose incomes under the new agricultural policies exceed 10,000-yuan a year.

Ten years of turmoil. Refers to the 1966–1976 Cultural Revolution.

Ten year calamity. Refers to the 1966–1976 Cultural Revolution.

"Three good" students. Students who are good in study, morality, and health.

Two educational systems. Proposed by Liu Shaoqi in 1958 and once again in 1964. Schools were to be divided into two categories: whole-day schools and half-work, half-study schools. Students in the former schools would concentrate on academic work in order to raise educational standards; those in the latter schools would be required to perform a considerable amount of labor, in part to help train the labor force, in part to help pay their educational expenses. Criticized during the

Cultural Revolution as a copy of the capitalist double-track system in education.

Two kinds of households. In agriculture, "specialized" and "key" households. "Key" households pursued economic activity independently, buying grain as they needed it on the market, and paying "taxes" to the production team. See "specialized" household.

Two whatevers. Whatever Mao said must be obeyed and whatever Mao decided must be upheld. Around this slogan, opposed by Deng Xiaoping, the "two whatevers" faction grouped in 1977.

Two work systems. See "two educational systems."

"Unrequited Love." Play written by PLA writer Bai Hua, which was severely criticized in April 1981.

Xiangxiang (Hunan) Experience. The subject of Central Committee document No. 37, issued in June 1978; authorities argued that burdens on the peasantry should be lifted, levels of accumulation should be reduced, and peasant incomes should be increased. Criticizing the failure of cadres to tie incomes to output, authorities focused attention on the experience of this county in a campaign launched in 1979.

Xidan. The Beijing street on which activists displayed wall posters during the Democracy Movement, 1978–1979.

Yuan. Approximately US $0.50 for the mid-1980s.

CHRONOLOGY OF EVENTS
1976–1985

1976

January   Death of Premier Zhou Enlai.

February   Hua Guofeng appointed acting premier.

April   Tiananmen riots. Politburo dismisses Deng Xiaoping from posts as vice-chairman of Party and vice-premier, and appoints Hua Guofeng as Party first vice-chairman and also premier.

July   Tangshan earthquake.

September   Death of Mao Zedong.

October   Arrest of "Gang of Four." Hua Guofeng named chairman of Party, and of Military Affairs Committee.

December   Second Dazhai Conference held in Beijing; leftist policies in agriculture continued.

1977

February   Wang Dongxing publishes "Two Whatevers" endorsing whatever Mao said.

March   Party work conference agrees that Deng Xiaoping should be restored to office.

April   National Conference on Learning from Daqing in Industry convened.

May   Hua Guofeng endorses "Two Whatevers."

July   *Third Plenum of Tenth Central Committee* reinstates Deng Xiaoping as Party vice-chairman and vice-premier.

August   *Eleventh Party Congress* reelects Hua Guofeng as Party chairman, and Ye Jianying, Deng Xiaoping, Li Xiannian, and Wang Dongxing as Party vice-chairmen. A new Party constitution is adopted. Although the end of the Cultural Revolution is announced, reports by Hua and Ye affirm that movement was a success.

October   *Fourth Session of the Standing Committee of Fourth NPC* convened.

1978

January	"Key" primary and secondary schools are restored.
February	*Fifth NPC* meets, elects Hua Guofeng premier, approves his Ten-Year National Development Plan. National Conference on Science and Technology meets, during which Deng Xiaoping defines intellectuals as members of the working class.
May	*Guangming ribao* publishes "Practice Is the Sole Criterion for Testing Truth."
June	Deng Xiaoping endorses "practice is the sole criterion for testing truth."
October	Authorities in Sichuan conduct experiments granting substantial autonomy to industrial enterprises.
November	Deng Xiaoping criticizes Hua Guofeng at a Central Work Conference. Reevaluation of Tiananmen riots from counterrevolutionary to revolutionary incident. Democracy Movement steps up activities in Beijing.
December	*Third Plenum of Eleventh Central Committee* meets. Decides to cease using the slogan "take class struggle as the key link" and shifts Party work to socialist modernization. Abolishes previous practice of discriminating against people of "bad" class backgrounds, such as former landlords and rich peasants, and their offspring. Sweeping personnel changes bring into Politburo four Deng Xiaoping supporters (Chen Yun, Deng Yingchao, Hu Yaobang, and Wang Zhen). Repudiates the "Two Whatevers" policy. Hua Guofeng's Ten-Year Development Plan replaced with new economic development policies, including major changes in agricultural policy and a relaxation of controls over privately owned businesses.

1979

January	China and United States officially establish diplomatic relations. Promotion of "One-Child-Per-Couple" policy formally announced.
February–March	Sino-Vietnam conflict escalates with border skirmishes and Chinese "advance" into Vietnam.
March	Wei Jingsheng publishes "On the Fifth Modernization." Deng criticizes the Democracy Movement and reaffirms the "Four Basic Principles." A National Capital Construction Conference halts many projects.
April	Wei Jingsheng and other "dissidents" are arrested. China decides not to extend its thirty-year "Friendship, Alliance, and Mutual Assistance Treaty" with the Soviet Union beyond its 1980 expiration date. Party work conference sets forth the principle of "readjusting, restructuring, consolidating, and improving" the national economy.
June–July	*Second Session of Fifth NPC* passes new "Organic Law on Local People's Congresses and Local People's Governments," "Electoral Law of the PRC for the NPC and Local People's Congresses of All Levels," "Criminal Law and Law of Criminal Procedures of the PRC," and "Foreign Investment Joint Venture Law."
July	Central Committee and State Council approve special policies and flexible measures by Guangdong and Fujian provinces to attract foreign investment. Establishment of four Special Economic Zones in these two provinces.

September	*Fourth Plenum of Eleventh Central Committee* meets. Zhao Ziyang and Peng Zhen enter Politburo.
October	Ye Jianying criticizes the Cultural Revolution and refers to Mao's mistakes.
November	Democracy Movement activists Wei Jingsheng and Fu Yuehua sentenced to prison terms; Liu Qing arrested.

1980

February	*Fifth Plenum of Eleventh Central Committee* meets. Reestablishes Secretariat of Central Committee, elects Hu Yaobang General Secretary of Central Committee and Hu Yaobang and Zhao Ziyang to Standing Committee of Politburo; adopts the Guiding Principles for Inner-Party Political Life; rehabilitates late former vice-chairman of the Party Central Committee and chairman of the PRC, Liu Shaoqi; approves resignations of Wang Dongxing and three other "whateverists" from leading Party and state posts.
April	State Council issues liberal directive on price control and market management. Beginning of 1980 county-level elections.
July-August	National Work Conference on "key" secondary schools affirms the necessity to develop first those schools with the best conditions.
August	Deng Xiaoping addresses Politburo on reforms.
August-September	*Third Session of Fifth NPC* meets. Zhao Ziyang replaces Hua Guofeng as premier of State Council. Document 75 endorses household contracting in agriculture. Resolution to revise text of Article 45 of Constitution banning the "Four Bigs" adopted, as are Nationality Law, revised Marriage Law, and Individual and Joint Venture Income Tax Law.
October	Liao Gailong addresses national Party school on the 1980 reforms.
November-December	Trial of ten "Gang of Four" and Lin Biao co-conspirators.
December	Deng Xiaoping attacks Democracy Movement at Party Work Conference and endorses the need for a high level of "spiritual civilization" in addition to material civilization. Central Committee work conference decides to give high priority to light industry and to down play heavy industry. Central Committee work conference clamps down on individual businesses.

1981

April	Bai Hua's screenplay "Unrequited Love" attacked.
May	*Renmin ribao* endorses some peasants "getting rich first."
June	*Sixth Plenum of Eleventh Central Committee* demotes Hua Guofeng to Party vice-chairman; Hu Yaobang elected chairman. Deng Xiaoping elected as chairman of the Military Commission under the CCP Central Committee. "Resolution on Some Questions in the History of Our Party since the Founding of the People's Republic of China," evaluating Mao and the Cultural Revolution, approved. State Council relaxes restrictions on individual entrepreneurs.

September	Ye Jianying elaborates on his nine-point proposal on peaceful reunification with Taiwan and proposes talks between the CCP and the Nationalist Party (KMT), calling for a "third cooperation" between the two parties.
October	Advocates of heavy industry reemerge.
November	National Commercial Work Conference permits individual entrepreneurs to hire labor.
November- December	*Fourth Session of Fifth NPC* meets. Zhao Ziyang sets forth ten principles for economic construction and announces State Council's decision to restructure the administration.

1982

January	Central Committee releases summary of National Conference on Rural Work held in October 1981, reporting that 90 percent of the country's production teams have adopted some form of the responsibility system. Public ownership of land and the responsibility system will remain "for a long time to come."
March	The Standing Committee of Fifth NPC approves proposals for reforming state institutions, beginning with State Council. Attack on "bourgeois liberalism" and stress on spiritual civilization.
July	Third nationwide census since 1949 undertaken.
August	*Seventh Plenum of Eleventh Central Committee* meets, approves a new Party constitution; Joint Communique between China and United States on gradually reducing U.S. arms sales to Taiwan.
September	*Twelfth Party Congress* meets, adopts new Party constitution. Decides to launch three-year Party rectification campaign. Hua Guofeng demoted from Politburo; Hu Yaobang is Party secretary-general. Post of chairman eliminated.
November	National Commercial Work Conference further relaxes controls on individual entrepreneurs.
December	*Fifth Session of Fifth NPC* adopts new state constitution and revises local government and local election laws.

1983

January	Document No. 1 permits peasants to hire labor.
May	State Council reimposes tight regulations on free markets.
June	*Sixth NPC* meets, approves new state constitution. Li Xiannian is new head of state, Deng Xiaoping is head of new State Military Commission, and Zhao Ziyang continues as premier. Peng Zhen becomes NPC chairman.
July	Deng Xiaoping's "Selected Works" published.
October	*Second Plenum of Twelfth Central Committee* meets, approves Party rectification plans and deals with problem of "spiritual pollution."

1984

January	Document No. 1 stresses the commercialization of agriculture.
March	Beginning of 1984 county-level elections.

May
Second Session of Sixth NPC approves a new Military Law, reintroducing ranks.

September
Party rectification campaign enters final stage.

October
Third Plenum of Twelfth Central Committee meets and endorses a plan to reform the economic structure.

December
Renmin ribao declares that China "cannot depend on the works of Marx and Lenin to solve our modern-day questions." The newspaper later amends this to read " . . . solve all our modern-day questions." Joint Declaration between China and the United Kingdom on the Question of Hong Kong signed.

1985

January
Meeting of Fourth Congress of the Chinese Writers' Association, December 29, 1984-January 5, 1985. Hu Qili stresses "freedom of creation" for writers. Document No. 1 includes ten measures to shift the emphasis from state planning to market demand in farm production and from administrative to economic means in rural management.

March
Third Session of Sixth NPC meets from March 27 to April 10. Enacts Inheritance Law and approves draft resolution on Joint Declaration on Hong Kong. Central Committee issues decision on the Reform of the Science and Technology Management System. State Council circular bans lottery tickets.

May
Decision of the Central Committee on Reform of the Educational System.

June
Ministry of Education replaced by State Education Commission headed by Vice-Premier Li Peng. Deng Xiaoping announces army to be cut by one million men over a two-year period.

July
Announcement that ten of the fourteen coastal cities opened to foreign investors in April 1984 will "slow down" the signing of contracts with outsiders.

September
Fourth and Fifth Plenums of the Twelfth Central Committee meet; National Conference of Party meets. Proposal for Seventh Five-Year Plan (1986–90) adopted. Reaffirms commitment to foreign investment, limited private enterprise, and decentralization of economic decision-making. Major personnel changes in Central Commission for Discipline Inspection announced. Sixty-four members or alternate members of Central Committee resign and are replaced. Ten of twenty-four Politburo members resign, including standing committee member Ye Jianying. Hu Qili, Li Peng, Tian Jiyun, Wu Xueqian, and Qiao Shi enter Politburo. Five new members join Central Committee Secretariat; three members resign.

ABOUT THE EDITORS

A graduate of St. Olaf College and Oxford University, JOHN P. BURNS received his Ph.D. in political science from Columbia University. Since 1979 he has taught in the Political Science Department of the University of Hong Kong where he is a senior lecturer.

Mr. Burns has written widely on various aspects of Chinese rural politics and on administrative questions in both China and Hong Kong. His works include *The Hong Kong Civil Service: Personnel Policies and Practices* (edited with Ian Scott, 1984) and *Political Participation in Rural China* (forthcoming).

A graduate of the University of North Carolina (Chapel Hill), STANLEY ROSEN received his Ph.D. from UCLA in political science. He began his teaching career at the Chinese University of Hong Kong and the University of California, San Diego. Since 1979 he has been on the faculty of the University of Southern California where he is an associate professor of political science.

Mr. Rosen has written widely on various aspects of Chinese affairs, particularly on youth, education, and social policy. His works include *The Role of Sent-Down Youth in the Chinese Cultural Revolution* (1981); *Red Guard Factionalism and the Cultural Revolution in Guangzhou* (1982); and *On Socialist Democracy and the Chinese Legal System: The Li Yizhe Debates* (co-edited with Anita Chan and Jonathan Unger, 1985). He is the editor of the journal *Chinese Education*.